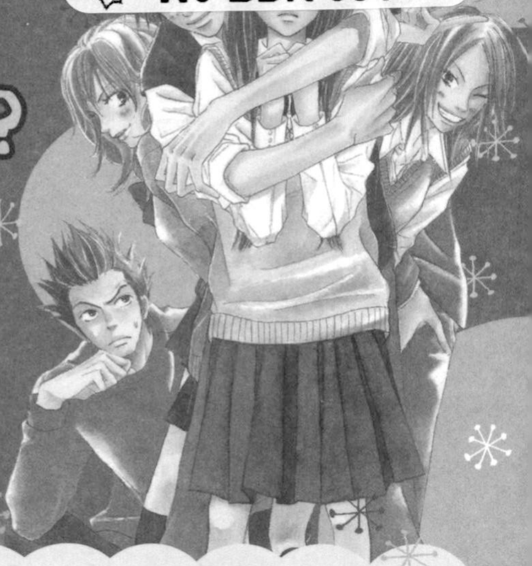



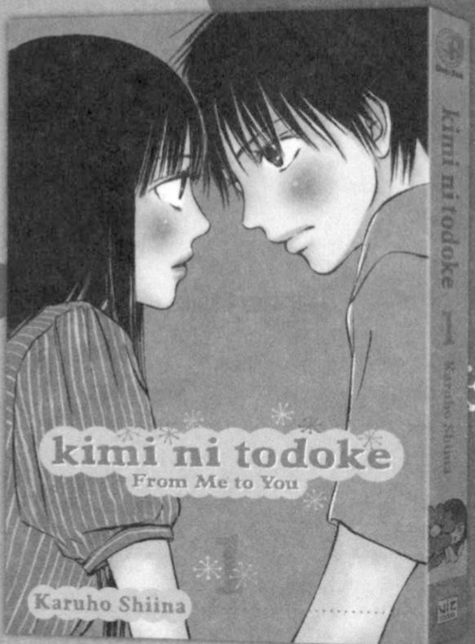
kimi ni todoke
From Me to You
Karuho Shiina

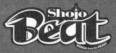

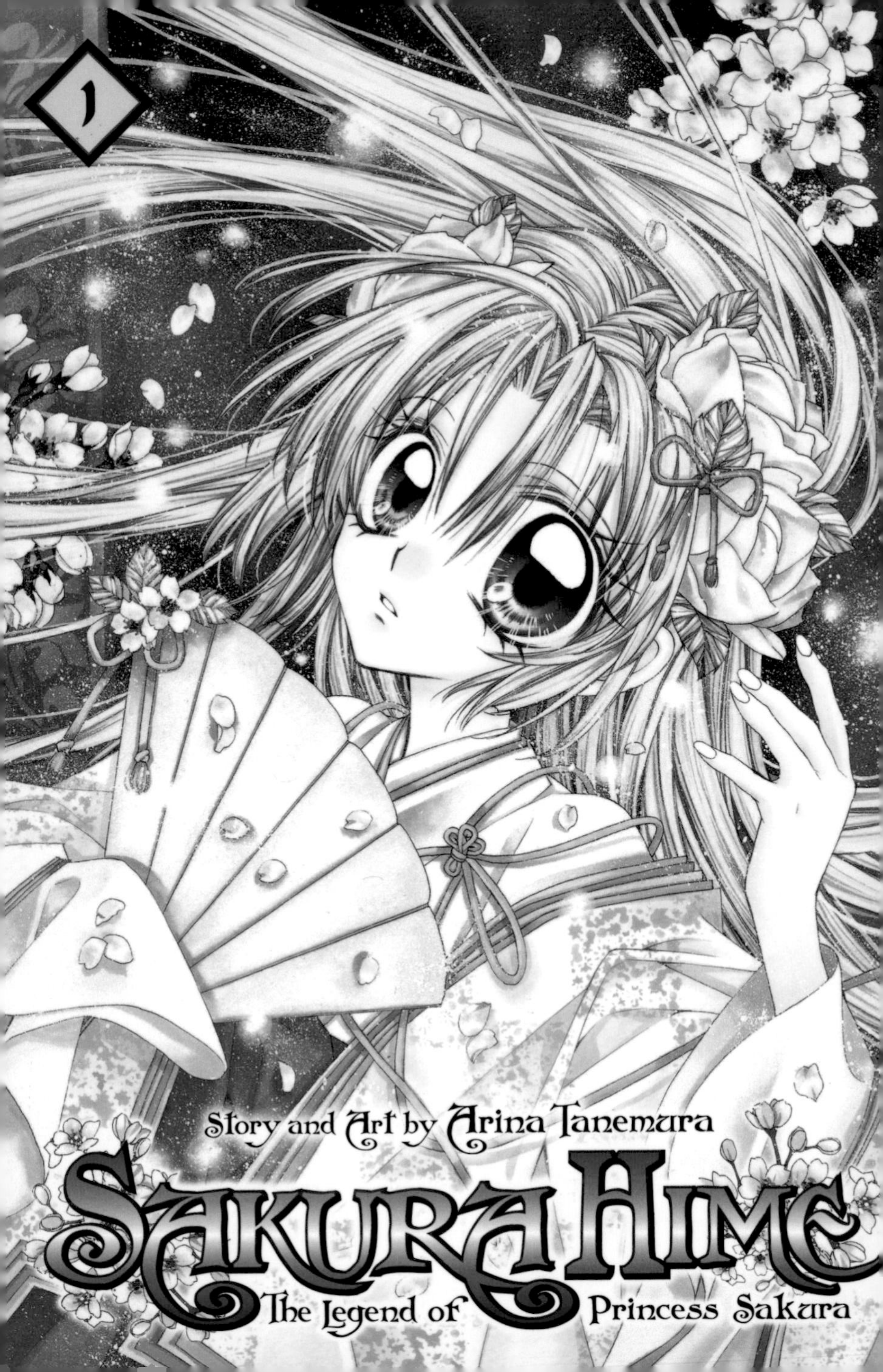
1
Story and Art by Arina Tanemura
SAKURA HIME
The Legend of Princess Sakura

Art book featuring
216 pages of beautiful
color images personally
selected by Tanemura

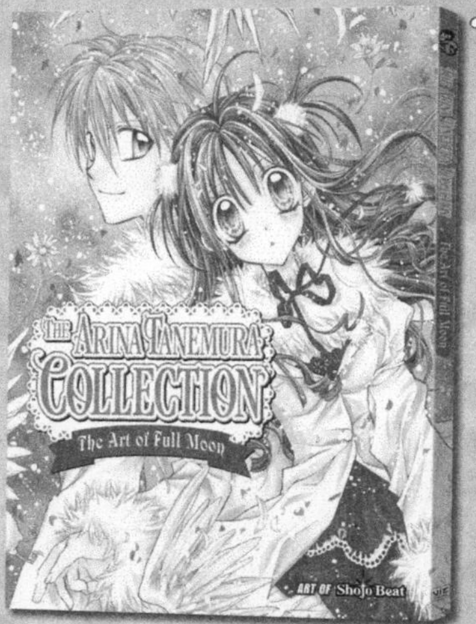
The Arina Tanemura Collection
The Art of Full Moon
ART OF Shojo Beat

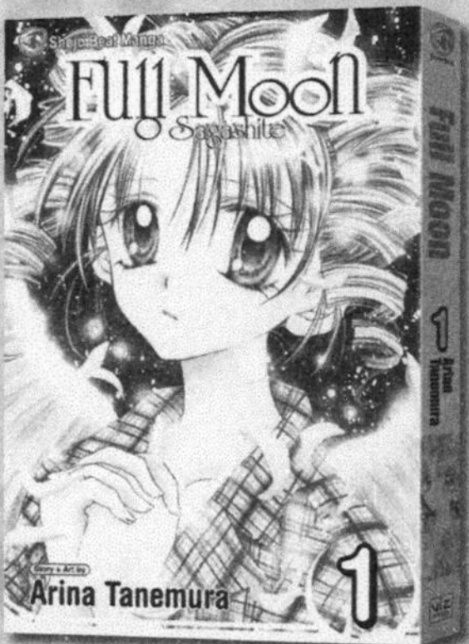
Shojo Beat Manga
FULL MOON
O Sagashite
Full Moon
1
Arina Tanemura
Story & Art by
Arina Tanemura
1

Read where Mitsuki's
pop dreams began
in the manga—all 7
volumes now available

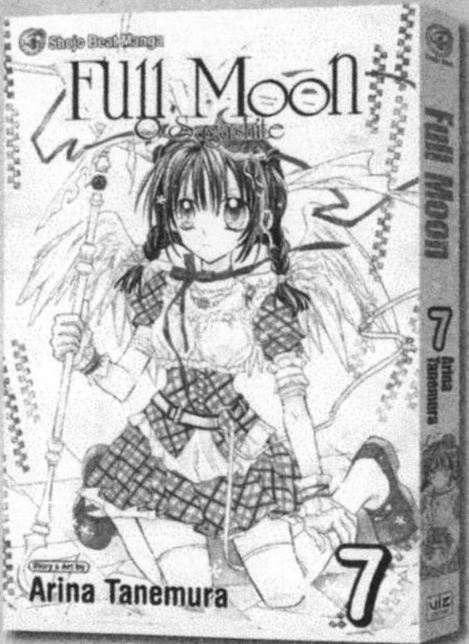
Shojo Beat Manga
FULL MOON
O Sagashite
Full Moon
7
Arina Tanemura
Story & Art by
Arina Tanemura
7

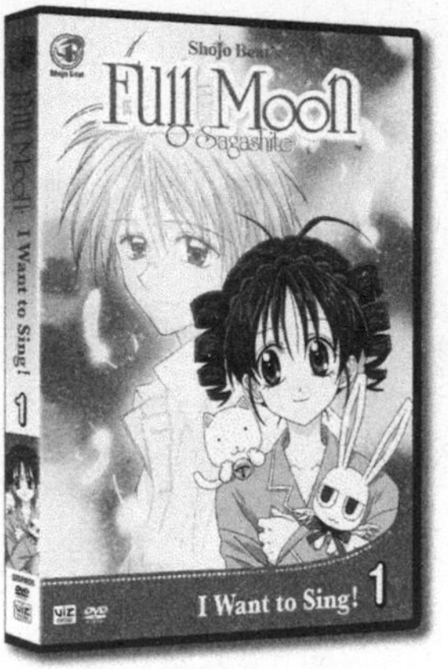
Shojo Beat
FULL MOON
O Sagashite
Full Moon I Want to Sing! 1
I Want to Sing! 1

Complete your
collection with the
anime, now on DVD

**WELCOME** to Imperial Academy:
a private school where trying to become
**SUPERIOR** can make you feel **INFERIOR**!

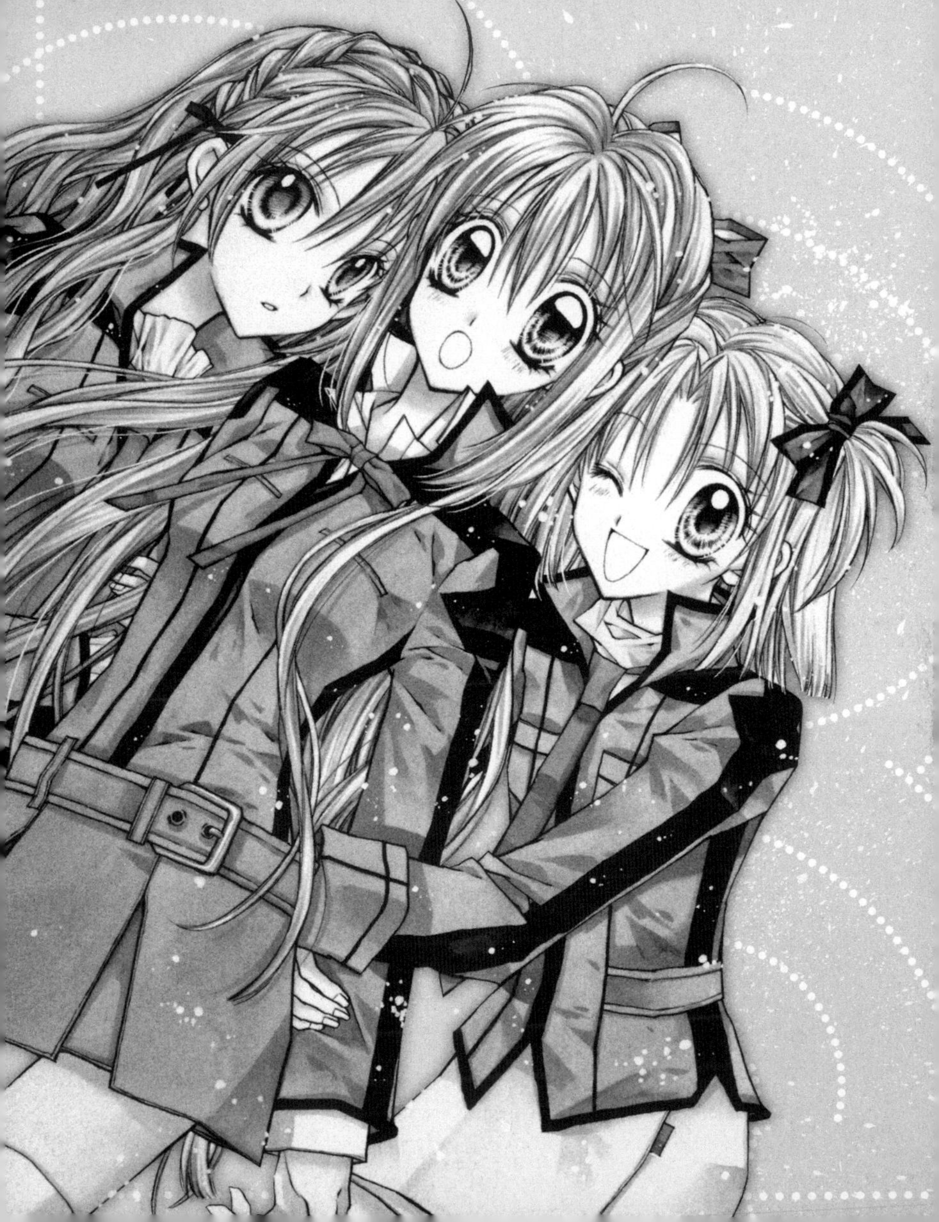

# I·O·N

**BY ARINA TANEMURA,**
CREATOR OF *FULL MOON*
AND *THE GENTLEMEN'S
ALLIANCE* †

Ion Tsuburagi is a normal junior high girl with normal junior high problems. But when a mysterious substance grants her telekinetic powers, she finds herself struggling to keep everything together! Are her new abilities a blessing...or a curse?

Find out in *I·O·N*—manga on sale now!

Sakura Hime: The Legend of Princess Sakura
Volume 1
Shojo Beat Edition

STORY AND ART BY
Arina Tanemura

Translation & Adaptation/Tetsuichiro Miyaki
Touch-up Art & Lettering/Inori Fukuda Trant
Design/Sam Elzway
Editor/Nancy Thistlethwaite

SAKURA-HIME KADEN © 2008 by Arina Tanemura
All rights reserved.
First published in Japan in 2008 by SHUEISHA Inc., Tokyo.
English translation rights arranged by SHUEISHA Inc.

Printed in the U.S.A.

Published by VIZ Media, LLC
P.O. Box 77010
San Francisco, CA 94107

10 9 8 7 6 5 4 3 2 1
First printing, April 2011

## ARINA TANEMURA

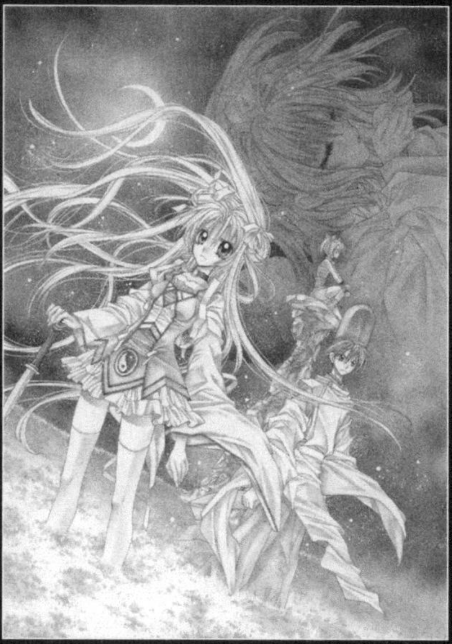

This is my first Heian Era fantasy. I had an inkling it would be difficult, but the period limits what kind of clothes I can have the characters wear. I'd like to try and create original designs for Japanese-style clothes on the title pages to add variety. Princess Sakura's battle has just started. Please support her growth, romance, struggles and fate.

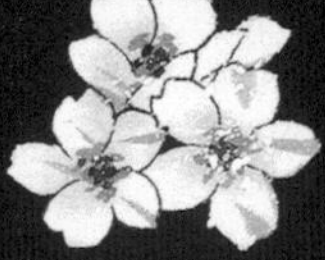

Arina Tanemura began her manga career in 1996 when her short stories debuted in *Ribon* magazine. She gained fame with the 1997 publication of *I•O•N*, and ever since her debut Tanemura has been a major force in shojo manga with popular series *Kamikaze Kaito Jeanne*, *Time Stranger Kyoko*, *Full Moon*, and *The Gentlemen's Alliance †*. Both *Kamikaze Kaito Jeanne* and *Full Moon* have been adapted into animated TV series.

Story and Art by Arina Tanemura

# SAKURA HIME
## The Legend of Princess Sakura

1

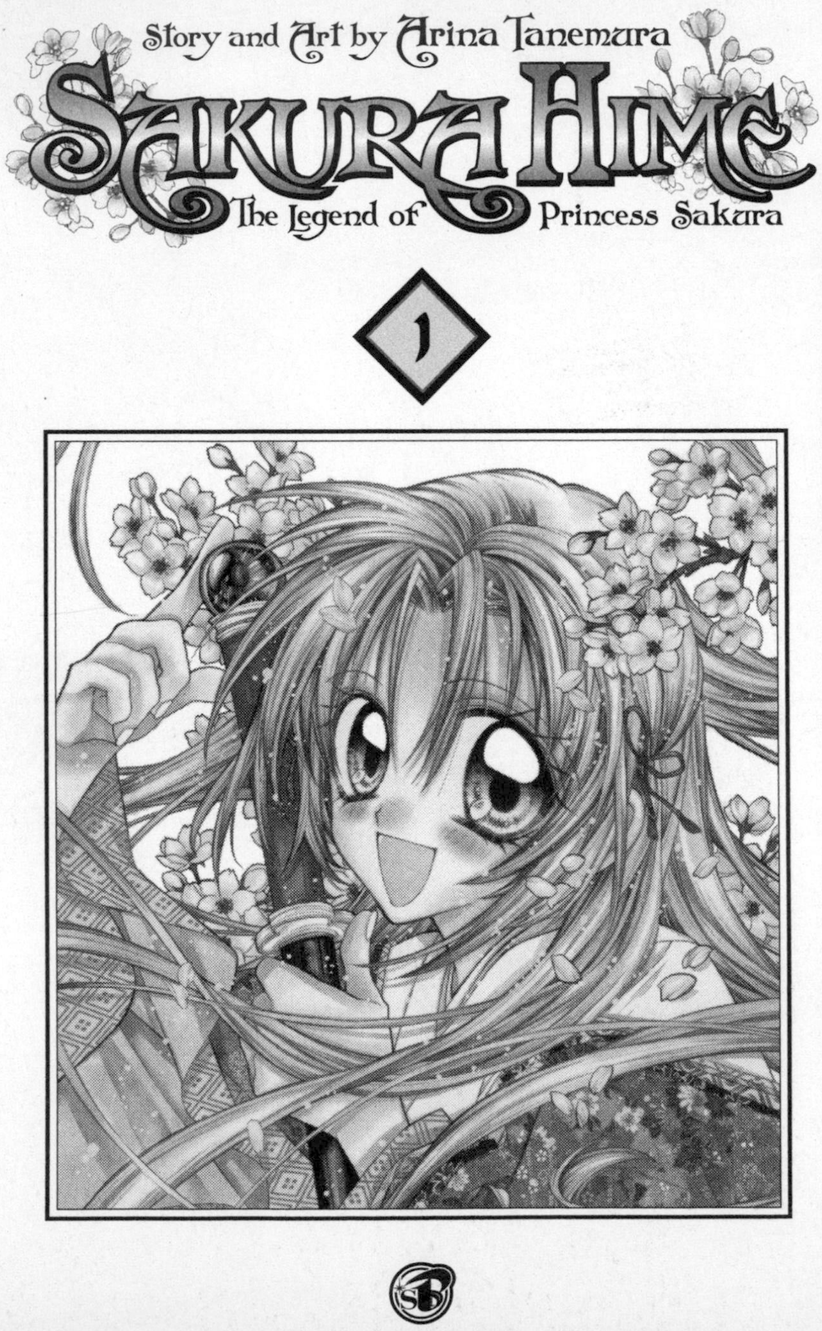

# Sakura Hime
## The Legend of Princess Sakura

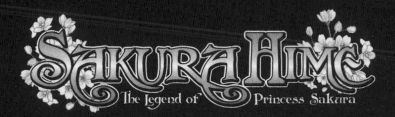

Contents

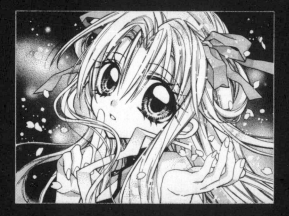

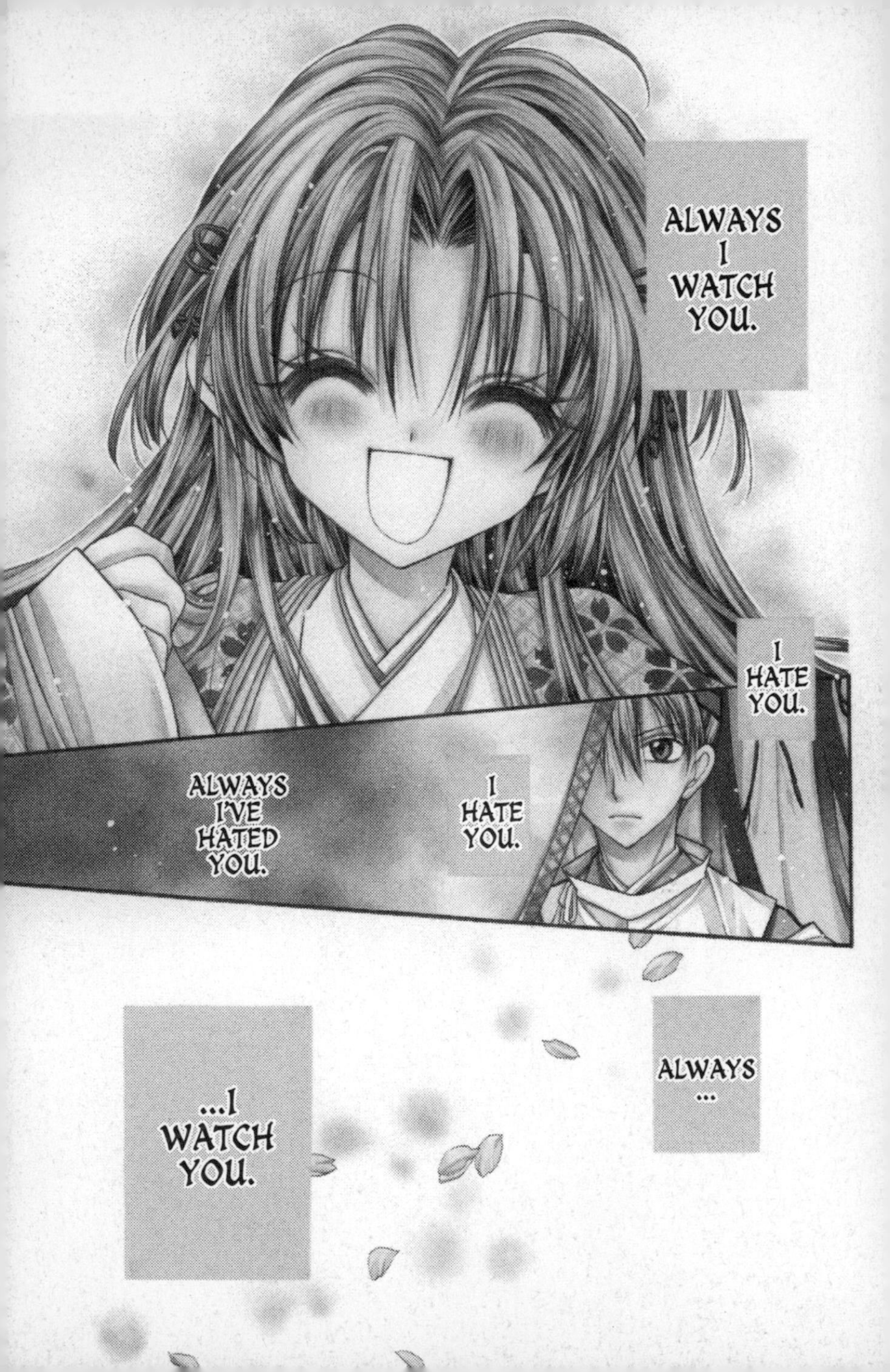
ALWAYS I WATCH YOU.
I HATE YOU.
I HATE YOU.
ALWAYS I'VE HATED YOU.
ALWAYS...
...I WATCH YOU.

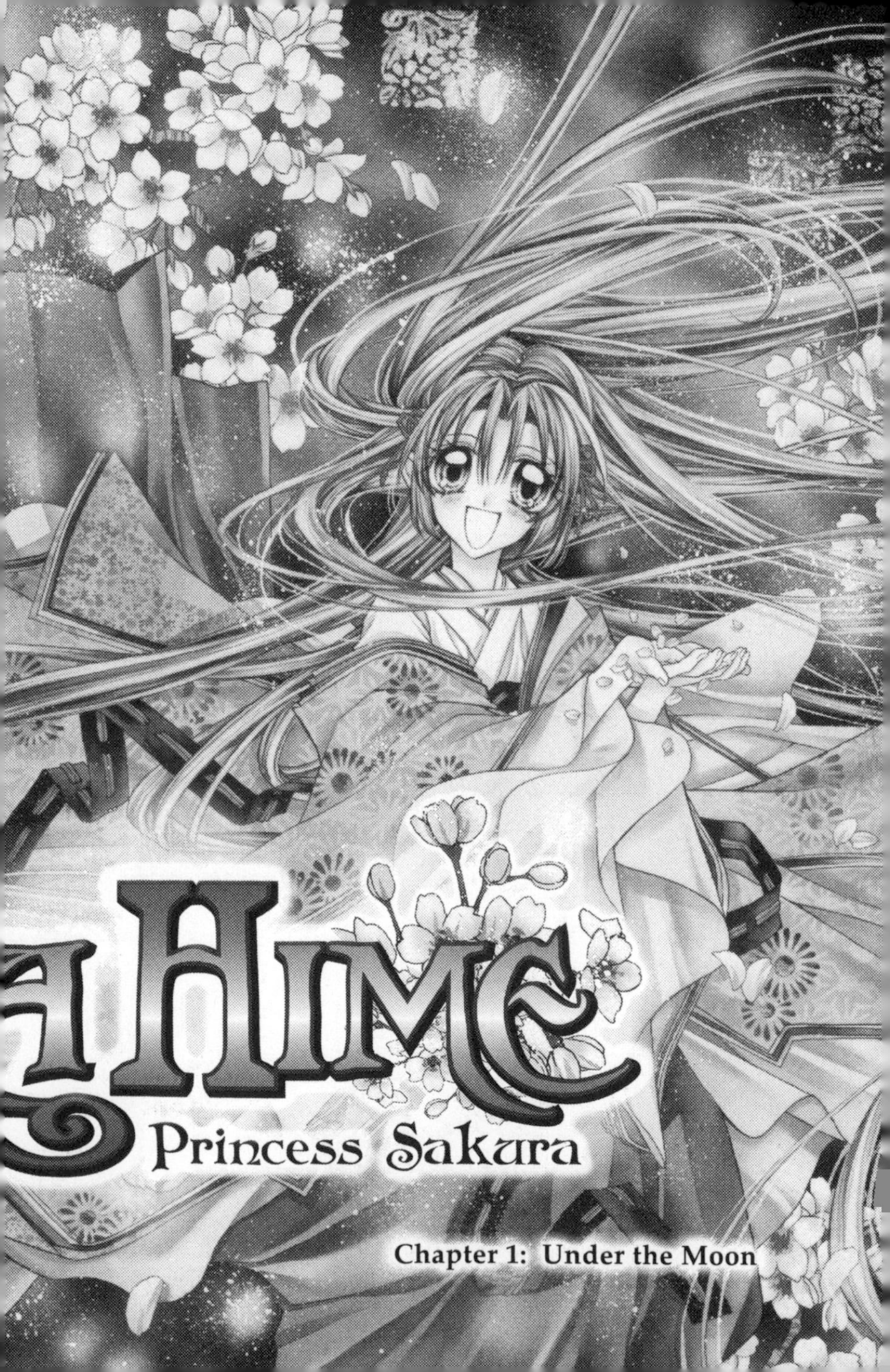
Hime
Princess Sakura
Chapter 1: Under the Moon

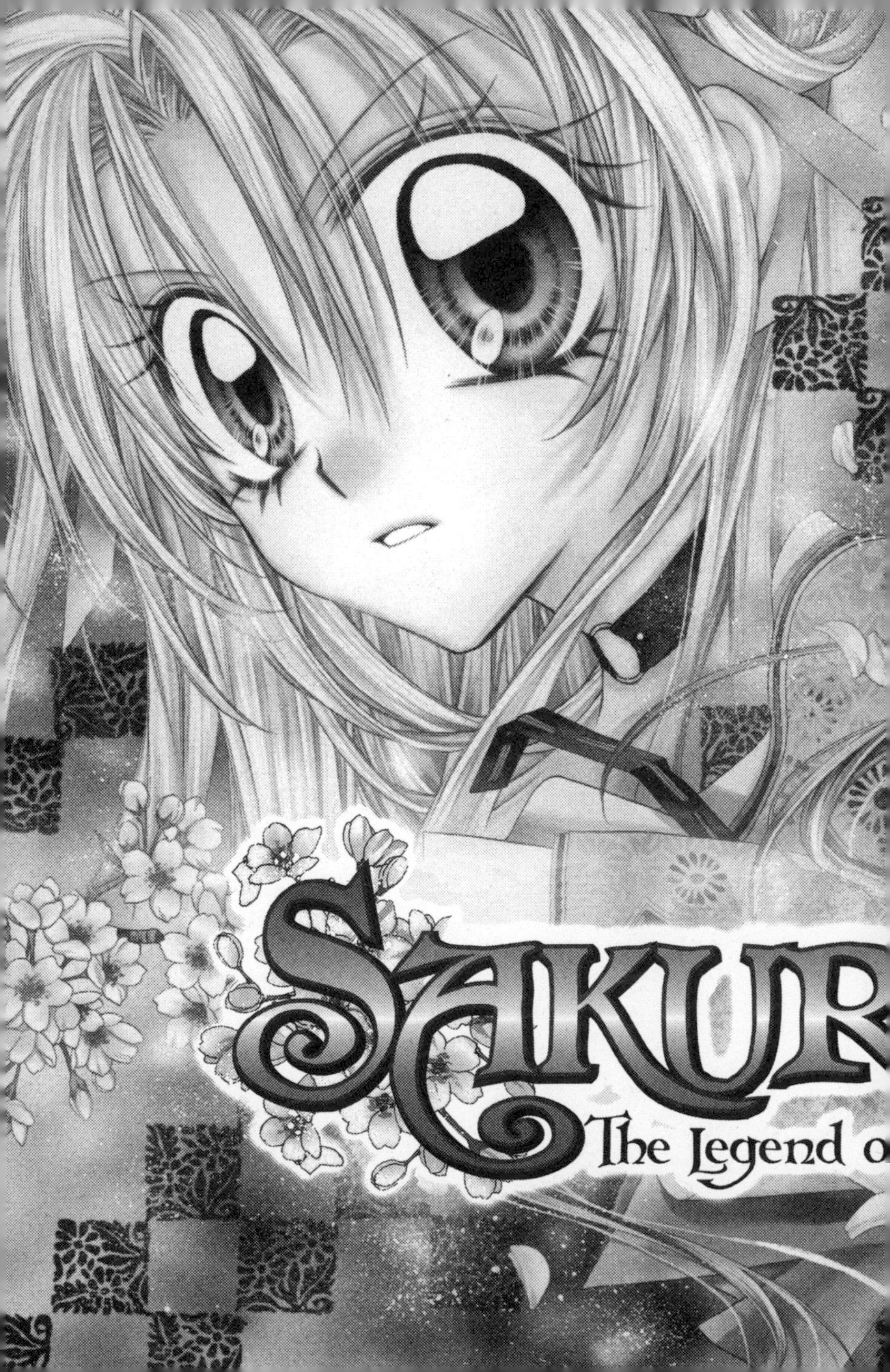
SAKUR
The Legend o

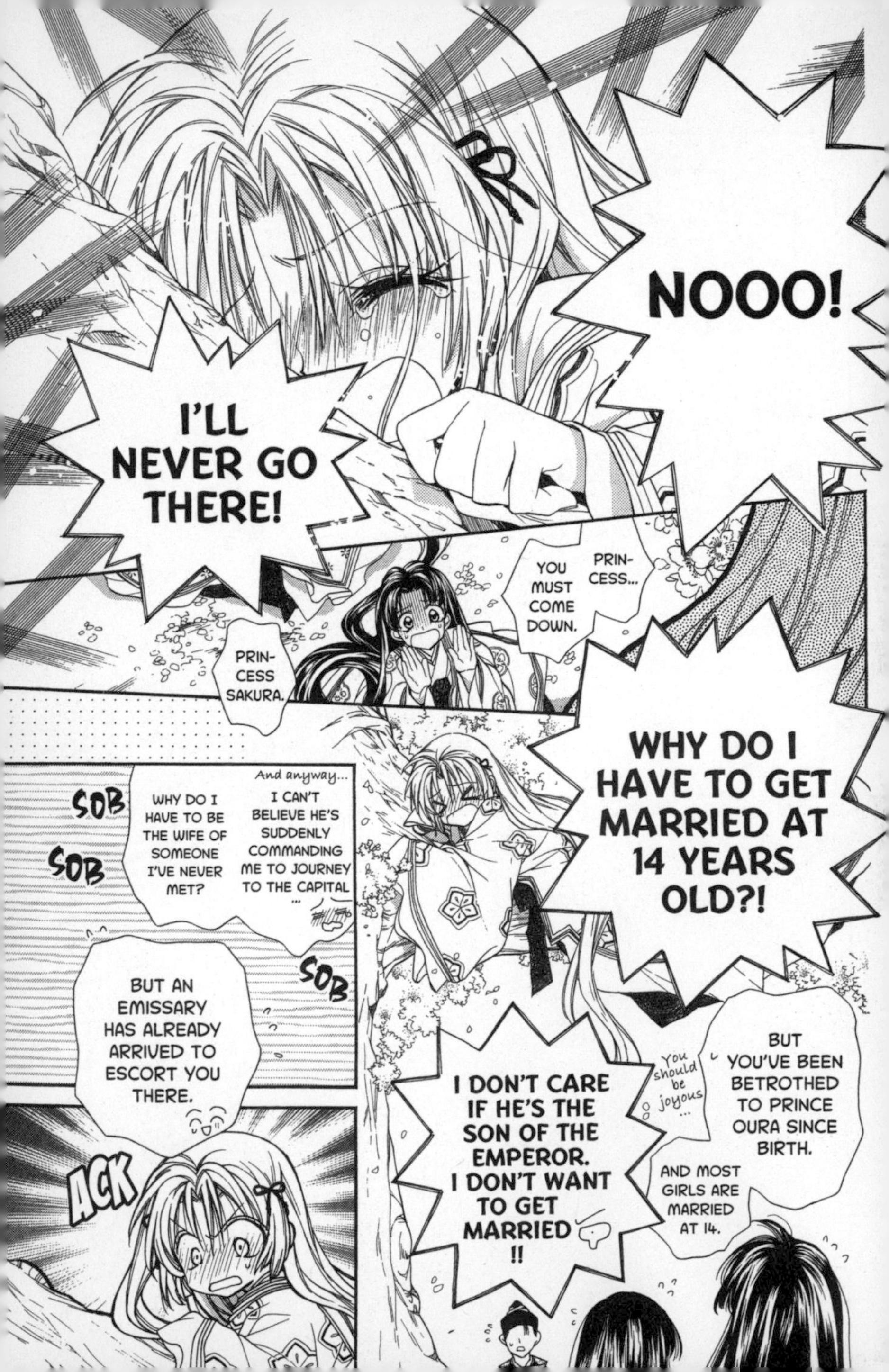
NOOO!
I'LL NEVER GO THERE!
PRIN-CESS...
YOU MUST COME DOWN.
PRIN-CESS SAKURA.
WHY DO I HAVE TO GET MARRIED AT 14 YEARS OLD?!
BUT YOU'VE BEEN BETROTHED TO PRINCE OURA SINCE BIRTH.
You should be joyous...
AND MOST GIRLS ARE MARRIED AT 14.
I DON'T CARE IF HE'S THE SON OF THE EMPEROR. I DON'T WANT TO GET MARRIED!!
And anyway... I CAN'T BELIEVE HE'S SUDDENLY COMMANDING ME TO JOURNEY TO THE CAPITAL...
WHY DO I HAVE TO BE THE WIFE OF SOMEONE I'VE NEVER MET?
SOB
SOB
SOB
BUT AN EMISSARY HAS ALREADY ARRIVED TO ESCORT YOU THERE.
ACK

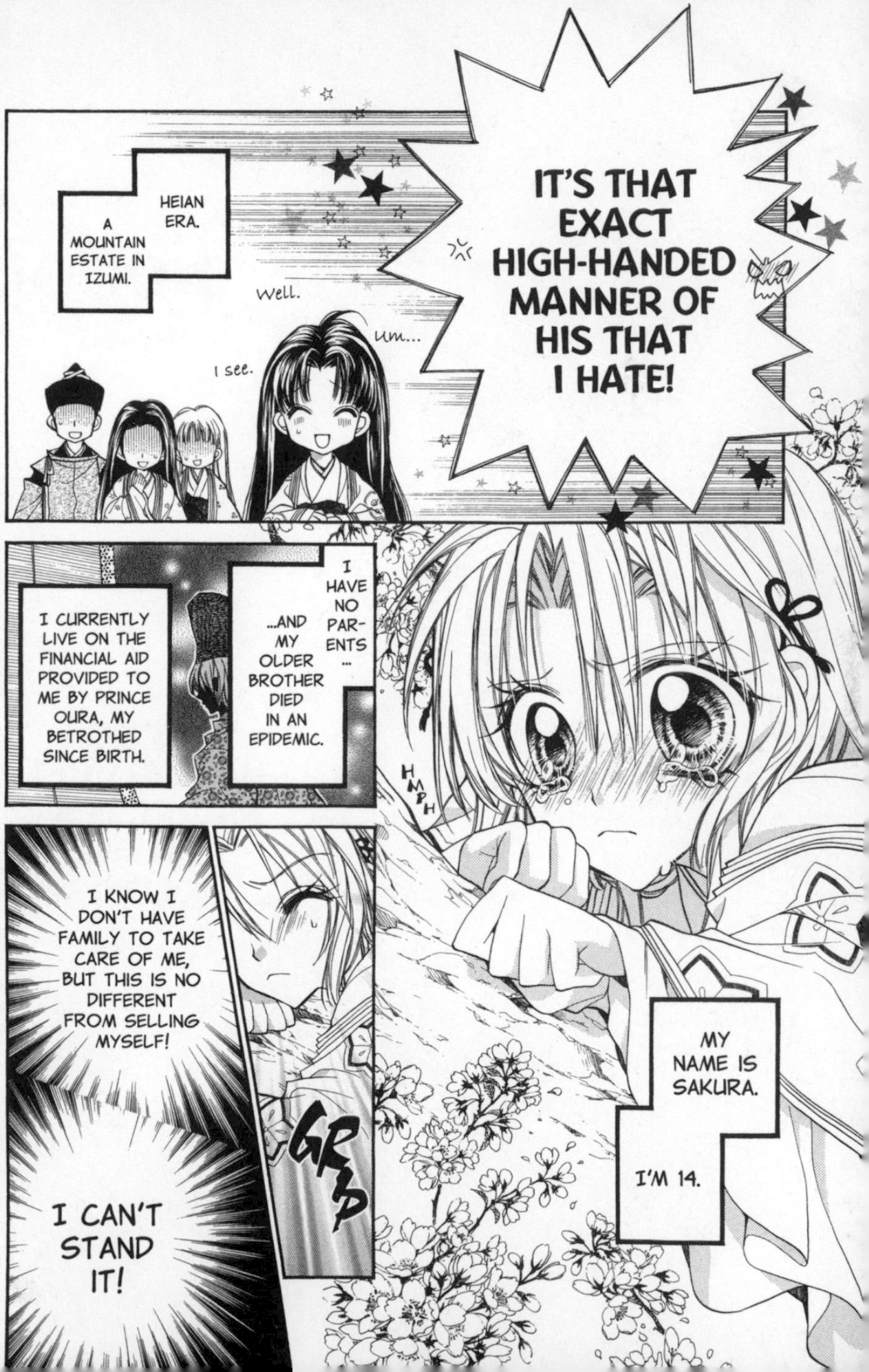
IT'S THAT EXACT HIGH-HANDED MANNER OF HIS THAT I HATE!
HEIAN ERA.
A MOUNTAIN ESTATE IN IZUMI.
Um...
Well.
I see.
HMPH
MY NAME IS SAKURA.
I'M 14.
I HAVE NO PARENTS...
...AND MY OLDER BROTHER DIED IN AN EPIDEMIC.
I CURRENTLY LIVE ON THE FINANCIAL AID PROVIDED TO ME BY PRINCE OURA, MY BETROTHED SINCE BIRTH.
GRP
I KNOW I DON'T HAVE FAMILY TO TAKE CARE OF ME, BUT THIS IS NO DIFFERENT FROM SELLING MYSELF!
I CAN'T STAND IT!

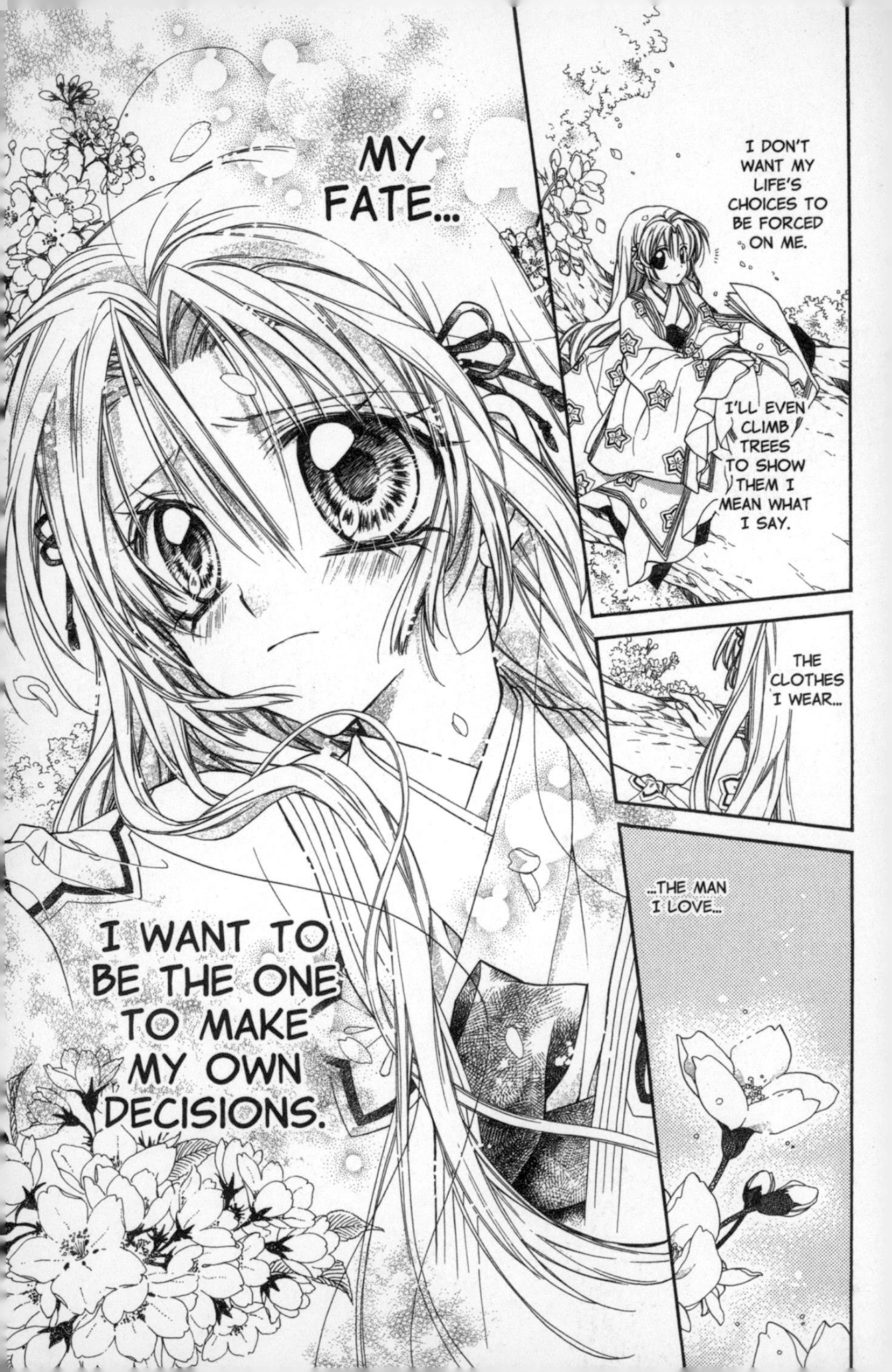
I DON'T WANT MY LIFE'S CHOICES TO BE FORCED ON ME.
I'LL EVEN CLIMB TREES TO SHOW THEM I MEAN WHAT I SAY.
THE CLOTHES I WEAR...
...THE MAN I LOVE...
MY FATE...
I WANT TO BE THE ONE TO MAKE MY OWN DECISIONS.

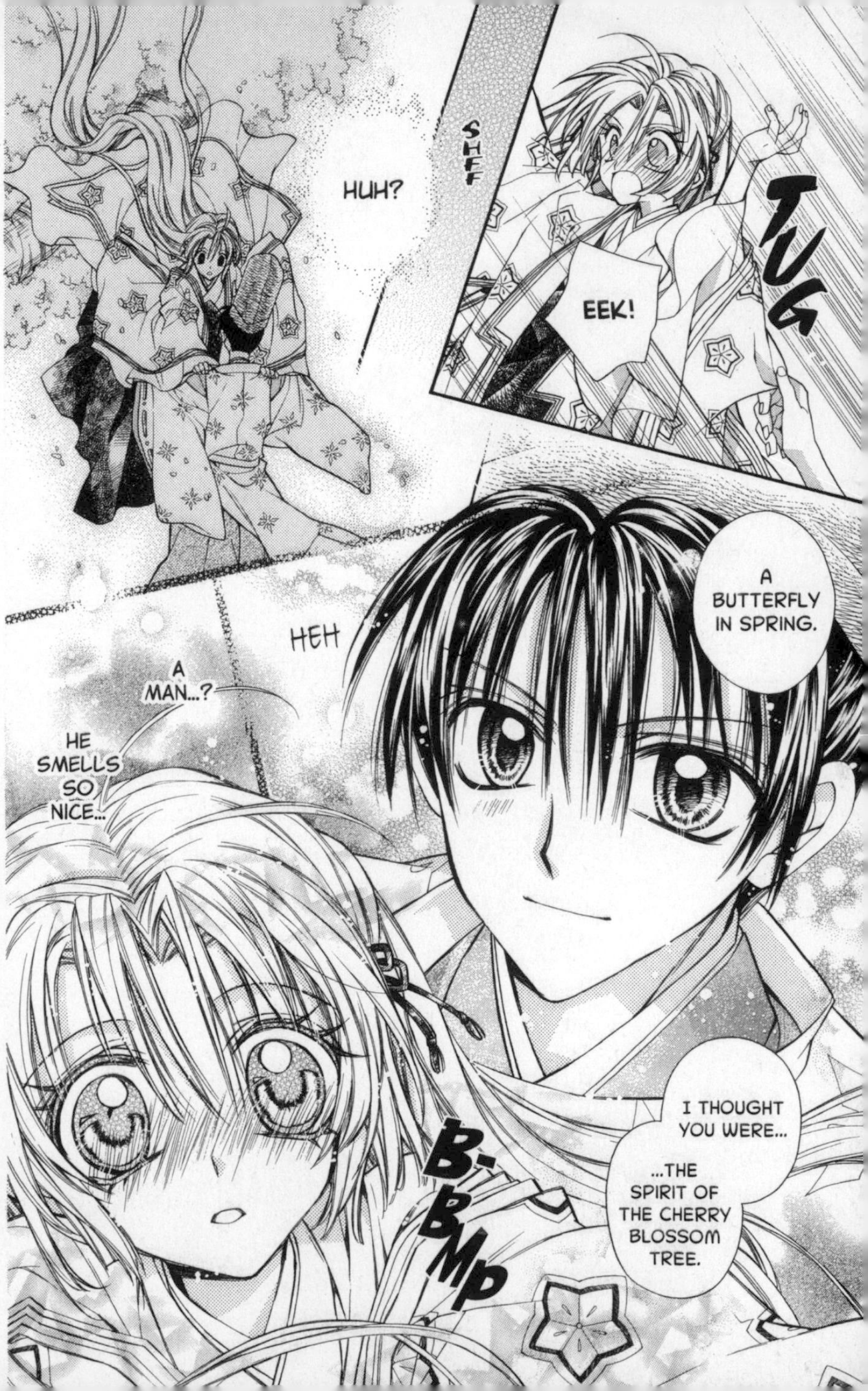
SHFF
EEK!
TUG
HUH?
A BUTTERFLY IN SPRING.
HEH
A MAN...?
HE SMELLS SO NICE...
I THOUGHT YOU WERE...
...THE SPIRIT OF THE CHERRY BLOSSOM TREE.
B-BMP

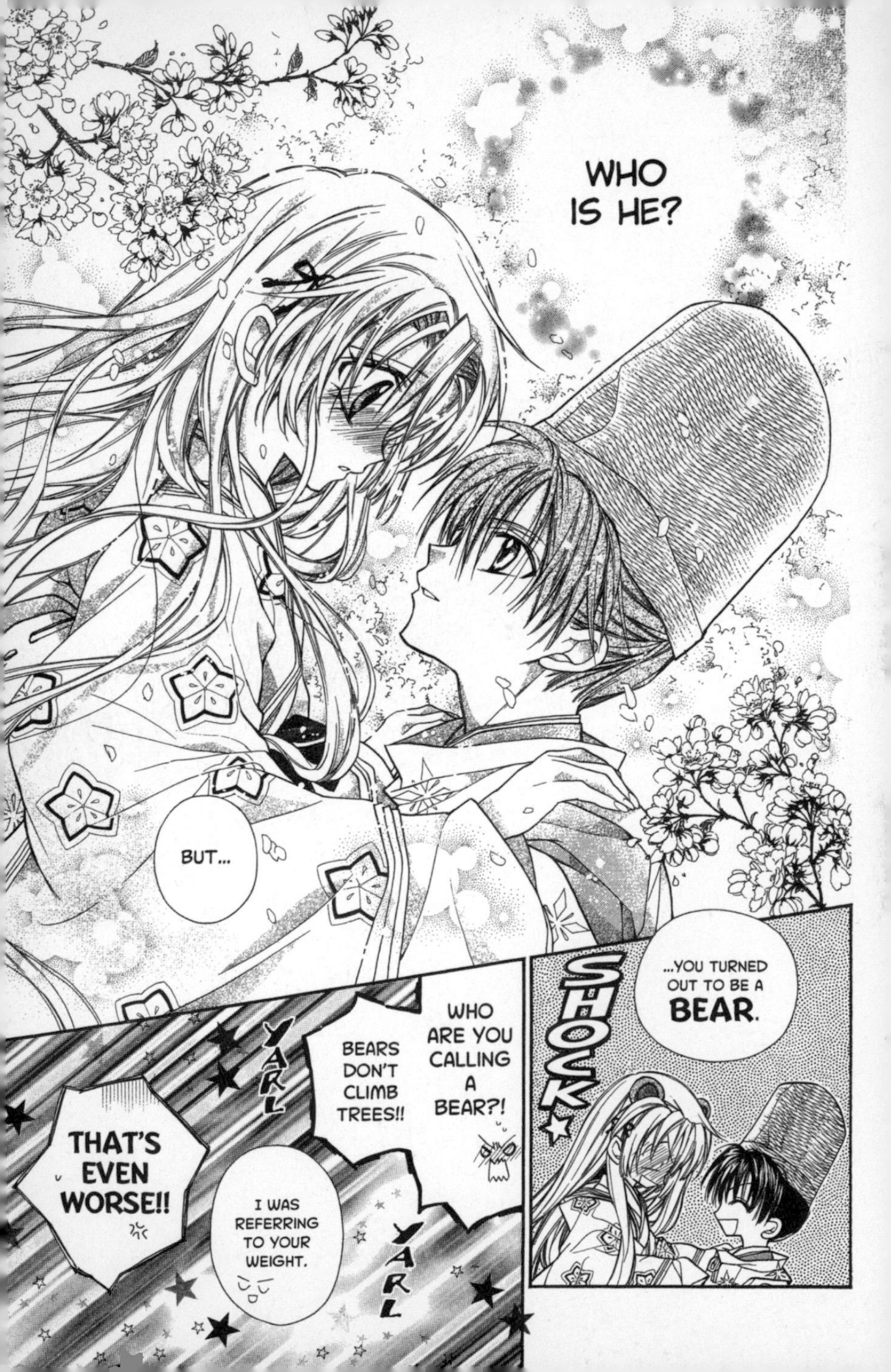
WHO IS HE?
BUT...
...YOU TURNED OUT TO BE A BEAR.
SHOCK
WHO ARE YOU CALLING A BEAR?!
BEARS DON'T CLIMB TREES!!
YARL
I WAS REFERRING TO YOUR WEIGHT.
THAT'S EVEN WORSE!!
YARL

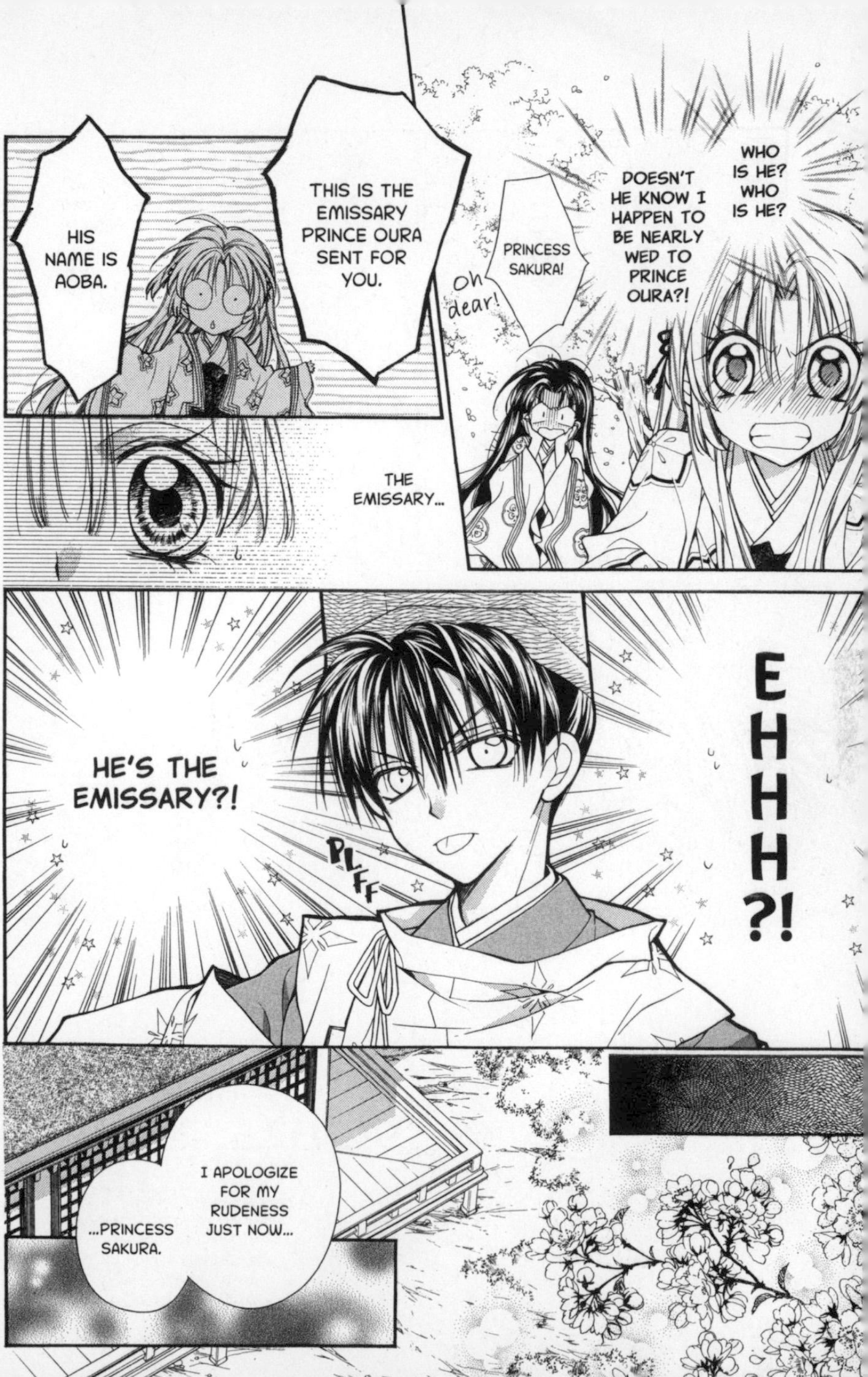
WHO IS HE? WHO IS HE?
DOESN'T HE KNOW I HAPPEN TO BE NEARLY WED TO PRINCE OURA?!
PRINCESS SAKURA!
Oh dear!
THIS IS THE EMISSARY PRINCE OURA SENT FOR YOU.
HIS NAME IS AOBA.
THE EMISSARY...
EHHH?!
HE'S THE EMISSARY?!
PLFF
I APOLOGIZE FOR MY RUDENESS JUST NOW...
...PRINCESS SAKURA.

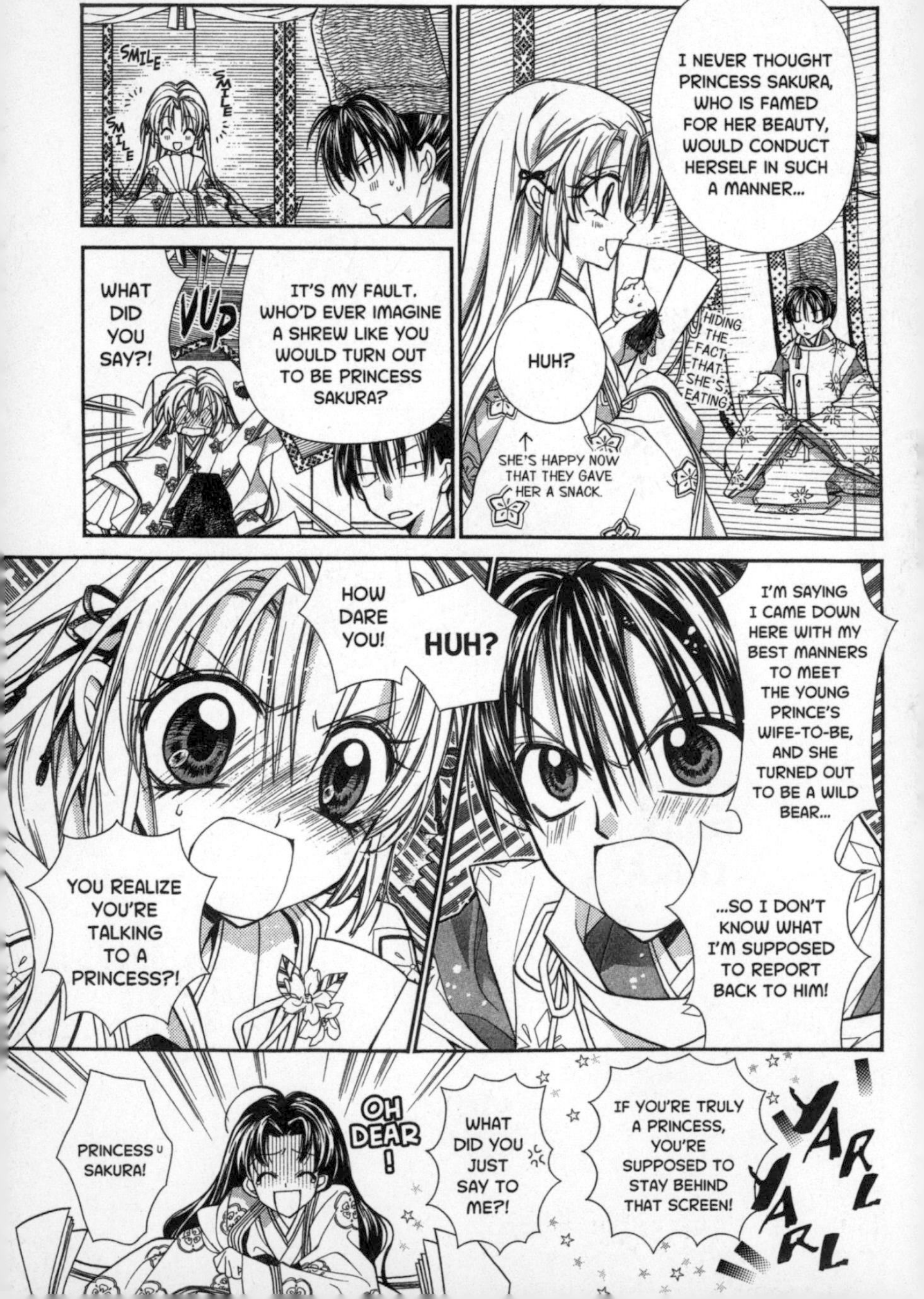
I NEVER THOUGHT PRINCESS SAKURA, WHO IS FAMED FOR HER BEAUTY, WOULD CONDUCT HERSELF IN SUCH A MANNER...
HIDING THE FACT THAT SHE'S EATING
HUH?
↑ SHE'S HAPPY NOW THAT THEY GAVE HER A SNACK.
SMILE
SMILE
SMILE
IT'S MY FAULT. WHO'D EVER IMAGINE A SHREW LIKE YOU WOULD TURN OUT TO BE PRINCESS SAKURA?
VUP
WHAT DID YOU SAY?!
I'M SAYING I CAME DOWN HERE WITH MY BEST MANNERS TO MEET THE YOUNG PRINCE'S WIFE-TO-BE, AND SHE TURNED OUT TO BE A WILD BEAR...
...SO I DON'T KNOW WHAT I'M SUPPOSED TO REPORT BACK TO HIM!
HUH?
HOW DARE YOU!
YOU REALIZE YOU'RE TALKING TO A PRINCESS?!
YARL YARL
IF YOU'RE TRULY A PRINCESS, YOU'RE SUPPOSED TO STAY BEHIND THAT SCREEN!
WHAT DID YOU JUST SAY TO ME?!
OH DEAR!
PRINCESS SAKURA!

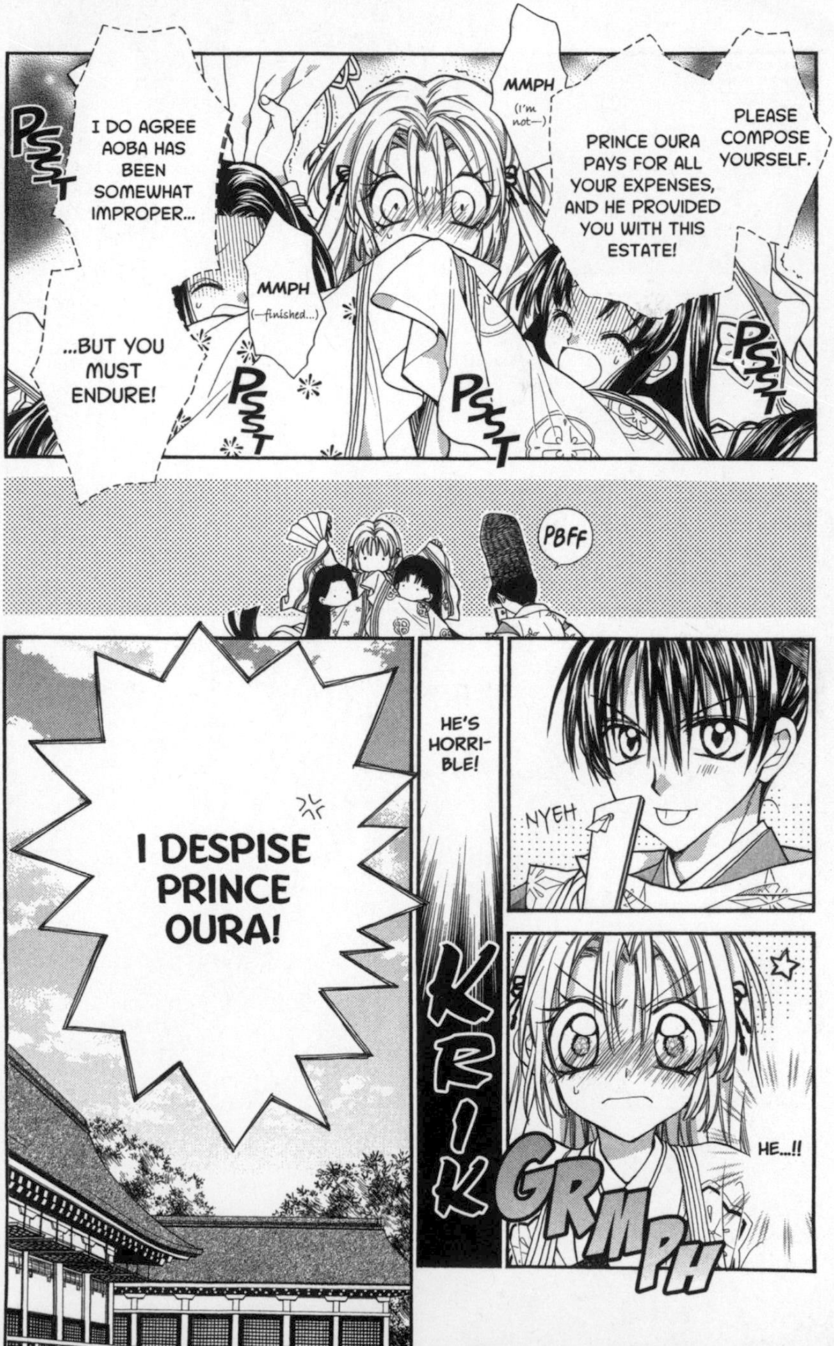
PLEASE COMPOSE YOURSELF.
PRINCE OURA PAYS FOR ALL YOUR EXPENSES, AND HE PROVIDED YOU WITH THIS ESTATE!
PSST
MMPH
(I'm not—)
PSST
MMPH
(—finished...)
PSST
I DO AGREE AOBA HAS BEEN SOMEWHAT IMPROPER...
...BUT YOU MUST ENDURE!
PSST
PBFF
NYEH
HE...!!
GRMPH
KRIK
HE'S HORRI-BLE!
I DESPISE PRINCE OURA!

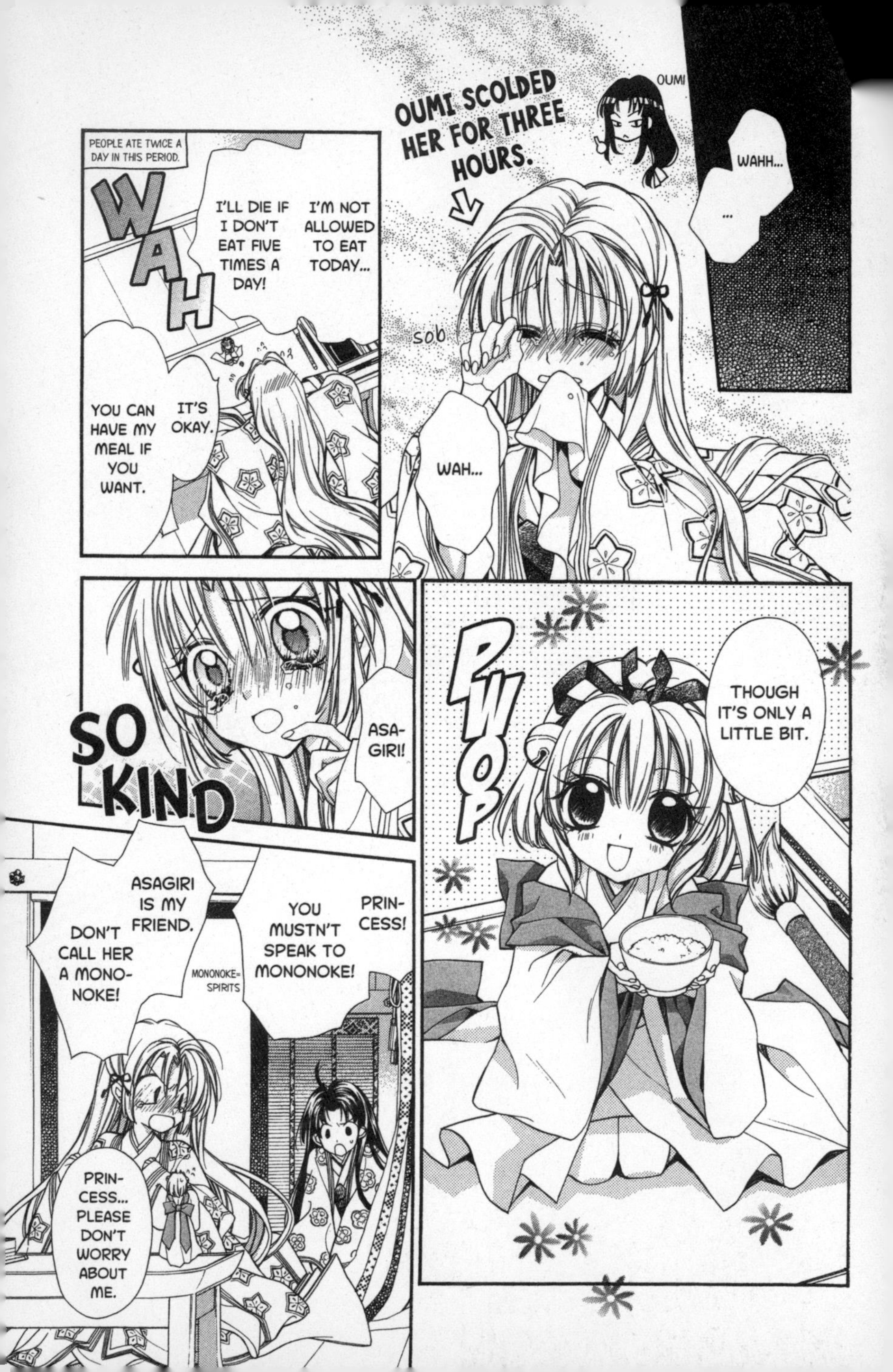
OUMI
WAHH...
...
OUMI SCOLDED HER FOR THREE HOURS.
sob
WAH...
PEOPLE ATE TWICE A DAY IN THIS PERIOD.
WAH
I'M NOT ALLOWED TO EAT TODAY...
I'LL DIE IF I DON'T EAT FIVE TIMES A DAY!
IT'S OKAY.
YOU CAN HAVE MY MEAL IF YOU WANT.
PWOP
THOUGH IT'S ONLY A LITTLE BIT.
ASA-GIRI!
SO KIND
PRIN-CESS!
YOU MUSTN'T SPEAK TO MONONOKE!
MONONOKE= SPIRITS
ASAGIRI IS MY FRIEND.
DON'T CALL HER A MONO-NOKE!
PRIN-CESS... PLEASE DON'T WORRY ABOUT ME.

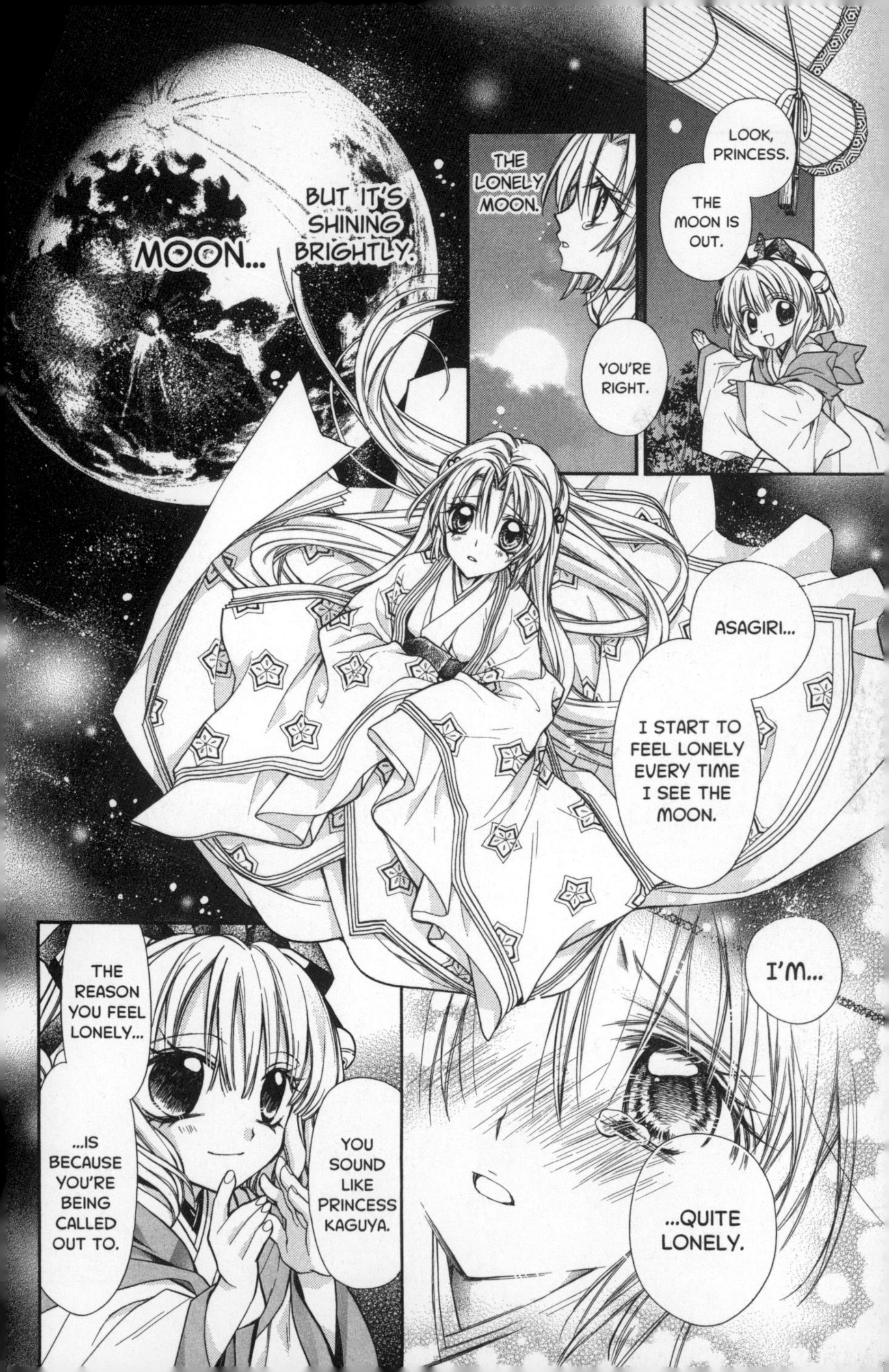
LOOK, PRINCESS.
THE MOON IS OUT.
THE LONELY MOON.
YOU'RE RIGHT.
BUT IT'S SHINING BRIGHTLY.
MOON...
ASAGIRI...
I START TO FEEL LONELY EVERY TIME I SEE THE MOON.
I'M...
...QUITE LONELY.
YOU SOUND LIKE PRINCESS KAGUYA.
THE REASON YOU FEEL LONELY...
...IS BECAUSE YOU'RE BEING CALLED OUT TO.

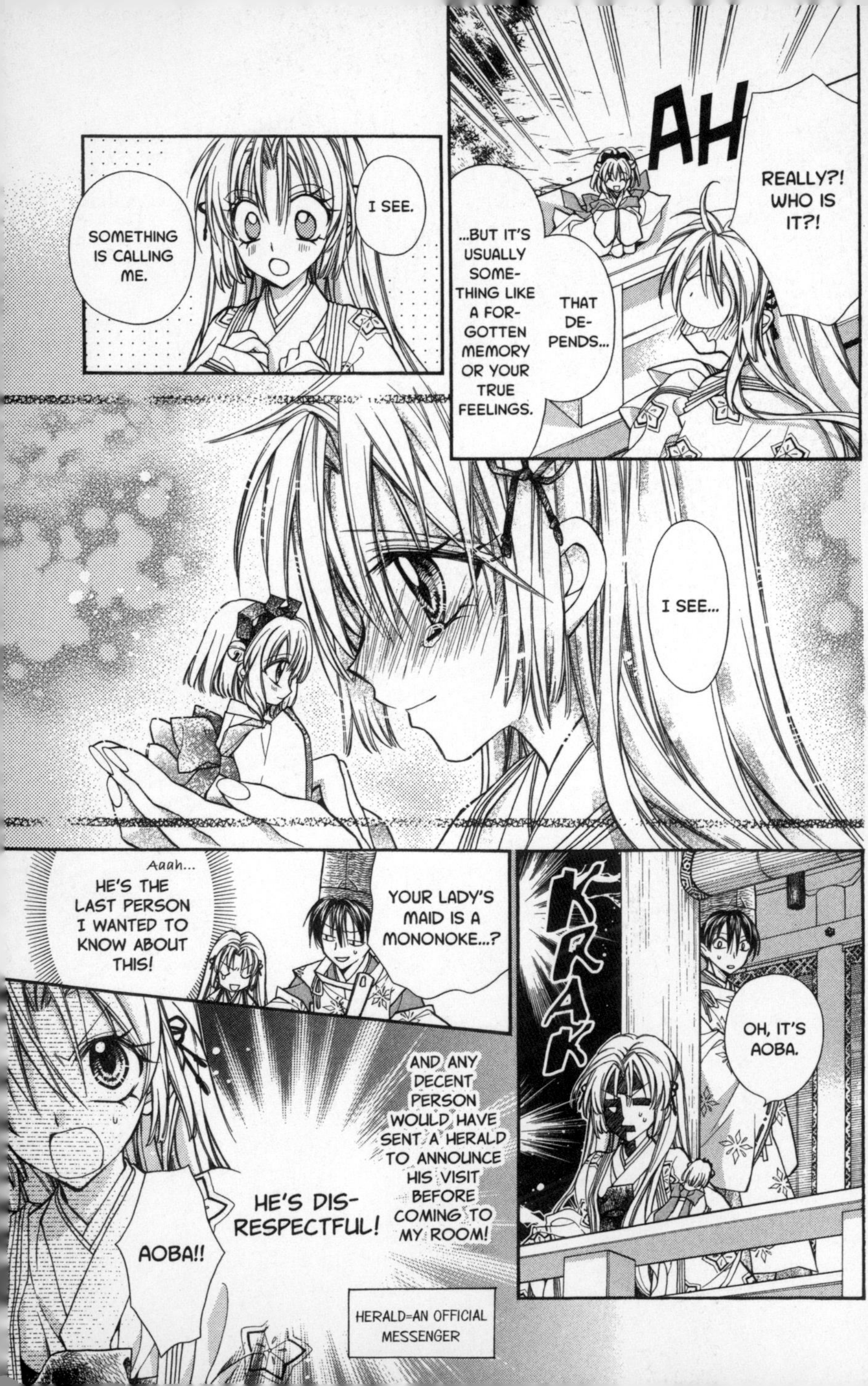
AH
REALLY?! WHO IS IT?!
THAT DE-PENDS...
...BUT IT'S USUALLY SOME-THING LIKE A FOR-GOTTEN MEMORY OR YOUR TRUE FEELINGS.
I SEE.
SOMETHING IS CALLING ME.
I SEE...
KRAK
OH, IT'S AOBA.
YOUR LADY'S MAID IS A MONONOKE...?
Aaah... HE'S THE LAST PERSON I WANTED TO KNOW ABOUT THIS!
AND ANY DECENT PERSON WOULD HAVE SENT A HERALD TO ANNOUNCE HIS VISIT BEFORE COMING TO MY ROOM!
HE'S DIS-RESPECTFUL!
AOBA!!
HERALD=AN OFFICIAL MESSENGER

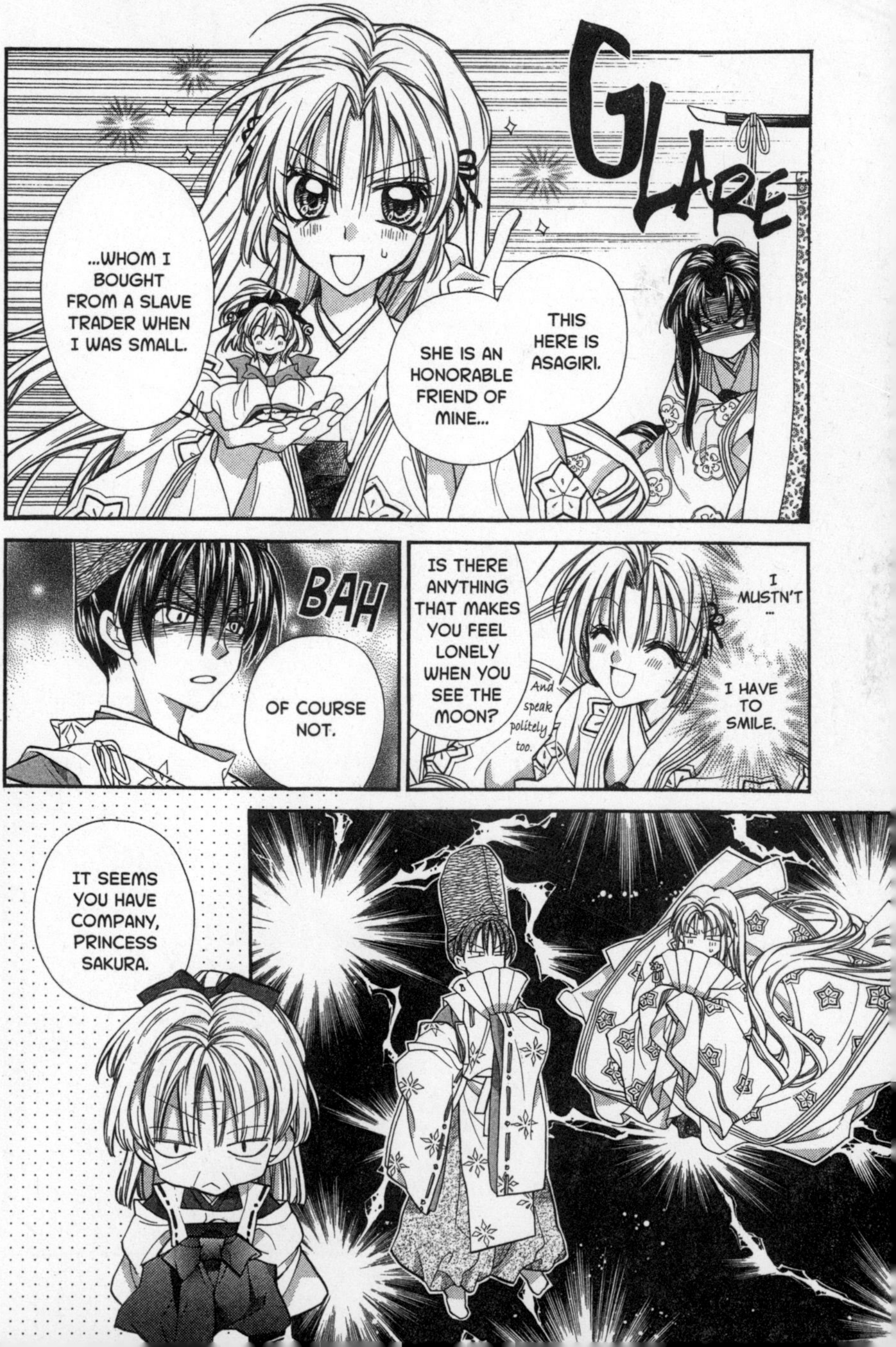
GLARE
THIS HERE IS ASAGIRI.
SHE IS AN HONORABLE FRIEND OF MINE...
...WHOM I BOUGHT FROM A SLAVE TRADER WHEN I WAS SMALL.
I MUSTN'T ...
I HAVE TO SMILE.
IS THERE ANYTHING THAT MAKES YOU FEEL LONELY WHEN YOU SEE THE MOON?
And speak politely too.
BAH
OF COURSE NOT.
IT SEEMS YOU HAVE COMPANY, PRINCESS SAKURA.

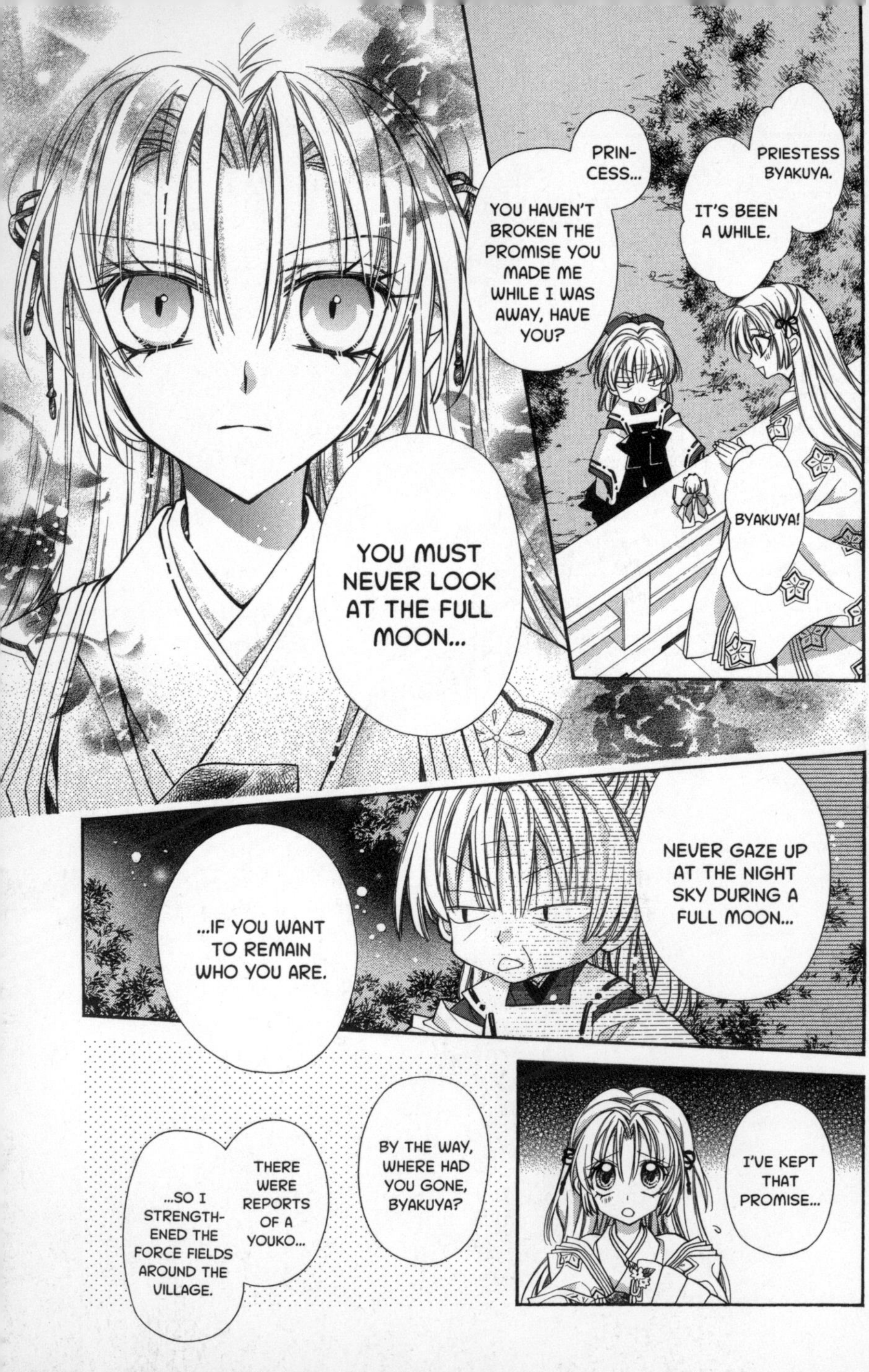
PRIESTESS BYAKUYA.
IT'S BEEN A WHILE.
PRIN-CESS...
YOU HAVEN'T BROKEN THE PROMISE YOU MADE ME WHILE I WAS AWAY, HAVE YOU?
BYAKUYA!
YOU MUST NEVER LOOK AT THE FULL MOON...
NEVER GAZE UP AT THE NIGHT SKY DURING A FULL MOON...
...IF YOU WANT TO REMAIN WHO YOU ARE.
I'VE KEPT THAT PROMISE...
BY THE WAY, WHERE HAD YOU GONE, BYAKUYA?
THERE WERE REPORTS OF A YOUKO...
...SO I STRENGTH-ENED THE FORCE FIELDS AROUND THE VILLAGE.

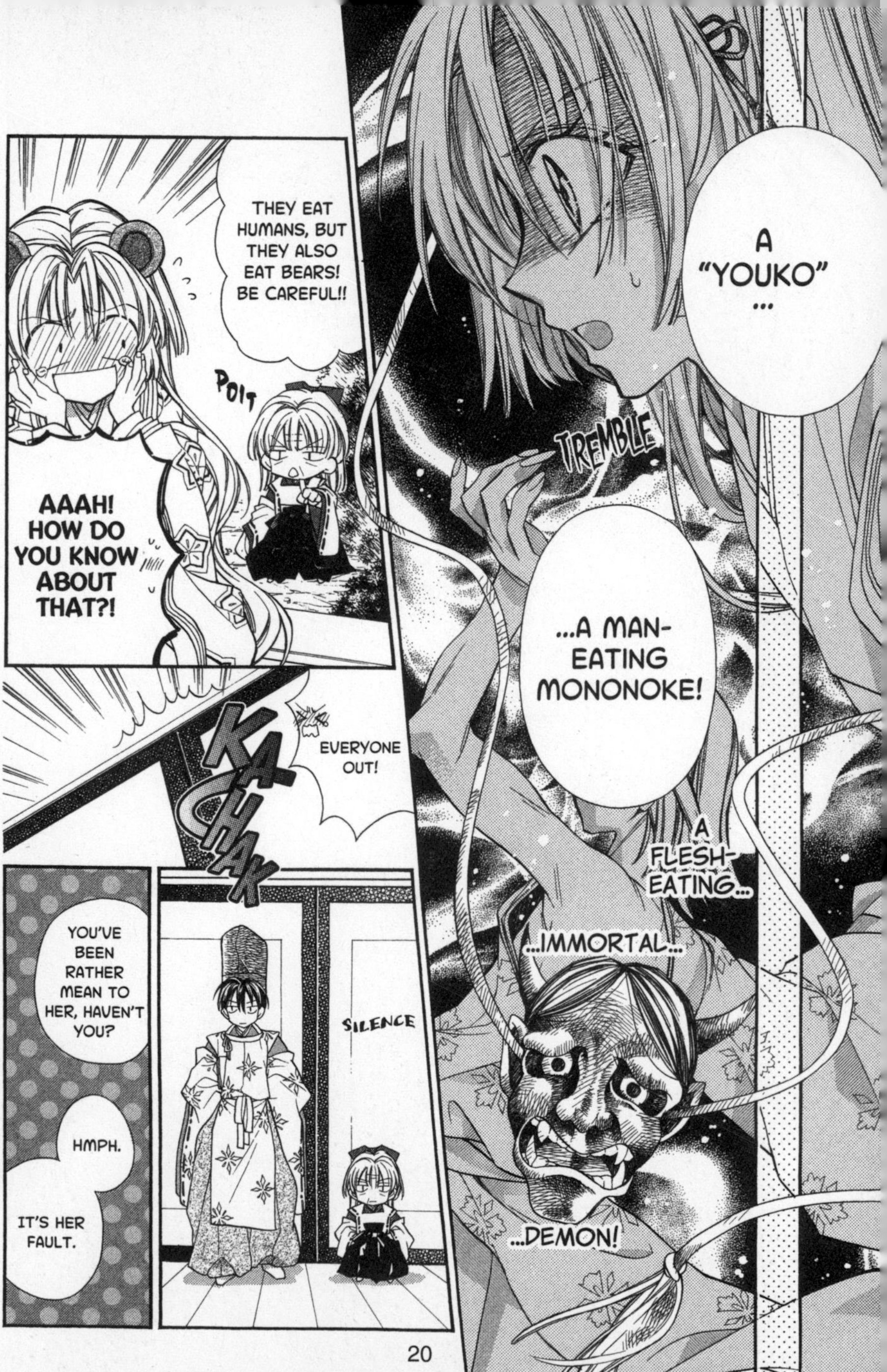
A "YOUKO" ...
TREMBLE
...A MAN-EATING MONONOKE!
A FLESH-EATING...
...IMMORTAL...
...DEMON!
THEY EAT HUMANS, BUT THEY ALSO EAT BEARS! BE CAREFUL!!
POIT
AAAH! HOW DO YOU KNOW ABOUT THAT?!
KA-CHAK
EVERYONE OUT!
SILENCE
YOU'VE BEEN RATHER MEAN TO HER, HAVEN'T YOU?
HMPH.
IT'S HER FAULT.

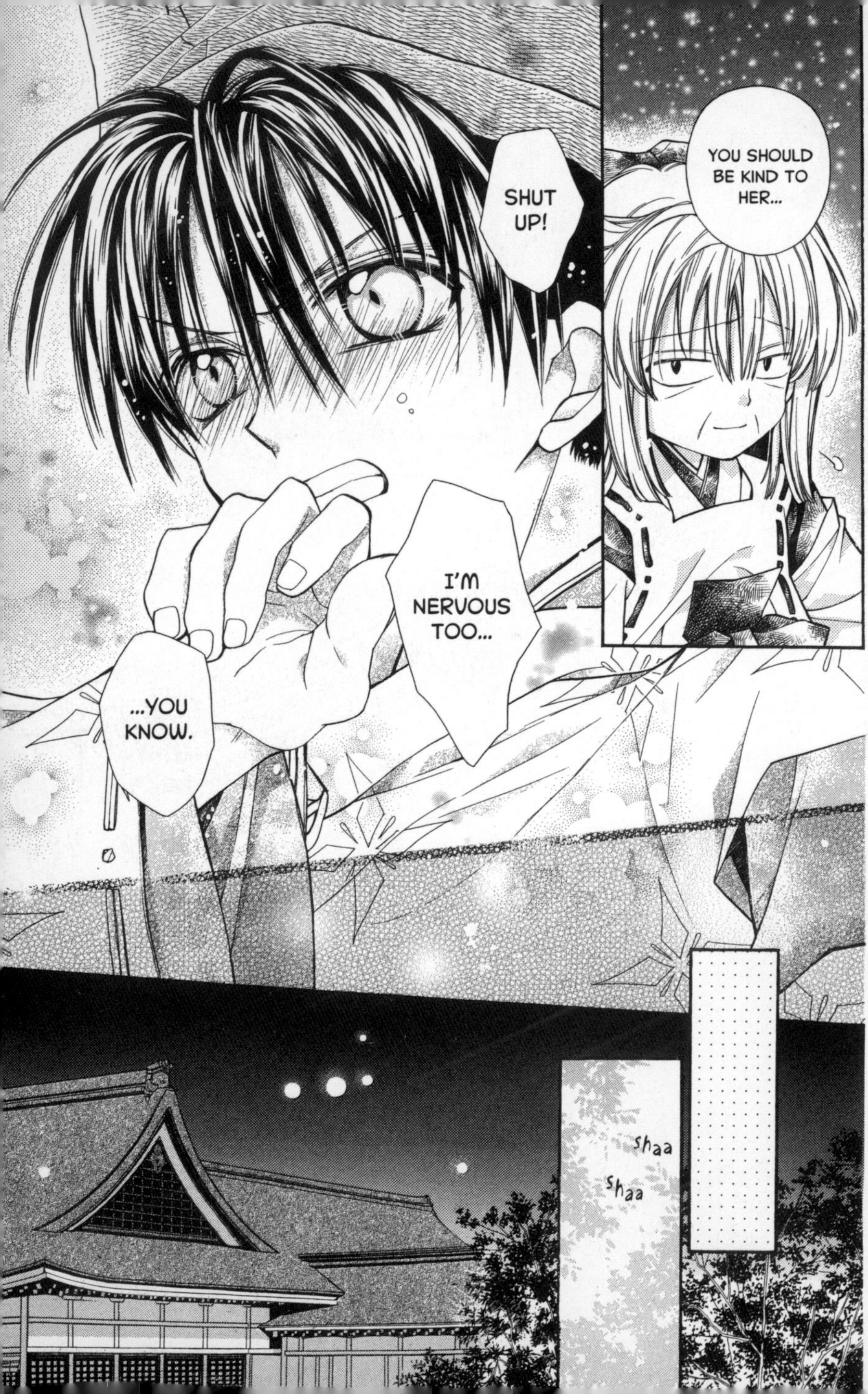
YOU SHOULD BE KIND TO HER...
SHUT UP!
I'M NERVOUS TOO...
...YOU KNOW.
shaa
shaa

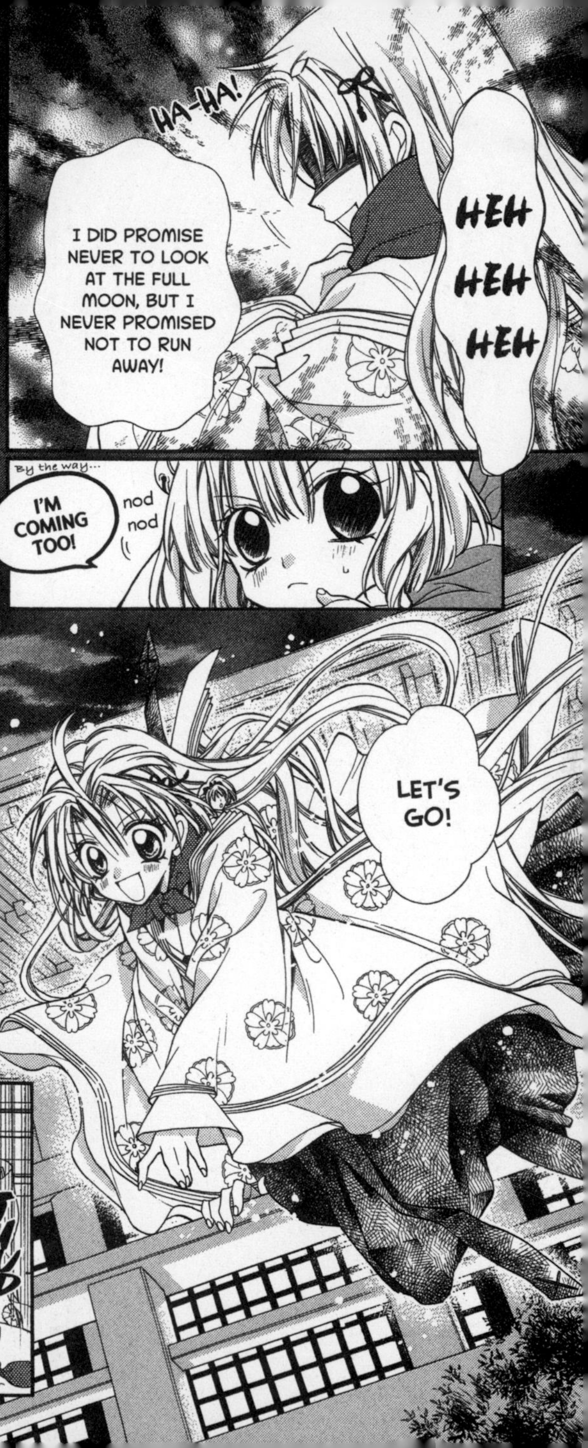
HA-HA!
I DID PROMISE NEVER TO LOOK AT THE FULL MOON, BUT I NEVER PROMISED NOT TO RUN AWAY!
HEH HEH HEH
By the way...
nod nod
I'M COMING TOO!
LET'S GO!

SAKURA HIME'S LETTER

I BID YOU FARE-WELL, MY DEAR EMISSARY.

I DO NOT WANT TO MARRY PRINCE OURA **ANYWAY**.

IF I TURNED OUT TO BE A WILD BEAR, AND YOU HAVE NO MEANS OF REPORTING TO HIM ABOUT IT...

...THEN TAKE THIS LETTER BACK TO THE CAPITAL AND TELL HIM THE TRUTH. ♡♡

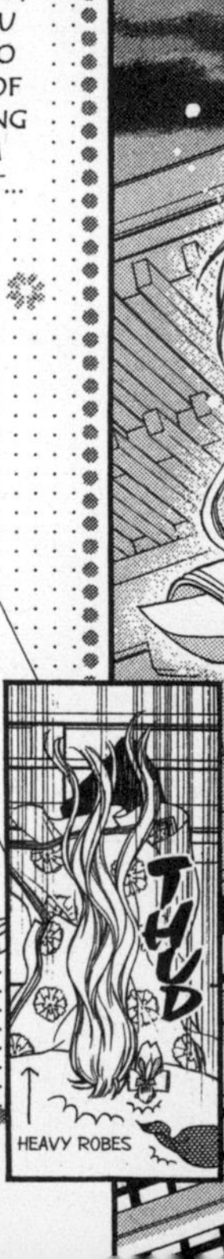
THUD
HEAVY ROBES

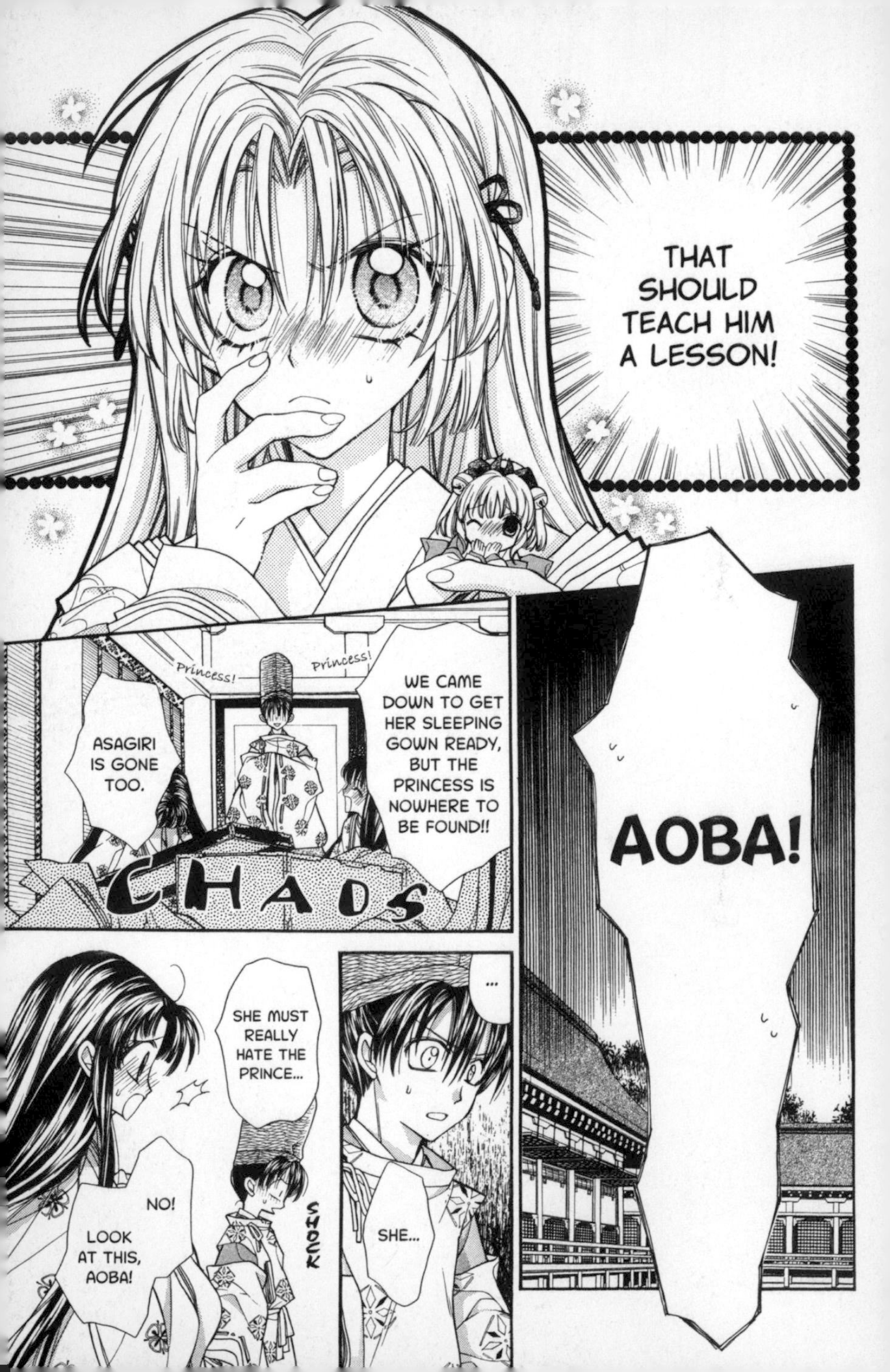
THAT SHOULD TEACH HIM A LESSON!
AOBA!
Princess!
Princess!
WE CAME DOWN TO GET HER SLEEPING GOWN READY, BUT THE PRINCESS IS NOWHERE TO BE FOUND!!
ASAGIRI IS GONE TOO.
CHAOS
...
SHE...
SHE MUST REALLY HATE THE PRINCE...
SHOCK
NO!
LOOK AT THIS, AOBA!

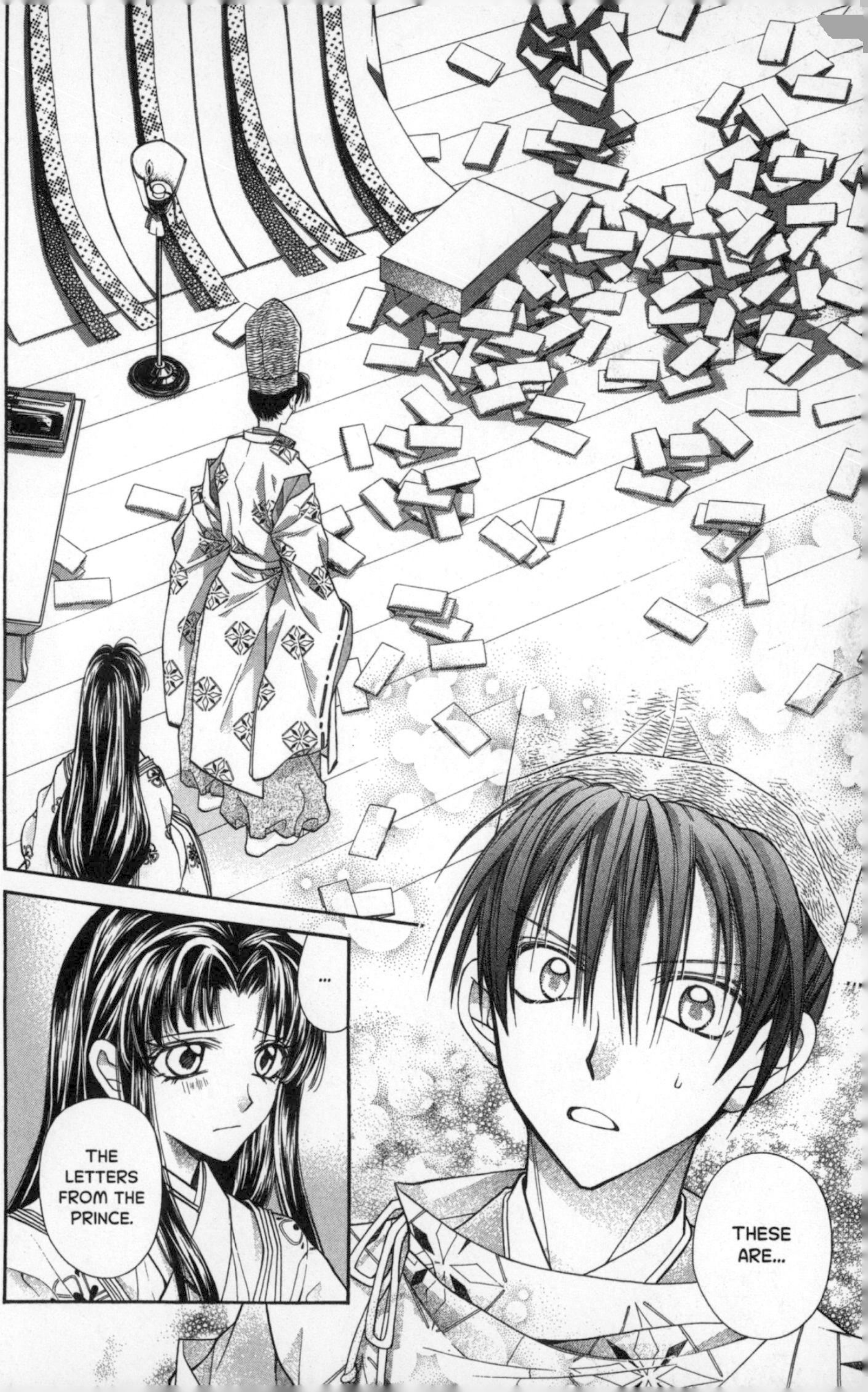
THESE ARE...
...
THE LETTERS FROM THE PRINCE.

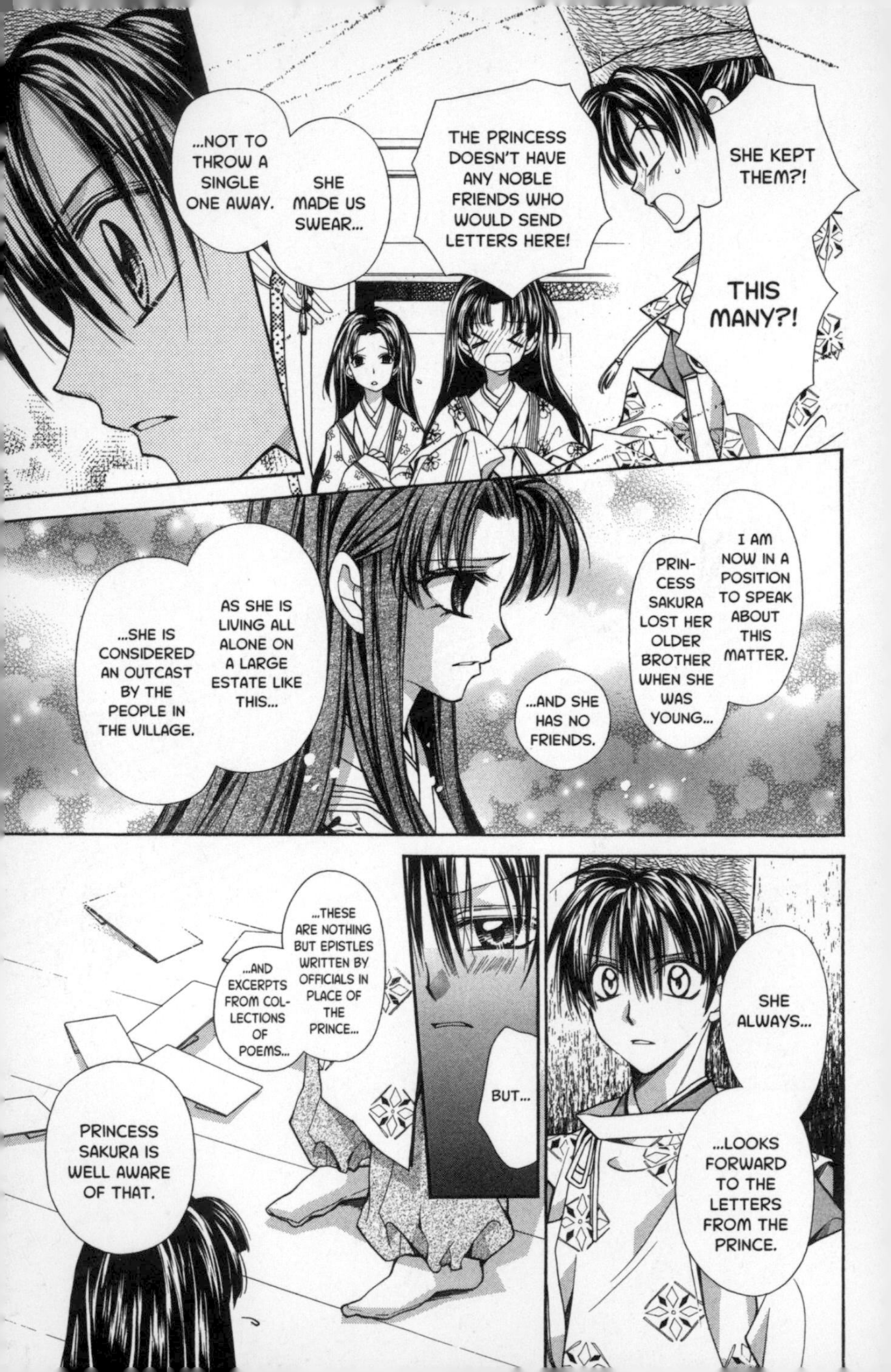
SHE KEPT THEM?!
THIS MANY?!
THE PRINCESS DOESN'T HAVE ANY NOBLE FRIENDS WHO WOULD SEND LETTERS HERE!
SHE MADE US SWEAR...
...NOT TO THROW A SINGLE ONE AWAY.
I AM NOW IN A POSITION TO SPEAK ABOUT THIS MATTER.
PRINCESS SAKURA LOST HER OLDER BROTHER WHEN SHE WAS YOUNG...
...AND SHE HAS NO FRIENDS.
AS SHE IS LIVING ALL ALONE ON A LARGE ESTATE LIKE THIS...
...SHE IS CONSIDERED AN OUTCAST BY THE PEOPLE IN THE VILLAGE.
SHE ALWAYS...
...LOOKS FORWARD TO THE LETTERS FROM THE PRINCE.
BUT...
...THESE ARE NOTHING BUT EPISTLES WRITTEN BY OFFICIALS IN PLACE OF THE PRINCE...
...AND EXCERPTS FROM COLLECTIONS OF POEMS...
PRINCESS SAKURA IS WELL AWARE OF THAT.

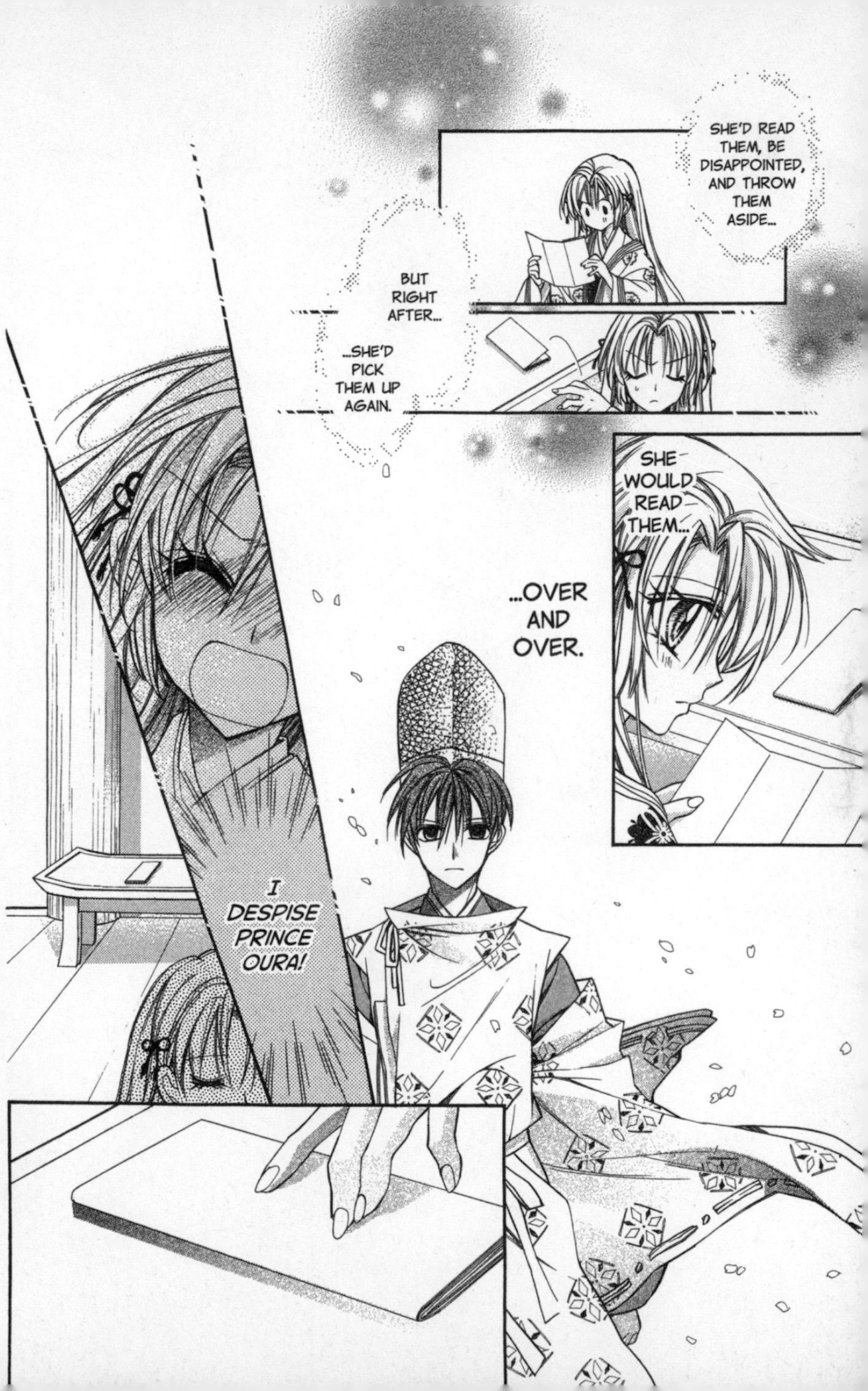
SHE'D READ THEM, BE DISAPPOINTED, AND THROW THEM ASIDE...
BUT RIGHT AFTER...
...SHE'D PICK THEM UP AGAIN.
SHE WOULD READ THEM...
...OVER AND OVER.
I DESPISE PRINCE OURA!

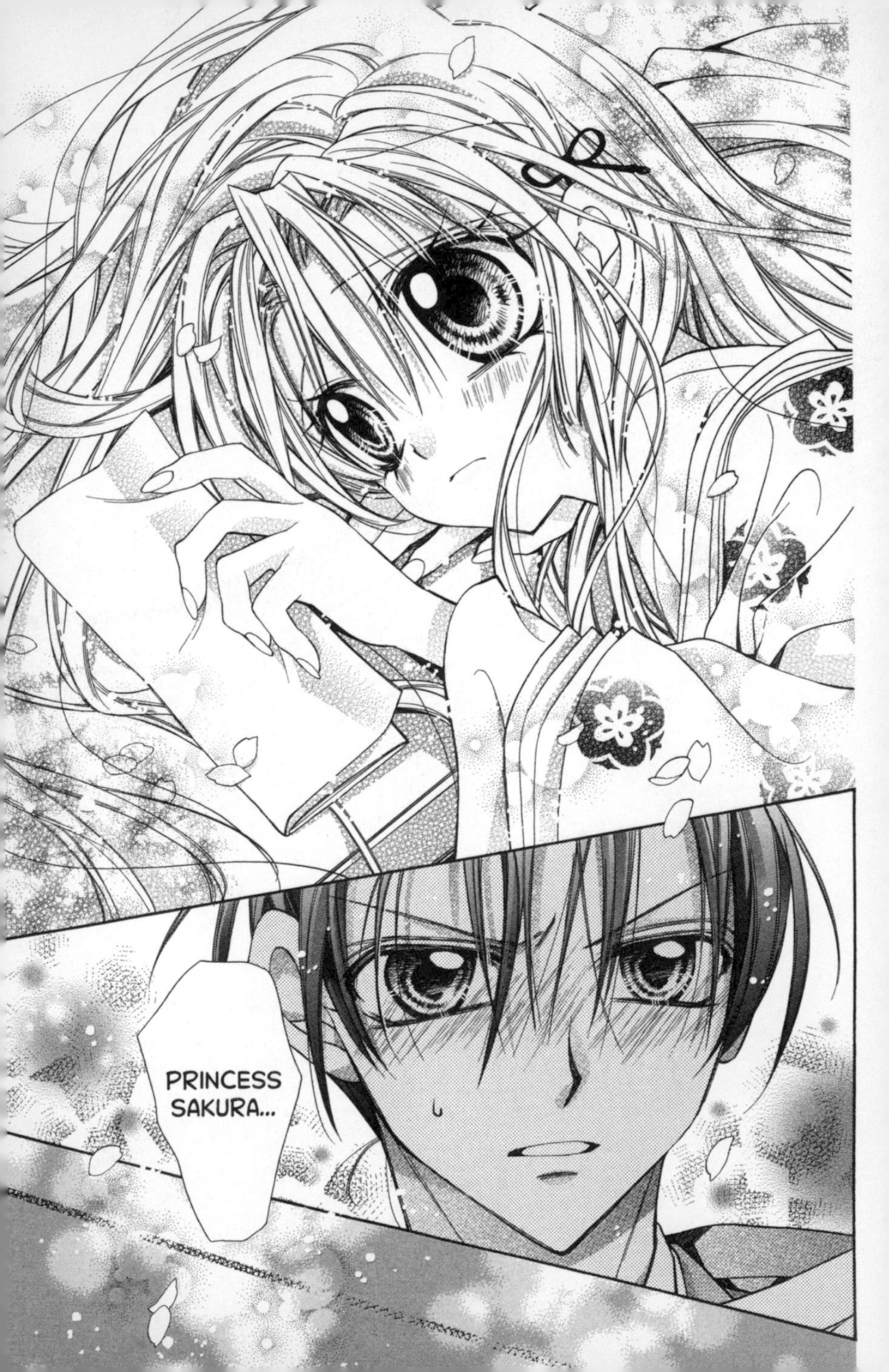
PRINCESS SAKURA...

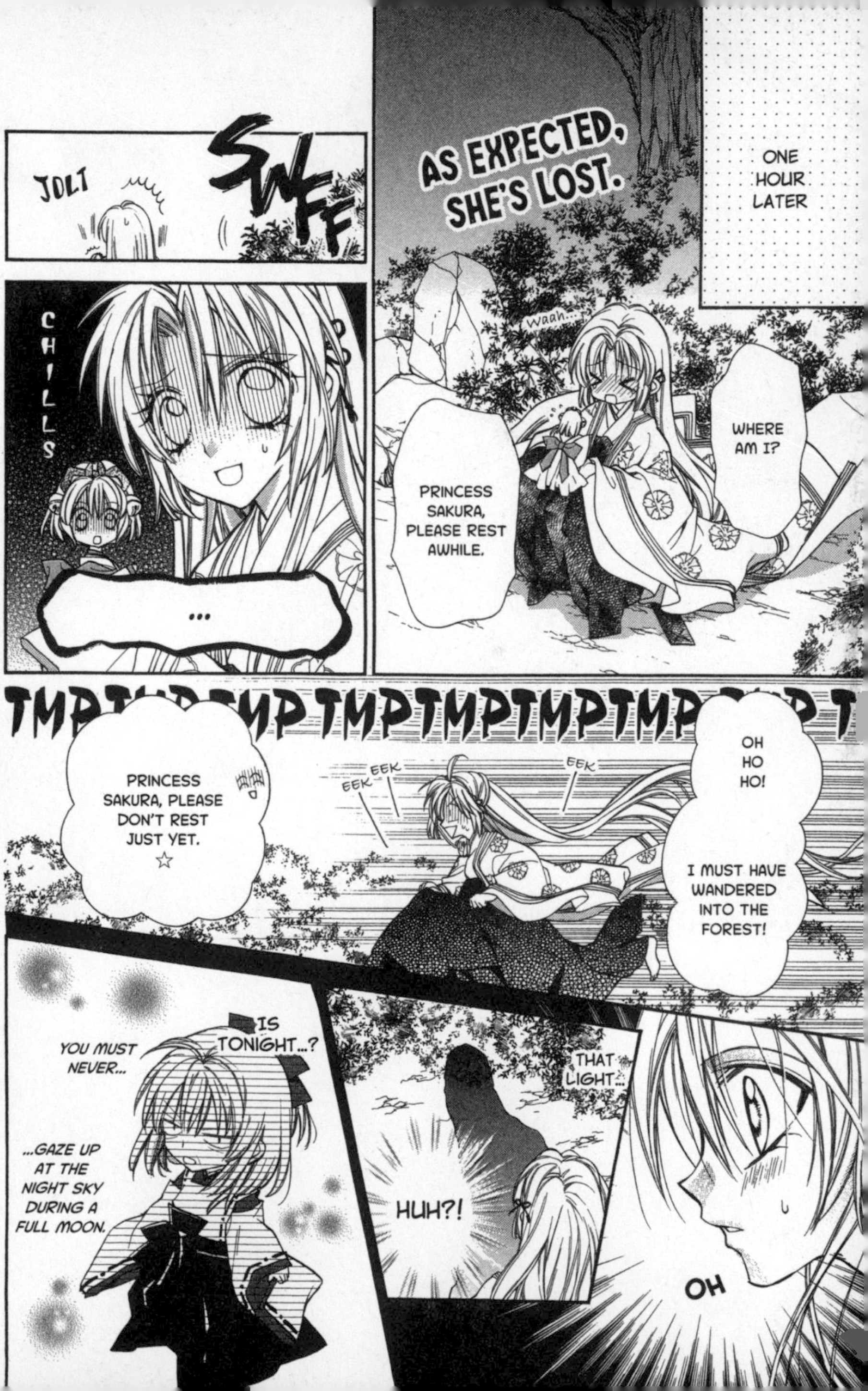
ONE HOUR LATER
AS EXPECTED, SHE'S LOST.
waah...
WHERE AM I?
PRINCESS SAKURA, PLEASE REST AWHILE.
SWFF
JOLT
CHILLS
...
TMP TMP TMP TMP
OH HO HO!
I MUST HAVE WANDERED INTO THE FOREST!
EEK
EEK
EEK
PRINCESS SAKURA, PLEASE DON'T REST JUST YET. ☆
OH
THAT LIGHT...
HUH?!
IS TONIGHT...?
YOU MUST NEVER...
...GAZE UP AT THE NIGHT SKY DURING A FULL MOON.

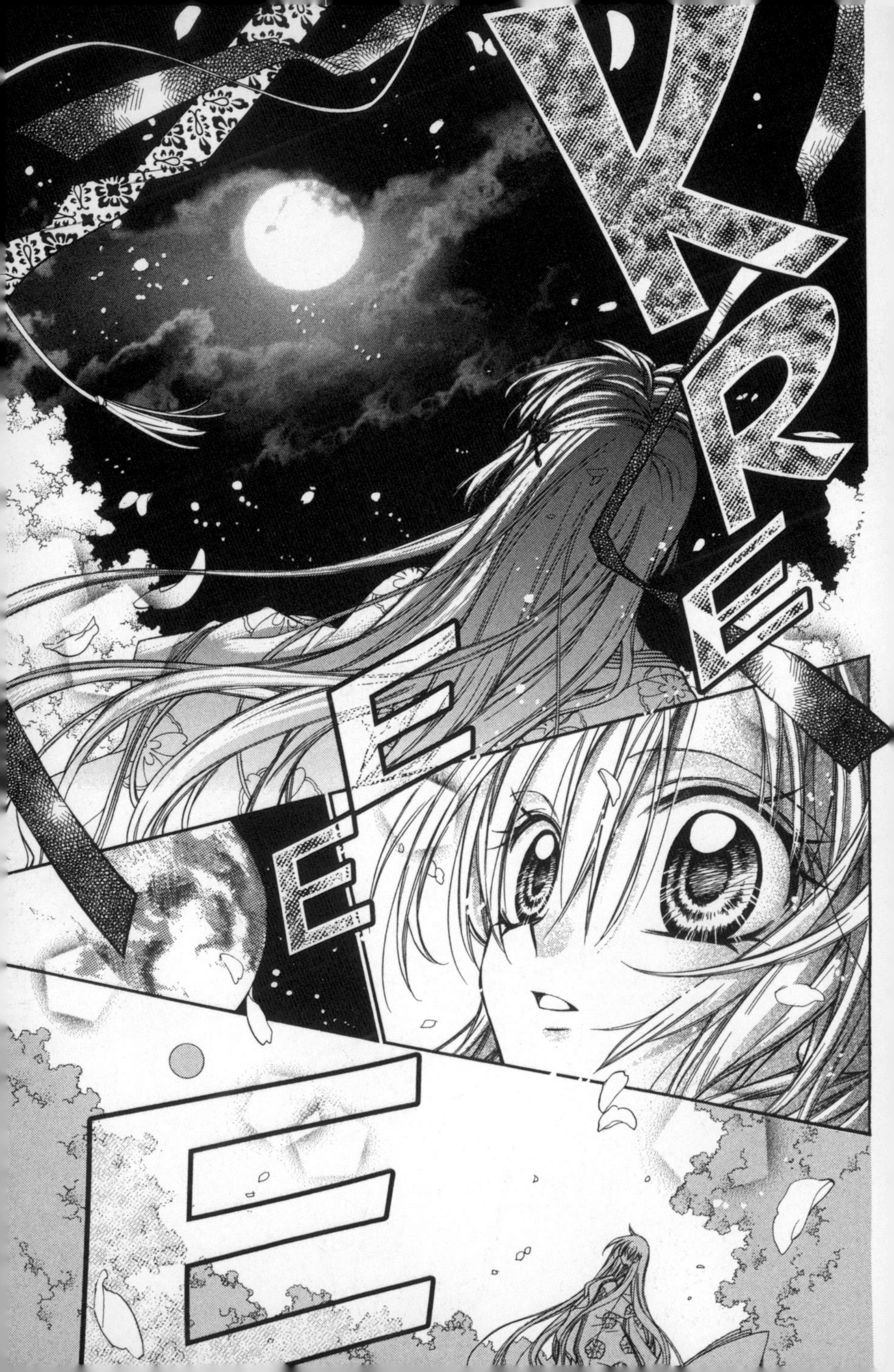
KREEEE

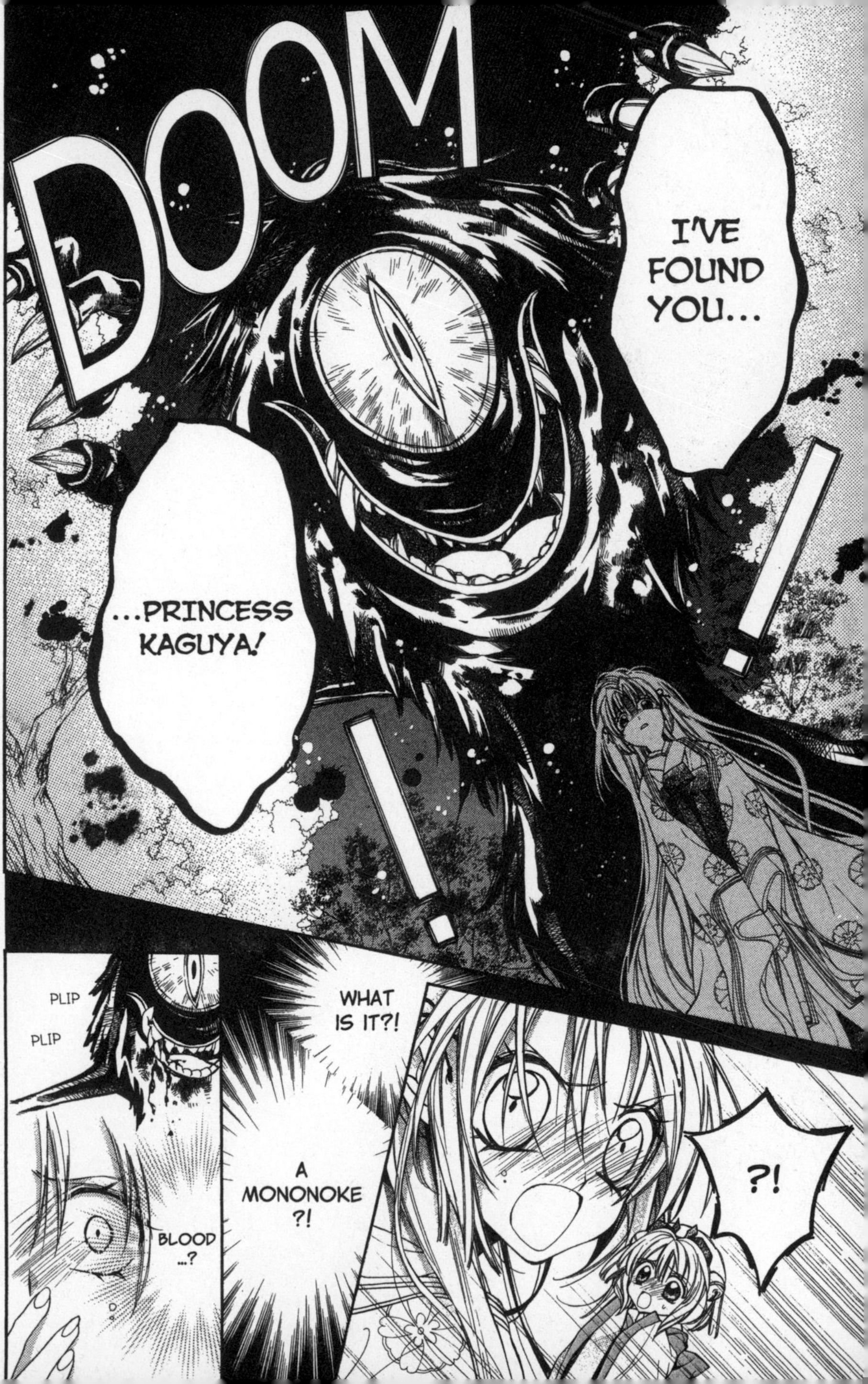
I'VE FOUND YOU...
DOOM
...PRINCESS KAGUYA!
?!
WHAT IS IT?!
A MONONOKE ?!
PLIP
PLIP
BLOOD ...?

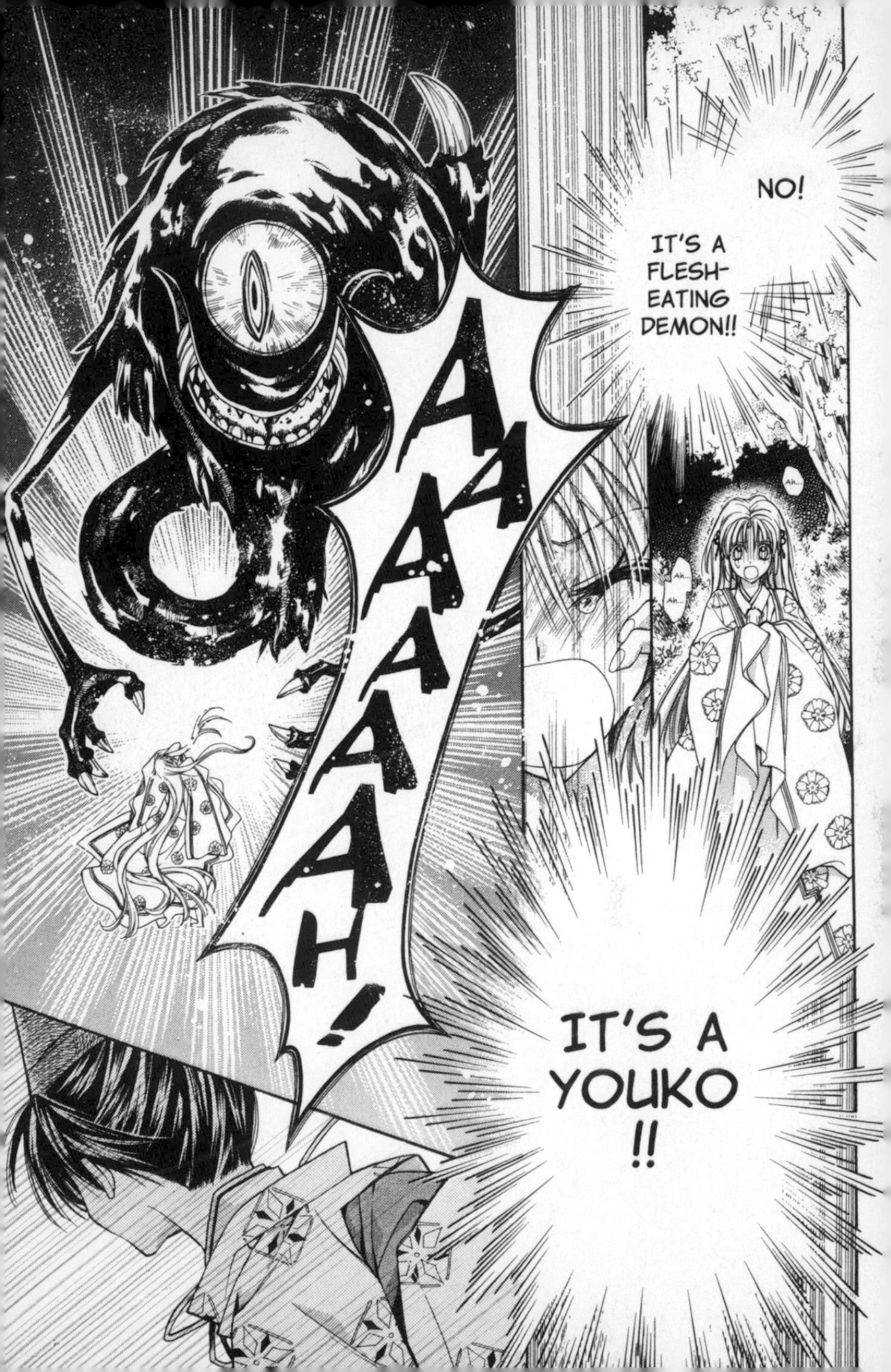
NO!
IT'S A FLESH-EATING DEMON!!
Ah...
Ah...
Ah...
AAAAAAAH!
IT'S A YOUKO !!

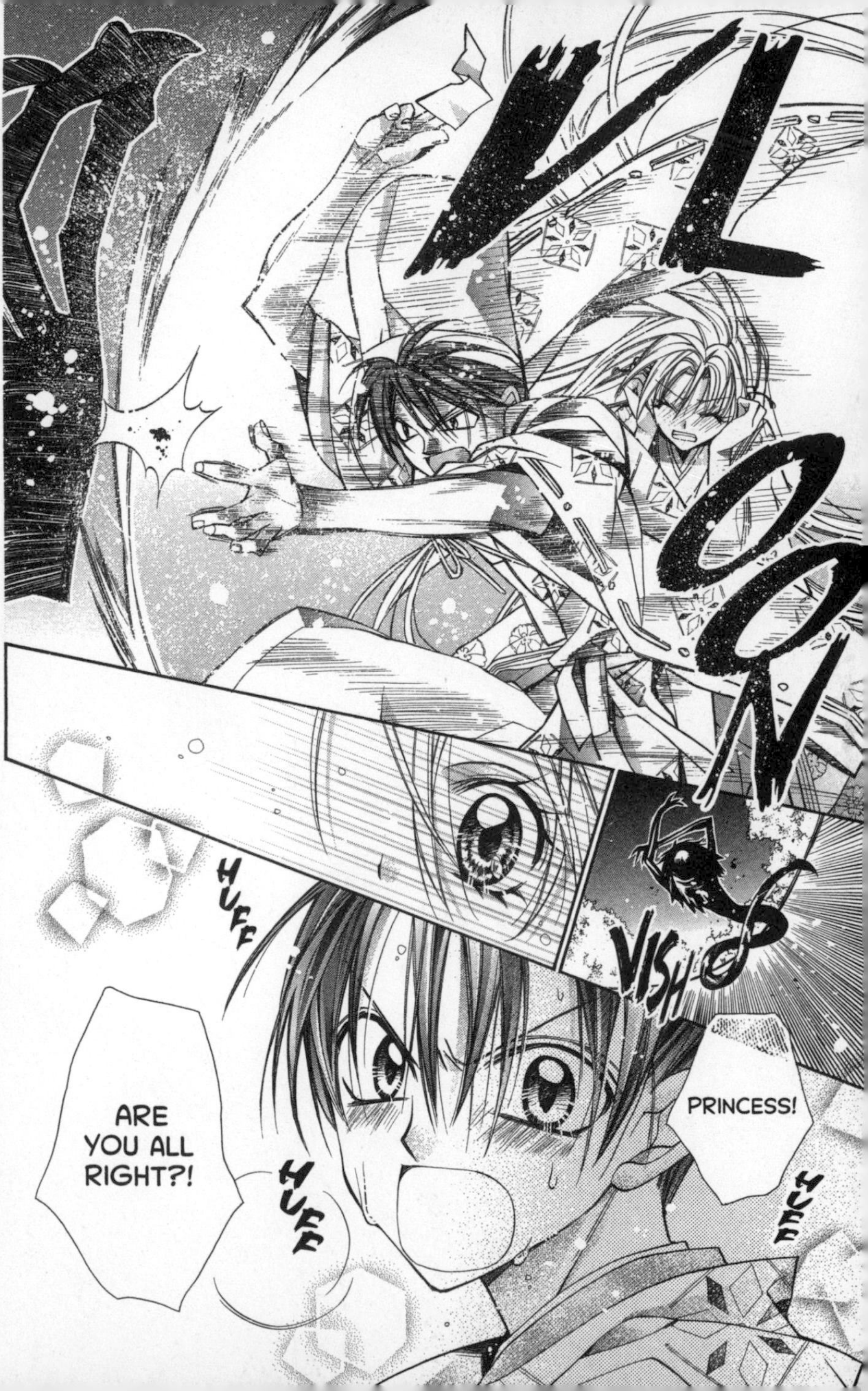
VISH
PRINCESS!
HUFF
HUFF
ARE YOU ALL RIGHT?!
HUFF

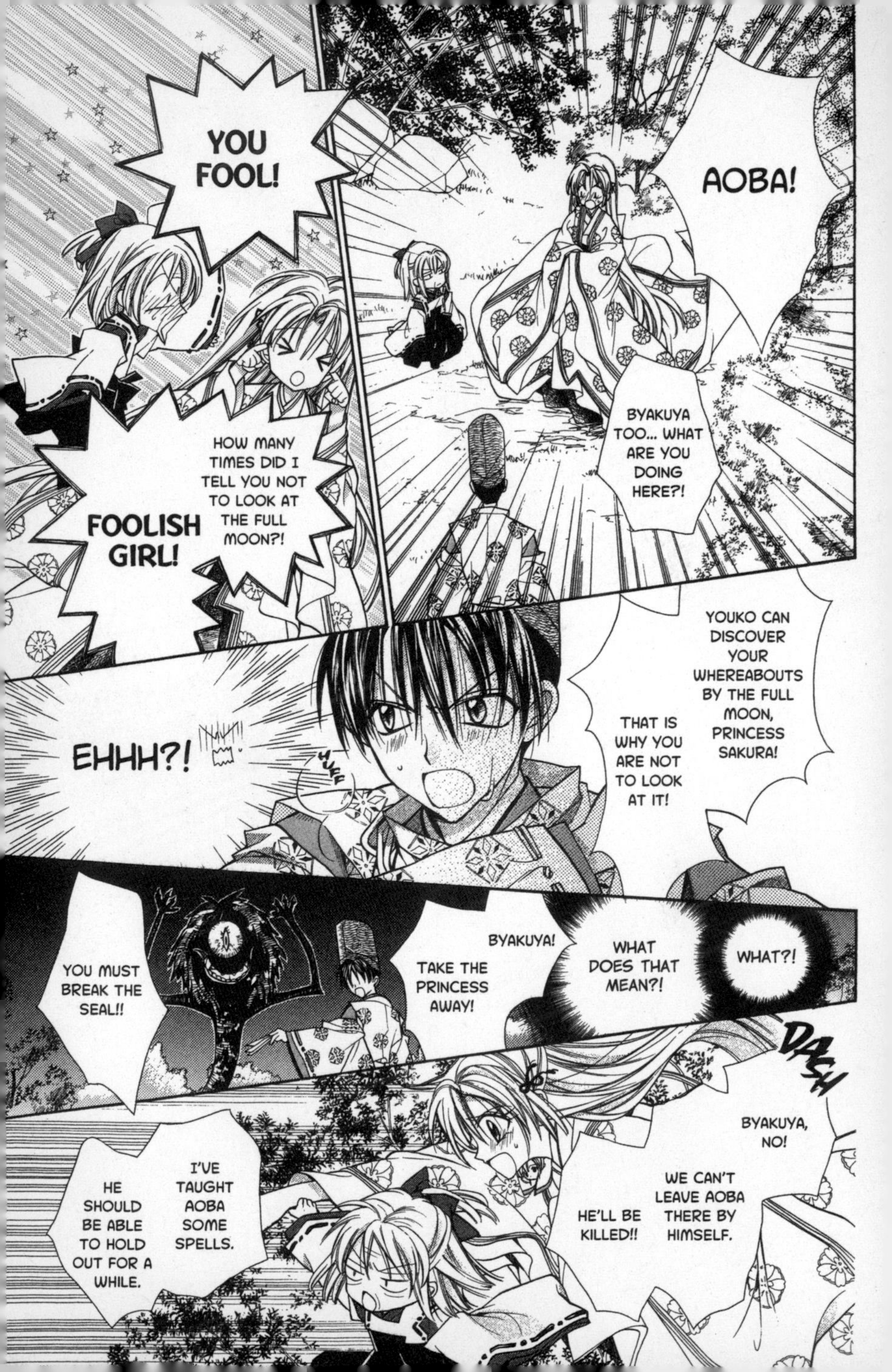
AOBA!
BYAKUYA TOO... WHAT ARE YOU DOING HERE?!
YOU FOOL!
HOW MANY TIMES DID I TELL YOU NOT TO LOOK AT THE FULL MOON?!
FOOLISH GIRL!
YOUKO CAN DISCOVER YOUR WHEREABOUTS BY THE FULL MOON, PRINCESS SAKURA!
THAT IS WHY YOU ARE NOT TO LOOK AT IT!
EHHH?!
WHAT?!
WHAT DOES THAT MEAN?!
BYAKUYA!
TAKE THE PRINCESS AWAY!
YOU MUST BREAK THE SEAL!!
DASH
BYAKUYA, NO!
WE CAN'T LEAVE AOBA THERE BY HIMSELF.
HE'LL BE KILLED!!
I'VE TAUGHT AOBA SOME SPELLS.
HE SHOULD BE ABLE TO HOLD OUT FOR A WHILE.

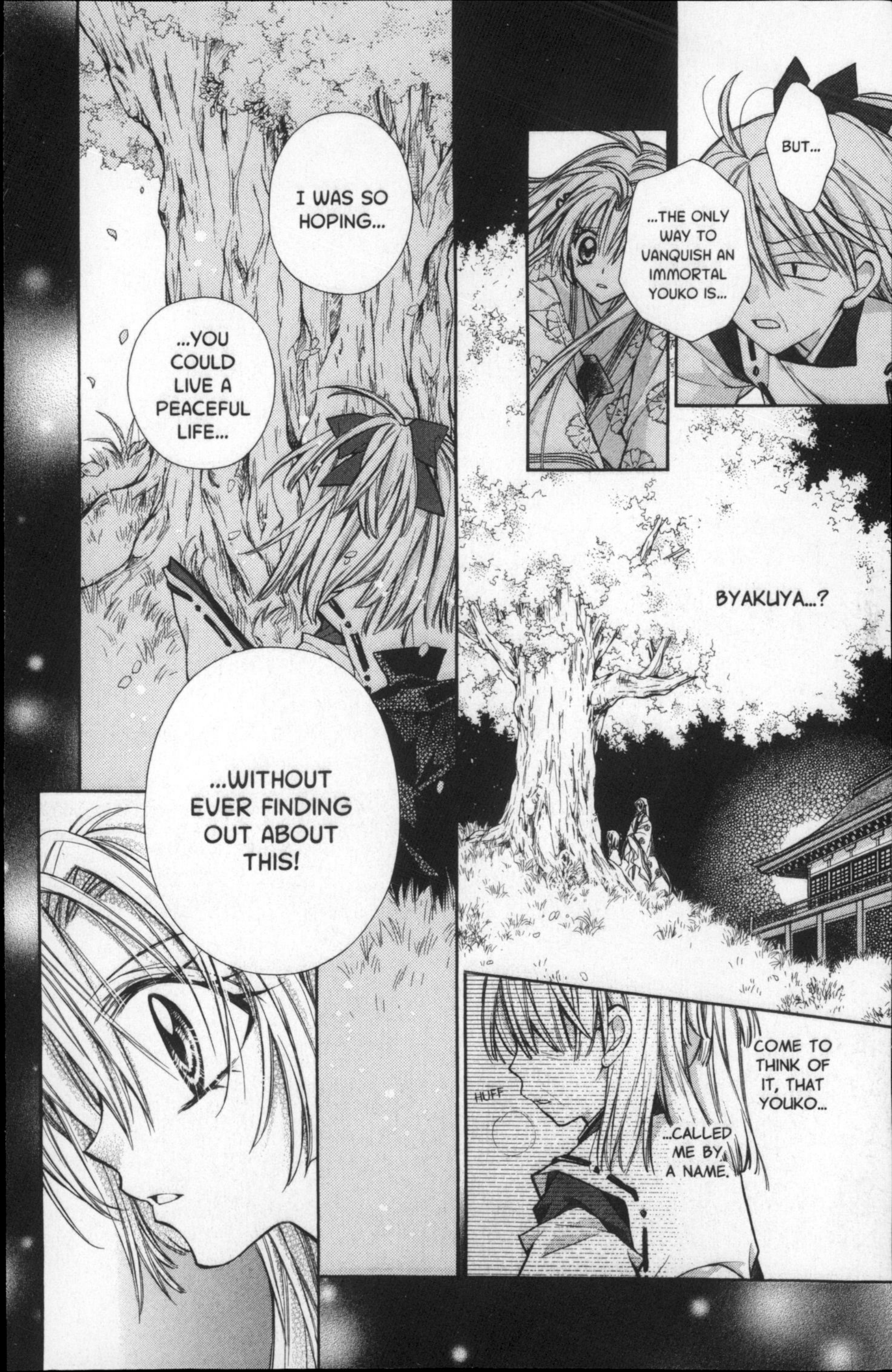
BUT...
...THE ONLY WAY TO VANQUISH AN IMMORTAL YOUKO IS...
I WAS SO HOPING...
...YOU COULD LIVE A PEACEFUL LIFE...
...WITHOUT EVER FINDING OUT ABOUT THIS!
BYAKUYA...?
COME TO THINK OF IT, THAT YOUKO...
...CALLED ME BY A NAME.
HUFF

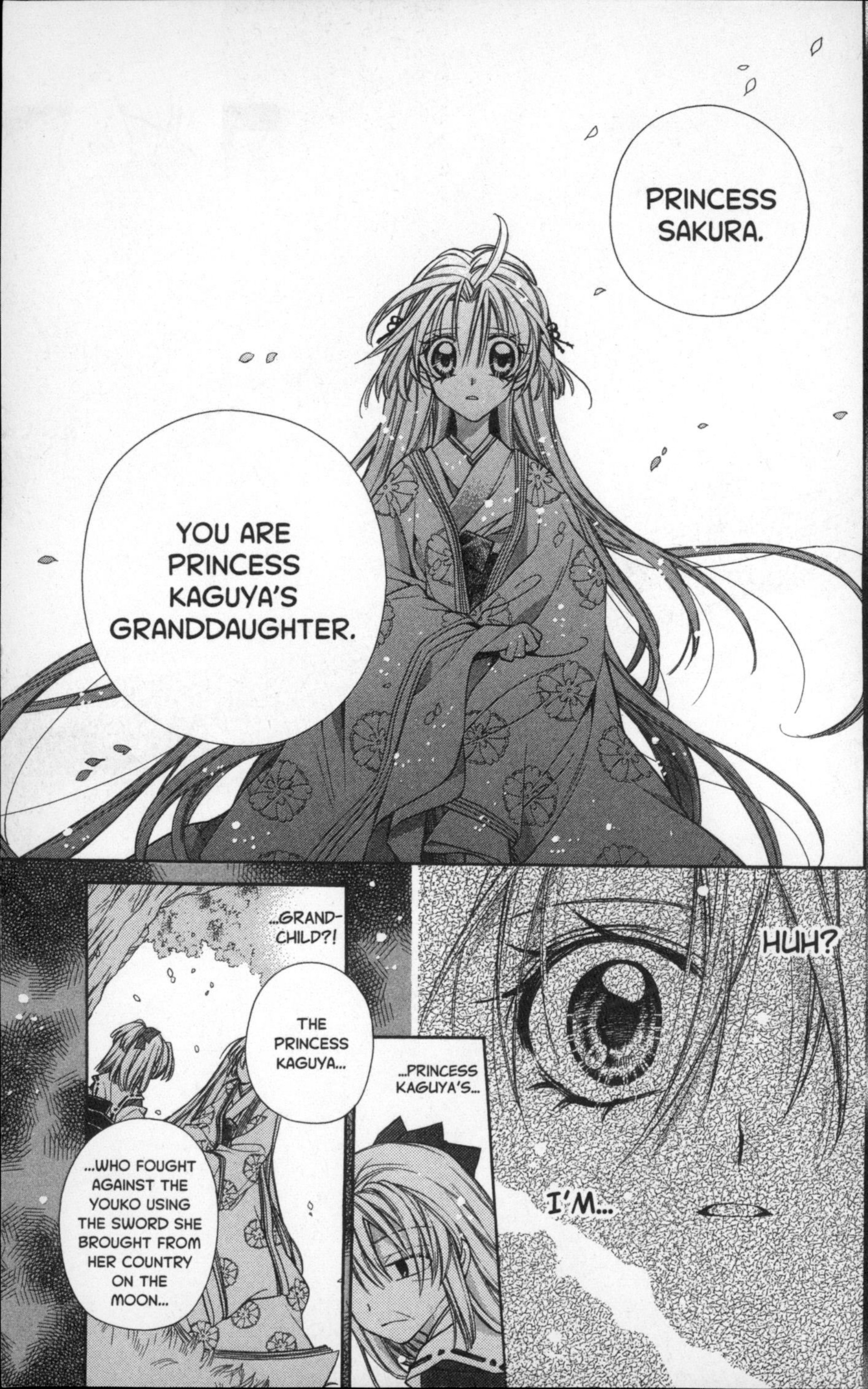
PRINCESS SAKURA.
YOU ARE PRINCESS KAGUYA'S GRANDDAUGHTER.
HUH?
I'M...
...GRAND-CHILD?!
...PRINCESS KAGUYA'S...
THE PRINCESS KAGUYA...
...WHO FOUGHT AGAINST THE YOUKO USING THE SWORD SHE BROUGHT FROM HER COUNTRY ON THE MOON...

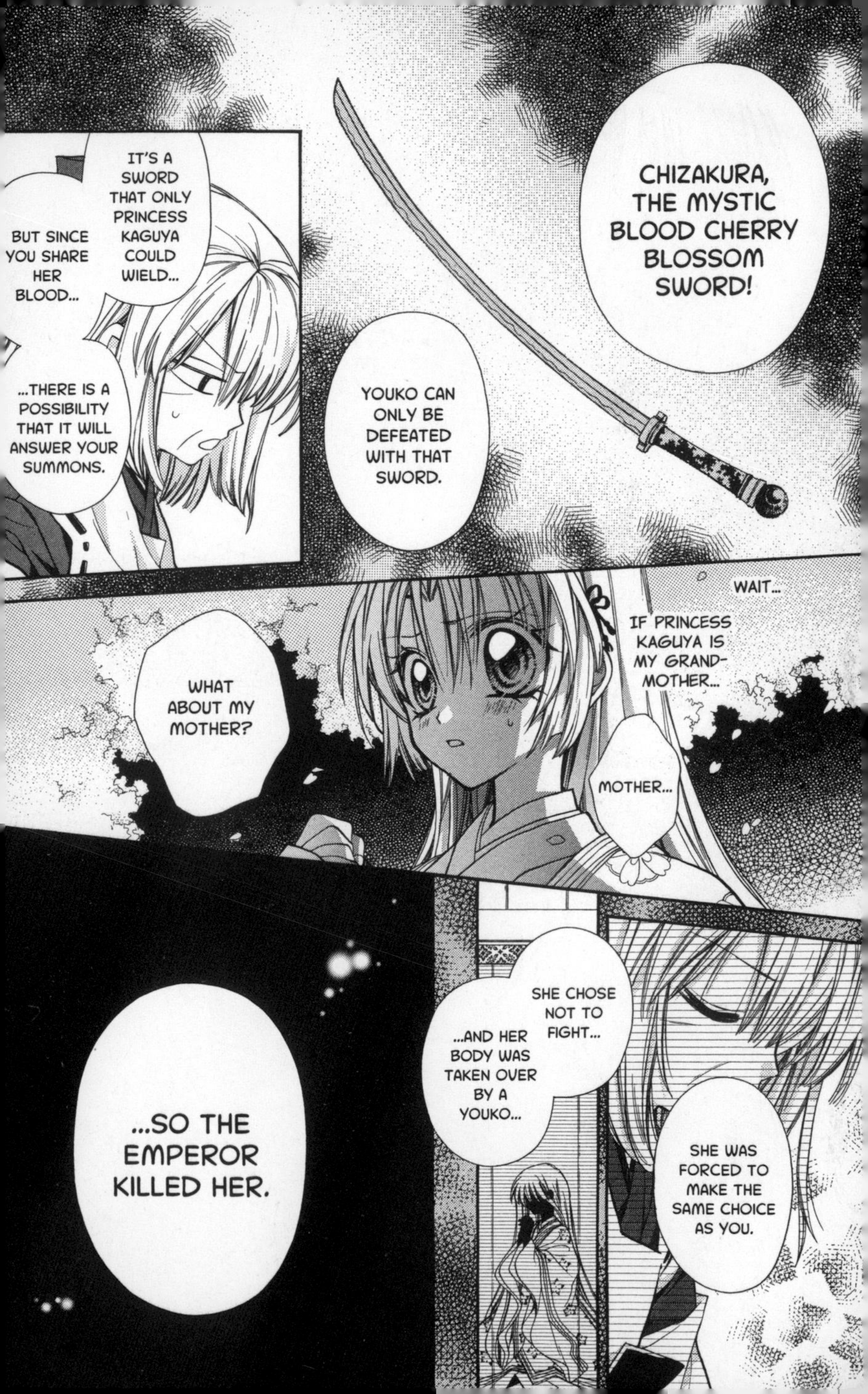
CHIZAKURA, THE MYSTIC BLOOD CHERRY BLOSSOM SWORD!
YOUKO CAN ONLY BE DEFEATED WITH THAT SWORD.
IT'S A SWORD THAT ONLY PRINCESS KAGUYA COULD WIELD...
BUT SINCE YOU SHARE HER BLOOD...
...THERE IS A POSSIBILITY THAT IT WILL ANSWER YOUR SUMMONS.
WAIT...
IF PRINCESS KAGUYA IS MY GRAND-MOTHER...
MOTHER...
WHAT ABOUT MY MOTHER?
SHE CHOSE NOT TO FIGHT...
...AND HER BODY WAS TAKEN OVER BY A YOUKO...
SHE WAS FORCED TO MAKE THE SAME CHOICE AS YOU.
...SO THE EMPEROR KILLED HER.

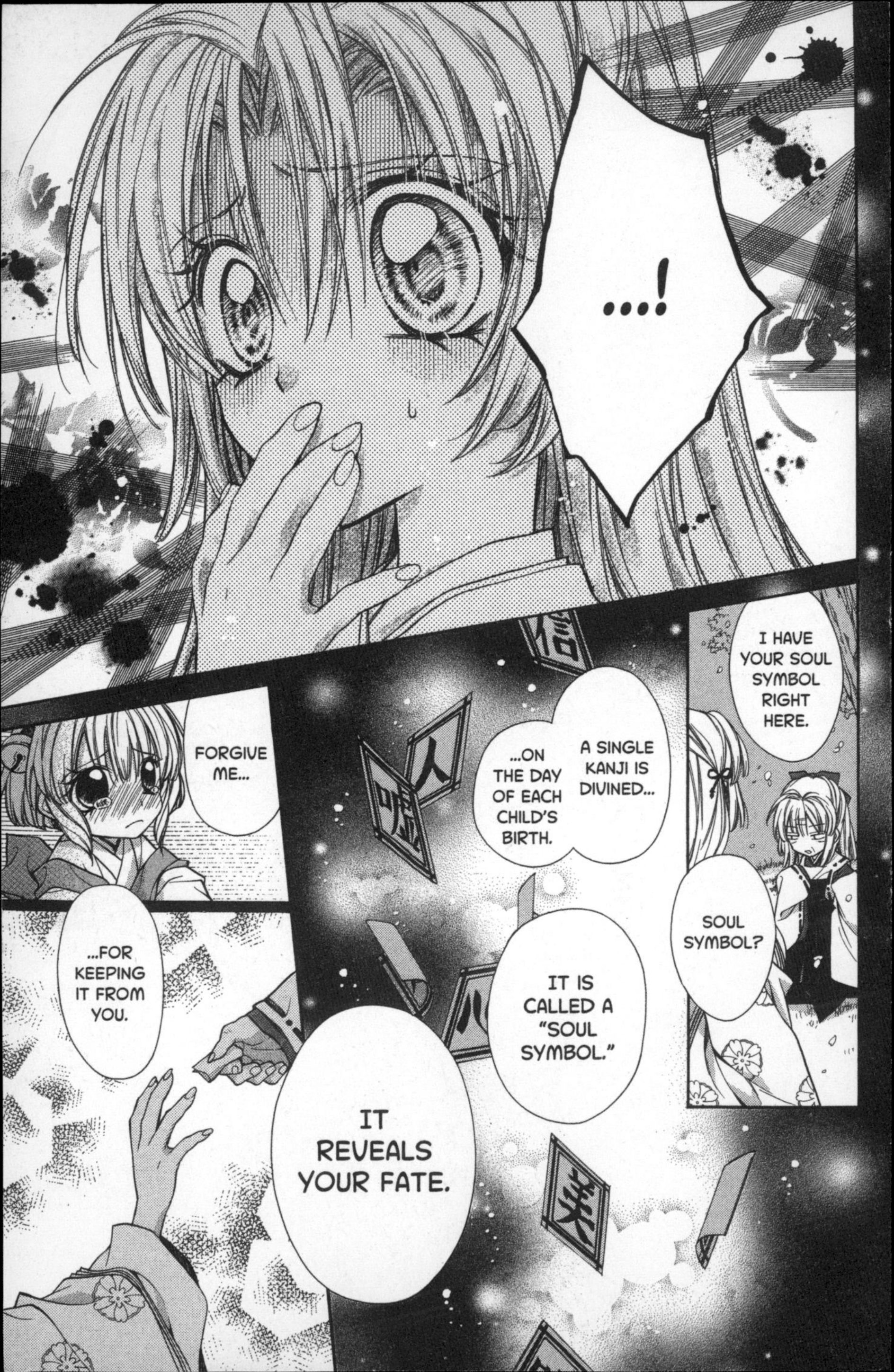
...!
I HAVE YOUR SOUL SYMBOL RIGHT HERE.
SOUL SYMBOL?
A SINGLE KANJI IS DIVINED...
...ON THE DAY OF EACH CHILD'S BIRTH.
IT IS CALLED A "SOUL SYMBOL."
IT REVEALS YOUR FATE.
FORGIVE ME...
...FOR KEEPING IT FROM YOU.

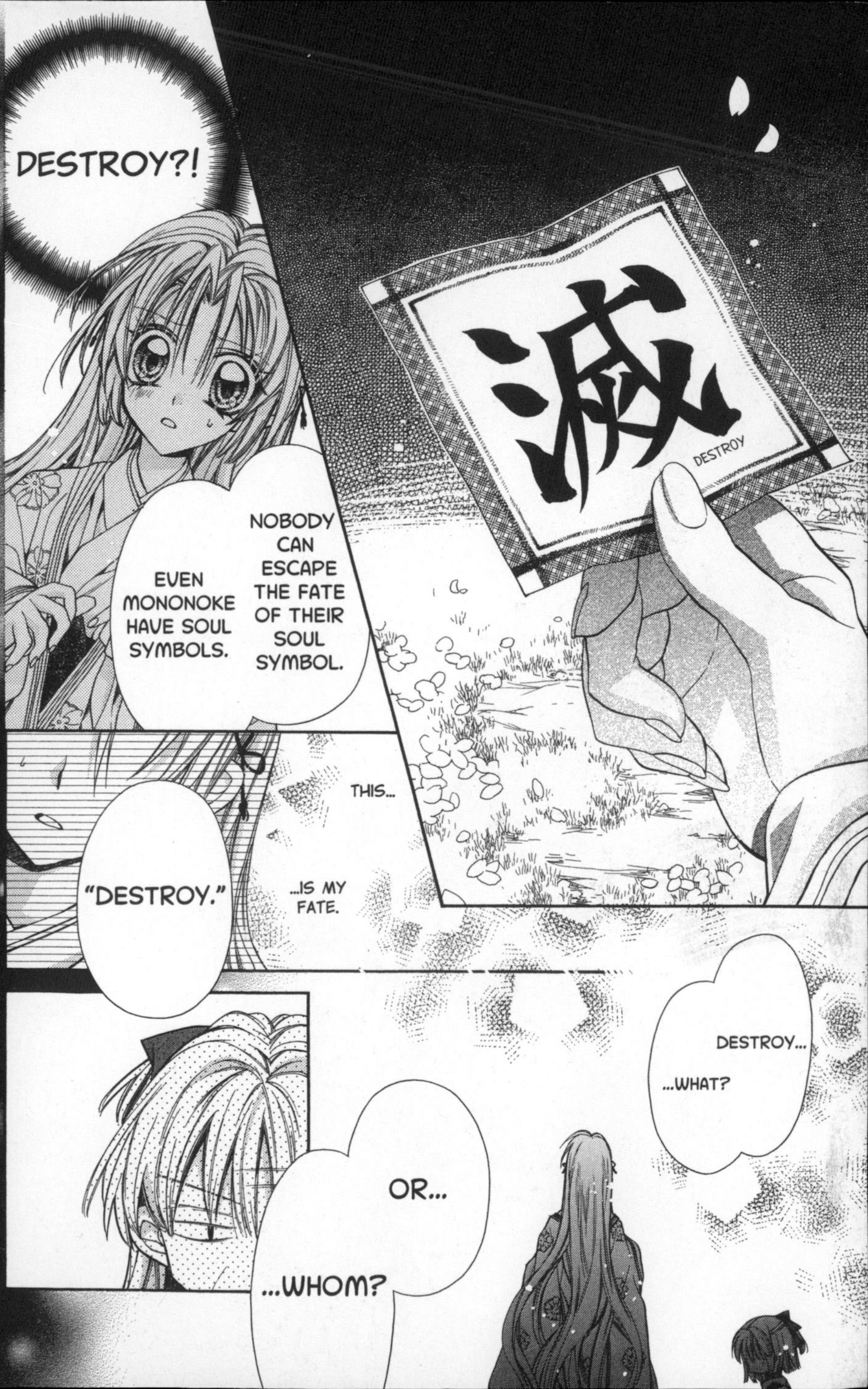
滅
DESTROY
DESTROY?!
EVEN MONONOKE HAVE SOUL SYMBOLS.
NOBODY CAN ESCAPE THE FATE OF THEIR SOUL SYMBOL.
THIS...
...IS MY FATE.
"DESTROY."
DESTROY...
...WHAT?
OR...
...WHOM?

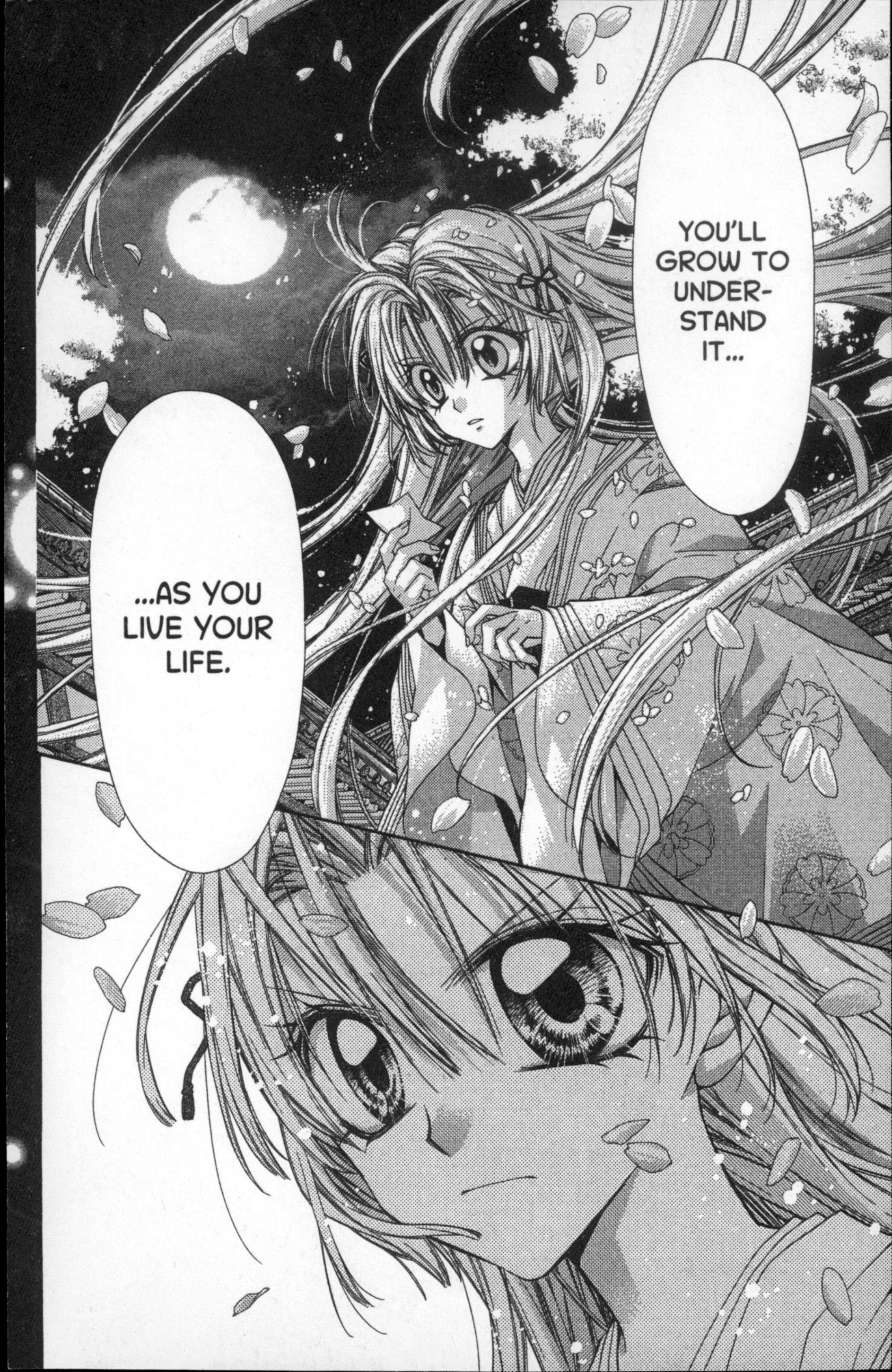
YOU'LL GROW TO UNDER-STAND IT...
...AS YOU LIVE YOUR LIFE.

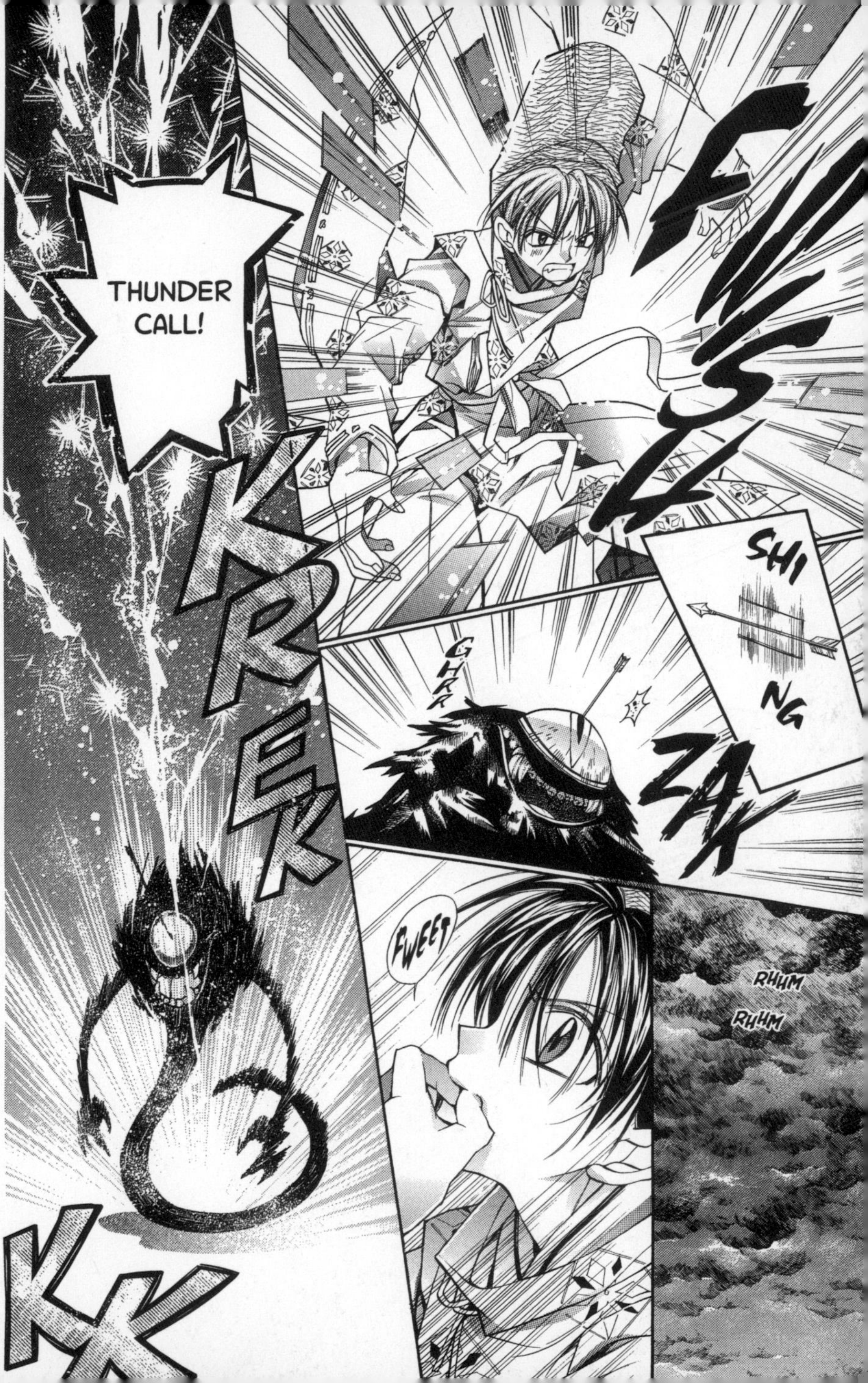

FWSSH
SHING
GHRR
ZAK
RHUM
RHUM
FWEET
THUNDER CALL!
KRREK
KK

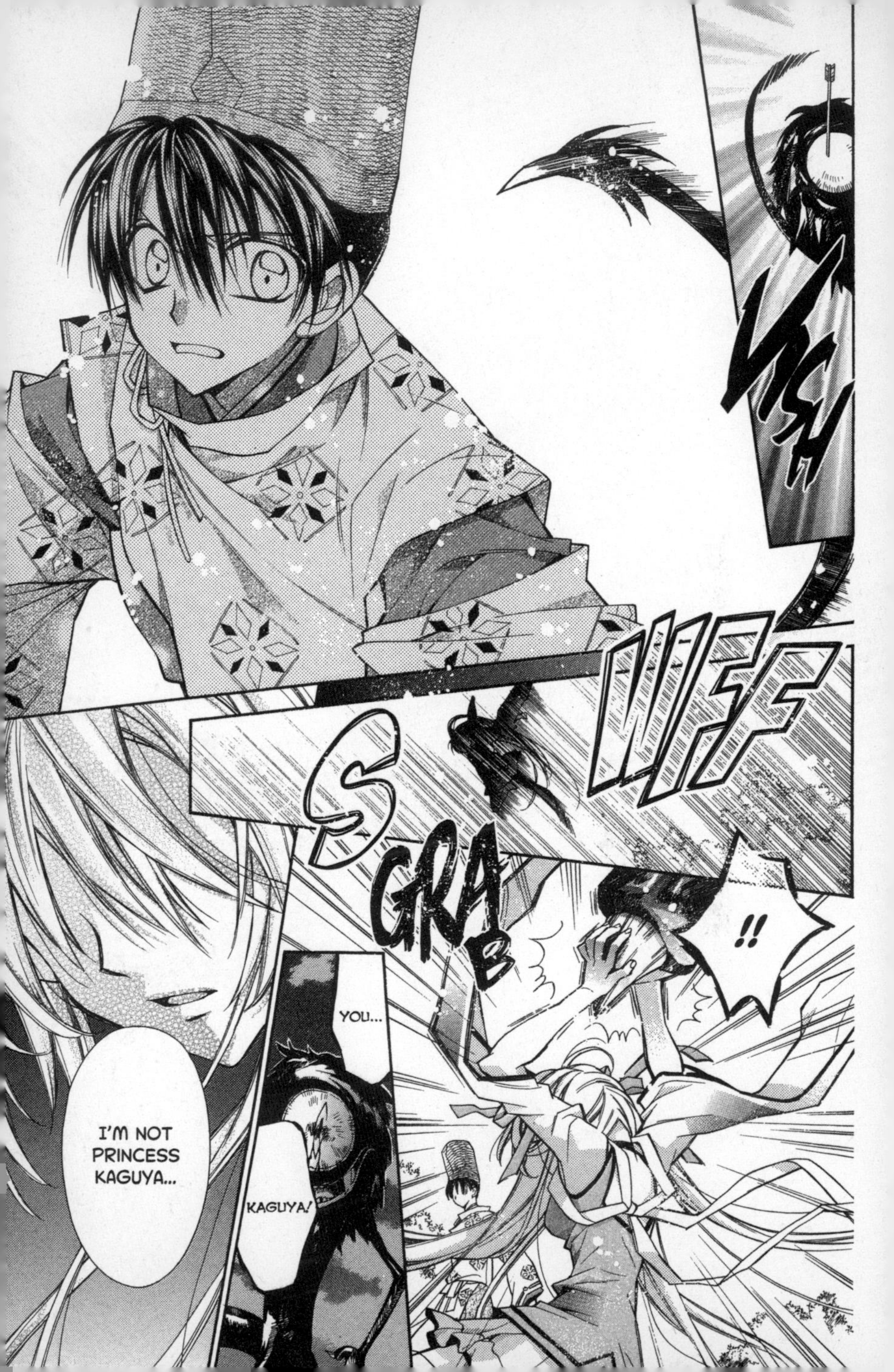
VISH
SWIFF
GRAB
!!
YOU...
KAGUYA!
I'M NOT PRINCESS KAGUYA...

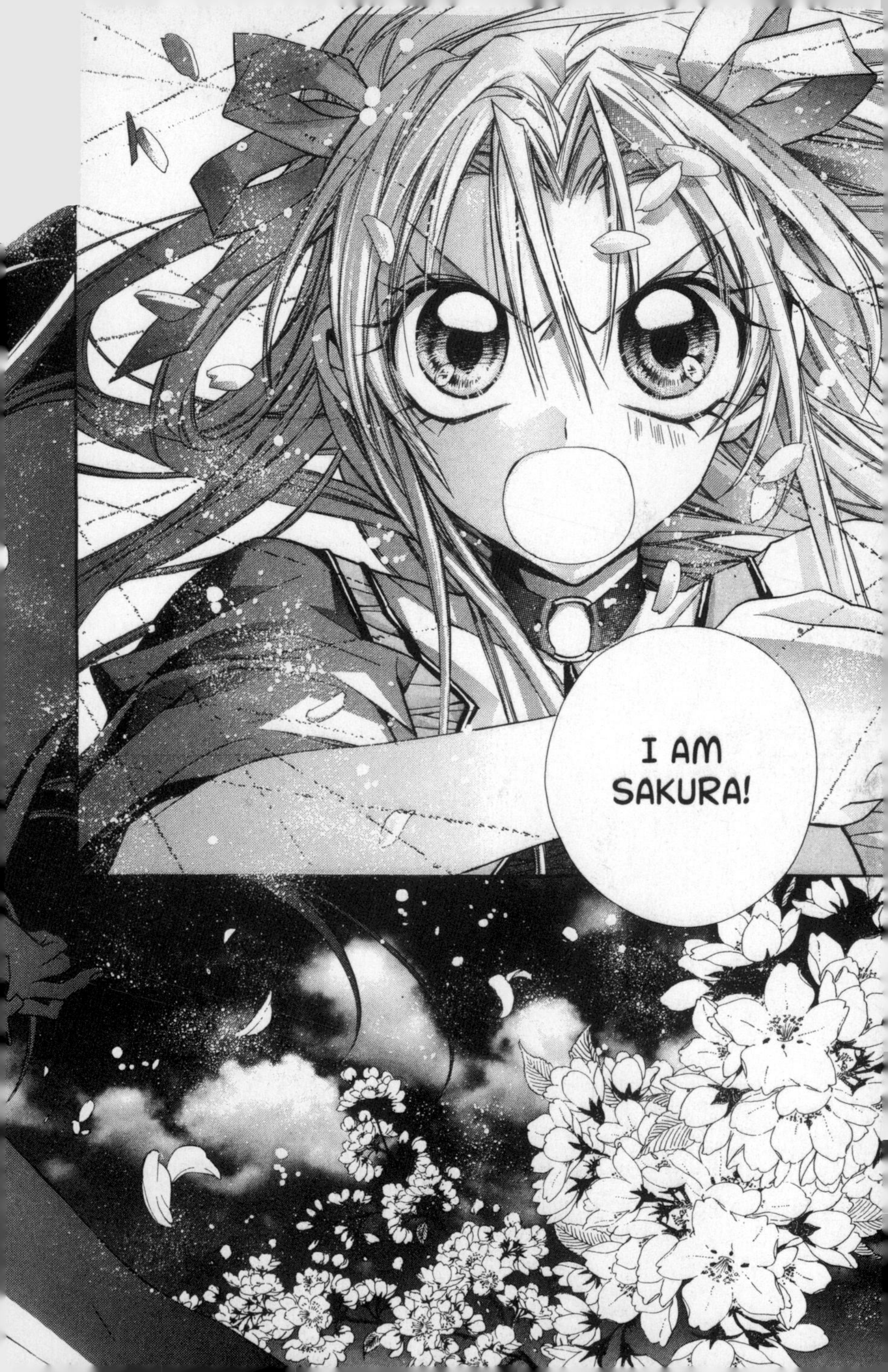
I AM SAKURA!

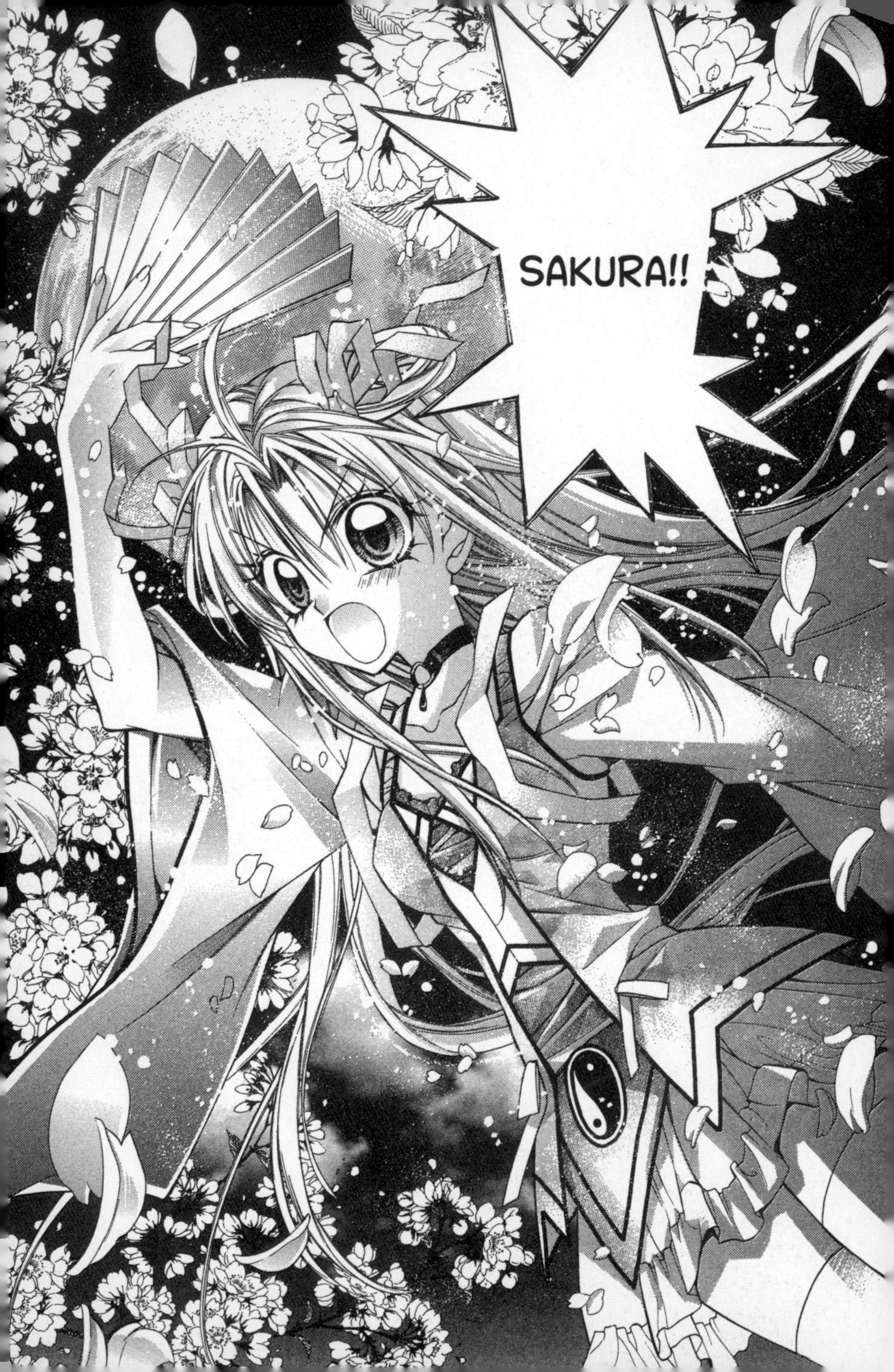
SAKURA!!

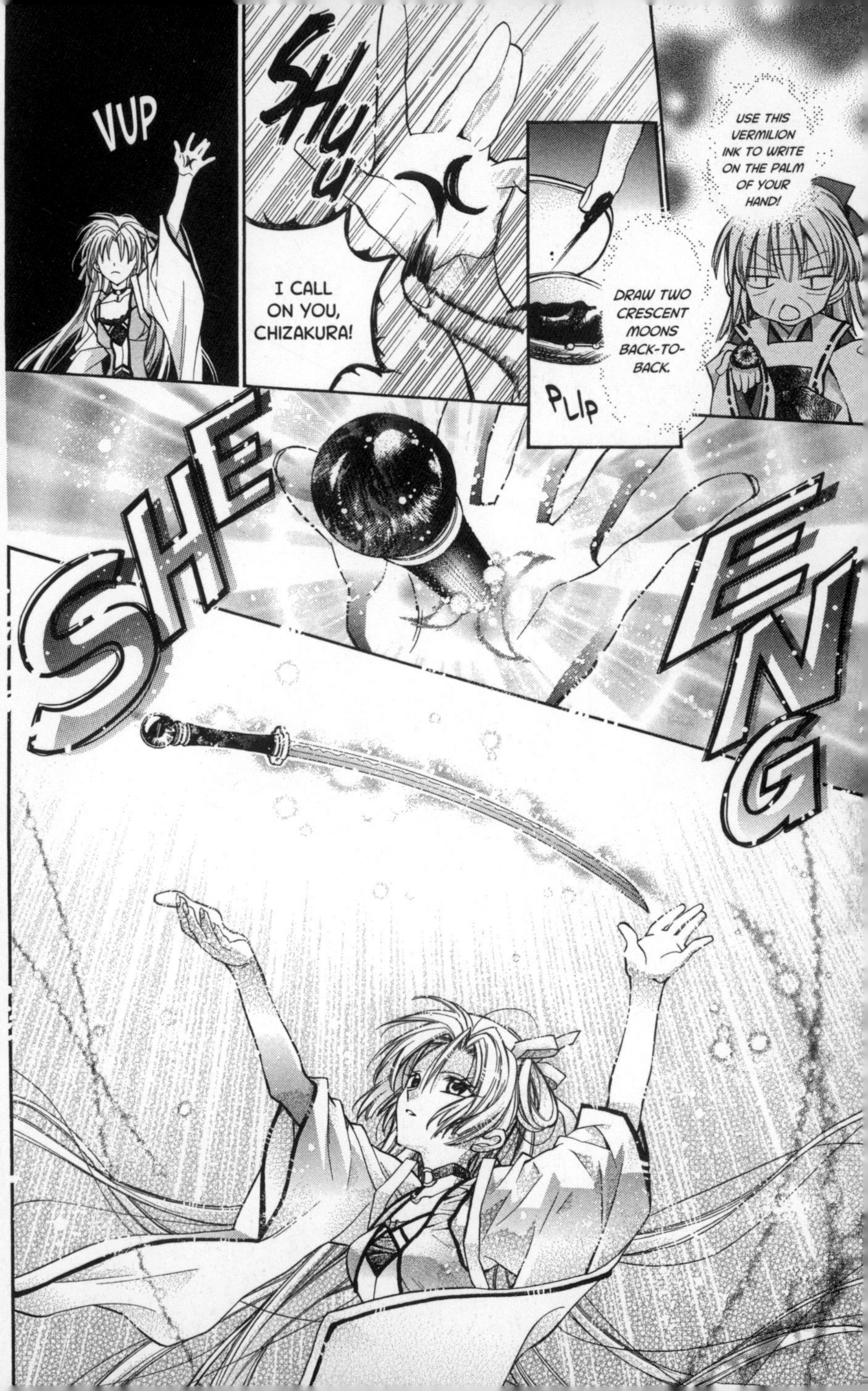
USE THIS VERMILION INK TO WRITE ON THE PALM OF YOUR HAND!
DRAW TWO CRESCENT MOONS BACK-TO-BACK.
PLIP
SHYU
I CALL ON YOU, CHIZAKURA!
VUP
SHEENG

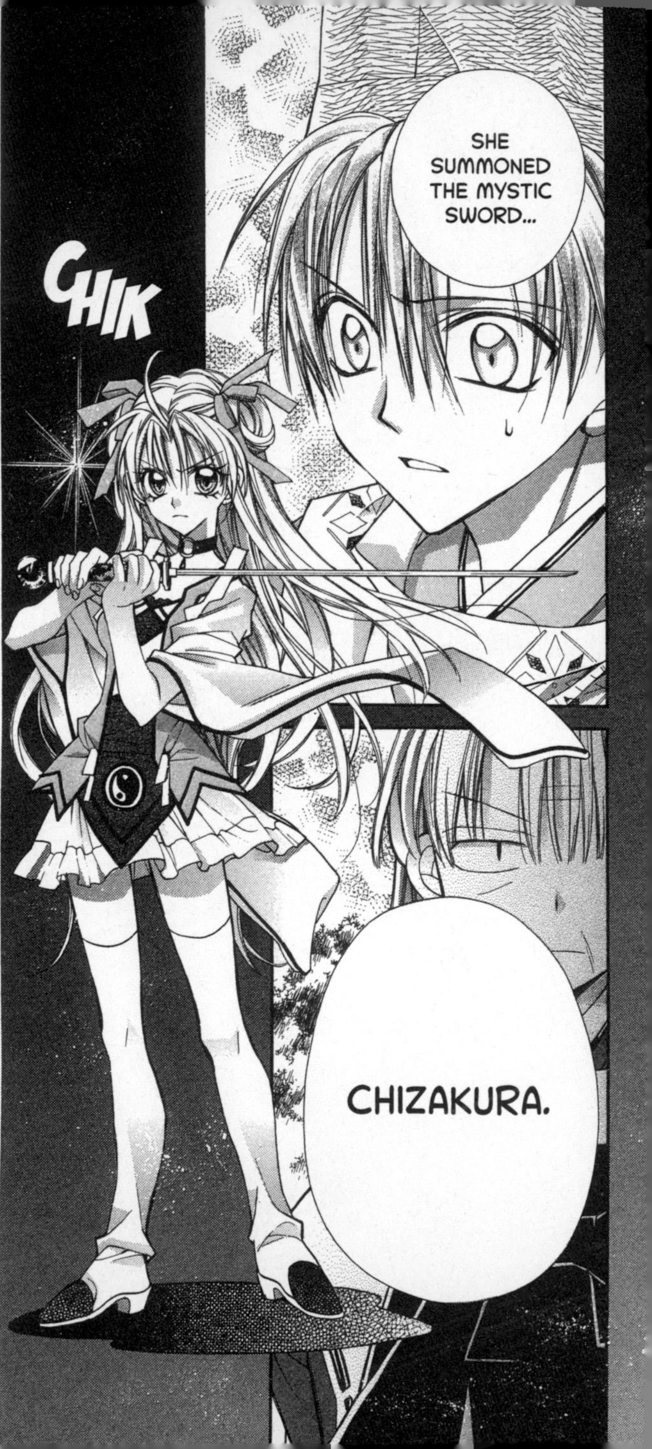
SHE SUMMONED THE MYSTIC SWORD...
CHIZAKURA.
CHIK

PRINCESS SAKURA

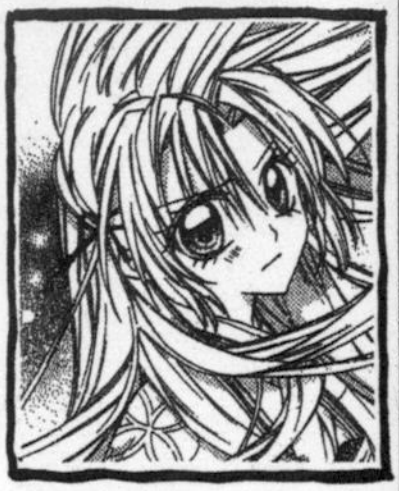

She's 14 years old and betrothed to Prince Oura. She is the granddaughter of Princess Kaguya, and her soul symbol is "destroy."

I worked backward from "Heian Period = Black Hair." She is a princess from the moon, after all. (I wanted to give her an otherworldly look).

As always, I haven't really decided exactly how she will be. I've been rather flexible about her. Unlike my other characters, she hasn't experienced any traumatizing events, nor does she have an inferiority complex.

This is a girl who has yet to experience those things.

But she's very strong inside. She's probably the strongest so far of the Arina characters.

She doesn't have anything important to her, or anything she really wants to protect yet...

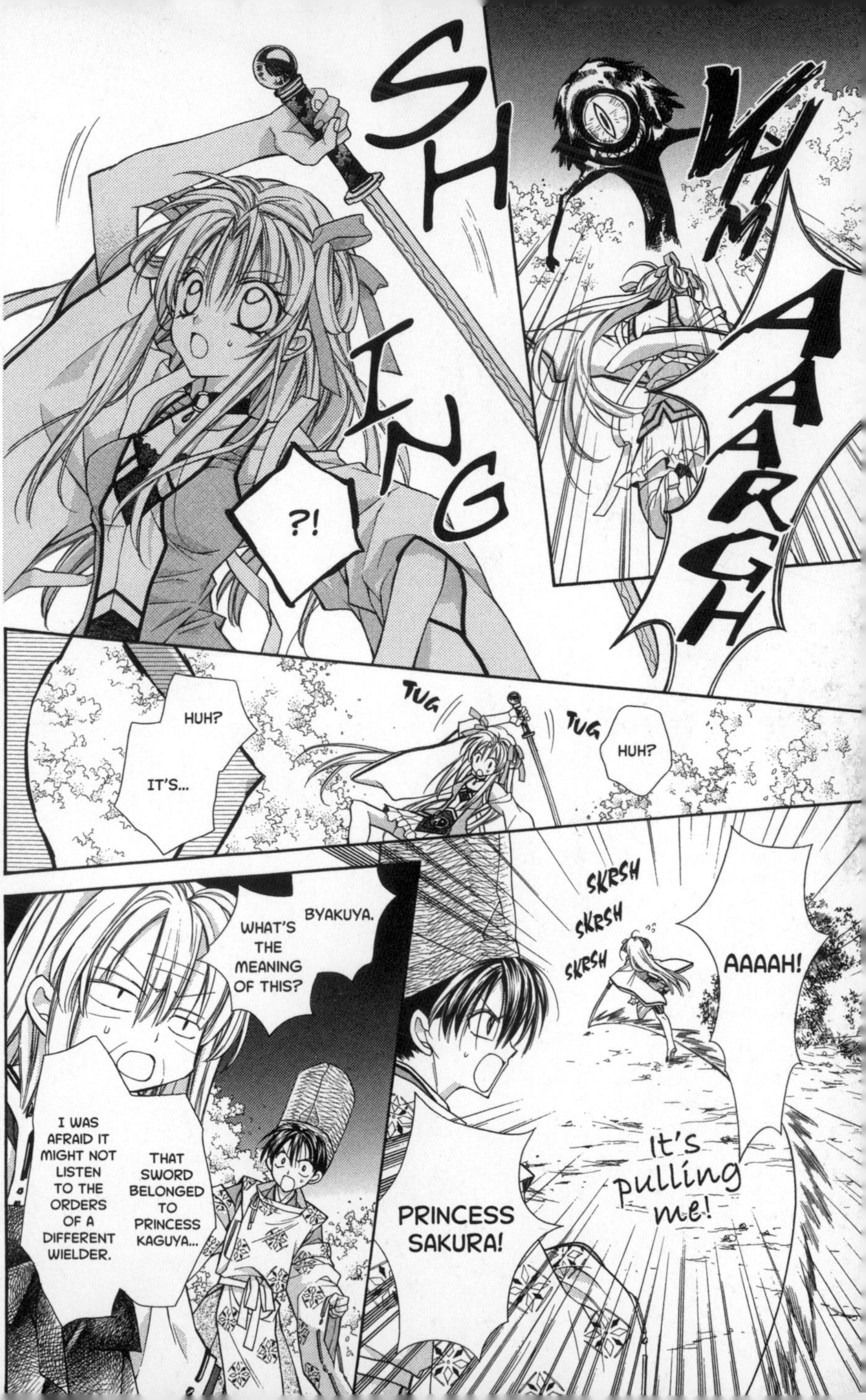
WHM
AAARGH
SHING
?!
TUG
TUG
HUH?
HUH?
IT'S...
SKRSH
SKRSH
SKRSH
AAAAH!
It's pulling me!
PRINCESS SAKURA!
BYAKUYA.
WHAT'S THE MEANING OF THIS?
THAT SWORD BELONGED TO PRINCESS KAGUYA...
I WAS AFRAID IT MIGHT NOT LISTEN TO THE ORDERS OF A DIFFERENT WIELDER.

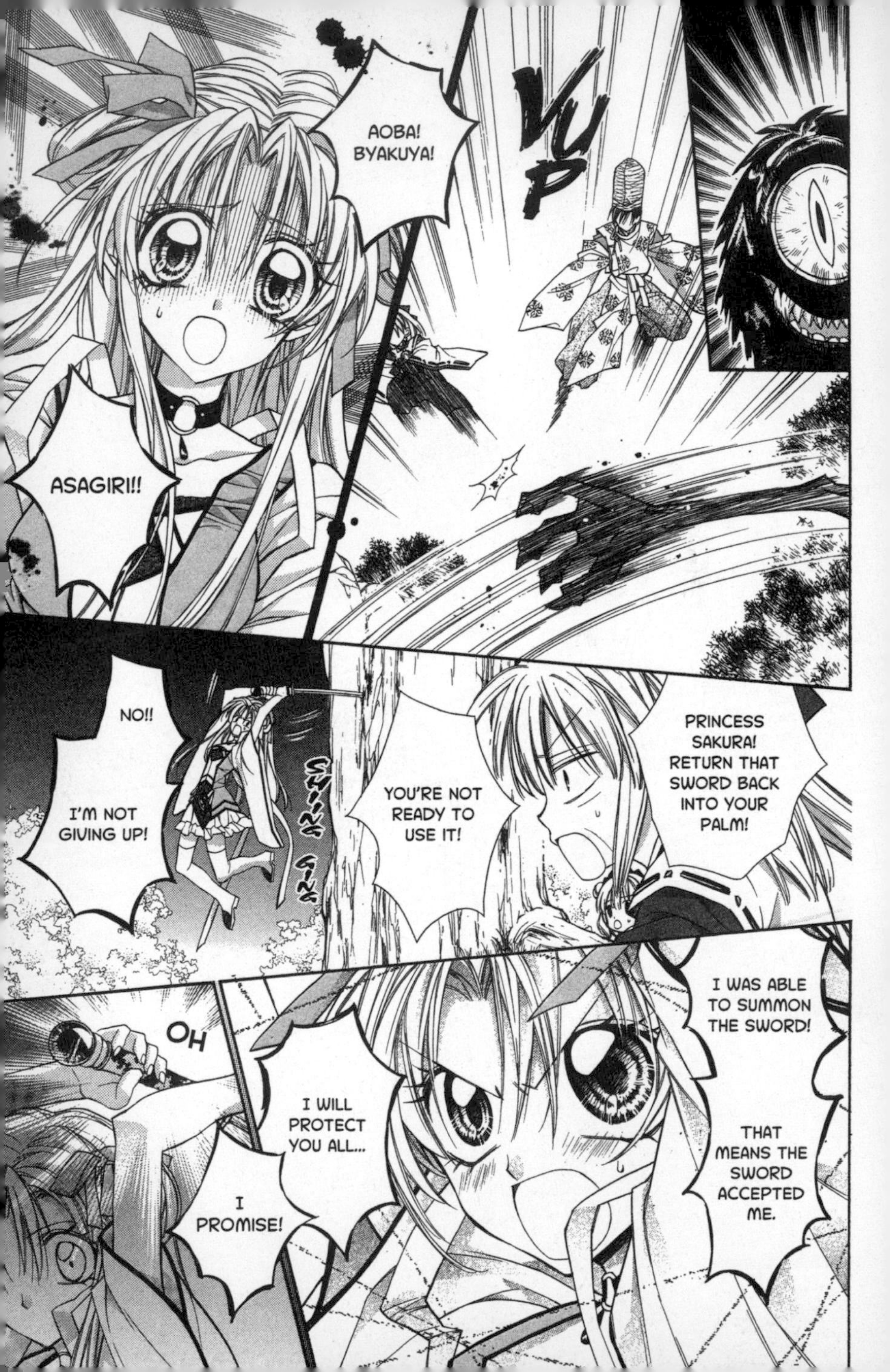
VUP
AOBA! BYAKUYA!
ASAGIRI!!
PRINCESS SAKURA! RETURN THAT SWORD BACK INTO YOUR PALM!
YOU'RE NOT READY TO USE IT!
SHIING
GING
NO!!
I'M NOT GIVING UP!
I WAS ABLE TO SUMMON THE SWORD!
THAT MEANS THE SWORD ACCEPTED ME.
I WILL PROTECT YOU ALL...
I PROMISE!
OH

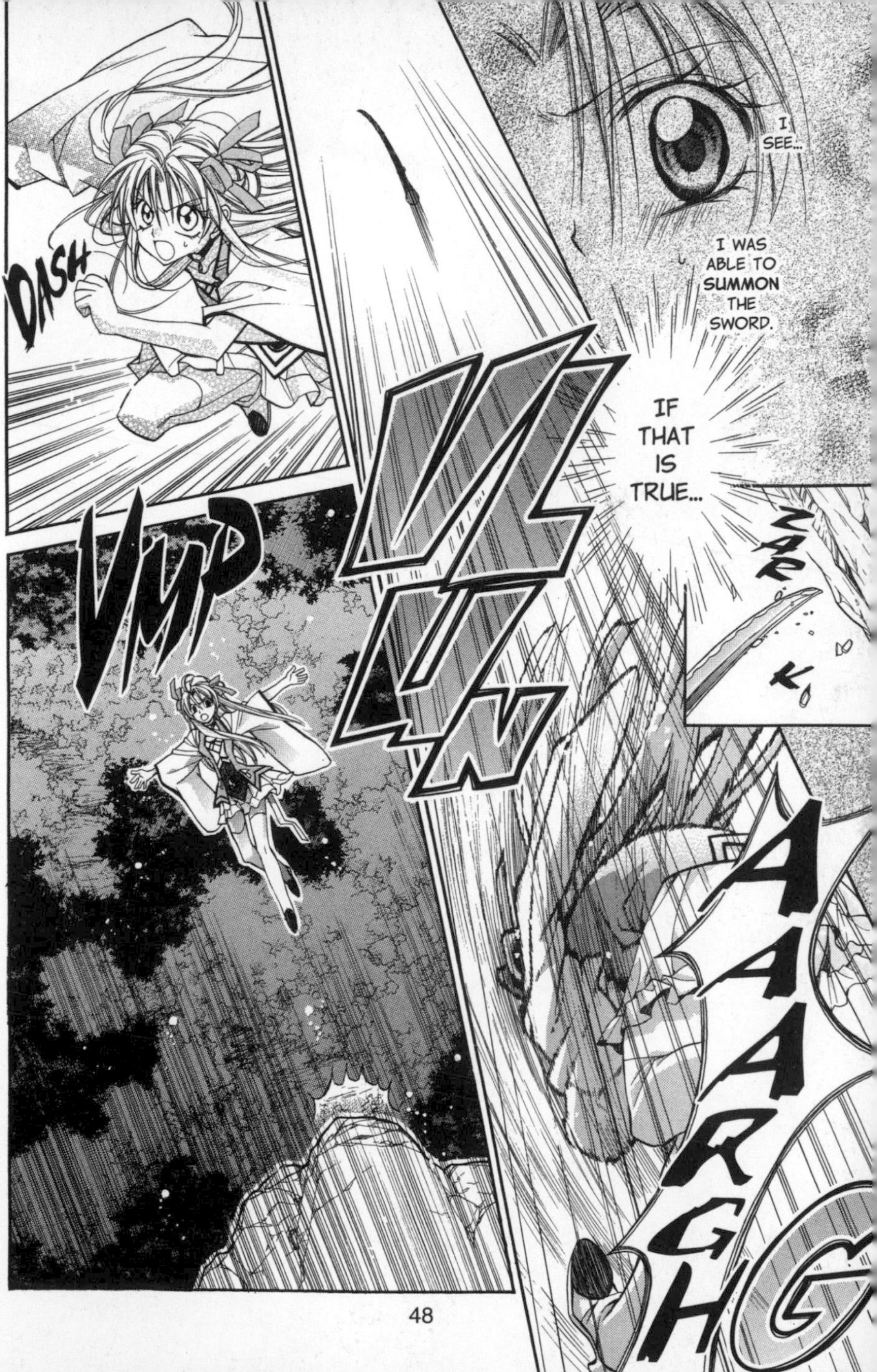
I SEE...
I WAS ABLE TO SUMMON THE SWORD.
IF THAT IS TRUE...
DASH
ZAP
K
VMP
AAARGHG

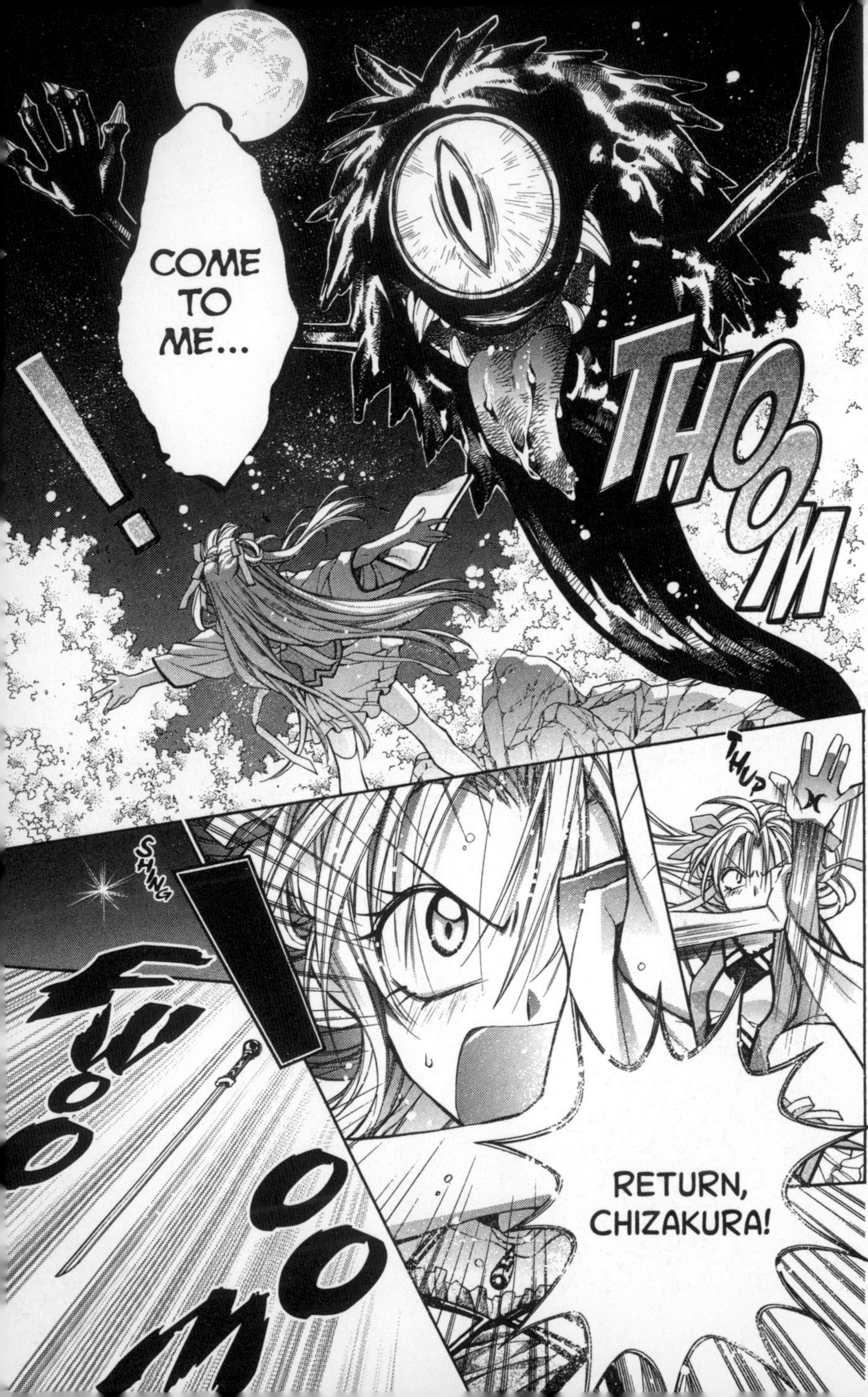
COME TO ME...
THOOM
!
THUP
RETURN, CHIZAKURA!
SHING
!

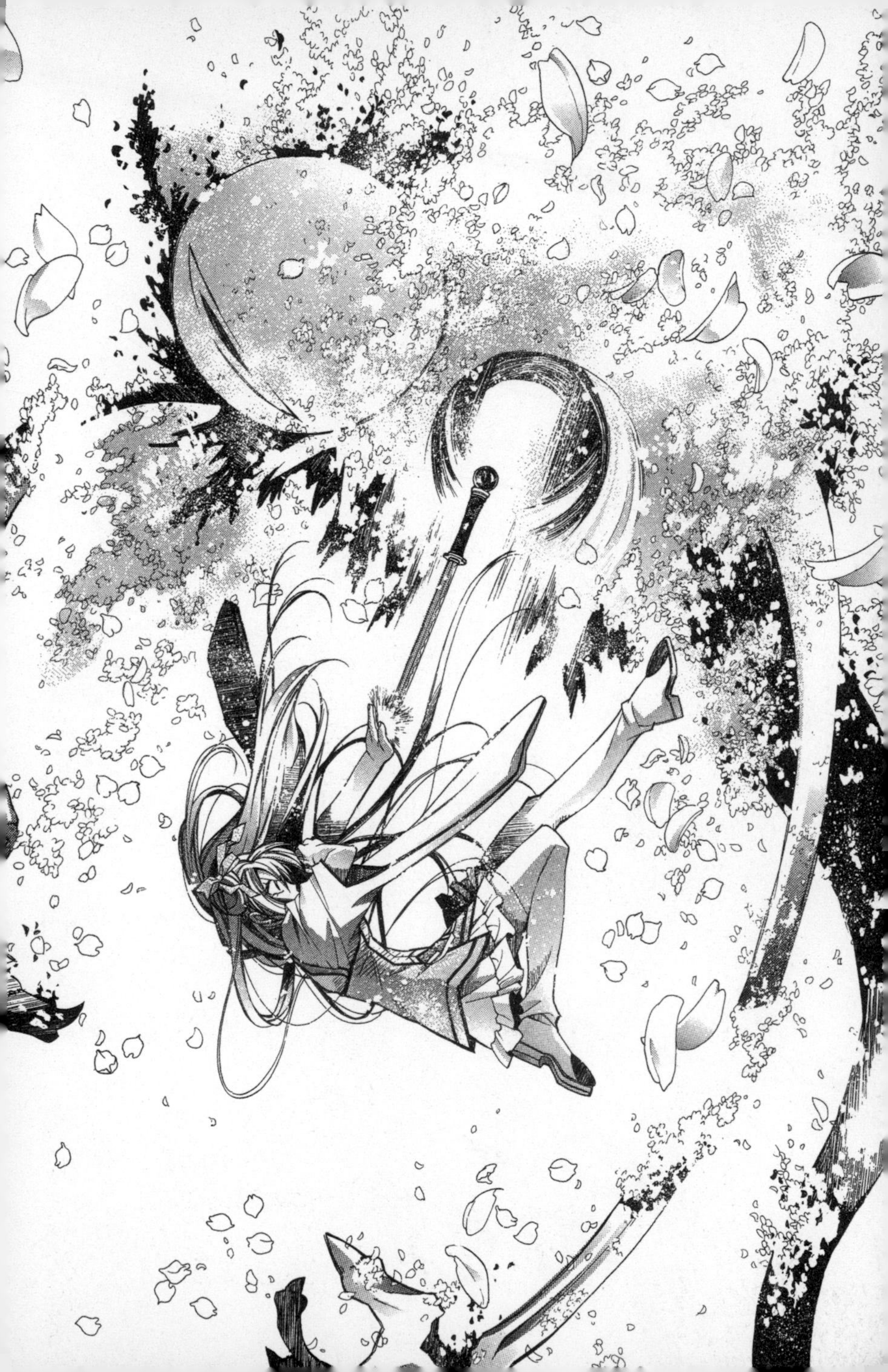

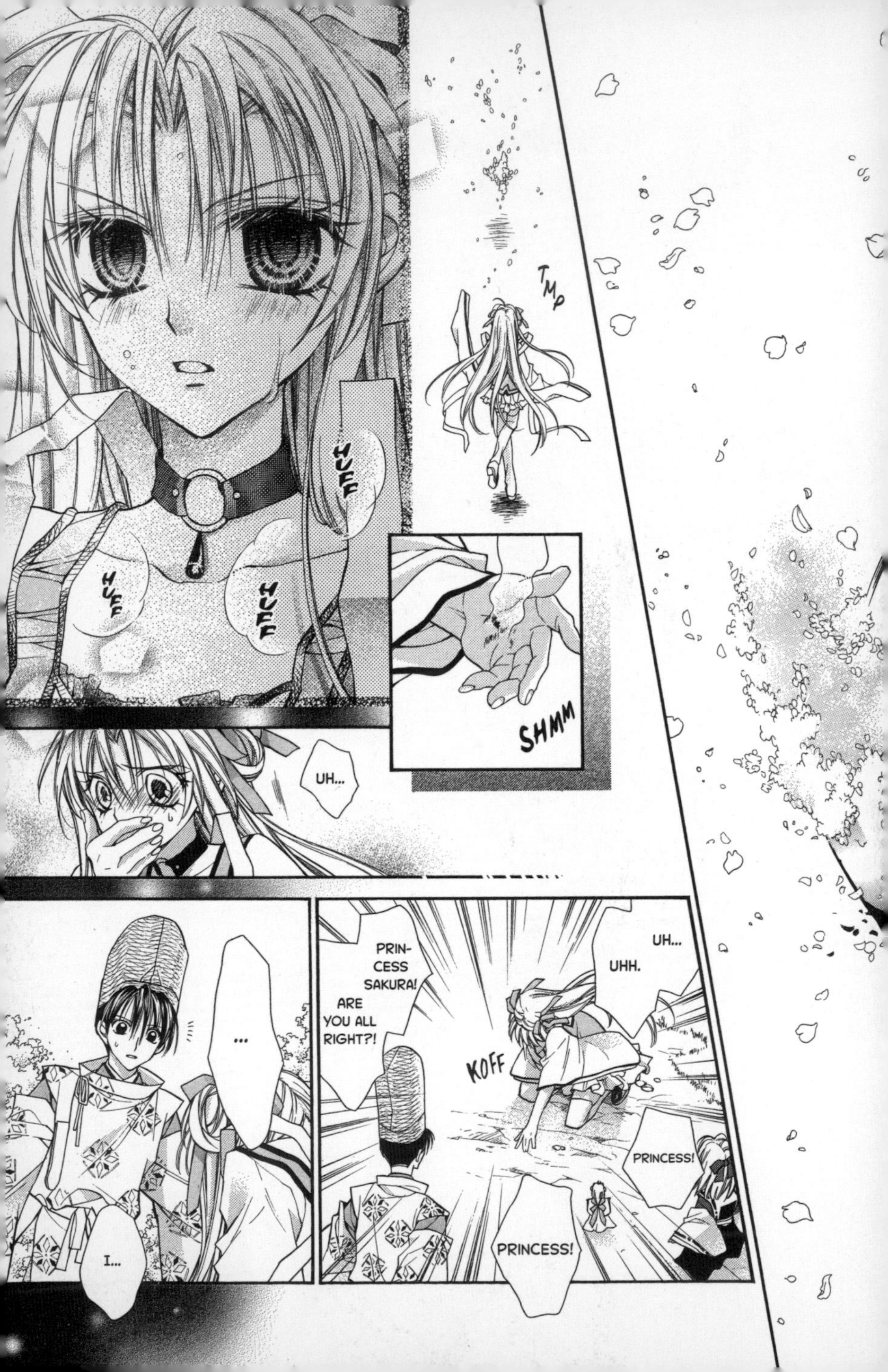
TMP
SHMM
HUFF
HUFF
HUFF
UH...
UH...
UHH.
PRIN-CESS SAKURA!
ARE YOU ALL RIGHT?!
KOFF
PRINCESS!
PRINCESS!
...
I...

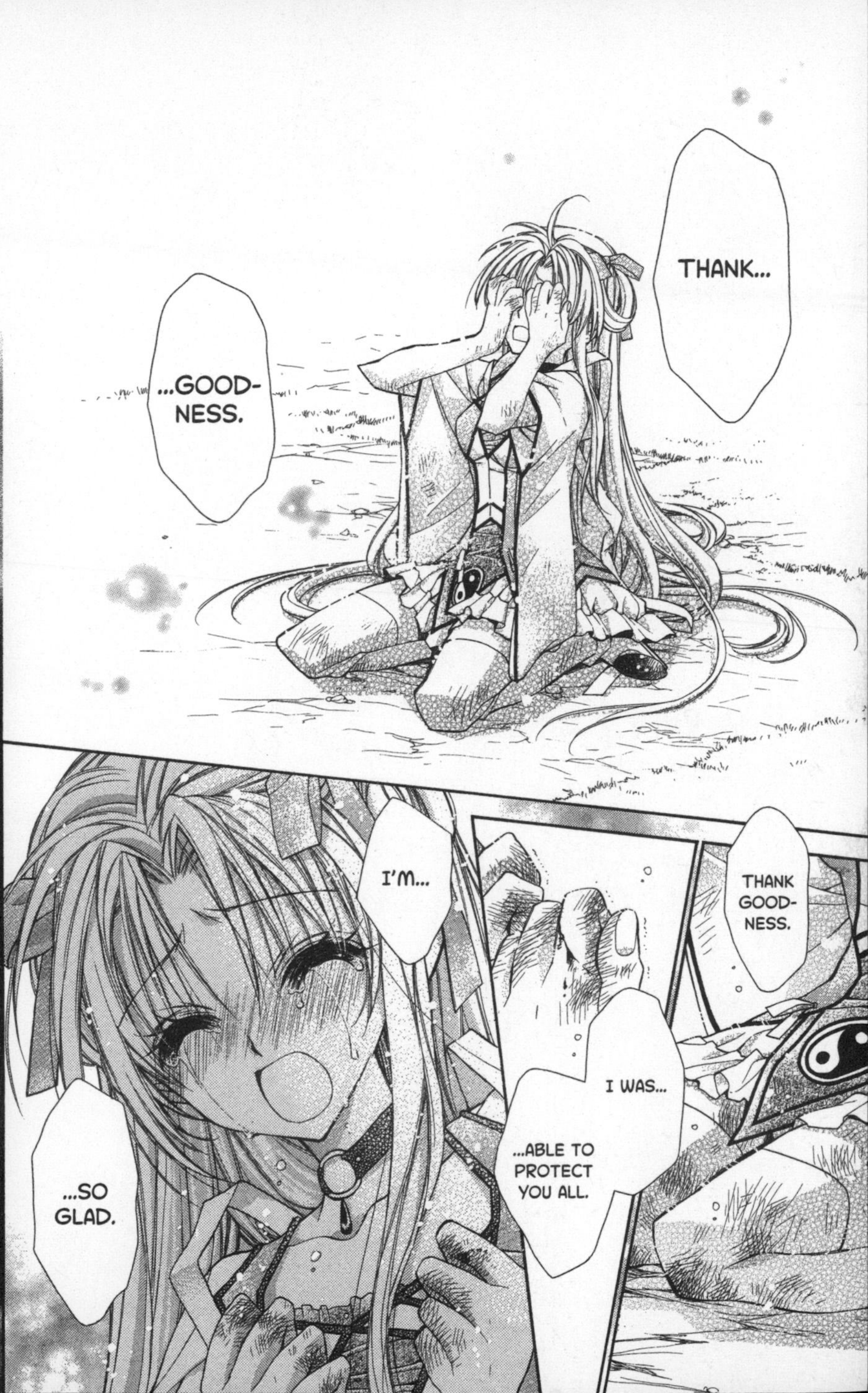
THANK...
...GOOD-NESS.
THANK GOOD-NESS.
I WAS...
...ABLE TO PROTECT YOU ALL.
I'M...
...SO GLAD.

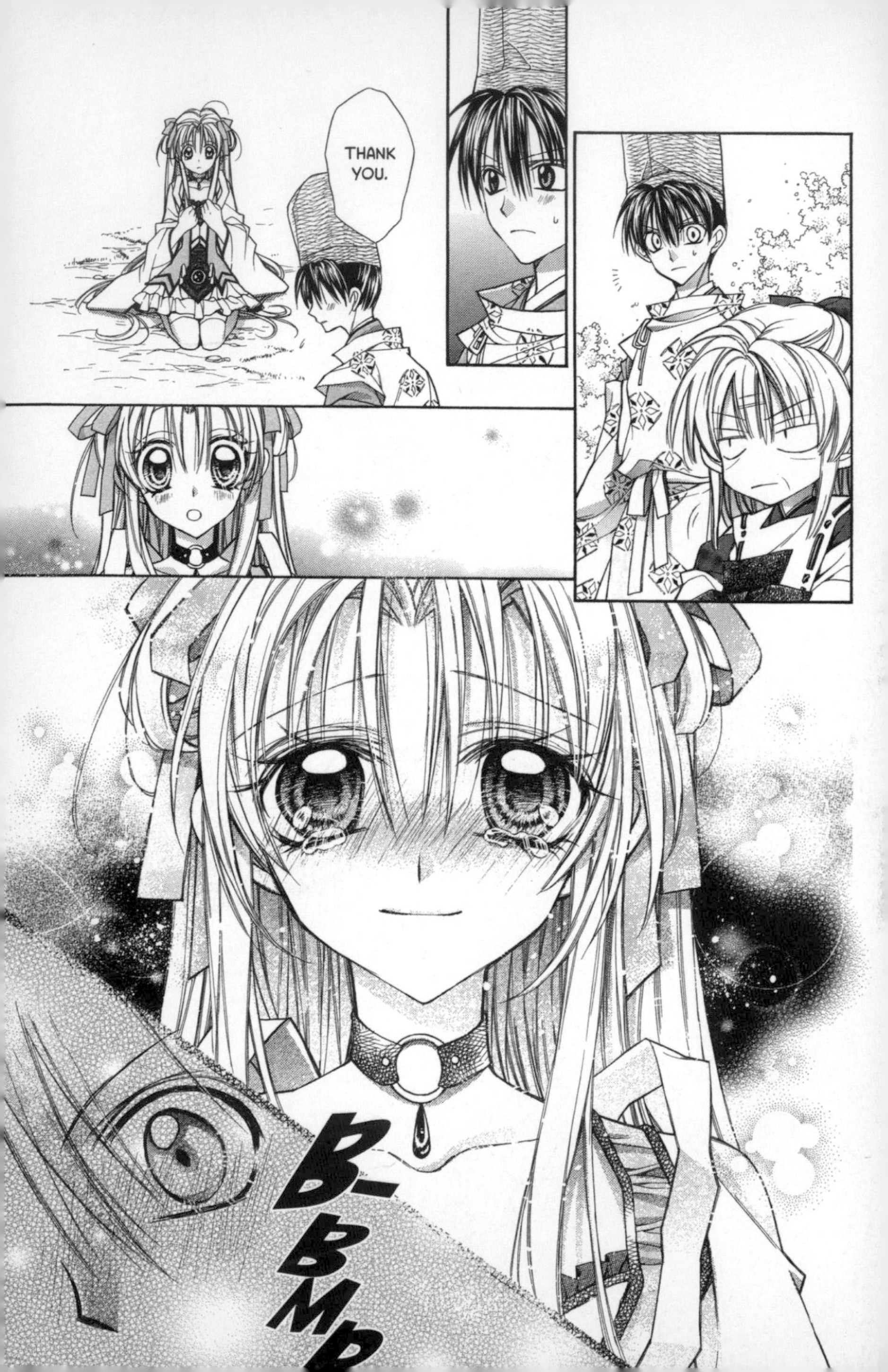
THANK YOU.
B-BMP

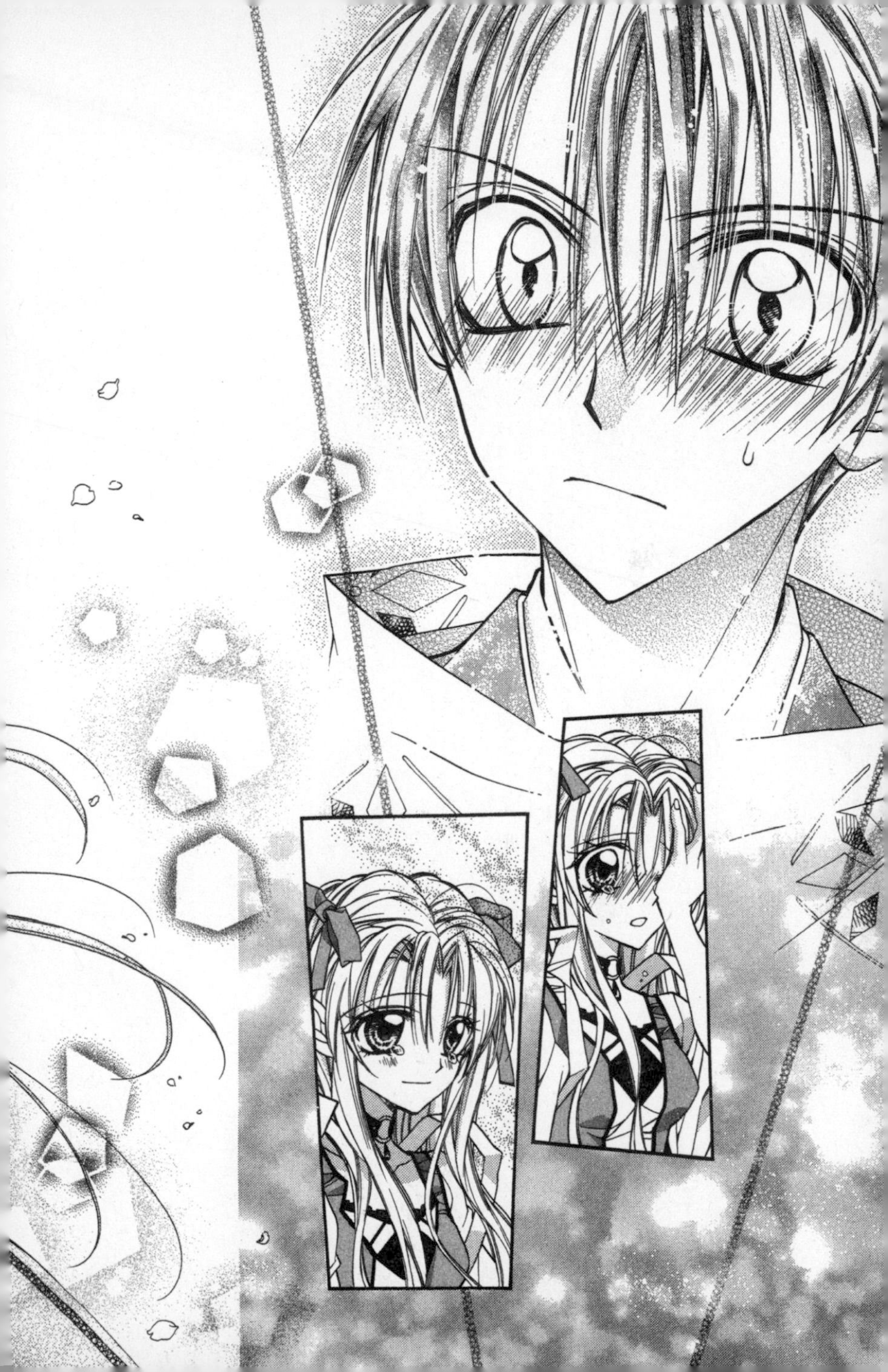

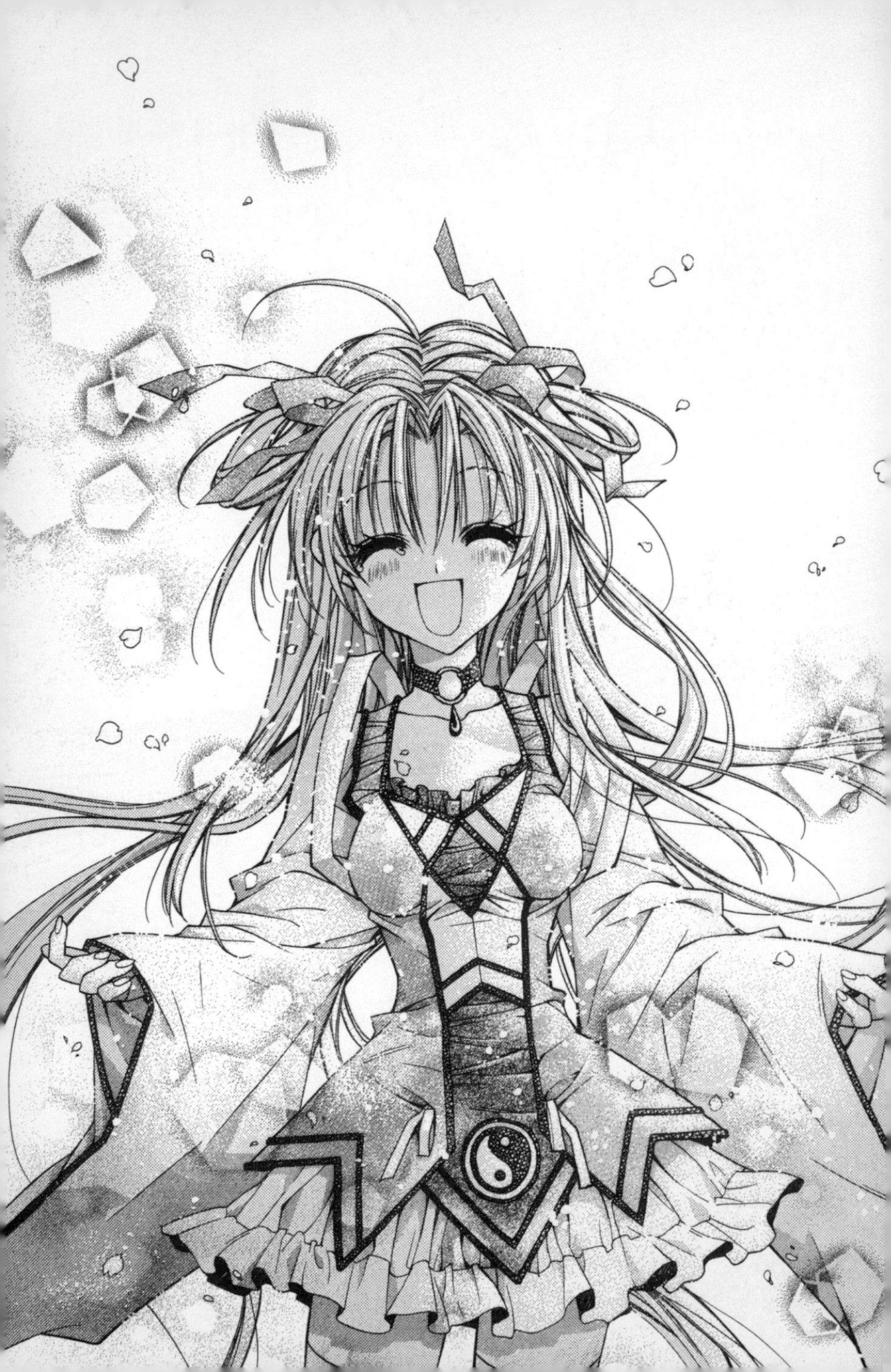

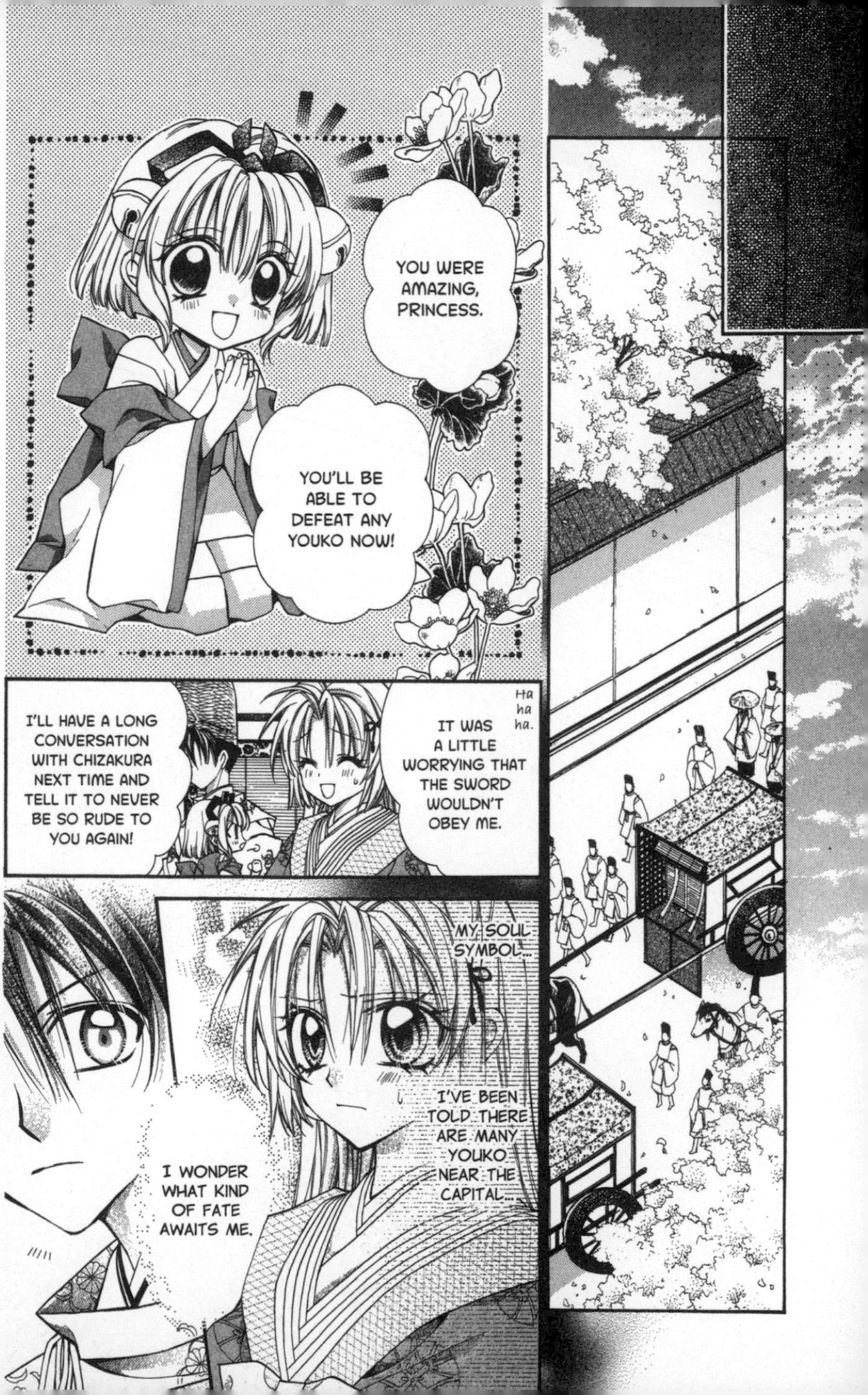
YOU WERE AMAZING, PRINCESS.
YOU'LL BE ABLE TO DEFEAT ANY YOUKO NOW!
Ha ha ha.
IT WAS A LITTLE WORRYING THAT THE SWORD WOULDN'T OBEY ME.
I'LL HAVE A LONG CONVERSATION WITH CHIZAKURA NEXT TIME AND TELL IT TO NEVER BE SO RUDE TO YOU AGAIN!
MY SOUL SYMBOL...
I'VE BEEN TOLD THERE ARE MANY YOUKO NEAR THE CAPITAL...
I WONDER WHAT KIND OF FATE AWAITS ME.

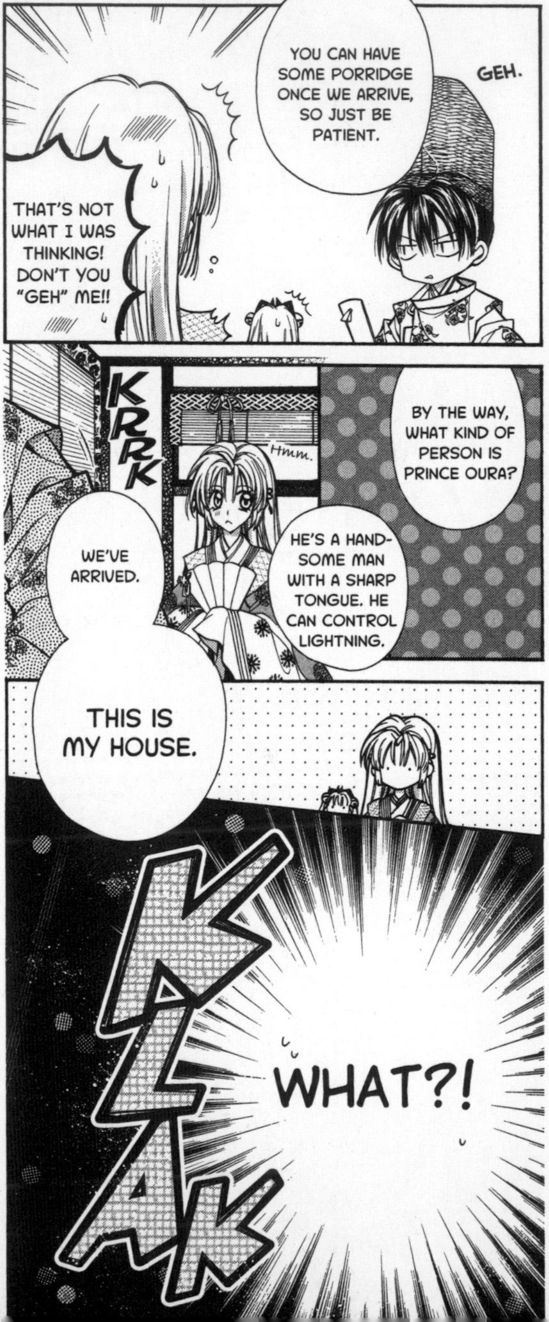
GEH.
YOU CAN HAVE SOME PORRIDGE ONCE WE ARRIVE, SO JUST BE PATIENT.
THAT'S NOT WHAT I WAS THINKING! DON'T YOU "GEH" ME!!
BY THE WAY, WHAT KIND OF PERSON IS PRINCE OURA?
HE'S A HAND-SOME MAN WITH A SHARP TONGUE. HE CAN CONTROL LIGHTNING.
Hmm.
WE'VE ARRIVED.
KRRK
THIS IS MY HOUSE.
WHAT?!
KLAK

## HELLO, HELLO.

Hello. I'm Arina Tanemura. I bring you *Sakura Hime: The Legend of Princess Sakura.* ♪

Ever since *Mistress* ☆ *Fortune* was published, I've received many letters asking for a sequel, but I'll be taking some time off from that for now, so please support *Princess Sakura* for me.

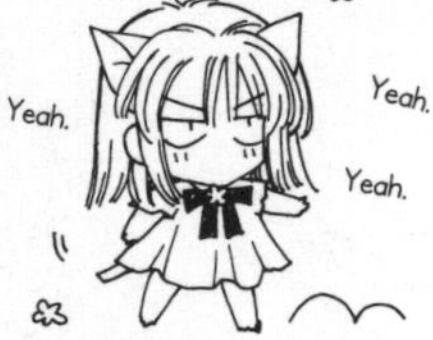
Yeah.
Yeah.
Yeah.

By the way, this volume has only three chapters, but each chapter is much longer than usual. (They are usually around 32 pages.)
↑ For *Ribon* magazine.

Each chapter is about twice as long.

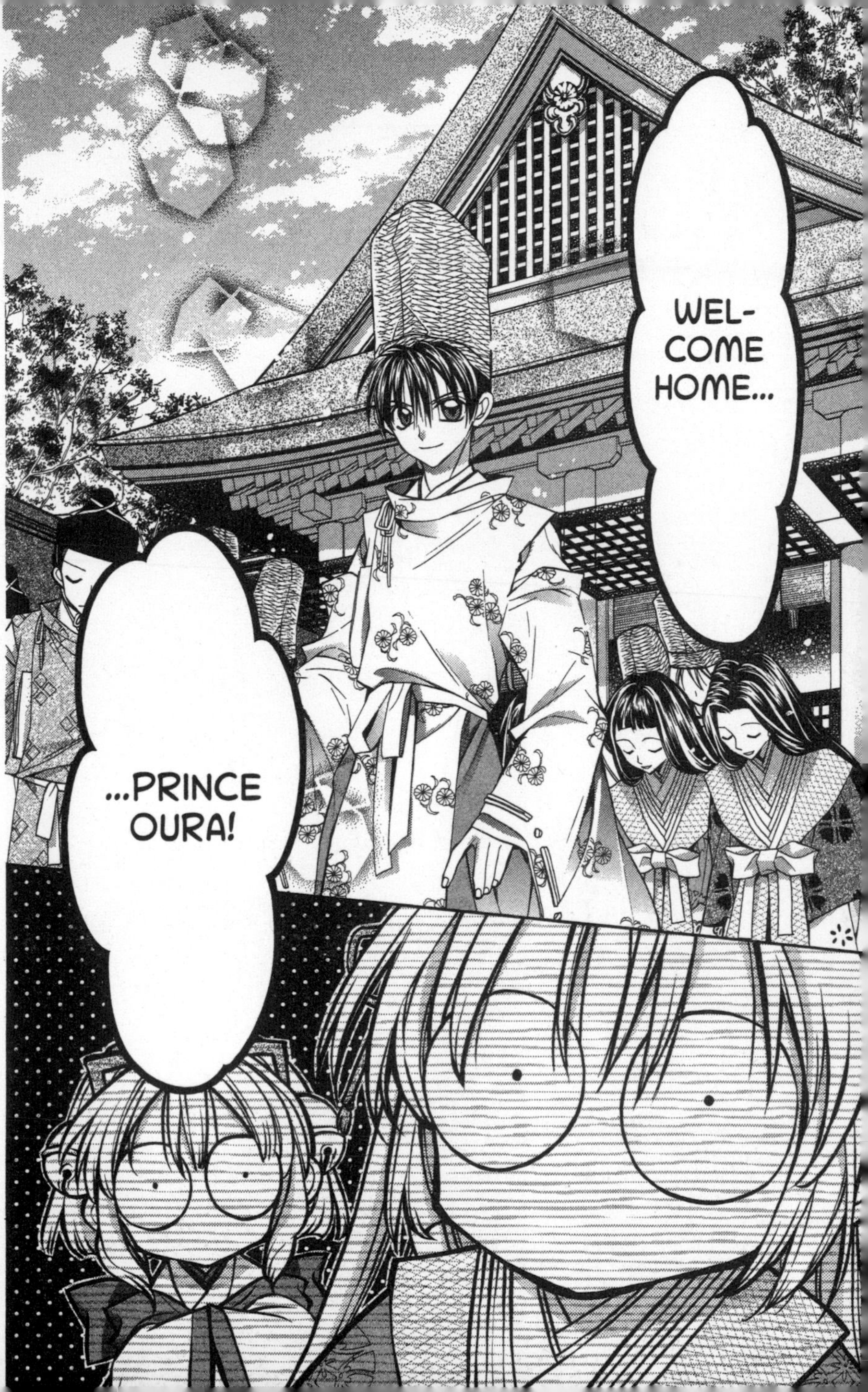
WEL-
COME
HOME...
...PRINCE
OURA!

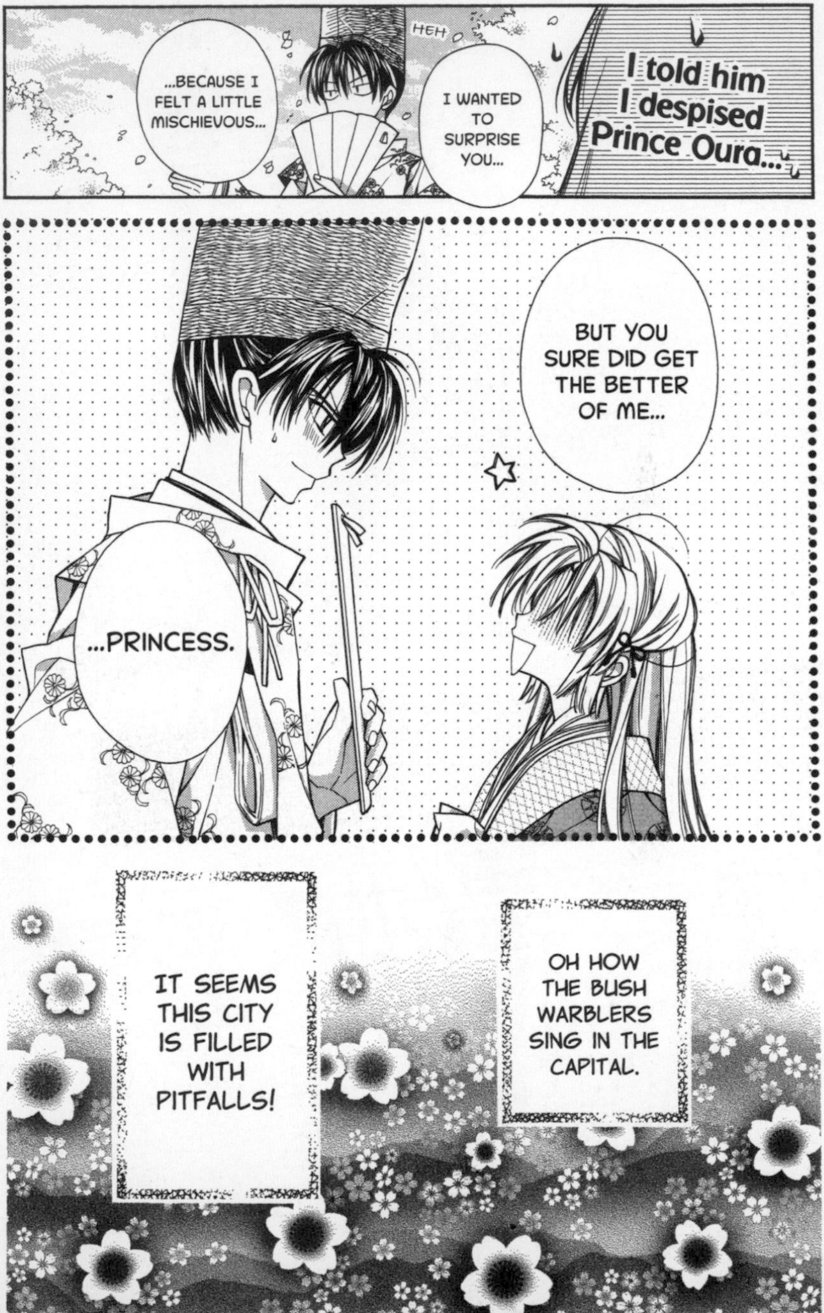
I told him I despised Prince Oura...
HEH
I WANTED TO SURPRISE YOU...
...BECAUSE I FELT A LITTLE MISCHIEVOUS...
BUT YOU SURE DID GET THE BETTER OF ME...
...PRINCESS.
OH HOW THE BUSH WARBLERS SING IN THE CAPITAL.
IT SEEMS THIS CITY IS FILLED WITH PITFALLS!

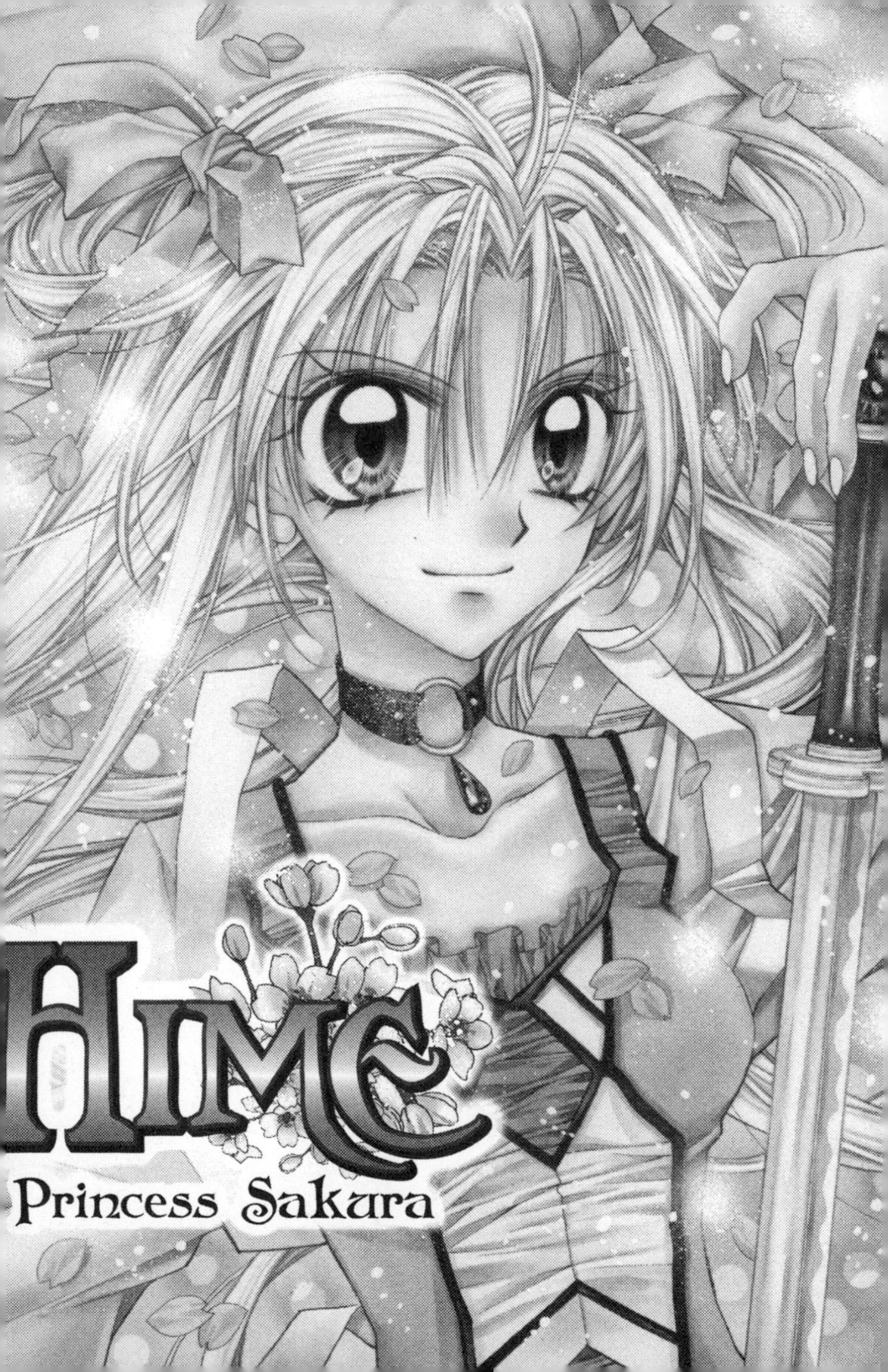
HIME
Princess Sakura

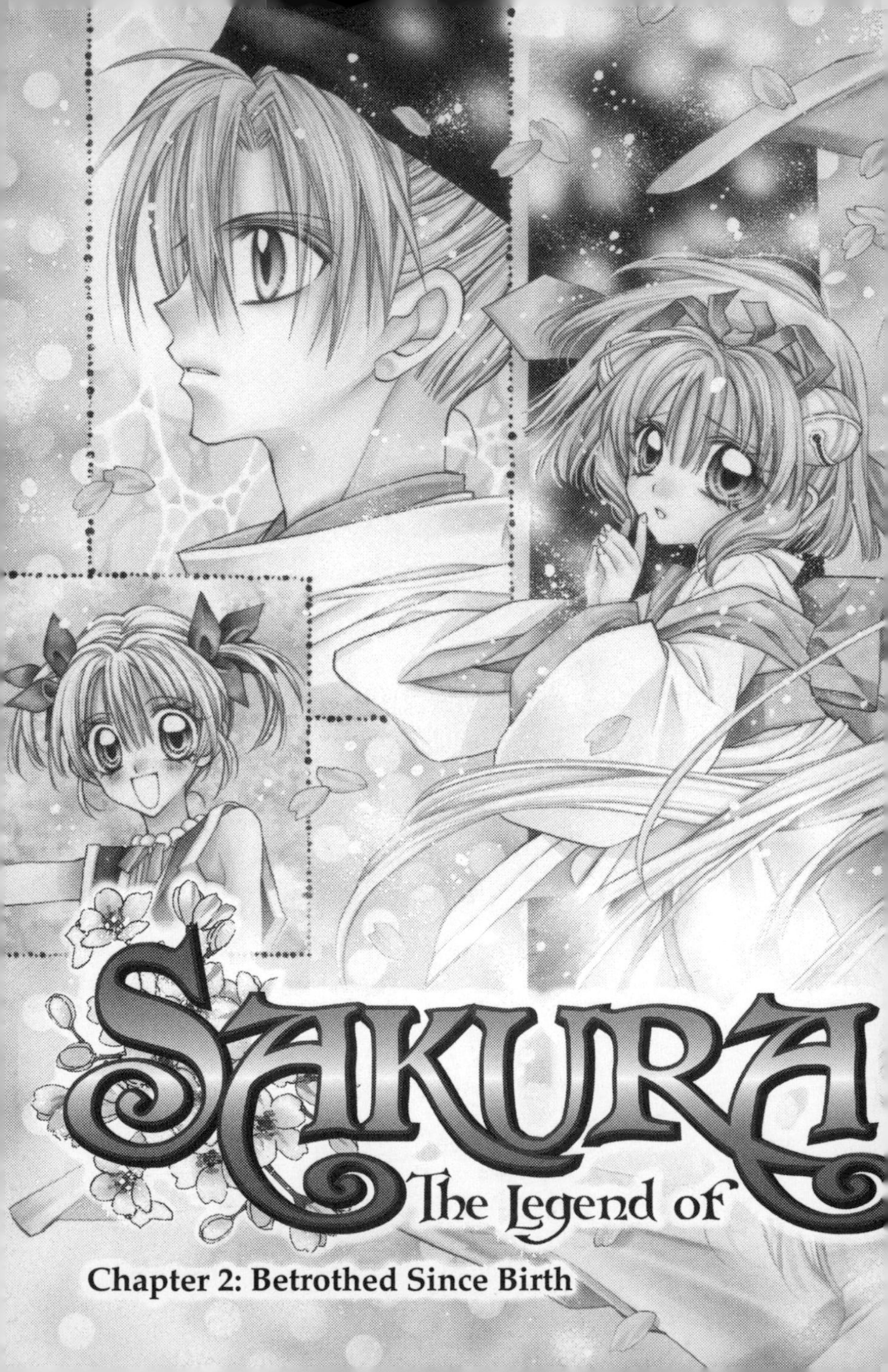
SAKURA
The Legend of
Chapter 2: Betrothed Since Birth

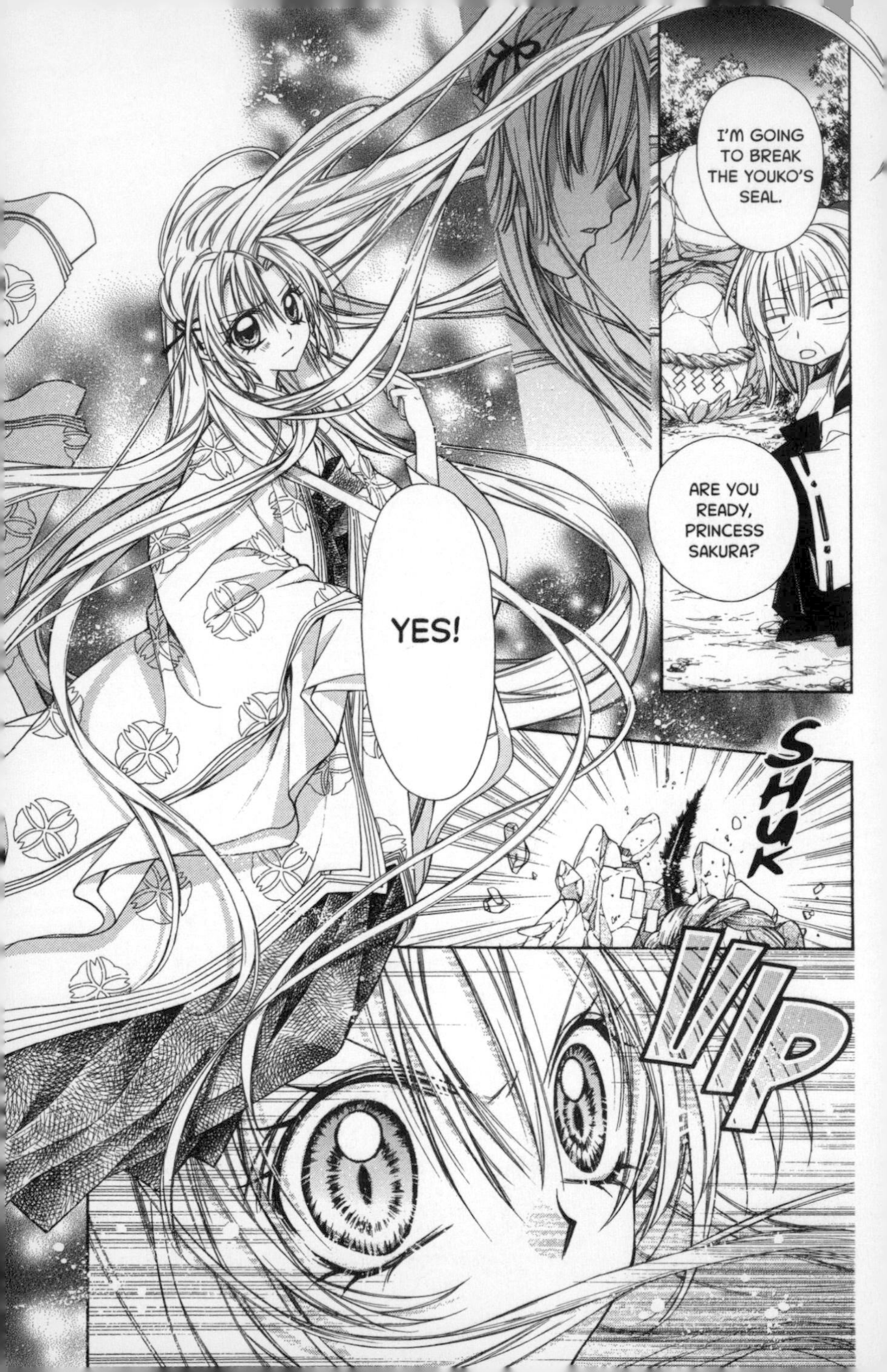
I'M GOING TO BREAK THE YOUKO'S SEAL.
ARE YOU READY, PRINCESS SAKURA?
YES!
SHUK
VIP

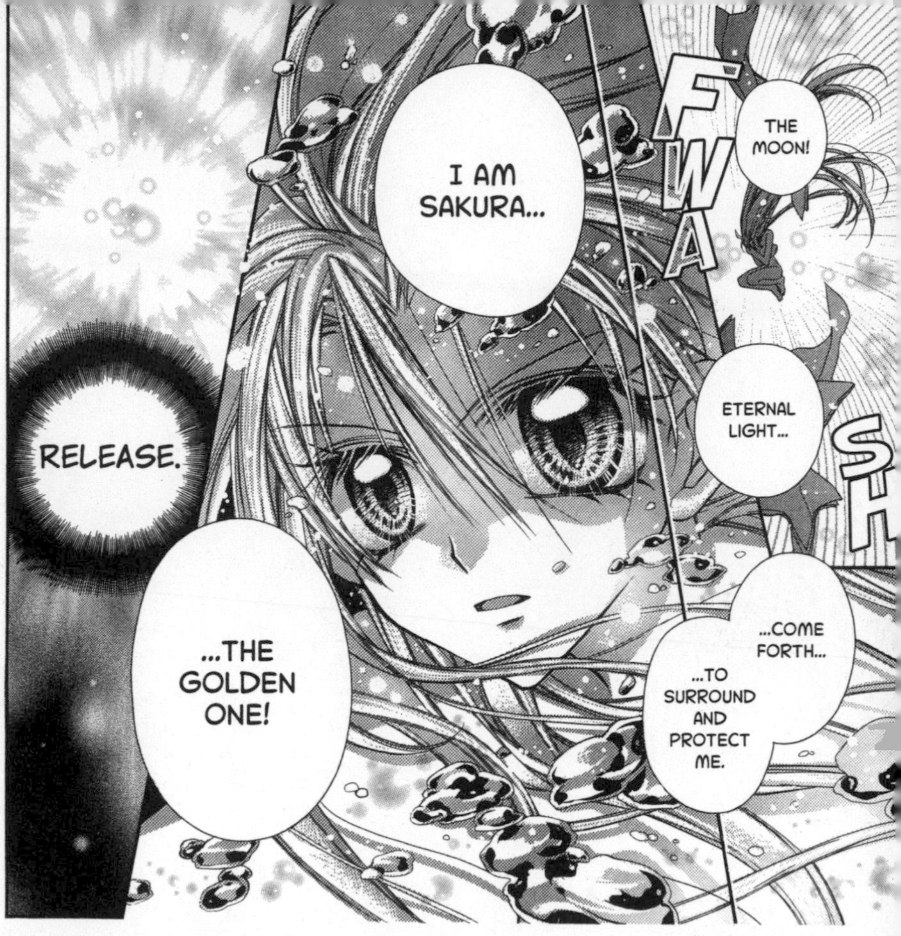
THE MOON!
FWA
ETERNAL LIGHT...
SH
...COME FORTH...
...TO SURROUND AND PROTECT ME.
I AM SAKURA...
RELEASE.
...THE GOLDEN ONE!

## Chapter 1: Under the Moon

The first chapter of the story... I was in a slump back then, and I remember making my editor very worried because I just could not come up with a storyboard for this. (For the past eight years or so, I've been able to create a story in about a day and get the go-ahead without fixing anything...)

But I kept thinking and thinking, trying to clear my mind, and this was what I got after some time. The biggest problem I had was thinking up "the reason for Sakura to fight"... But after I had a conversation with a female fan (a student at Aoyama Gakuin University whom I met in my private time ♥), I was quickly able to come up with something, and I finished it in one night. I've been a mangaka for some time now, so I'm able to create a complex story without thinking too hard, but a simple yet interesting story is rather tough, you know. I'm stubborn and proud, so... Hmm.

Anyway, thanks to all the effort I put into it, I like the first chapter a lot.

My editor told me, "The first chapter merely needs to be a promotional clip for the main character!" Do you think I succeeded? Hmm.

I put all my effort into drawing Sakura's facial expressions as best I could. I paid much more attention to that than I usually do.

Thanks to everyone's support, Sakura is the most popular character in chapter one by far. The next most popular character...was Asagiri. What a surprise.

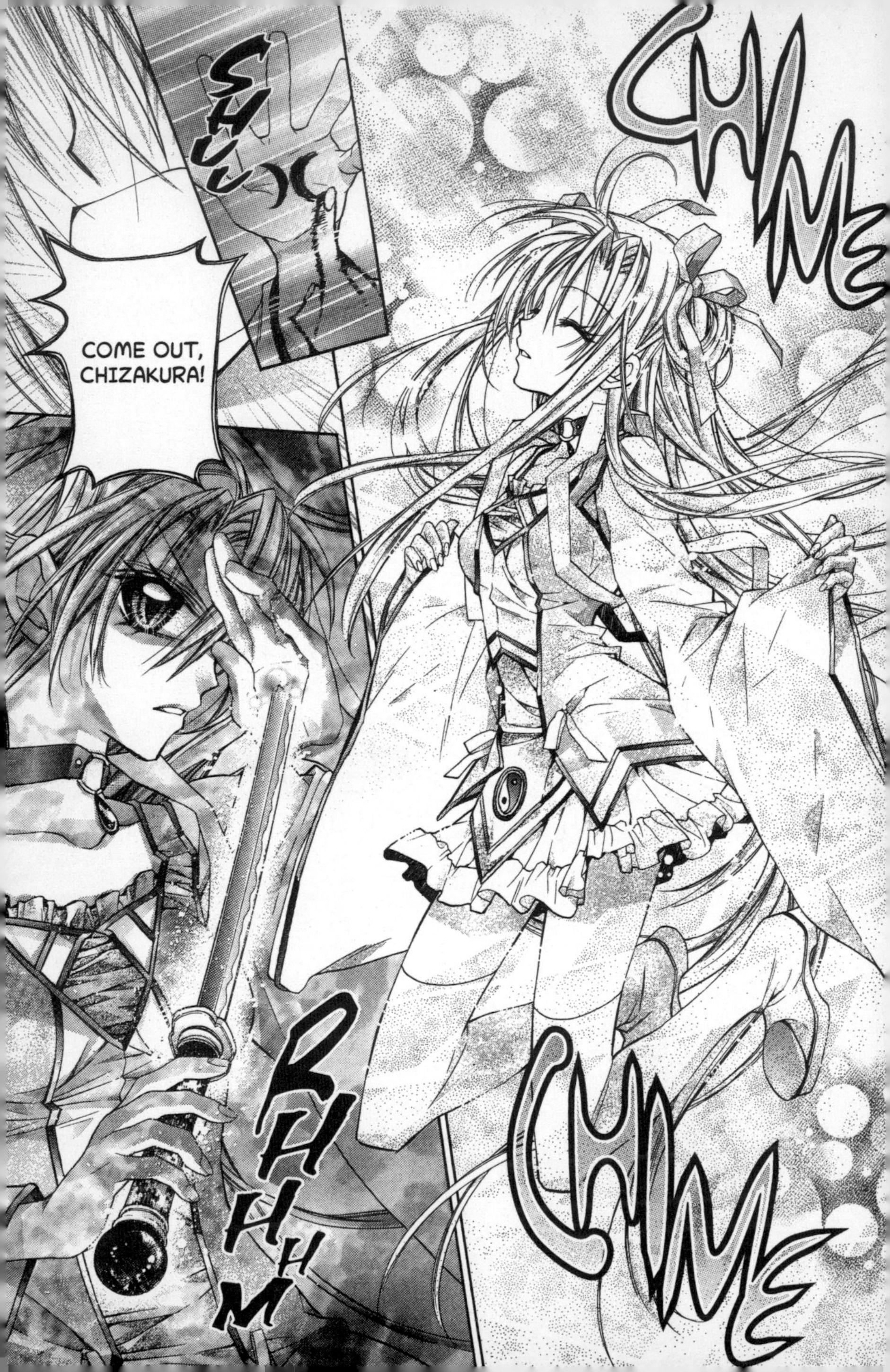
CHIME
CHIME
SHUU
COME OUT, CHIZAKURA!
RHHHM

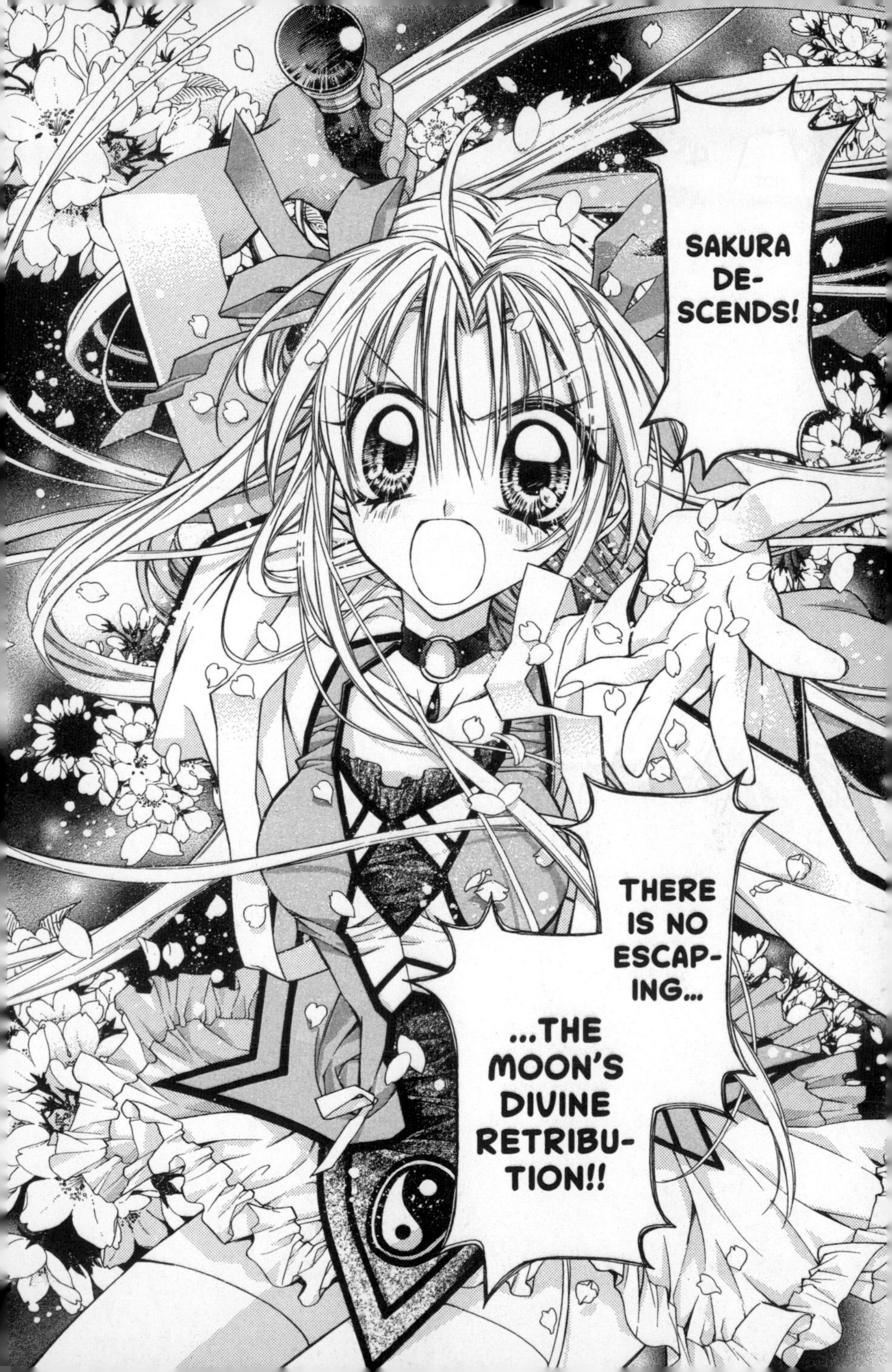
SAKURA DE-SCENDS!
THERE IS NO ESCAP-ING...
...THE MOON'S DIVINE RETRIBU-TION!!

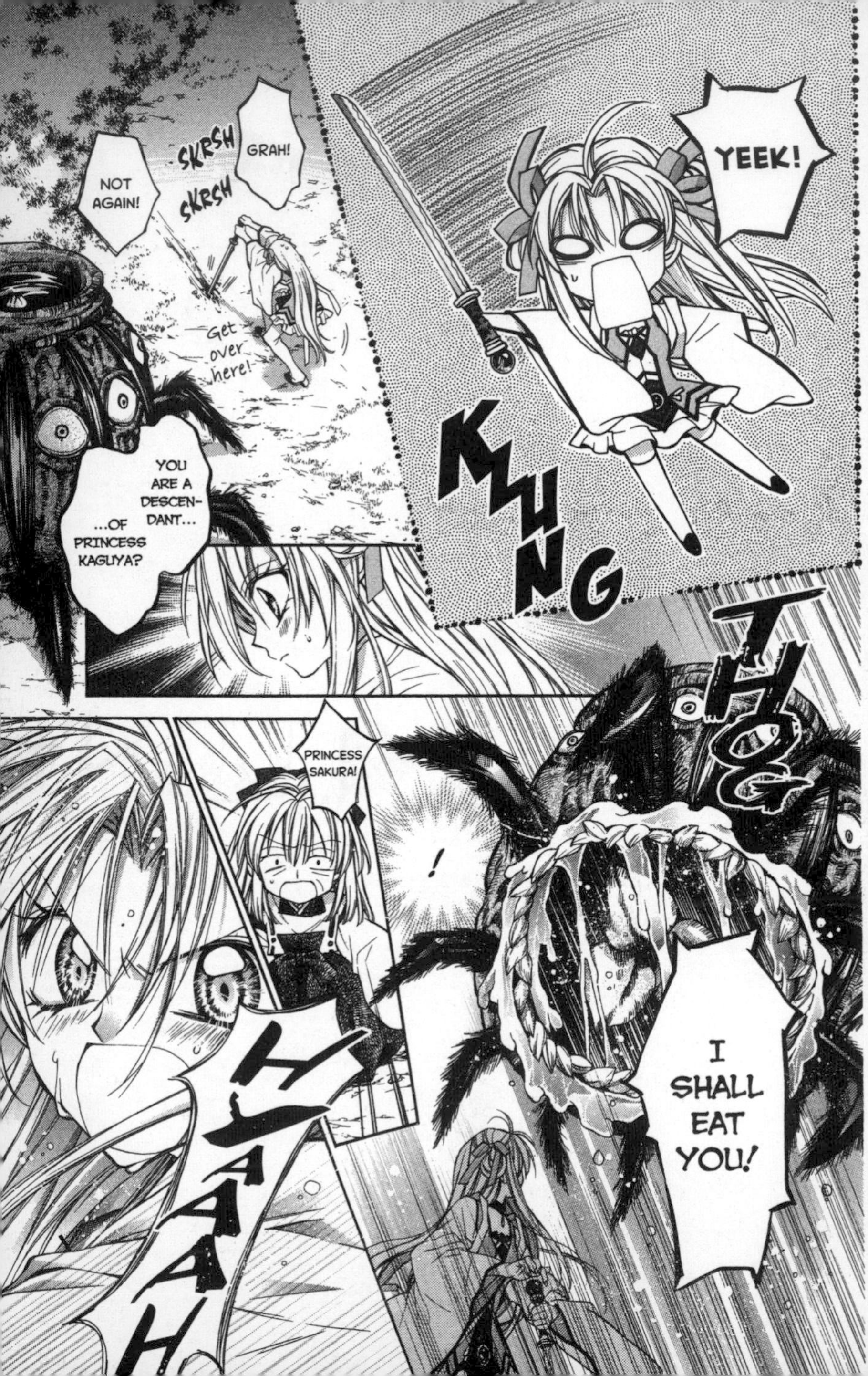
YEEK!
KNUNG
GRAH!
SKRSH SKRSH
NOT AGAIN!
Get over here!
YOU ARE A DESCENDANT...
...OF PRINCESS KAGUYA?
THOG
I SHALL EAT YOU!
PRINCESS SAKURA!
!
HYAAAAH

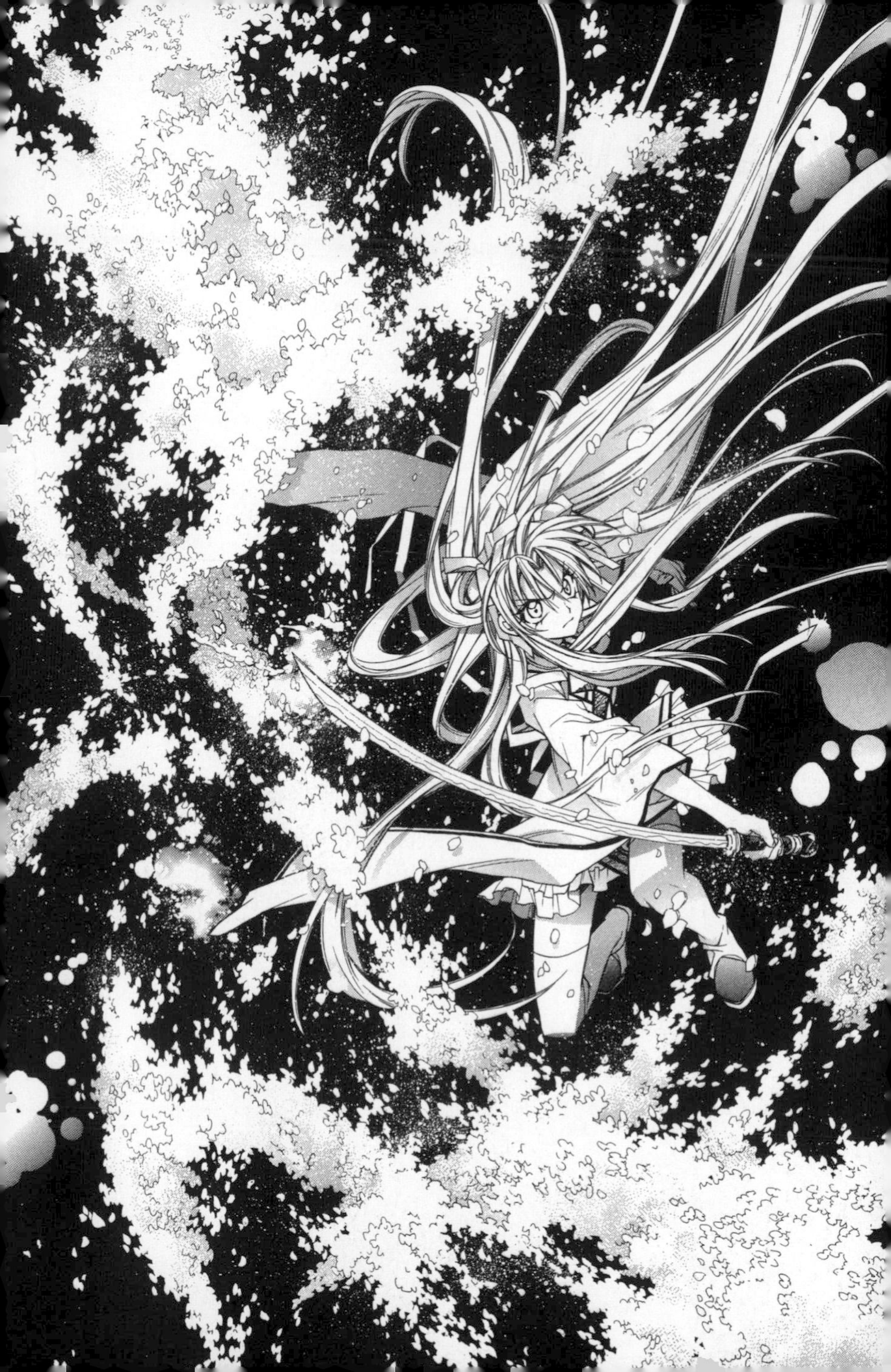

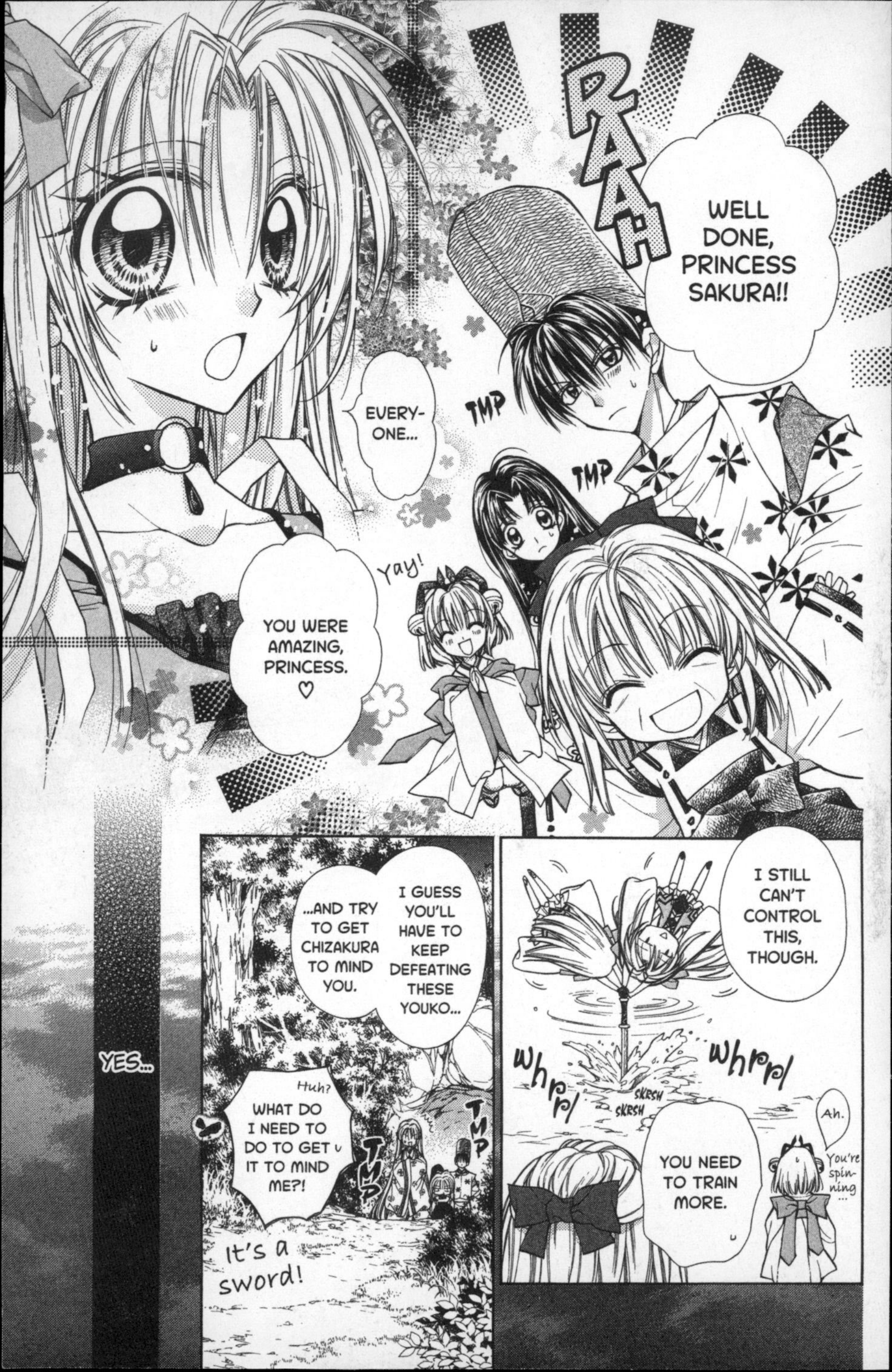
RAAH
WELL DONE, PRINCESS SAKURA!!
TMP
TMP
EVERY-ONE...
Yay!
YOU WERE AMAZING, PRINCESS. ♡
I STILL CAN'T CONTROL THIS, THOUGH.
whrrl
whrrl
SKRSH
SKRSH
Ah.
You're spin-ning...
YOU NEED TO TRAIN MORE.
I GUESS YOU'LL HAVE TO KEEP DEFEATING THESE YOUKO...
...AND TRY TO GET CHIZAKURA TO MIND YOU.
TMP
TMP
Huh?
WHAT DO I NEED TO DO TO GET IT TO MIND ME?!
It's a sword!
YES...

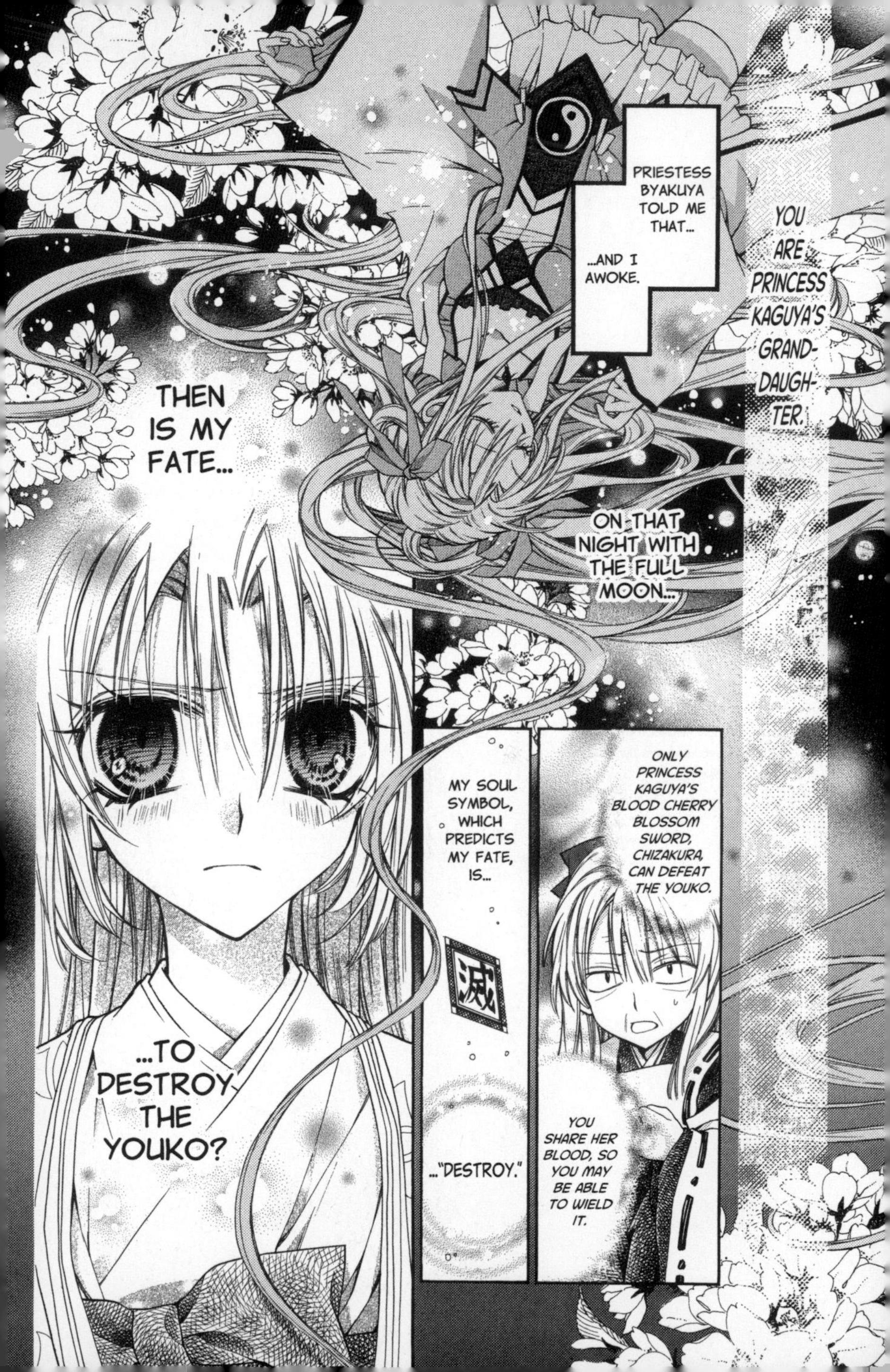
YOU ARE PRINCESS KAGUYA'S GRAND-DAUGHTER.
PRIESTESS BYAKUYA TOLD ME THAT...
...AND I AWOKE.
ON THAT NIGHT WITH THE FULL MOON...
THEN IS MY FATE...
ONLY PRINCESS KAGUYA'S BLOOD CHERRY BLOSSOM SWORD, CHIZAKURA, CAN DEFEAT THE YOUKO.
YOU SHARE HER BLOOD, SO YOU MAY BE ABLE TO WIELD IT.
MY SOUL SYMBOL, WHICH PREDICTS MY FATE, IS...
滅
..."DESTROY."
...TO DESTROY THE YOUKO?

## SINCE I STARTED THIS SERIES...

The troubles of creating a "Heian-Era Fantasy"...

✿ Princess Sakura's Costume

I was thinking about having her clothes change after her transformation. It would be too heavy if she was wearing a kouchigi.
(Although I'm sure it would look nice.)

But when it came to creating something she could easily move around in... I needed to create something with her legs showing. But then it wouldn't be authentic to the time... But after talking over it with my editor Kenken, we decided that she transforms into "clothes from the moon." Basically the country up on the moon is very advanced, so we came to the conclusion that we could make it modern and give her a "different" appearance.

✿ No Imported Words!!

I am trying not to be too strict on the types of words I use. There are a lot of modern words that did not exist in this time, but since I have problems making a point without using them, I've allowed myself to use those terms. But imported words have been forbidden.
You know, those foreign words written in katakana: *kisu* (kiss), *rizumu* (rhythm), *tenpo* (tempo), *sefu* (safe), etc.

It's pretty difficult... ~

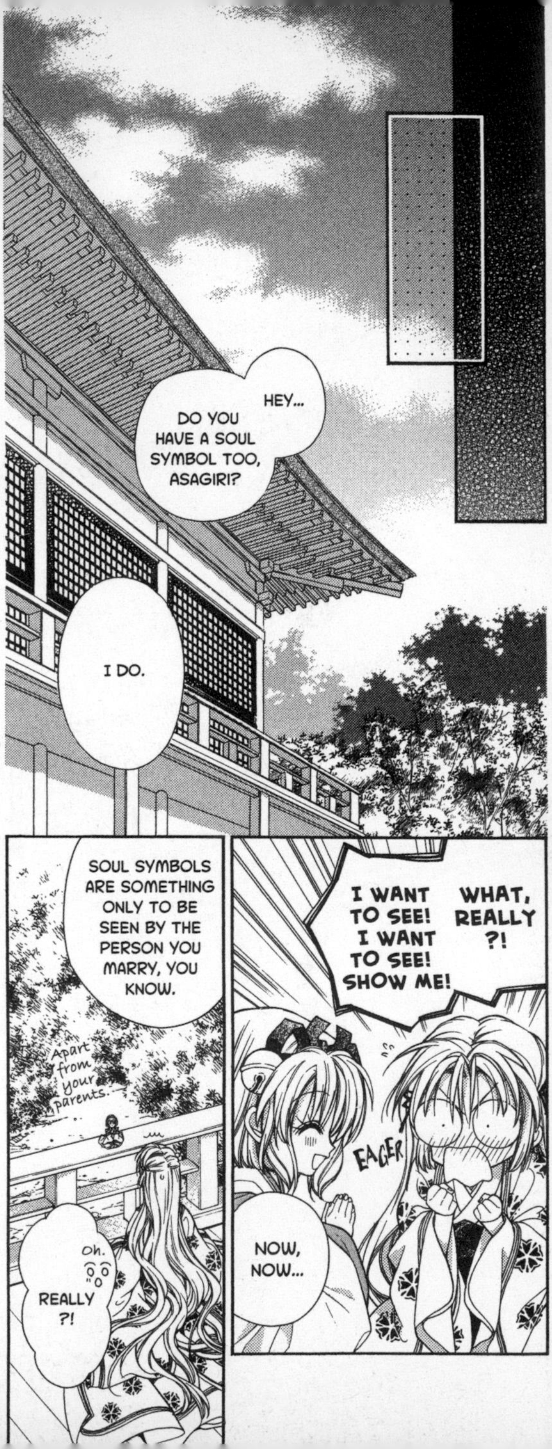
HEY... DO YOU HAVE A SOUL SYMBOL TOO, ASAGIRI?
I DO.
WHAT, REALLY ?!
I WANT TO SEE! I WANT TO SEE! SHOW ME!
EAGER
NOW, NOW...
SOUL SYMBOLS ARE SOMETHING ONLY TO BE SEEN BY THE PERSON YOU MARRY, YOU KNOW.
Apart from your parents.
Oh.
REALLY ?!

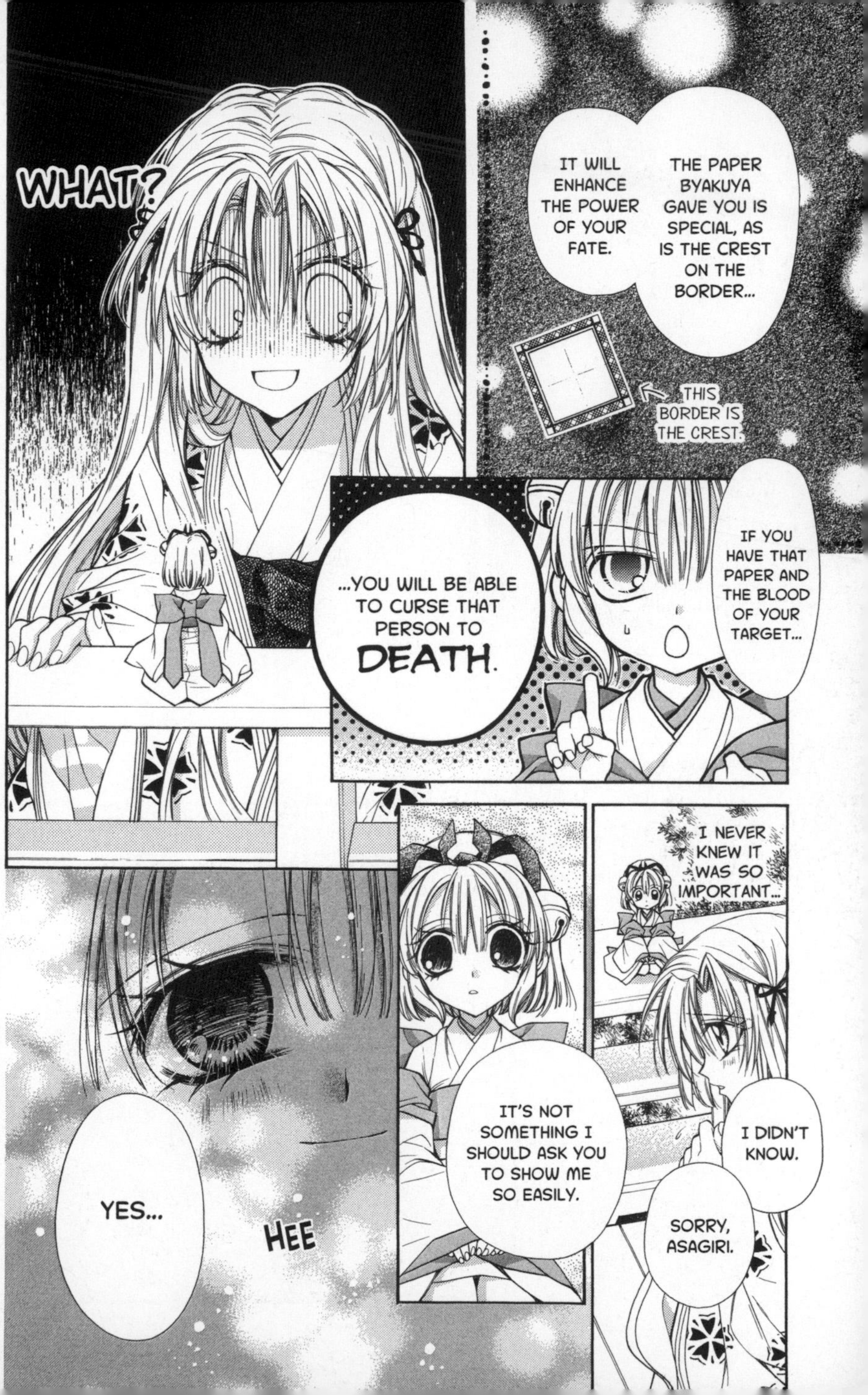
THE PAPER BYAKUYA GAVE YOU IS SPECIAL, AS IS THE CREST ON THE BORDER...
IT WILL ENHANCE THE POWER OF YOUR FATE.
THIS BORDER IS THE CREST.
IF YOU HAVE THAT PAPER AND THE BLOOD OF YOUR TARGET...
...YOU WILL BE ABLE TO CURSE THAT PERSON TO DEATH.
WHAT?
I NEVER KNEW IT WAS SO IMPORTANT...
I DIDN'T KNOW.
SORRY, ASAGIRI.
IT'S NOT SOMETHING I SHOULD ASK YOU TO SHOW ME SO EASILY.
YES...
HEE

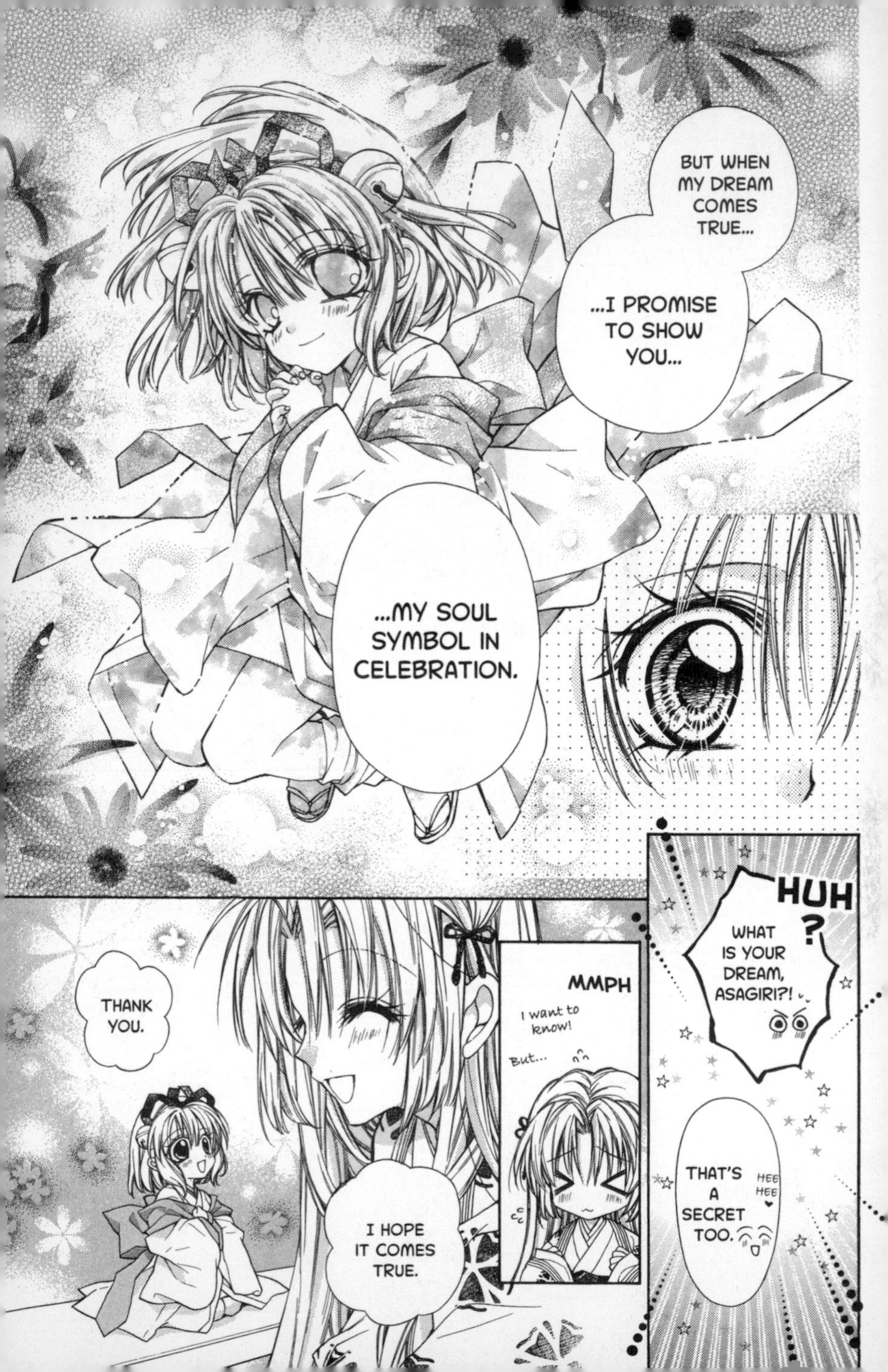

BUT WHEN MY DREAM COMES TRUE...
...I PROMISE TO SHOW YOU...
...MY SOUL SYMBOL IN CELEBRATION.
HUH?
WHAT IS YOUR DREAM, ASAGIRI?!
THAT'S A SECRET TOO.
HEE HEE
MMPH
I want to know!
But...
I HOPE IT COMES TRUE.
THANK YOU.

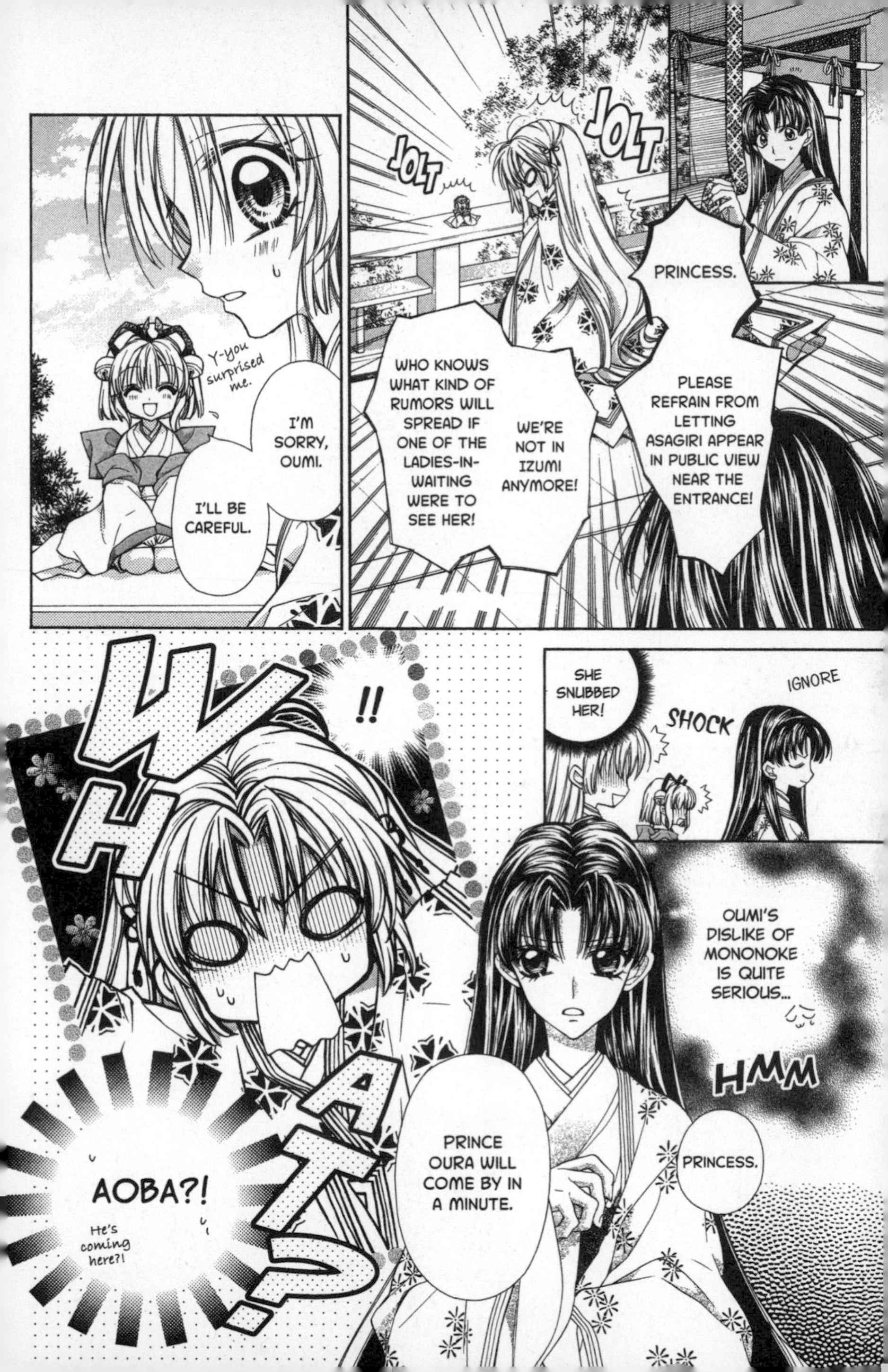
PRINCESS.
PLEASE REFRAIN FROM LETTING ASAGIRI APPEAR IN PUBLIC VIEW NEAR THE ENTRANCE!
JOLT
WE'RE NOT IN IZUMI ANYMORE!
WHO KNOWS WHAT KIND OF RUMORS WILL SPREAD IF ONE OF THE LADIES-IN-WAITING WERE TO SEE HER!
JOLT
Y-you surprised me.
I'M SORRY, OUMI.
I'LL BE CAREFUL.
IGNORE
SHE SNUBBED HER!
SHOCK
OUMI'S DISLIKE OF MONONOKE IS QUITE SERIOUS...
HMM
PRINCESS.
PRINCE OURA WILL COME BY IN A MINUTE.
!!
WHAT?!
AOBA?!
He's coming here?!

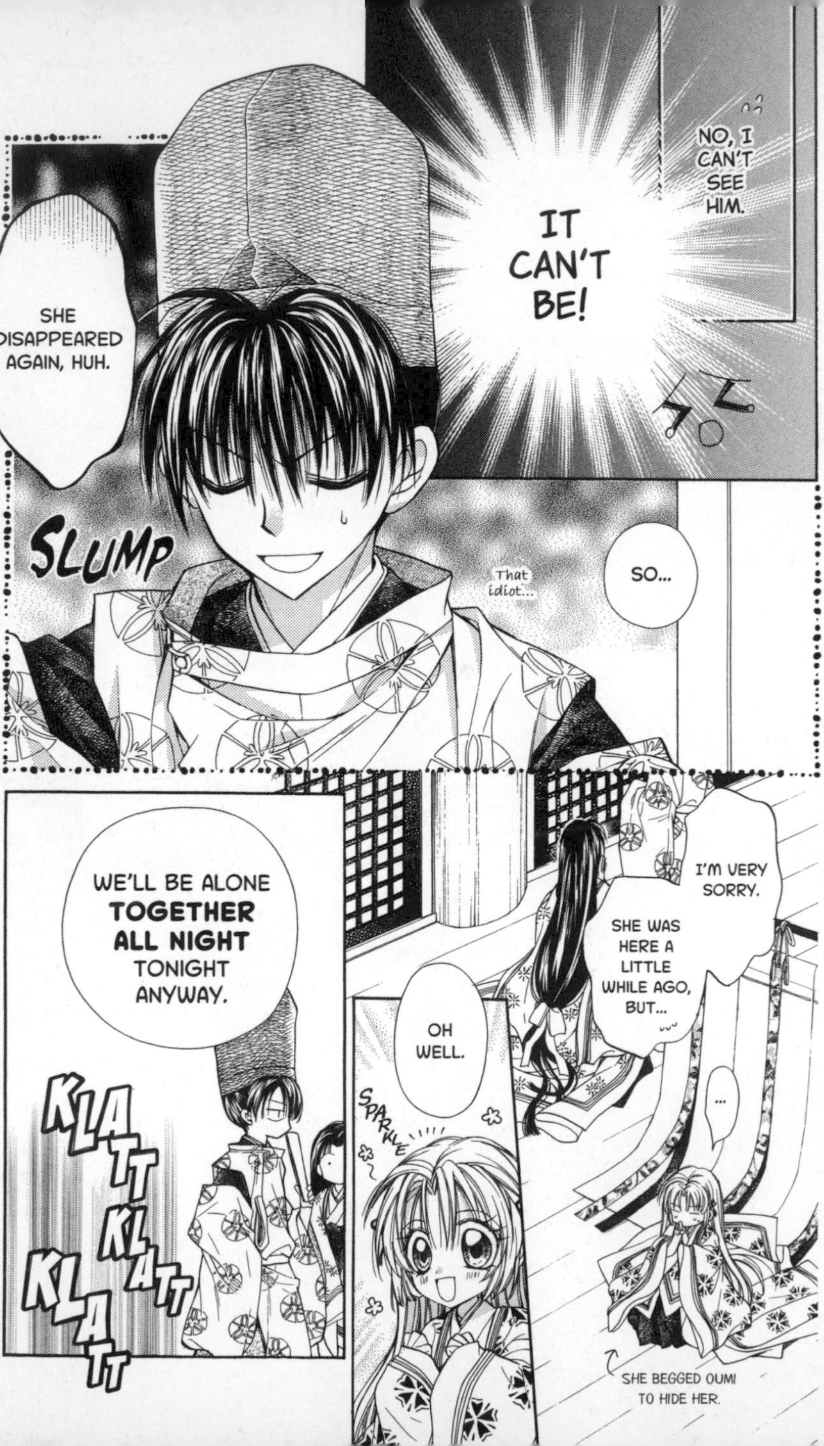
IT CAN'T BE!
NO, I CAN'T SEE HIM.
SHE DISAPPEARED AGAIN, HUH.
SLUMP
That idiot...
SO...
I'M VERY SORRY.
SHE WAS HERE A LITTLE WHILE AGO, BUT...
...
SHE BEGGED OUMI TO HIDE HER.
OH WELL.
SPARKLE
WE'LL BE ALONE **TOGETHER ALL NIGHT** TONIGHT ANYWAY.
KLATT KLATT KLATT

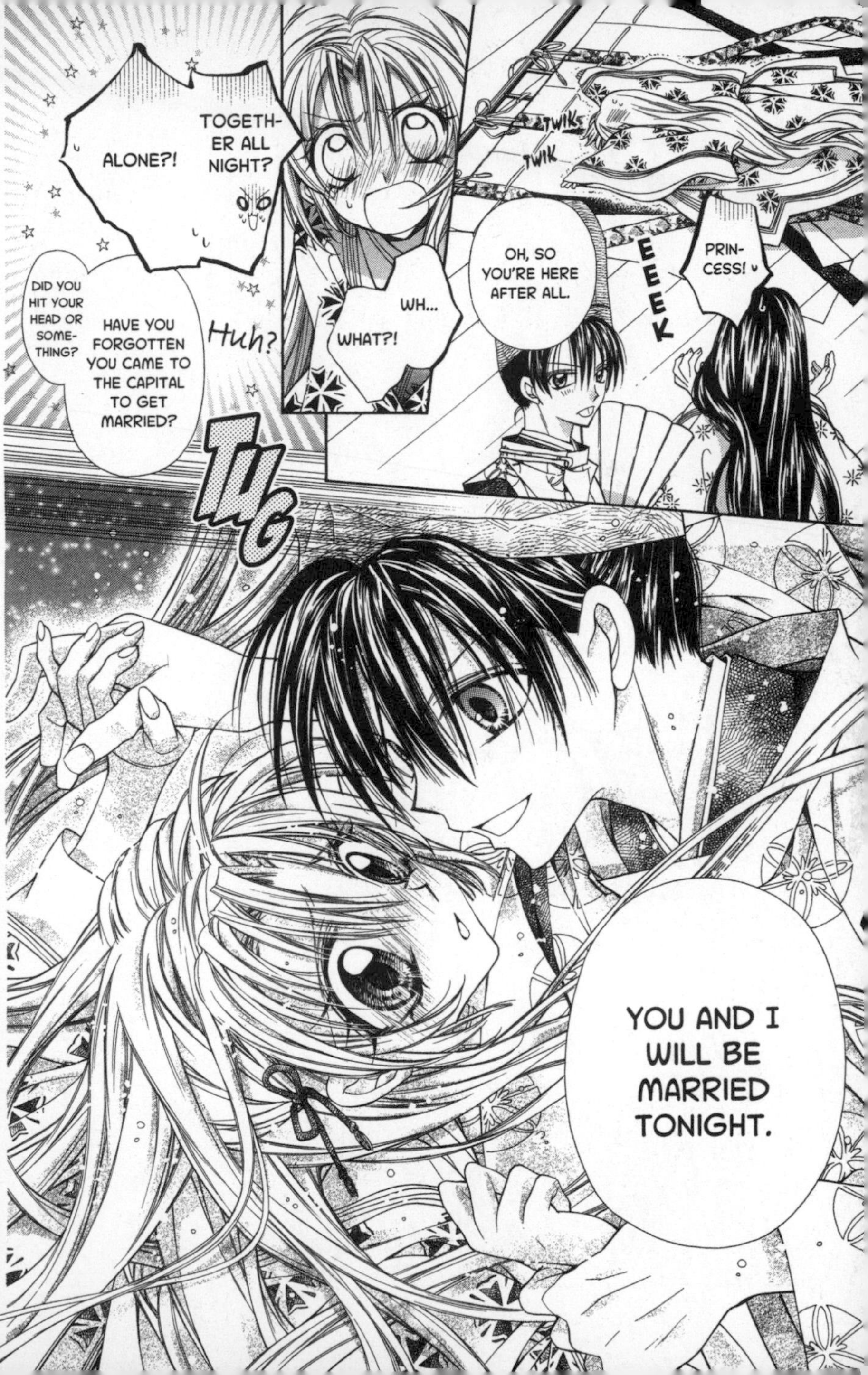
TWIK
TWIK
PRIN-CESS!
EEEK
OH, SO YOU'RE HERE AFTER ALL.
TOGETH-ER ALL NIGHT?
ALONE?!
WH...
WHAT?!
Huh?
HAVE YOU FORGOTTEN YOU CAME TO THE CAPITAL TO GET MARRIED?
DID YOU HIT YOUR HEAD OR SOME-THING?
TUG
YOU AND I WILL BE MARRIED TONIGHT.

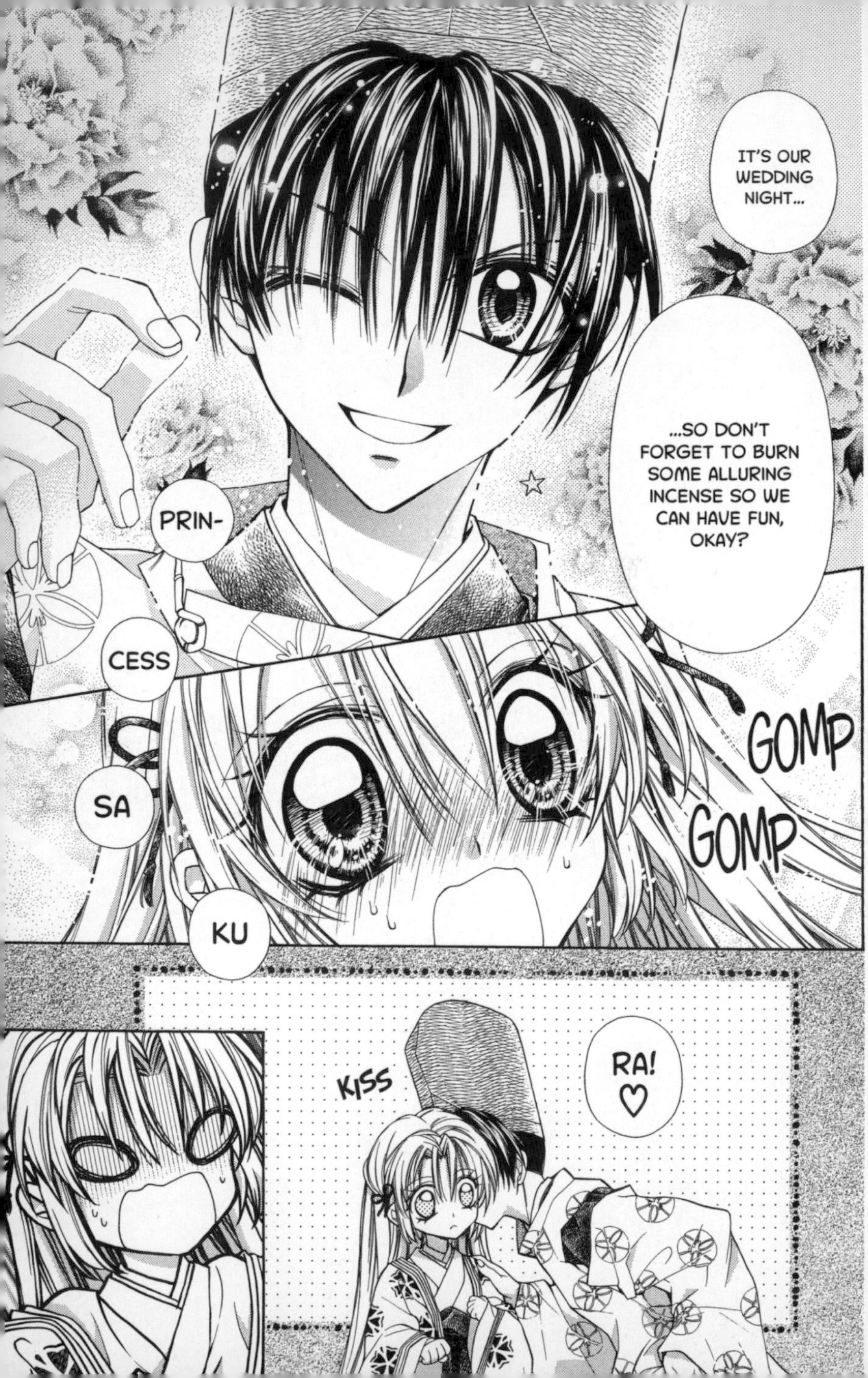
IT'S OUR WEDDING NIGHT...
...SO DON'T FORGET TO BURN SOME ALLURING INCENSE SO WE CAN HAVE FUN, OKAY?
PRIN-
CESS
GOMP
GOMP
SA
KU
RA! ♡
KISS

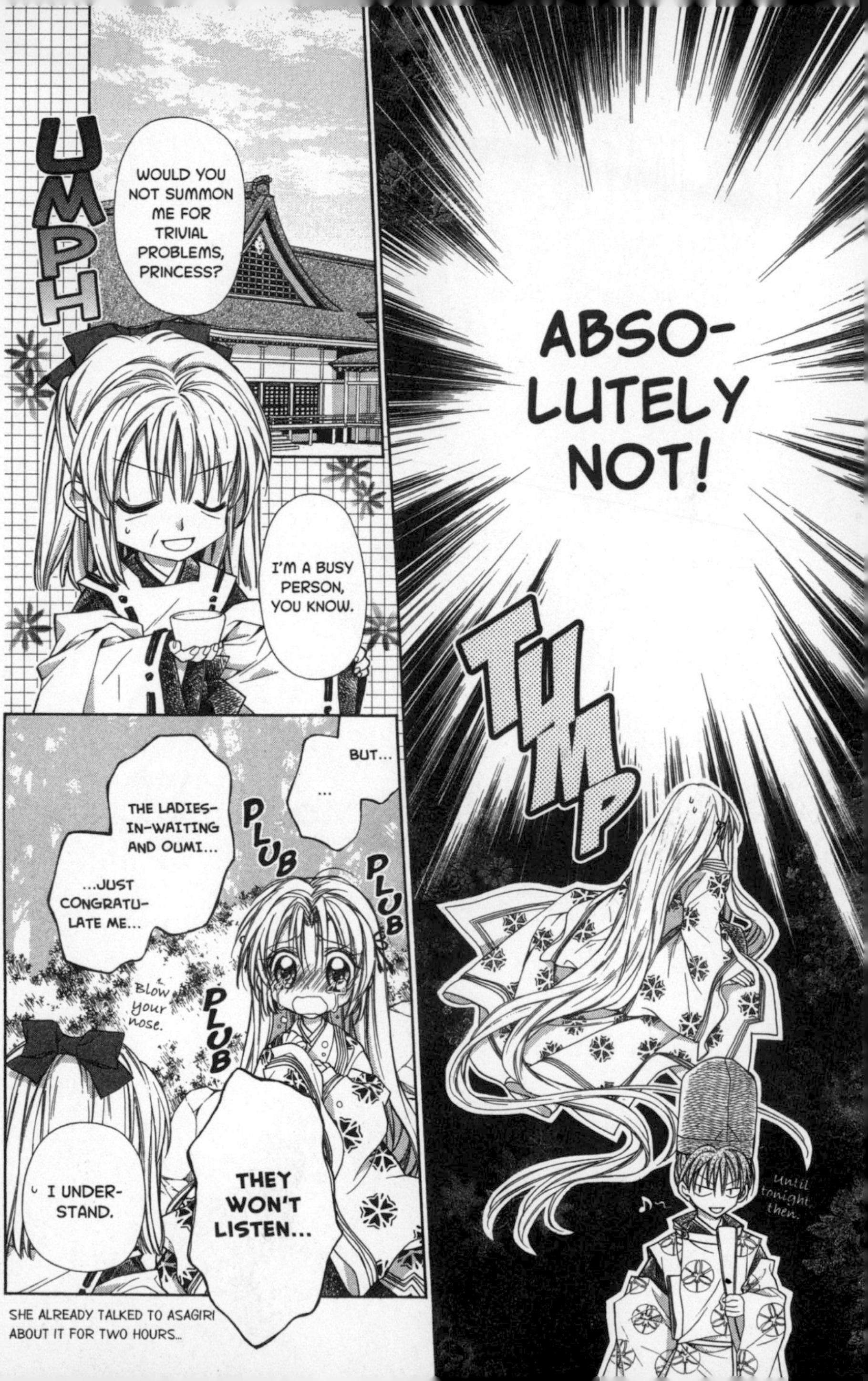
ABSO-LUTELY NOT!
THUMP
Until tonight, then.
UMPH
WOULD YOU NOT SUMMON ME FOR TRIVIAL PROBLEMS, PRINCESS?
I'M A BUSY PERSON, YOU KNOW.
BUT...
...
THE LADIES-IN-WAITING AND OUMI...
...JUST CONGRATULATE ME...
PLUB
PLUB
Blow your nose.
PLUB
THEY WON'T LISTEN...
I UNDER-STAND.
SHE ALREADY TALKED TO ASAGIRI ABOUT IT FOR TWO HOURS...

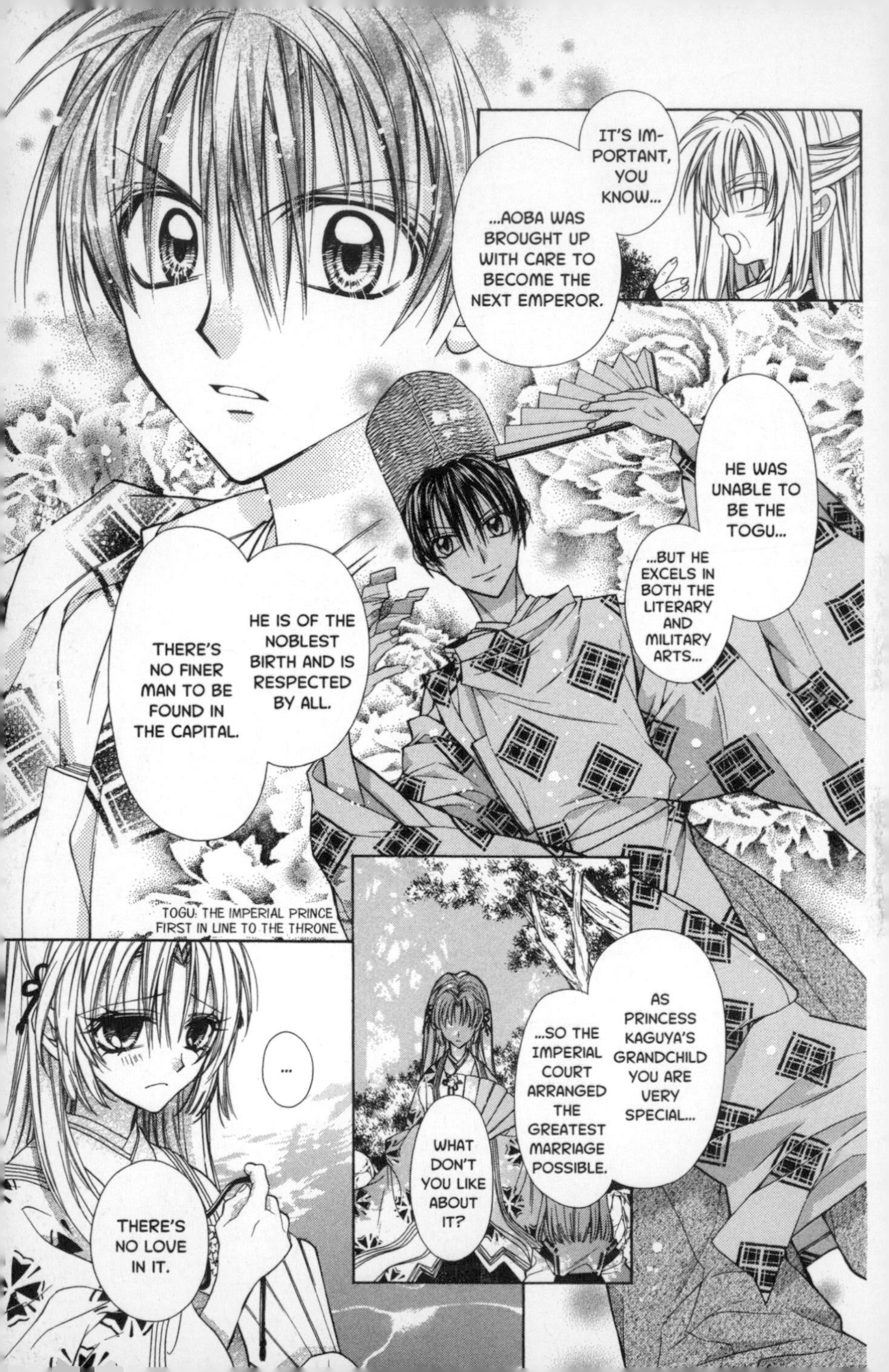
IT'S IM-PORTANT, YOU KNOW...
...AOBA WAS BROUGHT UP WITH CARE TO BECOME THE NEXT EMPEROR.
HE WAS UNABLE TO BE THE TOGU...
...BUT HE EXCELS IN BOTH THE LITERARY AND MILITARY ARTS...
HE IS OF THE NOBLEST BIRTH AND IS RESPECTED BY ALL.
THERE'S NO FINER MAN TO BE FOUND IN THE CAPITAL.
TOGU: THE IMPERIAL PRINCE FIRST IN LINE TO THE THRONE.
AS PRINCESS KAGUYA'S GRANDCHILD YOU ARE VERY SPECIAL...
...SO THE IMPERIAL COURT ARRANGED THE GREATEST MARRIAGE POSSIBLE.
WHAT DON'T YOU LIKE ABOUT IT?
...
THERE'S NO LOVE IN IT.

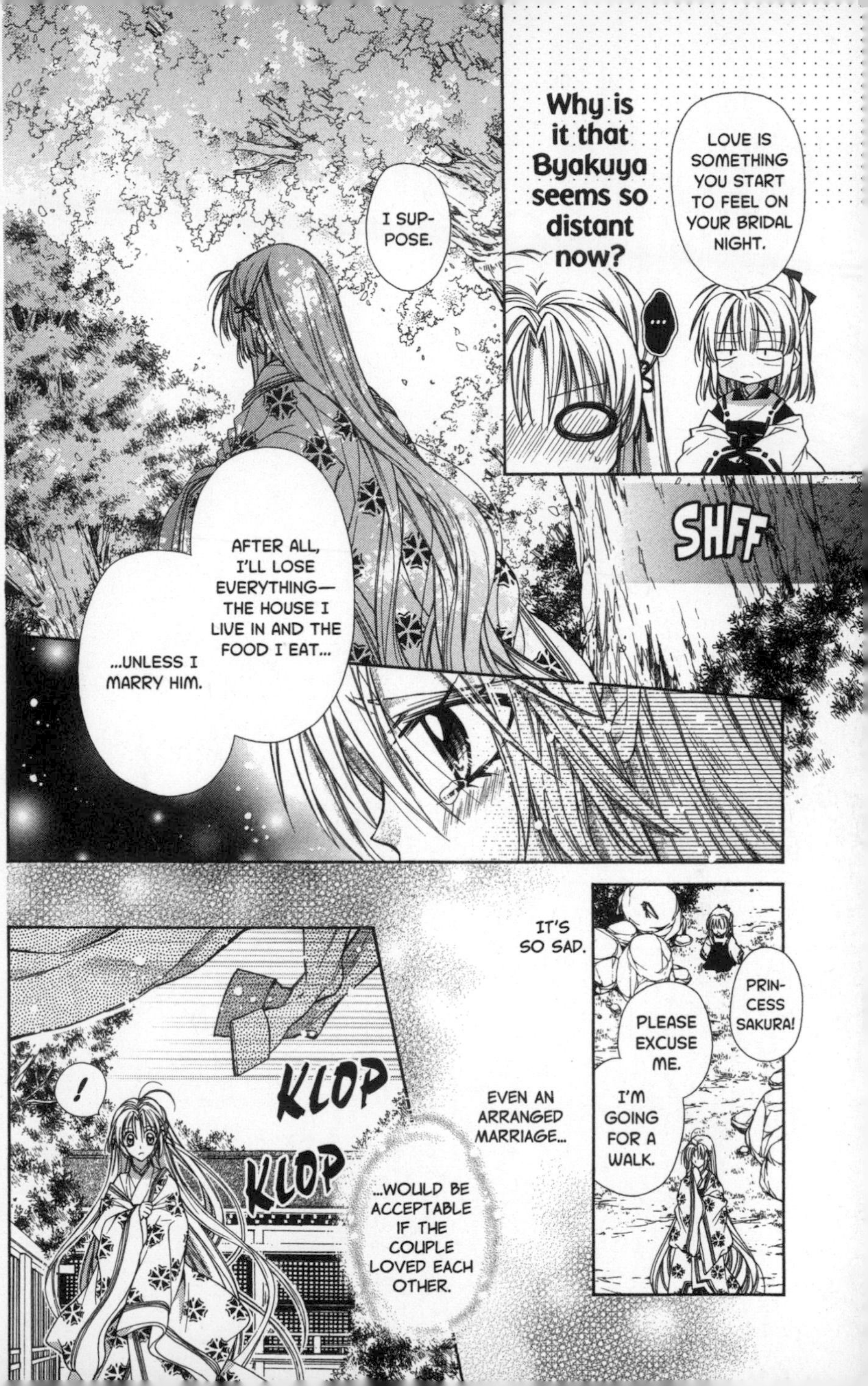
LOVE IS SOMETHING YOU START TO FEEL ON YOUR BRIDAL NIGHT.
Why is it that Byakuya seems so distant now?
...
I SUP-POSE.
AFTER ALL, I'LL LOSE EVERYTHING— THE HOUSE I LIVE IN AND THE FOOD I EAT...
...UNLESS I MARRY HIM.
SHFF
PRIN-CESS SAKURA!
PLEASE EXCUSE ME.
I'M GOING FOR A WALK.
IT'S SO SAD.
EVEN AN ARRANGED MARRIAGE...
...WOULD BE ACCEPTABLE IF THE COUPLE LOVED EACH OTHER.
KLOP
KLOP
!

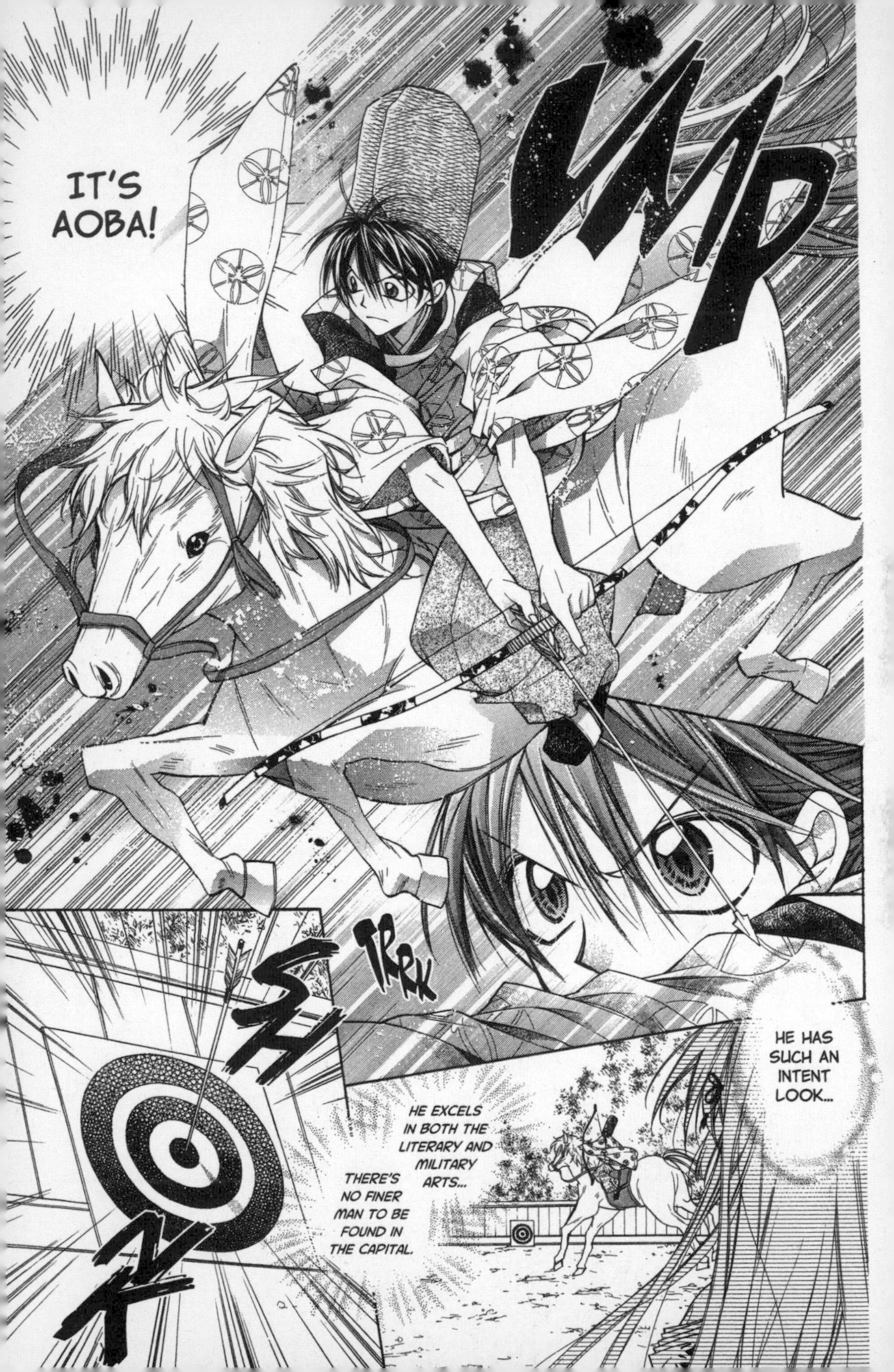
WMP
IT'S AOBA!
TRRK
HE HAS SUCH AN INTENT LOOK...
HE EXCELS IN BOTH THE LITERARY AND MILITARY ARTS...
THERE'S NO FINER MAN TO BE FOUND IN THE CAPITAL.
SHNK

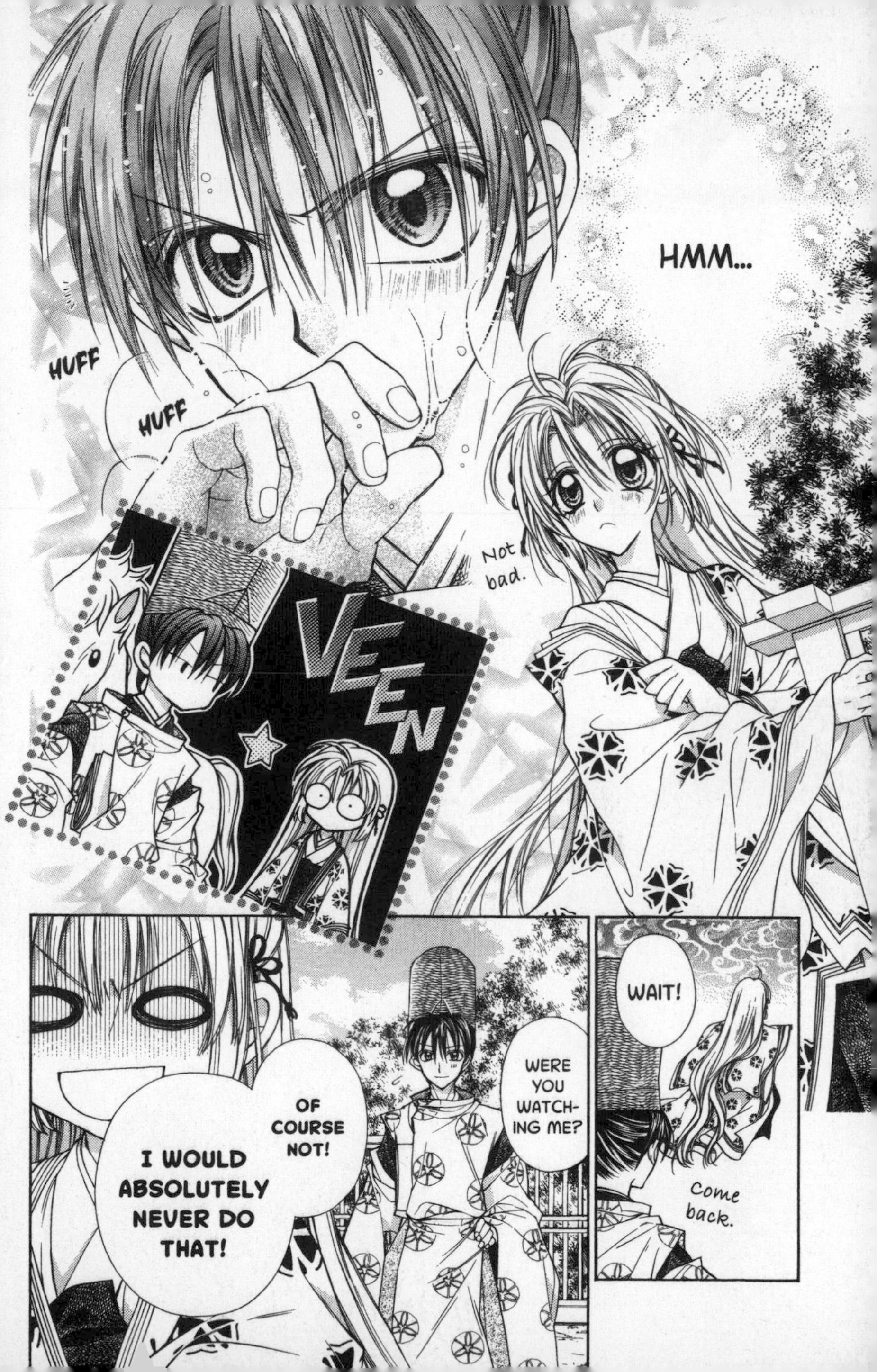
HMM...
Not bad.
HUFF
HUFF
VEEN
WAIT!
Come back.
WERE YOU WATCHING ME?
OF COURSE NOT!
I WOULD ABSOLUTELY NEVER DO THAT!

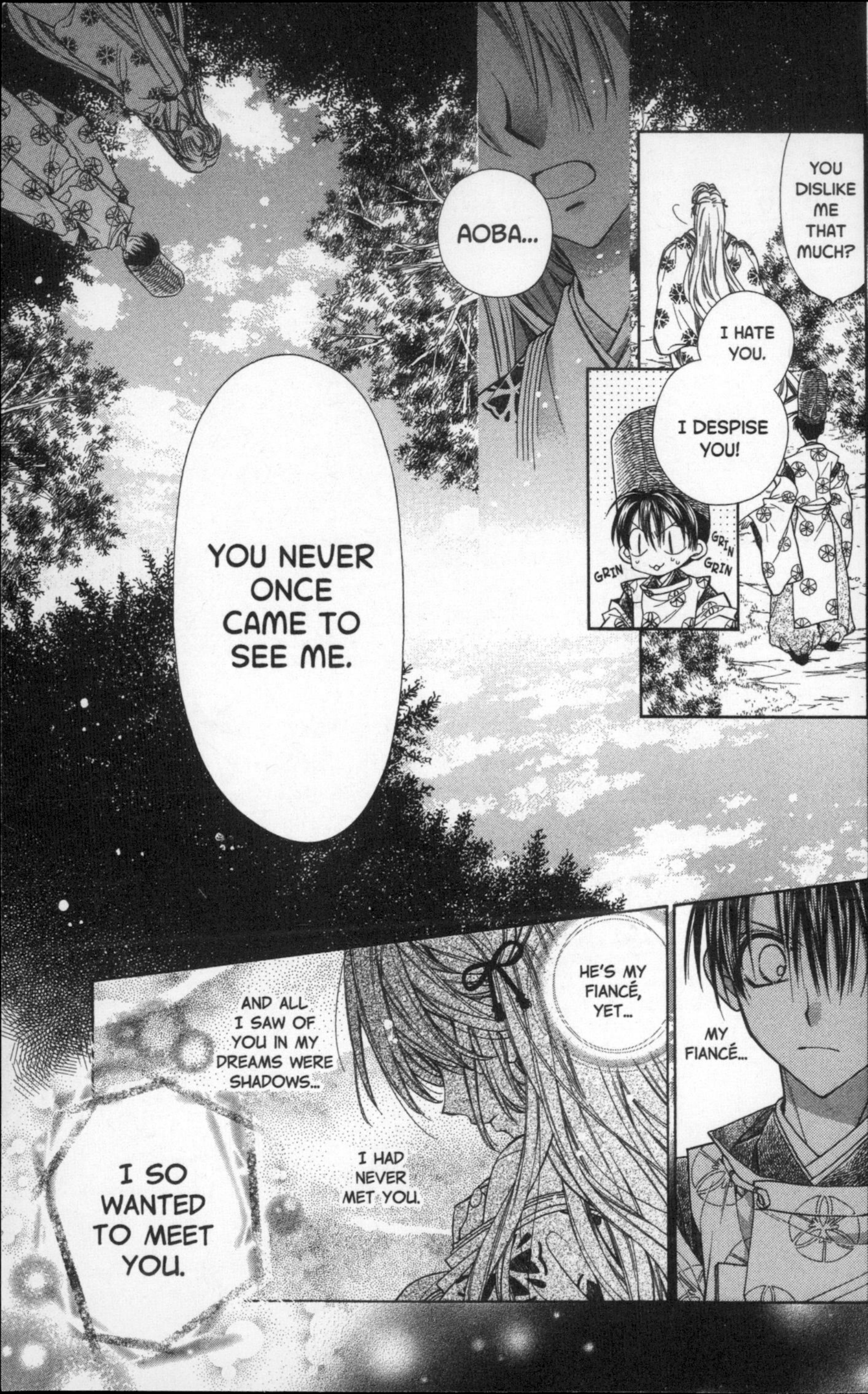

YOU DISLIKE ME THAT MUCH?
I HATE YOU.
I DESPISE YOU!
GRIN GRIN GRIN
AOBA...
YOU NEVER ONCE CAME TO SEE ME.
MY FIANCÉ...
HE'S MY FIANCÉ, YET...
AND ALL I SAW OF YOU IN MY DREAMS WERE SHADOWS...
I HAD NEVER MET YOU.
I SO WANTED TO MEET YOU.

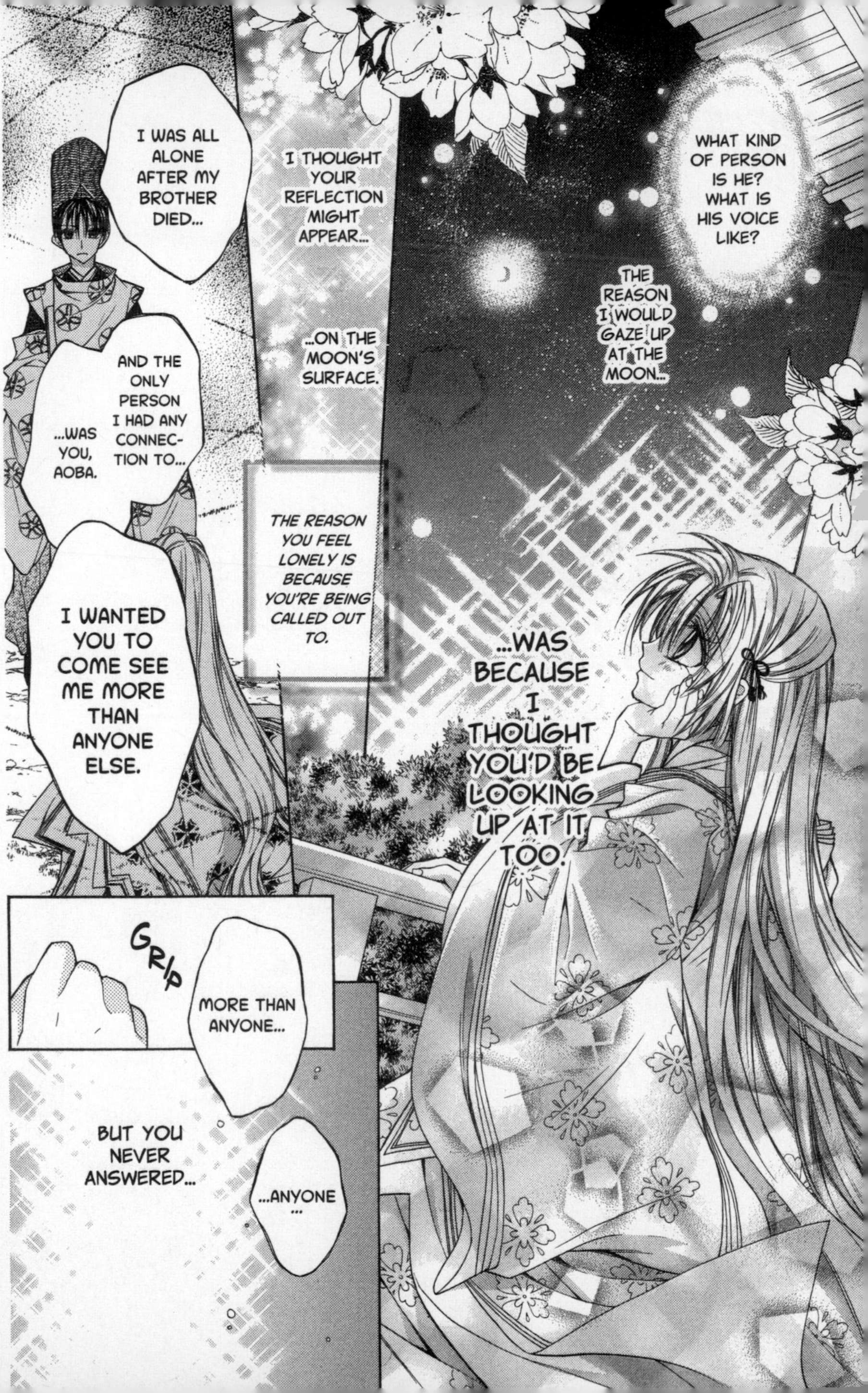
WHAT KIND OF PERSON IS HE? WHAT IS HIS VOICE LIKE?
THE REASON I WOULD GAZE UP AT THE MOON...
...WAS BECAUSE I THOUGHT YOU'D BE LOOKING UP AT IT TOO.
I THOUGHT YOUR REFLECTION MIGHT APPEAR...
...ON THE MOON'S SURFACE.
THE REASON YOU FEEL LONELY IS BECAUSE YOU'RE BEING CALLED OUT TO.
I WAS ALL ALONE AFTER MY BROTHER DIED...
AND THE ONLY PERSON I HAD ANY CONNECTION TO...
...WAS YOU, AOBA.
I WANTED YOU TO COME SEE ME MORE THAN ANYONE ELSE.
MORE THAN ANYONE...
GRIP
BUT YOU NEVER ANSWERED...
...ANYONE ...

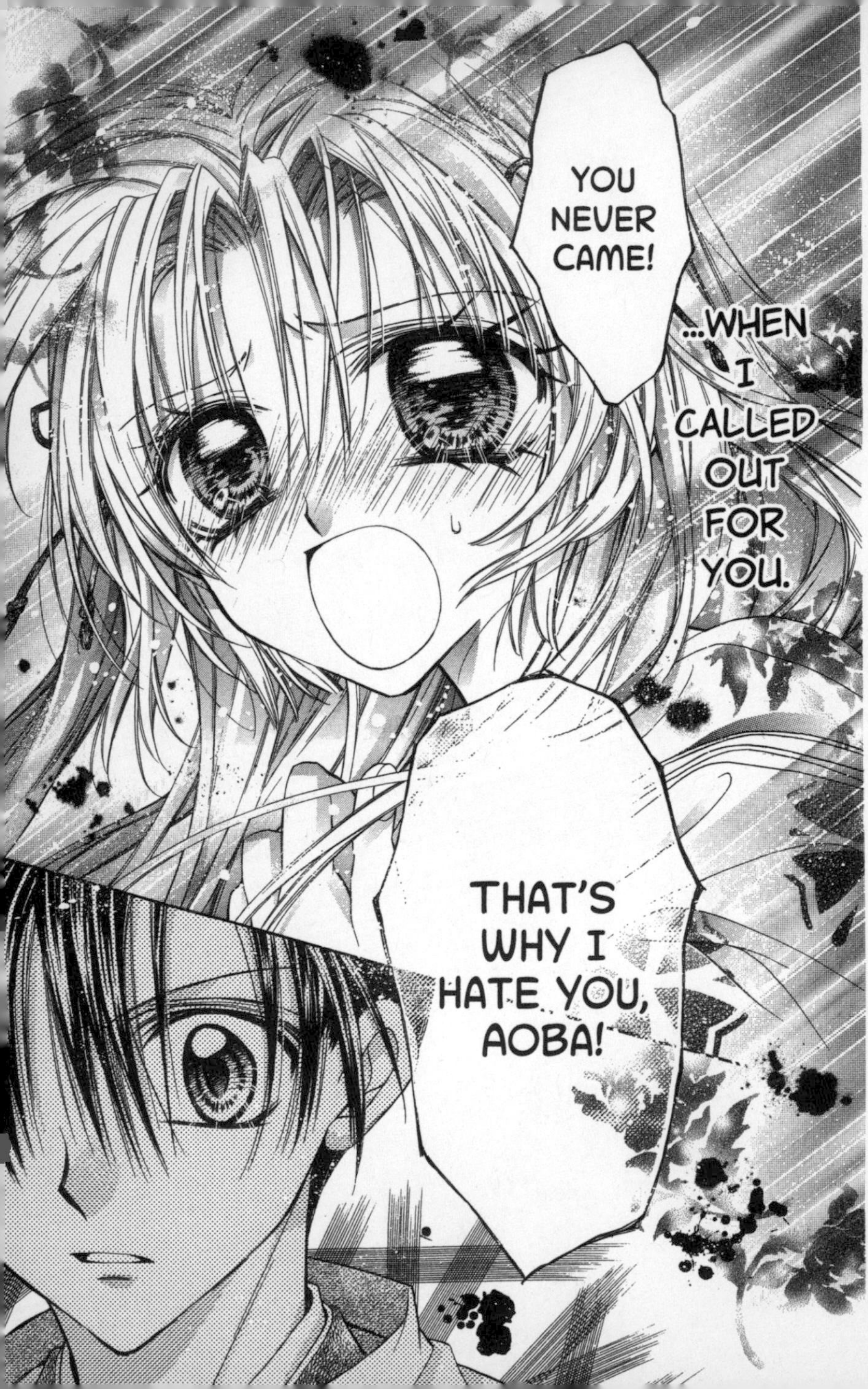
YOU NEVER CAME!
...WHEN I CALLED OUT FOR YOU.
THAT'S WHY I HATE YOU, AOBA!

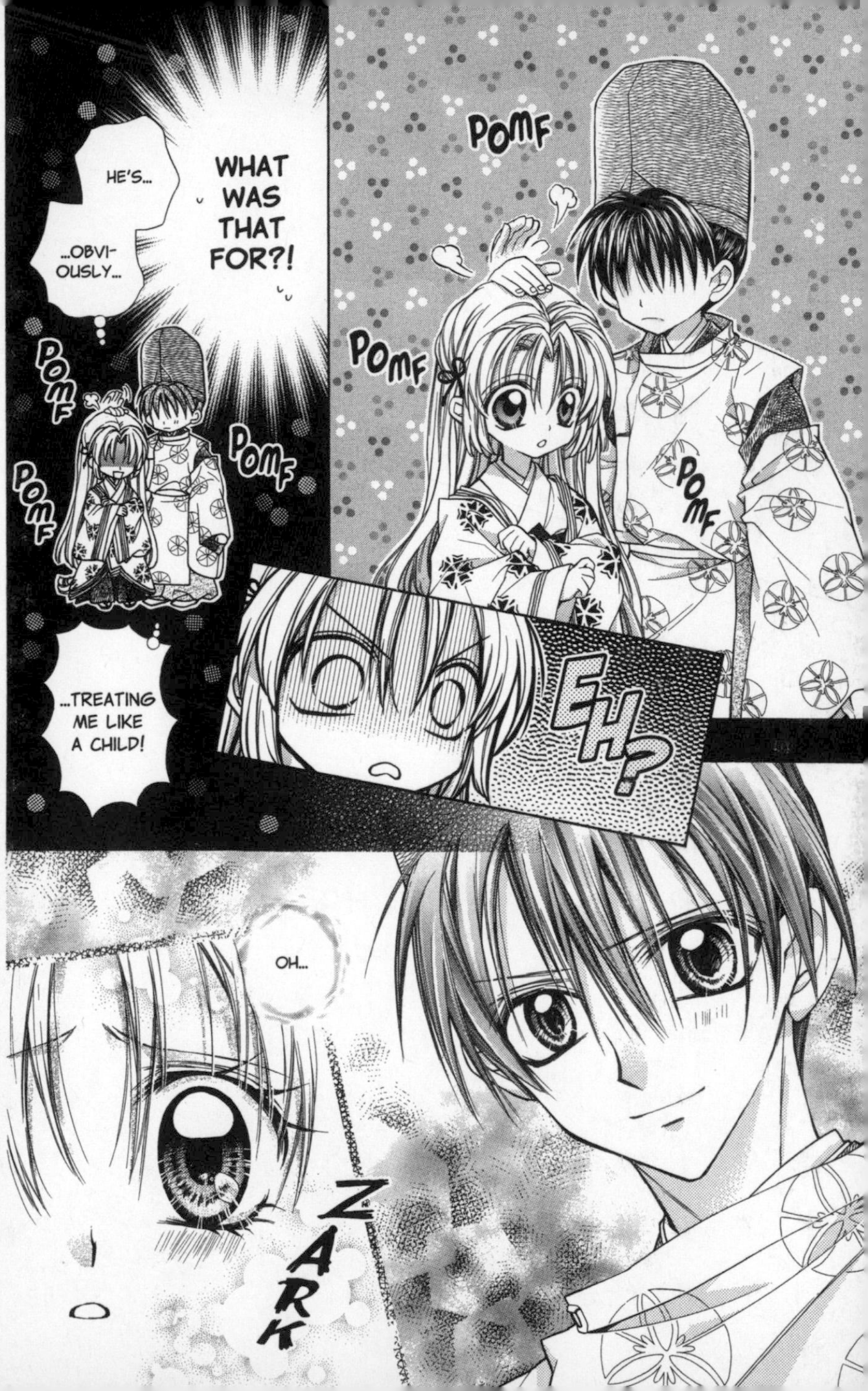
POMF
POMF
POMF
WHAT WAS THAT FOR?!
HE'S...
...OBVI-OUSLY...
POMF
POMF
POMF
...TREATING ME LIKE A CHILD!
EH?
OH...
ZARK

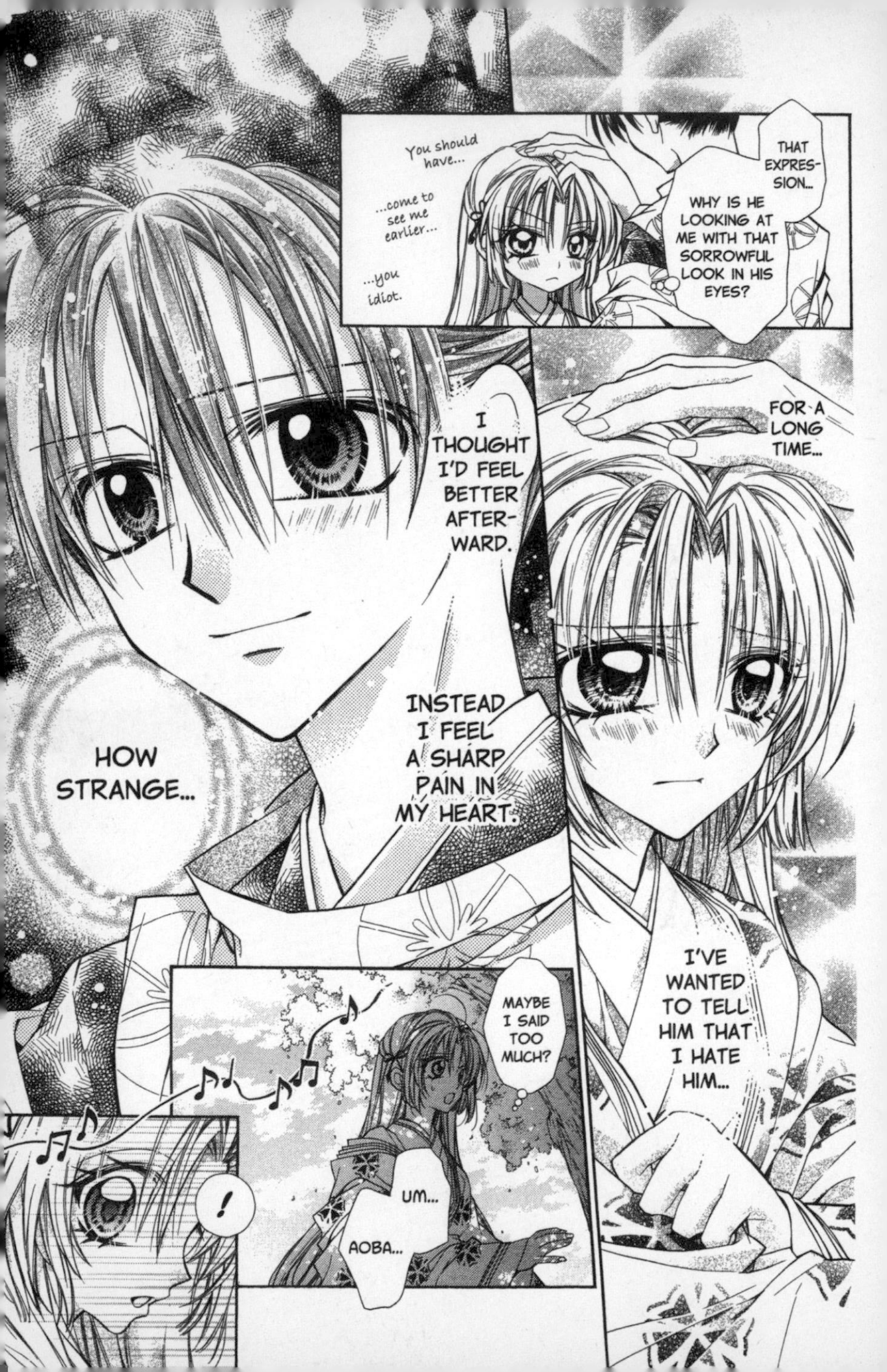
THAT EXPRESSION...
WHY IS HE LOOKING AT ME WITH THAT SORROWFUL LOOK IN HIS EYES?
You should have...
...come to see me earlier...
...you idiot.
FOR A LONG TIME...
I'VE WANTED TO TELL HIM THAT I HATE HIM...
I THOUGHT I'D FEEL BETTER AFTERWARD.
INSTEAD I FEEL A SHARP PAIN IN MY HEART.
HOW STRANGE...
MAYBE I SAID TOO MUCH?
UM...
AOBA...
!

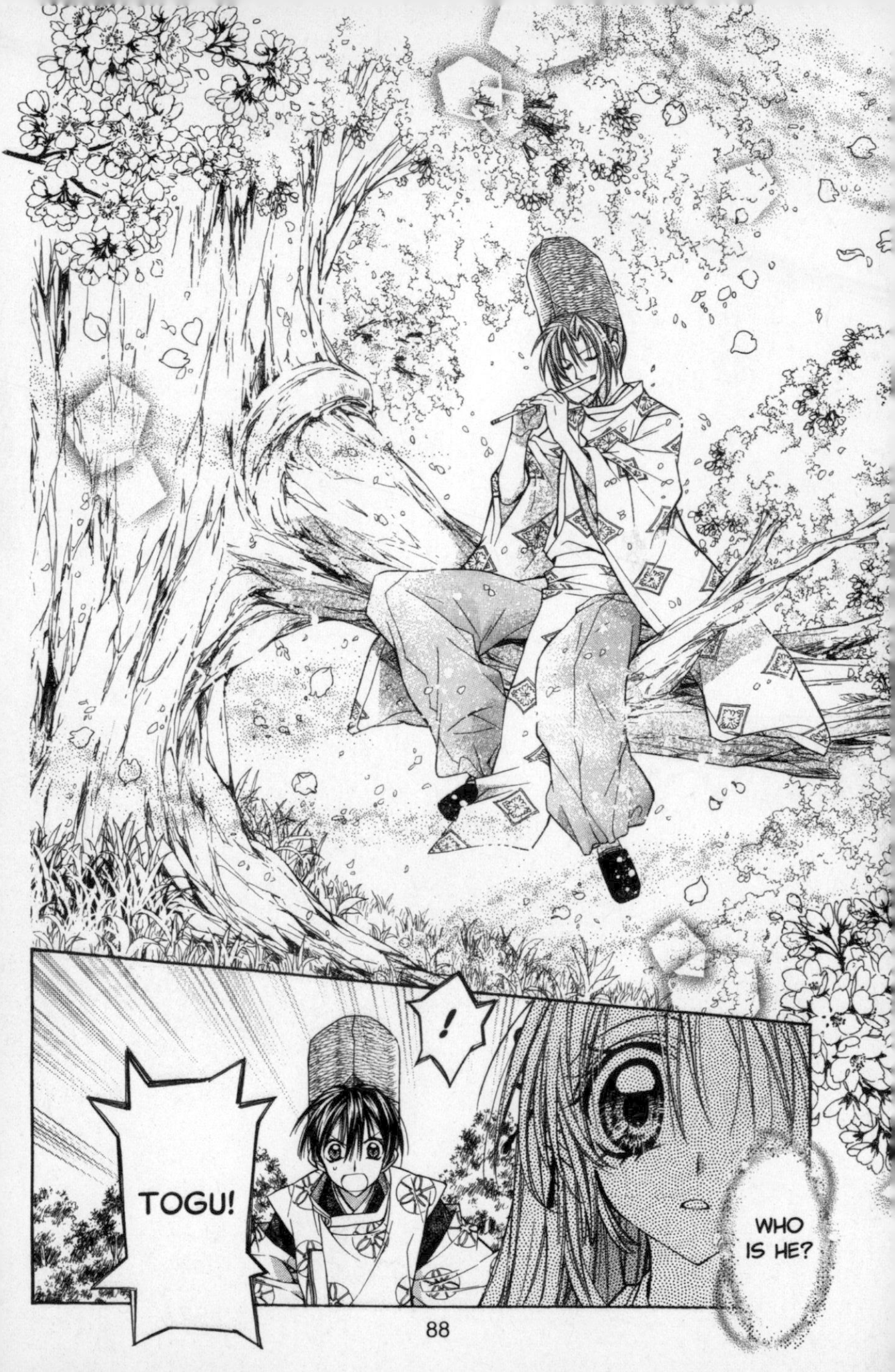
WHO IS HE?
!
TOGU!

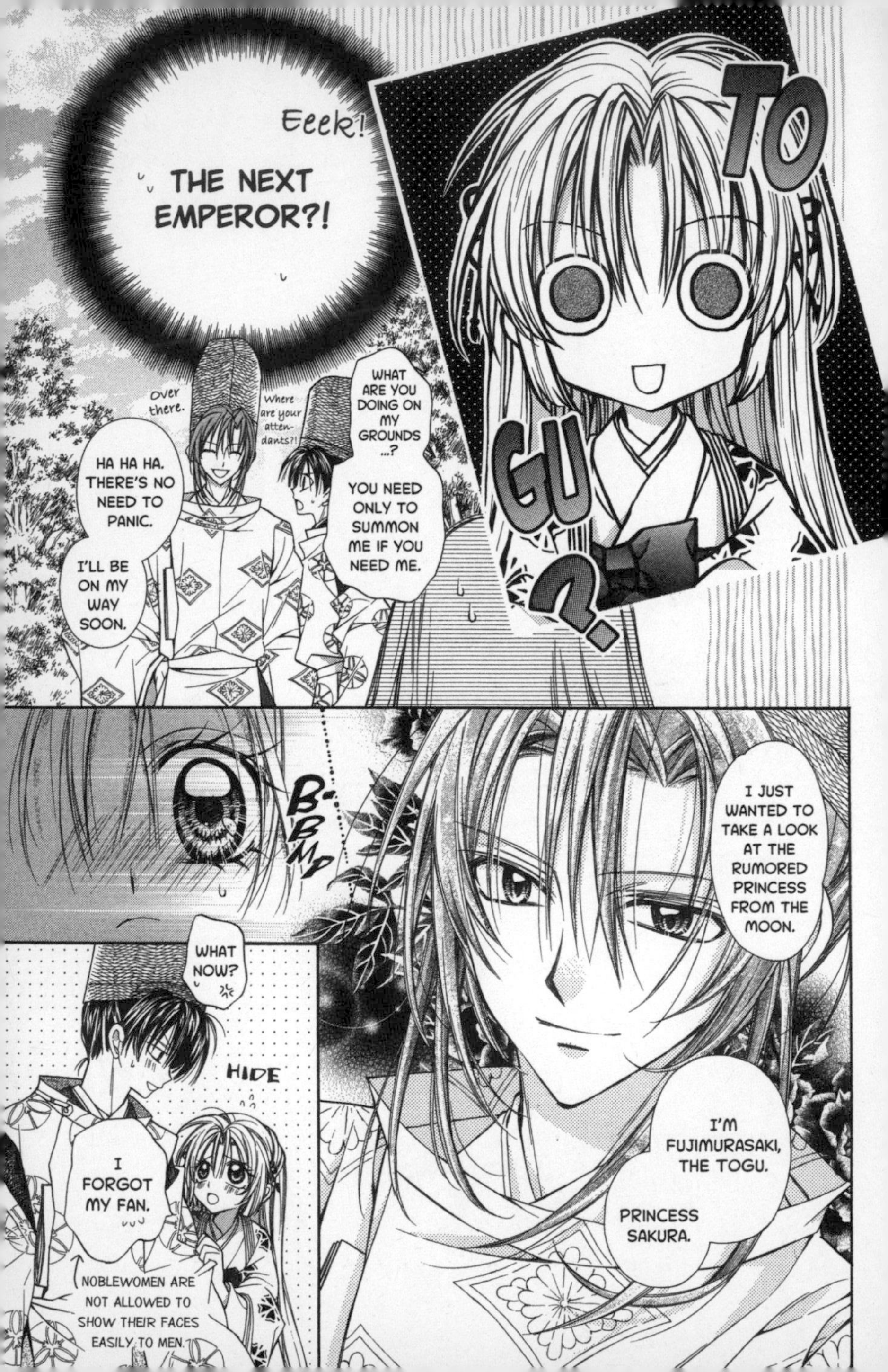
TO
GU
?
Eeek!
THE NEXT EMPEROR?!
WHAT ARE YOU DOING ON MY GROUNDS ...?
YOU NEED ONLY TO SUMMON ME IF YOU NEED ME.
Where are your atten-dants?!
Over there.
HA HA HA. THERE'S NO NEED TO PANIC.
I'LL BE ON MY WAY SOON.
I JUST WANTED TO TAKE A LOOK AT THE RUMORED PRINCESS FROM THE MOON.
I'M FUJIMURASAKI, THE TOGU.
PRINCESS SAKURA.
B-BUMP
WHAT NOW?
HIDE
I FORGOT MY FAN.
NOBLEWOMEN ARE NOT ALLOWED TO SHOW THEIR FACES EASILY TO MEN.

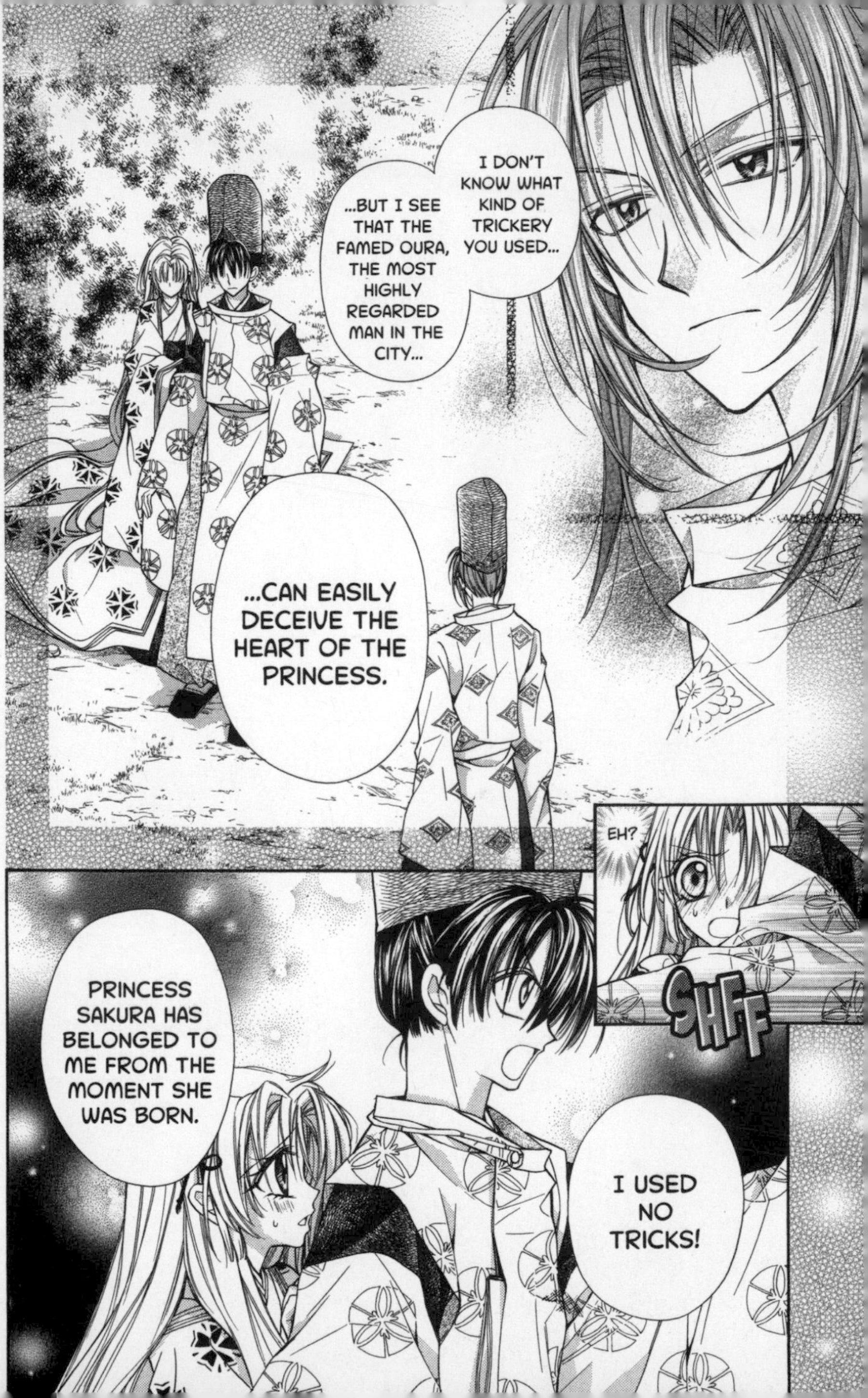
I DON'T KNOW WHAT KIND OF TRICKERY YOU USED...
...BUT I SEE THAT THE FAMED OURA, THE MOST HIGHLY REGARDED MAN IN THE CITY...
...CAN EASILY DECEIVE THE HEART OF THE PRINCESS.
EH?
SHFF
I USED NO TRICKS!
PRINCESS SAKURA HAS BELONGED TO ME FROM THE MOMENT SHE WAS BORN.

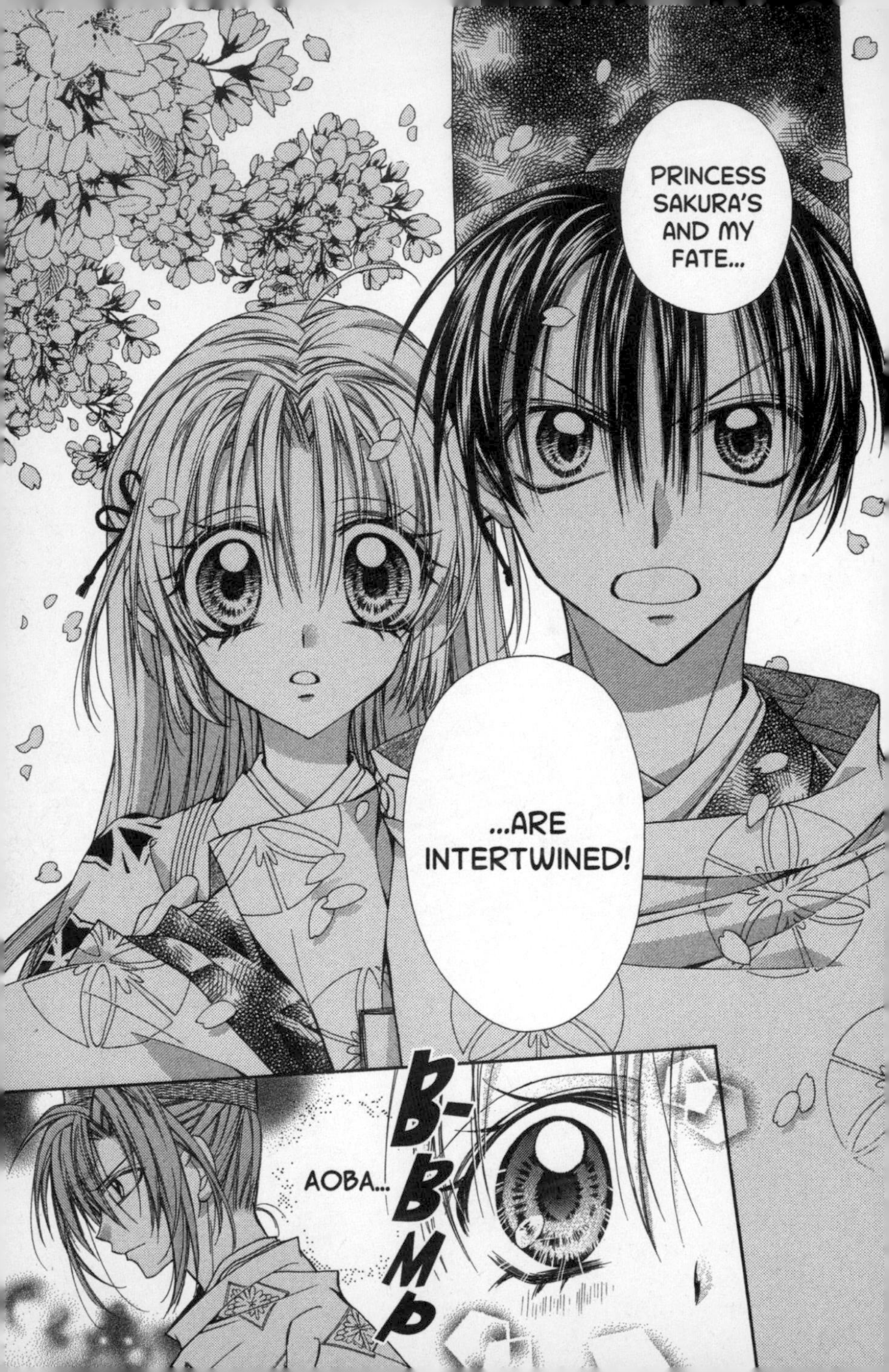
PRINCESS SAKURA'S AND MY FATE...
...ARE INTERTWINED!
B-B-BMP
AOBA...

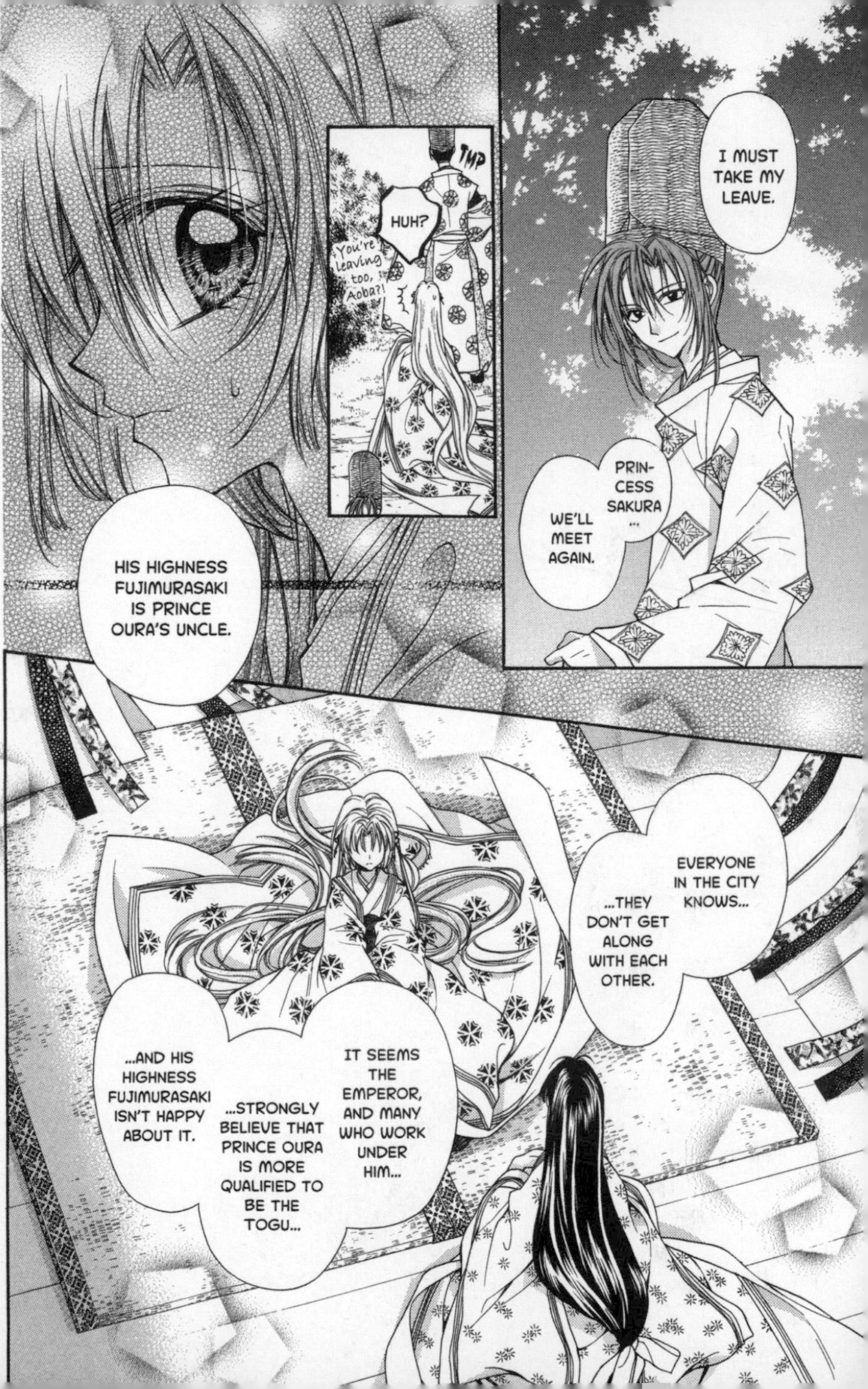
I MUST TAKE MY LEAVE.
PRINCESS SAKURA...
WE'LL MEET AGAIN.
TMP
HUH?
You're leaving too, Aoba?!
HIS HIGHNESS FUJIMURASAKI IS PRINCE OURA'S UNCLE.
EVERYONE IN THE CITY KNOWS...
...THEY DON'T GET ALONG WITH EACH OTHER.
IT SEEMS THE EMPEROR, AND MANY WHO WORK UNDER HIM...
...STRONGLY BELIEVE THAT PRINCE OURA IS MORE QUALIFIED TO BE THE TOGU...
...AND HIS HIGHNESS FUJIMURASAKI ISN'T HAPPY ABOUT IT.

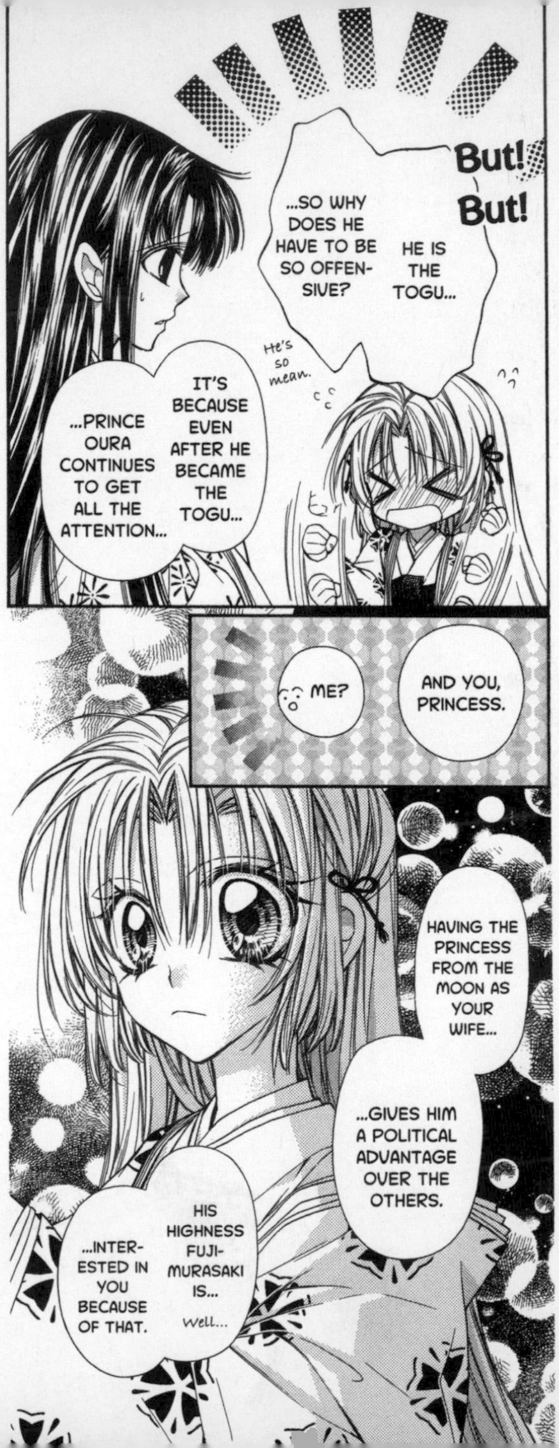
But!
But!
HE IS THE TOGU...
...SO WHY DOES HE HAVE TO BE SO OFFEN-SIVE?
He's so mean.
IT'S BECAUSE EVEN AFTER HE BECAME THE TOGU...
...PRINCE OURA CONTINUES TO GET ALL THE ATTENTION...
AND YOU, PRINCESS.
ME?
HAVING THE PRINCESS FROM THE MOON AS YOUR WIFE...
...GIVES HIM A POLITICAL ADVANTAGE OVER THE OTHERS.
HIS HIGHNESS FUJI-MURASAKI IS...
Well...
...INTER-ESTED IN YOU BECAUSE OF THAT.

**Macross F** (The songs...)

I bought the DVDs but I haven't gotten all the episodes yet, so I haven't watched it. But I've been listening to the CD over and over! My favorite is "Northern Cross."♥
I'd like to write a little review about it. ☆

I also love "Triangler" too!
I especially like Maaya's version!!!
The lyrics for the one they sing in unison have been changed, so I don't like it as much. I wonder why... Maybe it's for the live performances? I think it would be a little more exciting if she were to look over at the other girl during the chorus... But I guess there's a reason for that, huh?

"Empty Diamond Crevasse"
I like this version the best. I listened to it in Maldives under a star-filled sky, so I was able to really get into it.

"Sagittarius☆ 9 p.m. Don't Be Late"
I love listening to it and singing it. I heard this song in a TV commercial and decided to buy the CD for Macross F! Singing the "Infinitely" part is very hard! I just can't seem to lower my pitch there... The way May'n sings the second chorus is just electrifying ... ~

"Interstellar Flight"
I have the single for this as well. (The CD Jacket was too cute.)
I just love how cute and joyous she looks!
But the "Twinkle☆" is difficult...
The lyrics are nice too. Youth, huh...

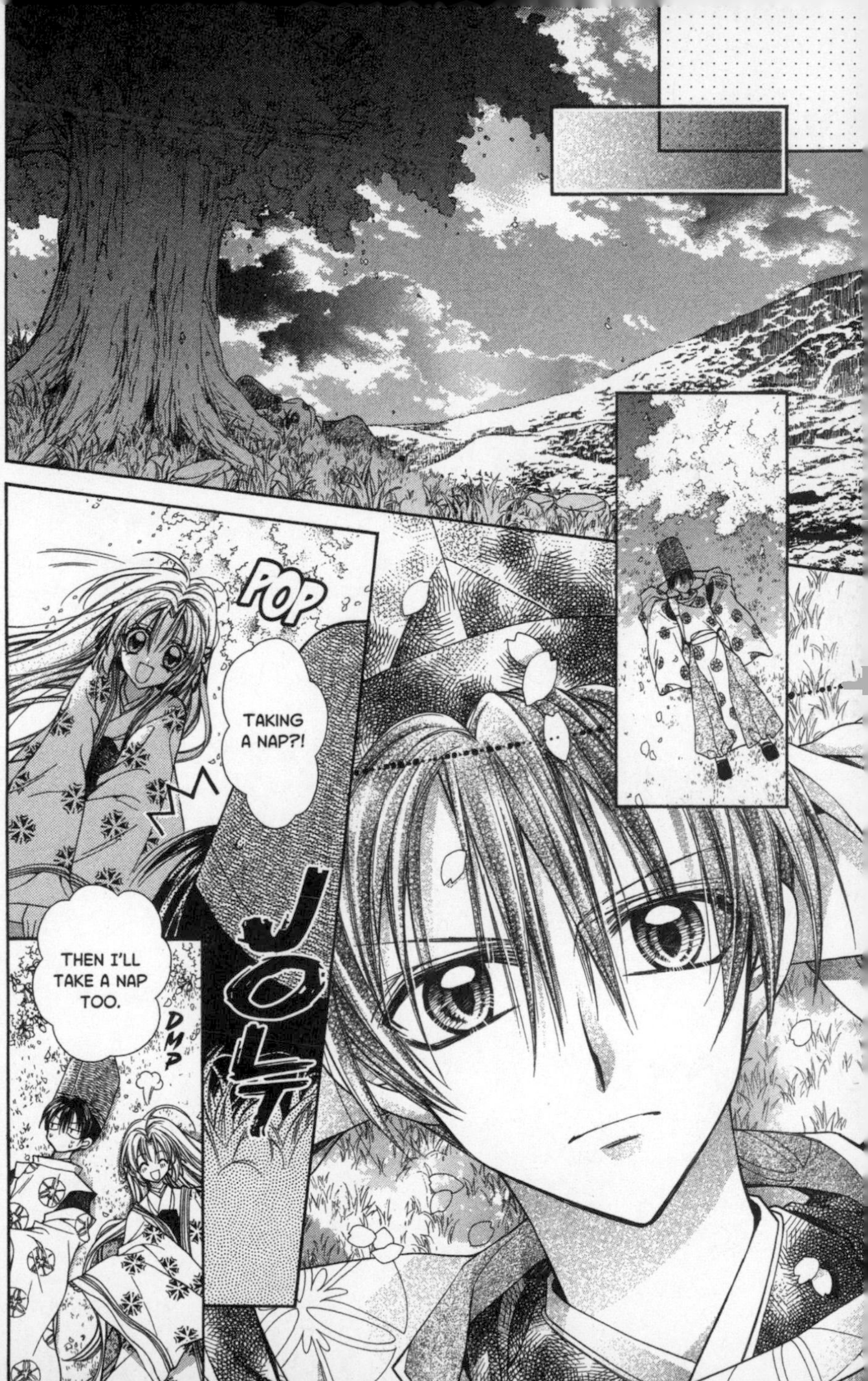
POP
TAKING A NAP?!
JOLT
THEN I'LL TAKE A NAP TOO.
DMP

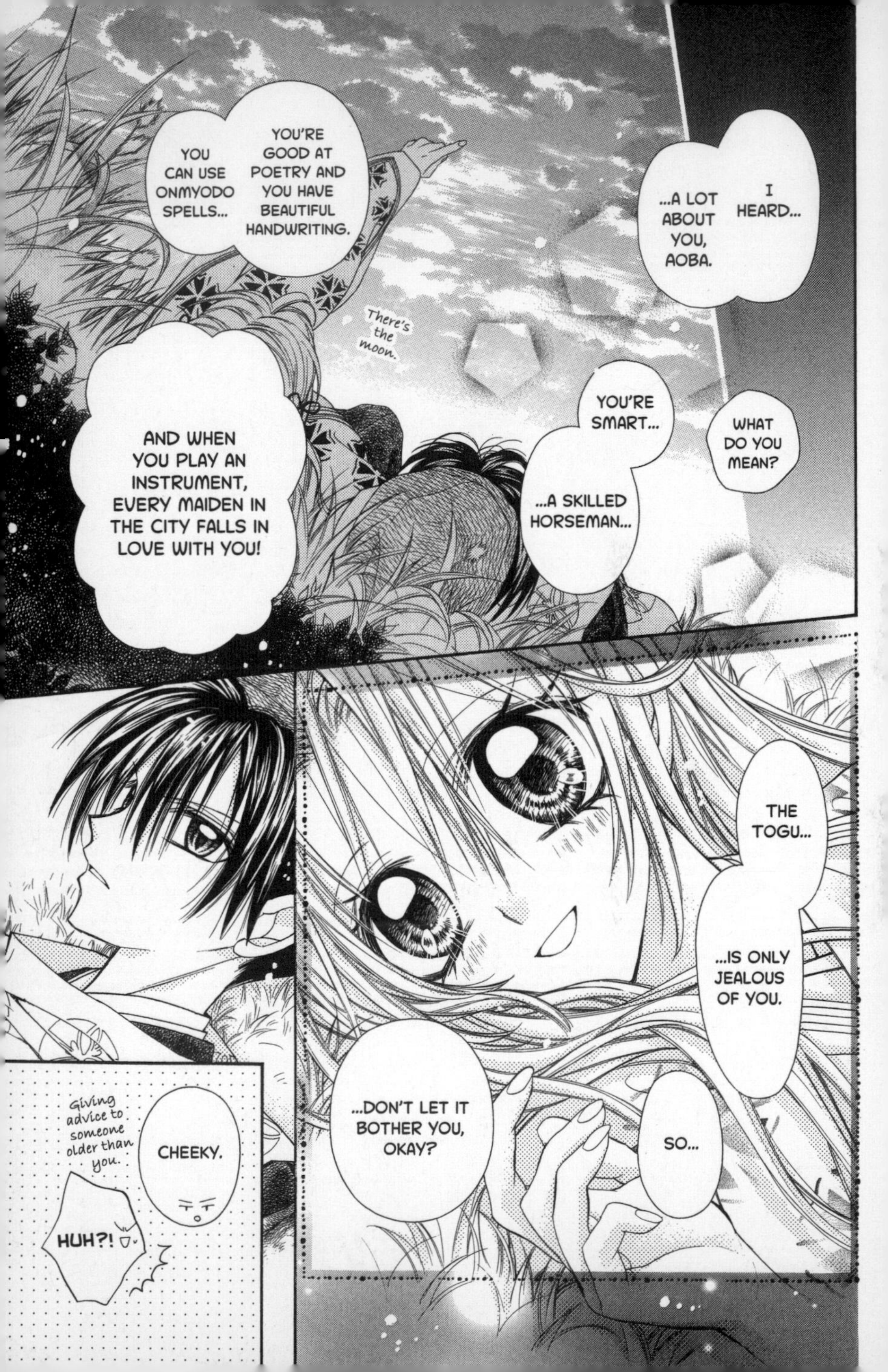
I HEARD...
...A LOT ABOUT YOU, AOBA.
WHAT DO YOU MEAN?
YOU'RE SMART...
...A SKILLED HORSEMAN...
YOU'RE GOOD AT POETRY AND YOU HAVE BEAUTIFUL HANDWRITING.
YOU CAN USE ONMYODO SPELLS...
AND WHEN YOU PLAY AN INSTRUMENT, EVERY MAIDEN IN THE CITY FALLS IN LOVE WITH YOU!
There's the moon.
THE TOGU...
...IS ONLY JEALOUS OF YOU.
SO...
...DON'T LET IT BOTHER YOU, OKAY?
CHEEKY.
Giving advice to someone older than you.
HUH?!

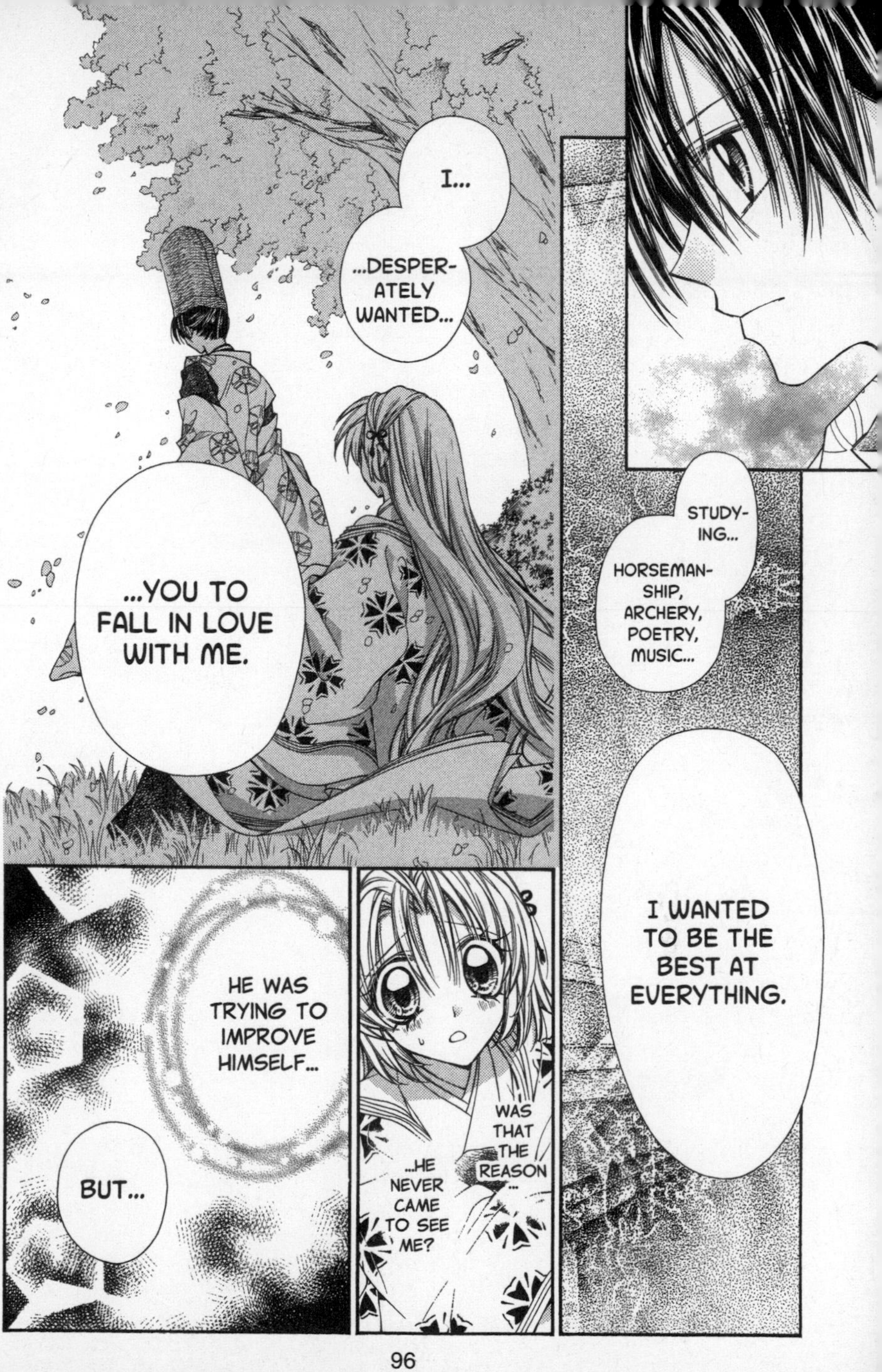
I...
...DESPER-ATELY WANTED...
...YOU TO FALL IN LOVE WITH ME.
STUDY-ING...
HORSEMAN-SHIP, ARCHERY, POETRY, MUSIC...
I WANTED TO BE THE BEST AT EVERYTHING.
WAS THAT THE REASON...
...HE NEVER CAME TO SEE ME?
HE WAS TRYING TO IMPROVE HIMSELF...
BUT...

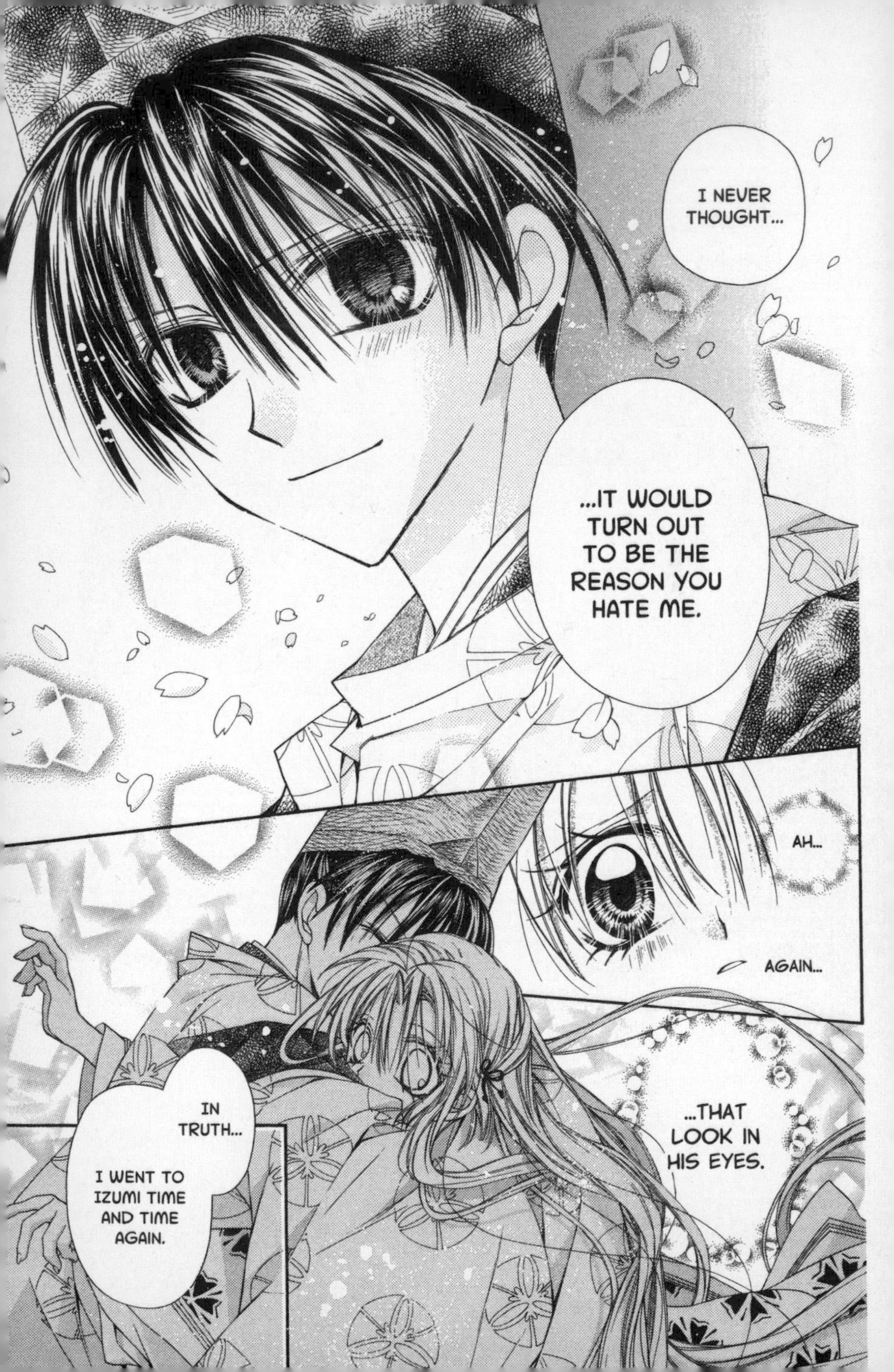
I NEVER THOUGHT...
...IT WOULD TURN OUT TO BE THE REASON YOU HATE ME.
AH...
AGAIN...
...THAT LOOK IN HIS EYES.
IN TRUTH...
I WENT TO IZUMI TIME AND TIME AGAIN.

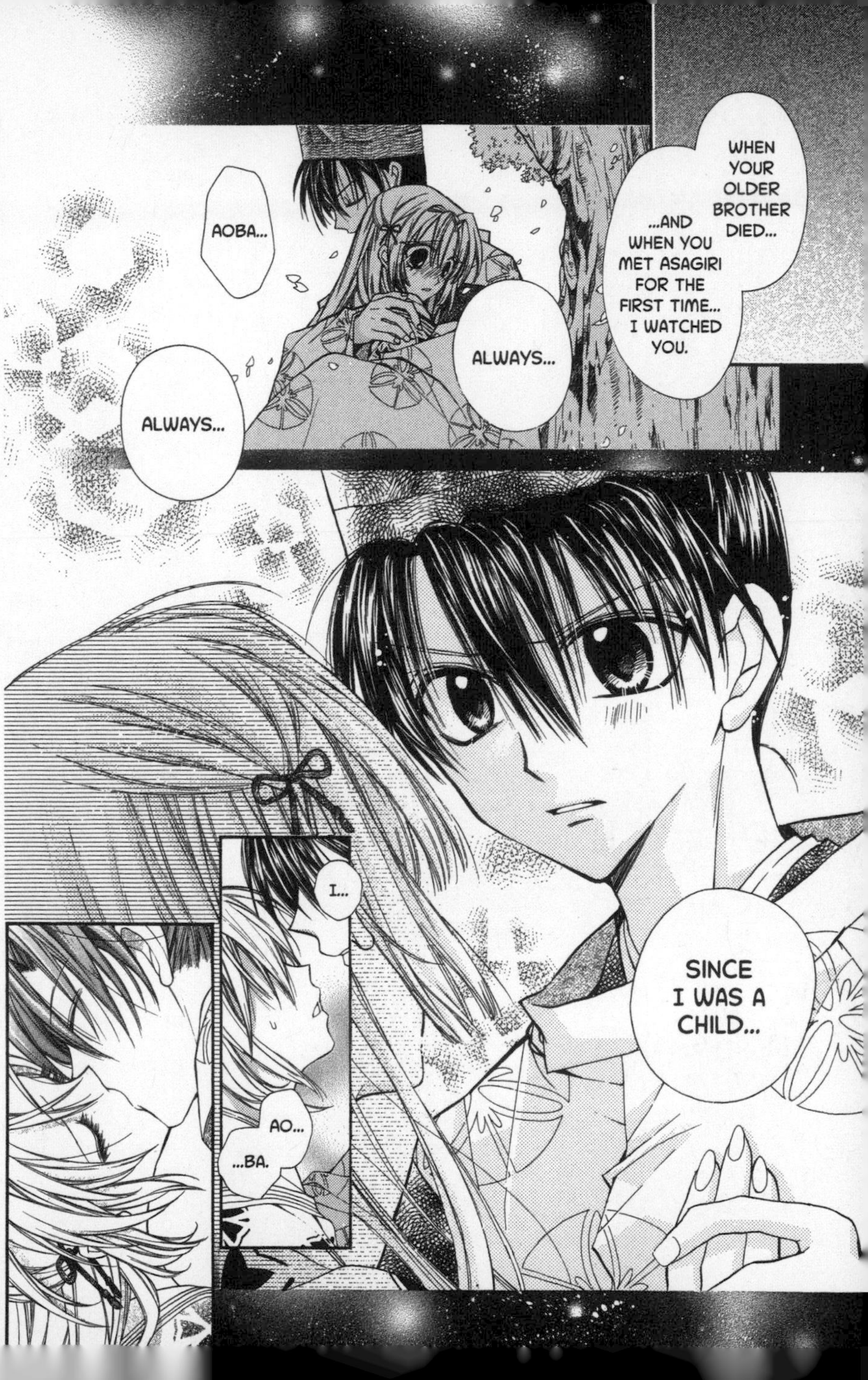
WHEN YOUR OLDER BROTHER DIED...
...AND WHEN YOU MET ASAGIRI FOR THE FIRST TIME... I WATCHED YOU.
AOBA...
ALWAYS...
ALWAYS...
SINCE I WAS A CHILD...
I...
AO...
...BA.

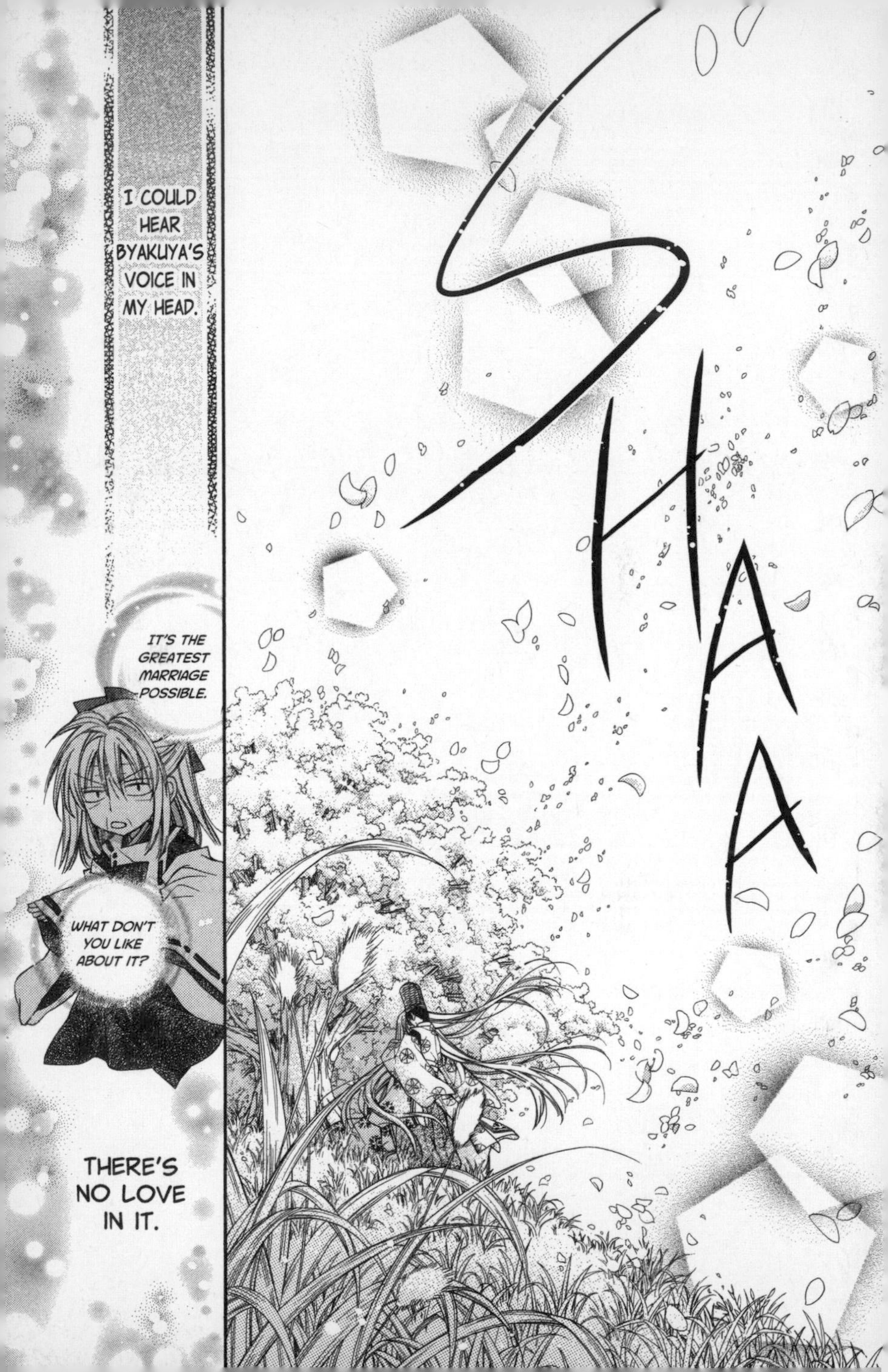
SHAAA
I COULD HEAR BYAKUYA'S VOICE IN MY HEAD.
IT'S THE GREATEST MARRIAGE POSSIBLE.
WHAT DON'T YOU LIKE ABOUT IT?
THERE'S NO LOVE IN IT.

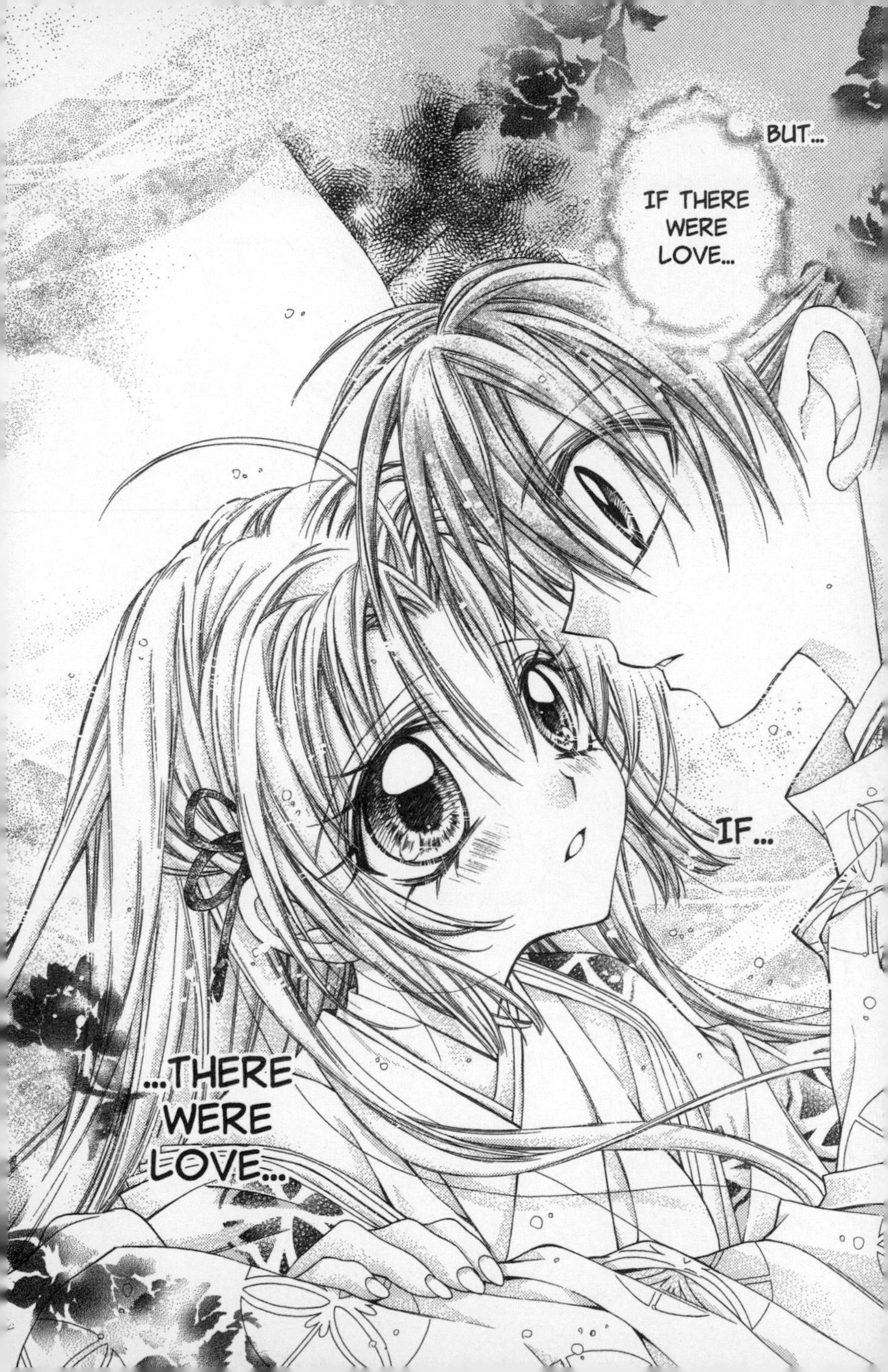
BUT...
IF THERE WERE LOVE...
IF...
...THERE WERE LOVE...

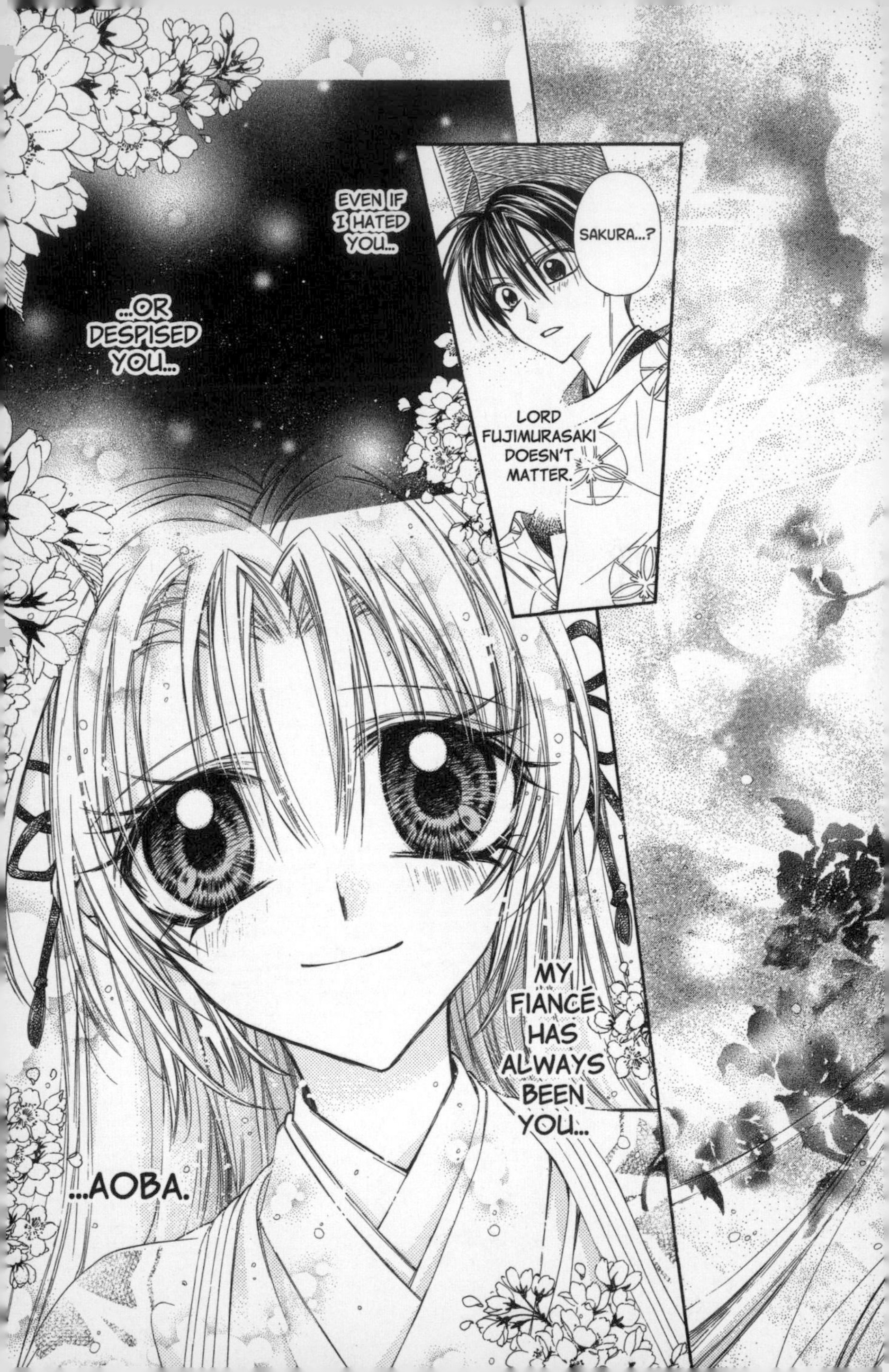
SAKURA...?
LORD FUJIMURASAKI DOESN'T MATTER.
EVEN IF I HATED YOU...
...OR DESPISED YOU...
MY FIANCÉ HAS ALWAYS BEEN YOU...
...AOBA.

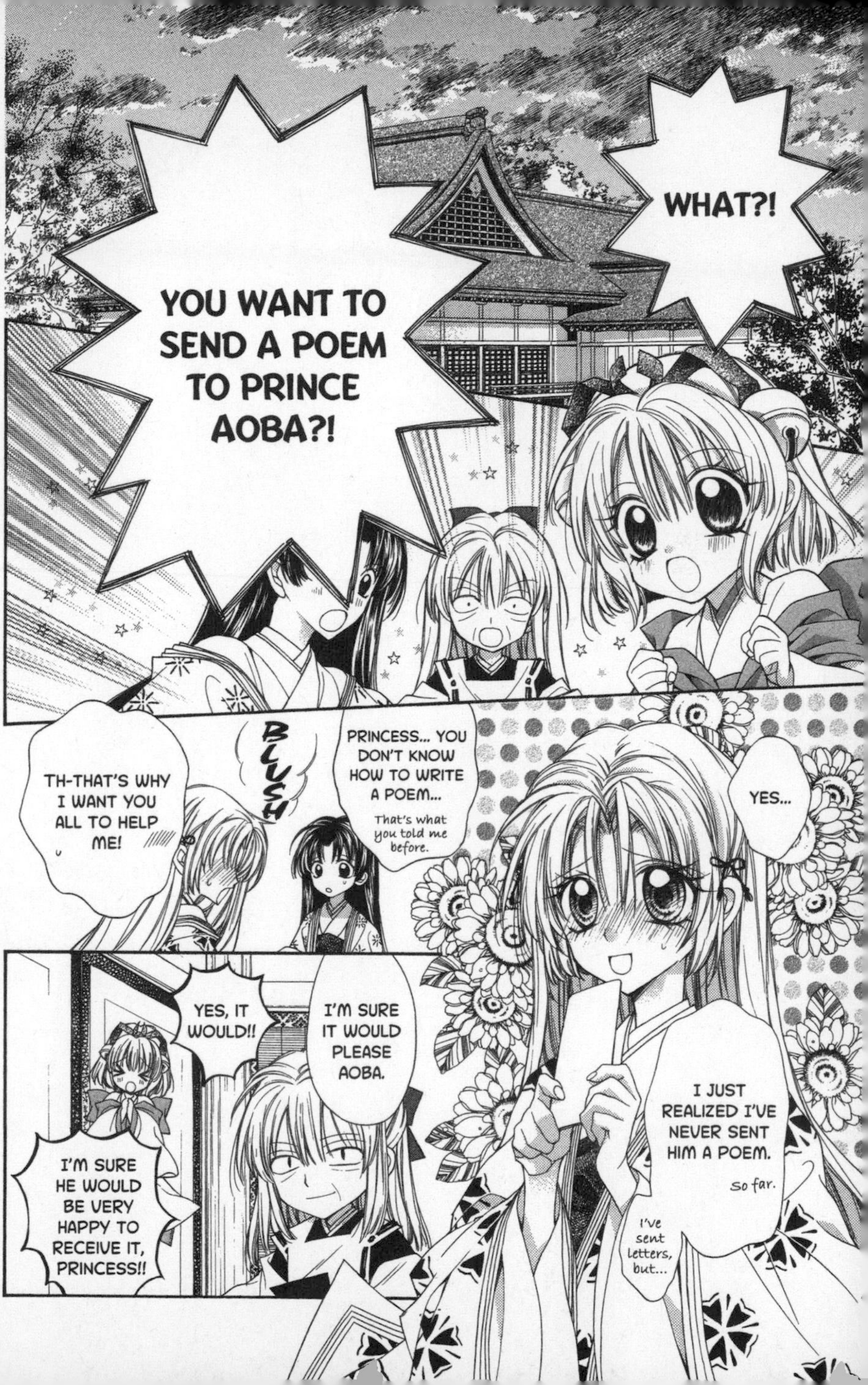
WHAT?!
YOU WANT TO SEND A POEM TO PRINCE AOBA?!
YES...
I JUST REALIZED I'VE NEVER SENT HIM A POEM.
So far.
I've sent letters, but...
PRINCESS... YOU DON'T KNOW HOW TO WRITE A POEM...
That's what you told me before.
BLUSH
TH-THAT'S WHY I WANT YOU ALL TO HELP ME!
I'M SURE IT WOULD PLEASE AOBA.
YES, IT WOULD!!
I'M SURE HE WOULD BE VERY HAPPY TO RECEIVE IT, PRINCESS!!

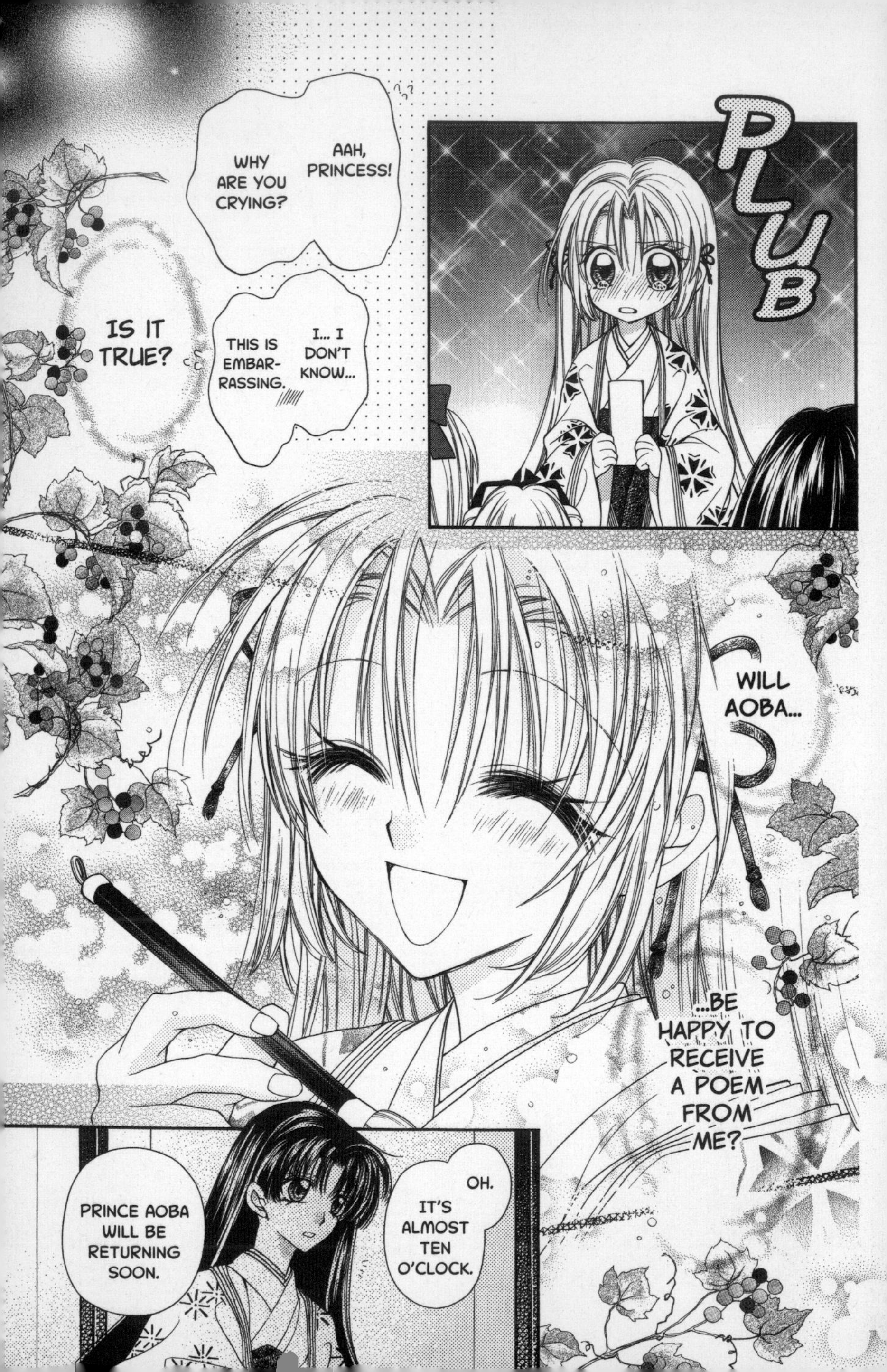
PLUB
AAH, PRINCESS!
WHY ARE YOU CRYING?
I... I DON'T KNOW...
THIS IS EMBARRASSING.
IS IT TRUE?
WILL AOBA...
...BE HAPPY TO RECEIVE A POEM FROM ME?
OH. IT'S ALMOST TEN O'CLOCK.
PRINCE AOBA WILL BE RETURNING SOON.

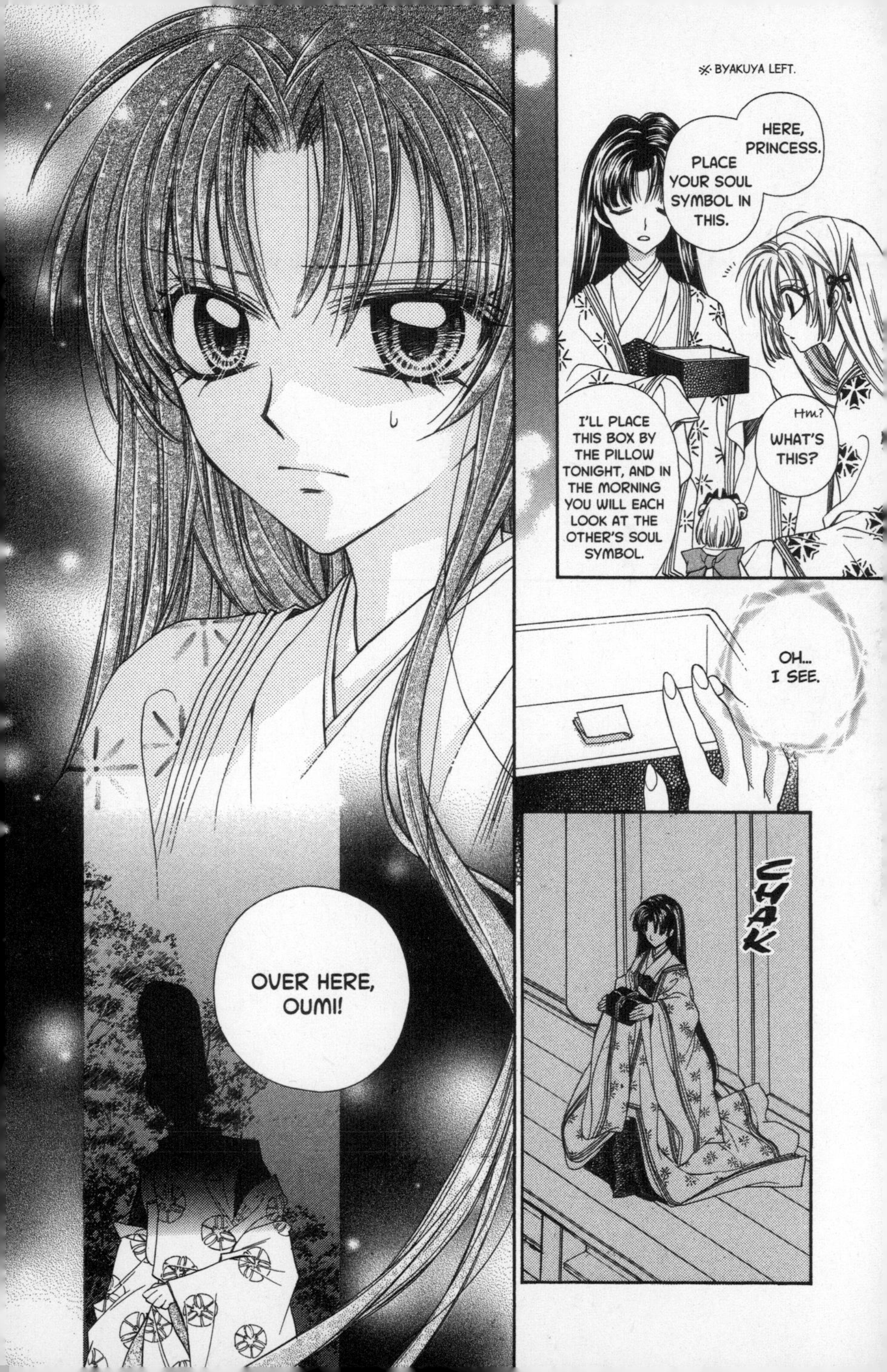
※ BYAKUYA LEFT.
HERE, PRINCESS. PLACE YOUR SOUL SYMBOL IN THIS.
Hm? WHAT'S THIS?
I'LL PLACE THIS BOX BY THE PILLOW TONIGHT, AND IN THE MORNING YOU WILL EACH LOOK AT THE OTHER'S SOUL SYMBOL.
OH... I SEE.
CHAK
OVER HERE, OUMI!

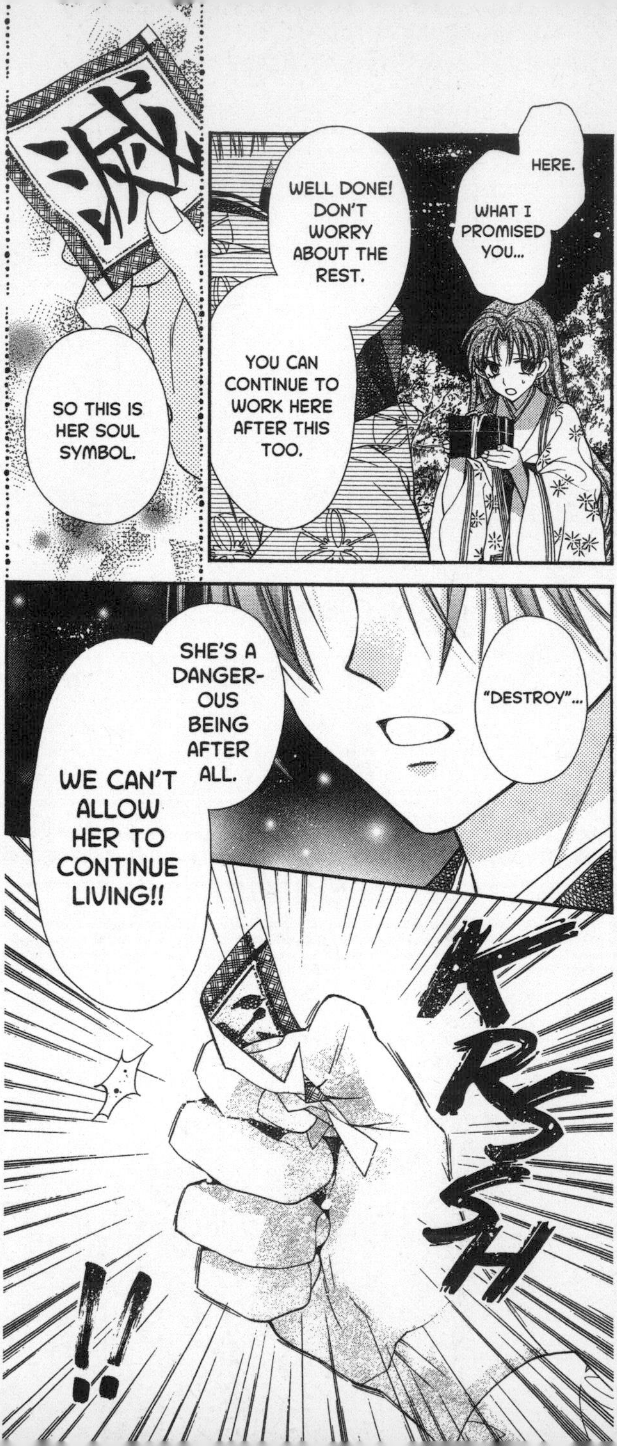
HERE.
WHAT I PROMISED YOU...
WELL DONE! DON'T WORRY ABOUT THE REST.
YOU CAN CONTINUE TO WORK HERE AFTER THIS TOO.
SO THIS IS HER SOUL SYMBOL.
"DESTROY"...
SHE'S A DANGER-OUS BEING AFTER ALL.
WE CAN'T ALLOW HER TO CONTINUE LIVING!!
KRSSH
!!

## ASAGIRI

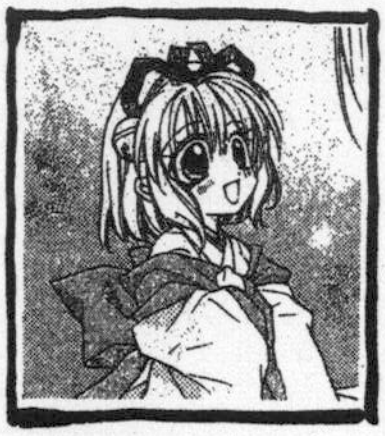

Age unknown.
The young Sakura got her from a slave trader.

Since the princess and ladies-in-waiting all have long hair, I gave her a bob. Sakura thinks of her as a friend, but Asagiri sees herself as a servant.

Unlike Sakura, she is the type of person who tries to hide her feelings entirely. I'm sure she has experienced several traumatizing incidents and that has affected her self-confidence.

When I created Ushio in *The Gentlemen's Alliance †* (a Tanemura manga), I felt I could then create the story. For this manga it was Asagiri.
I would like many second helpings of them. (What kind of expression is that?)

She is the most popular of the supporting characters. She's my favorite too.

I hope she evolves into a great character.

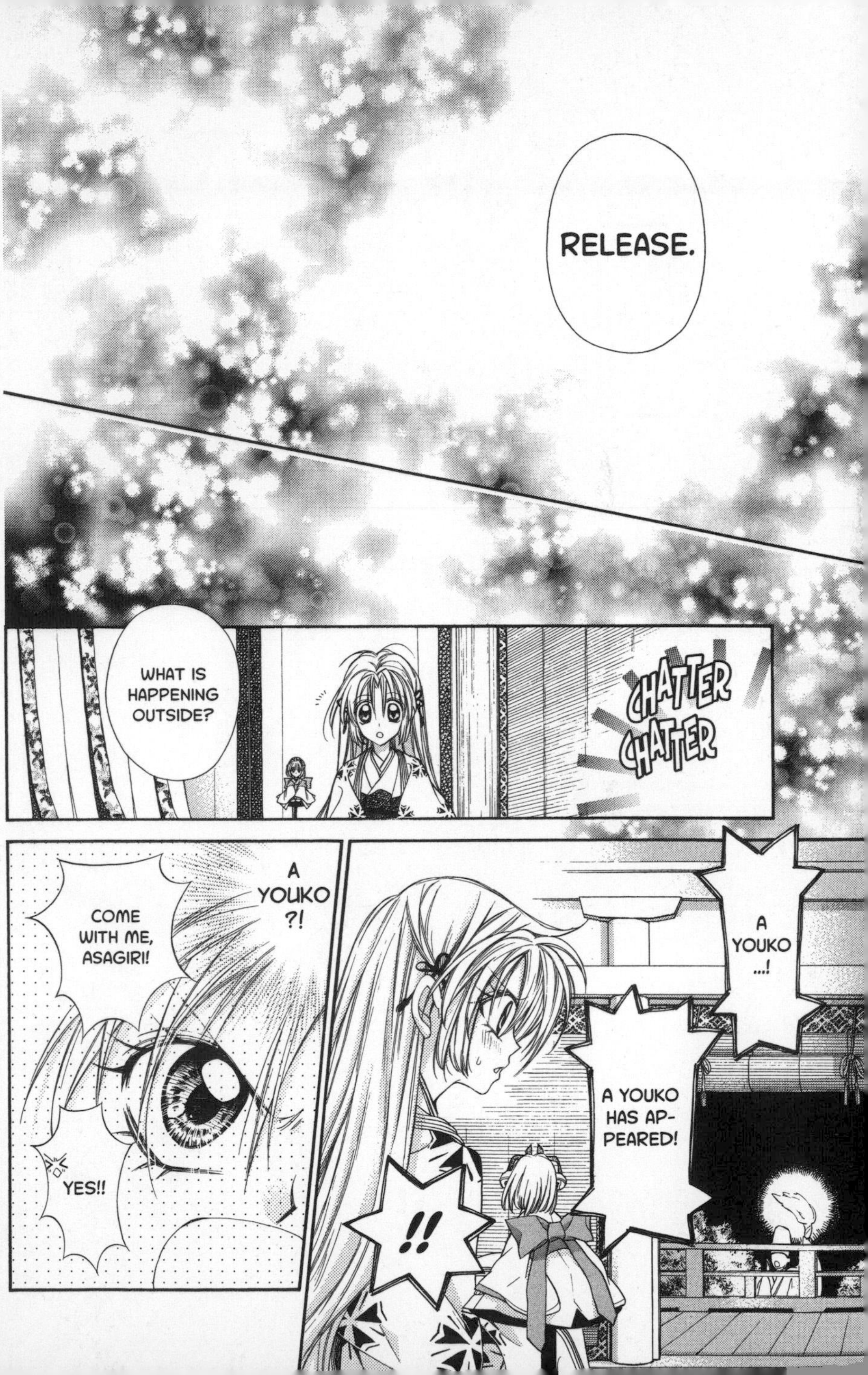
RELEASE.
CHATTER CHATTER
WHAT IS HAPPENING OUTSIDE?
A YOUKO ...!
A YOUKO HAS AP- PEARED!
!!
A YOUKO ?!
COME WITH ME, ASAGIRI!
YES!!

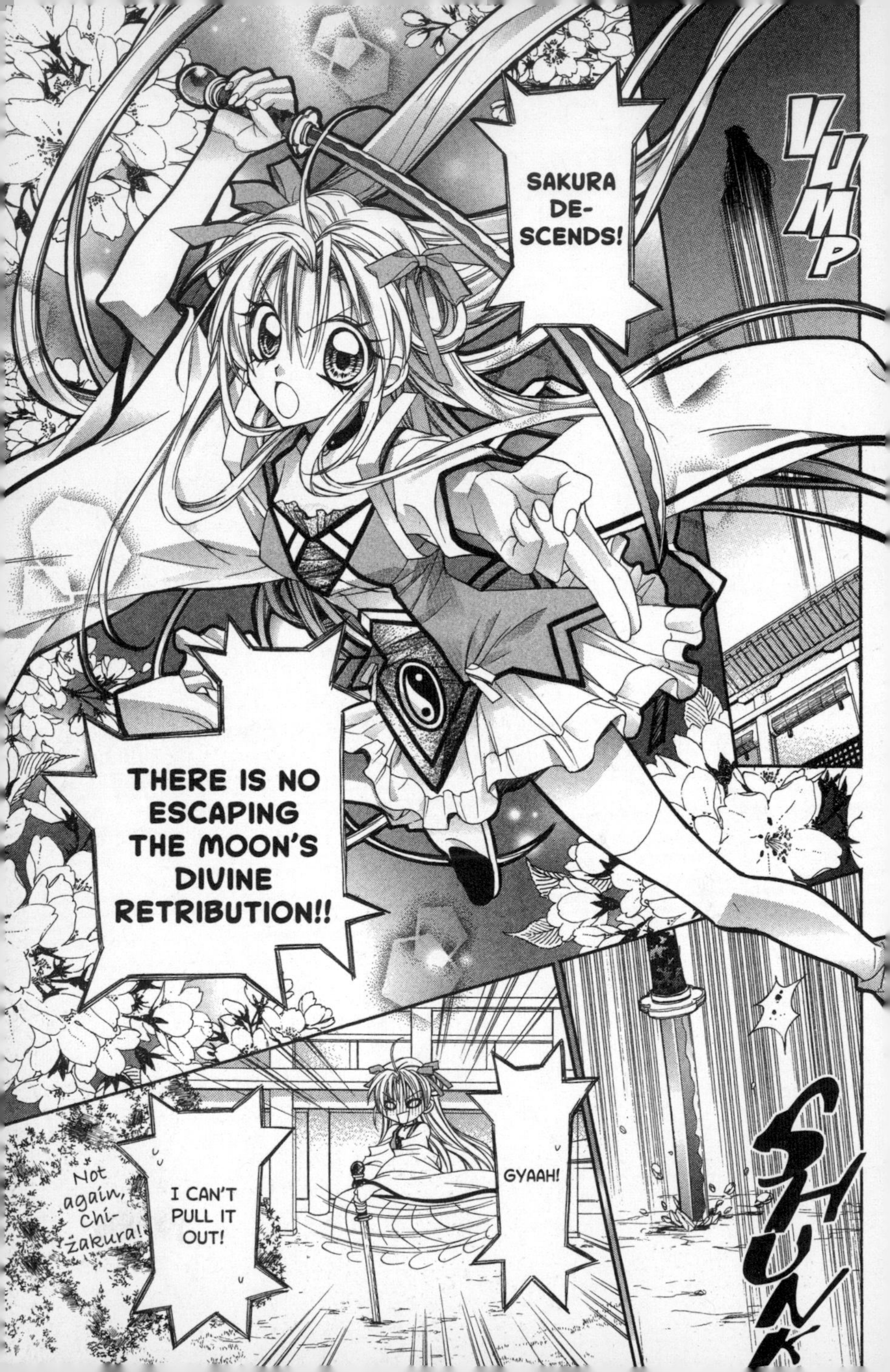
VUMP
SAKURA DE-SCENDS!
THERE IS NO ESCAPING THE MOON'S DIVINE RETRIBUTION!!
SHUNK
GYAAH!
I CAN'T PULL IT OUT!
Not again, Chi-zakura!

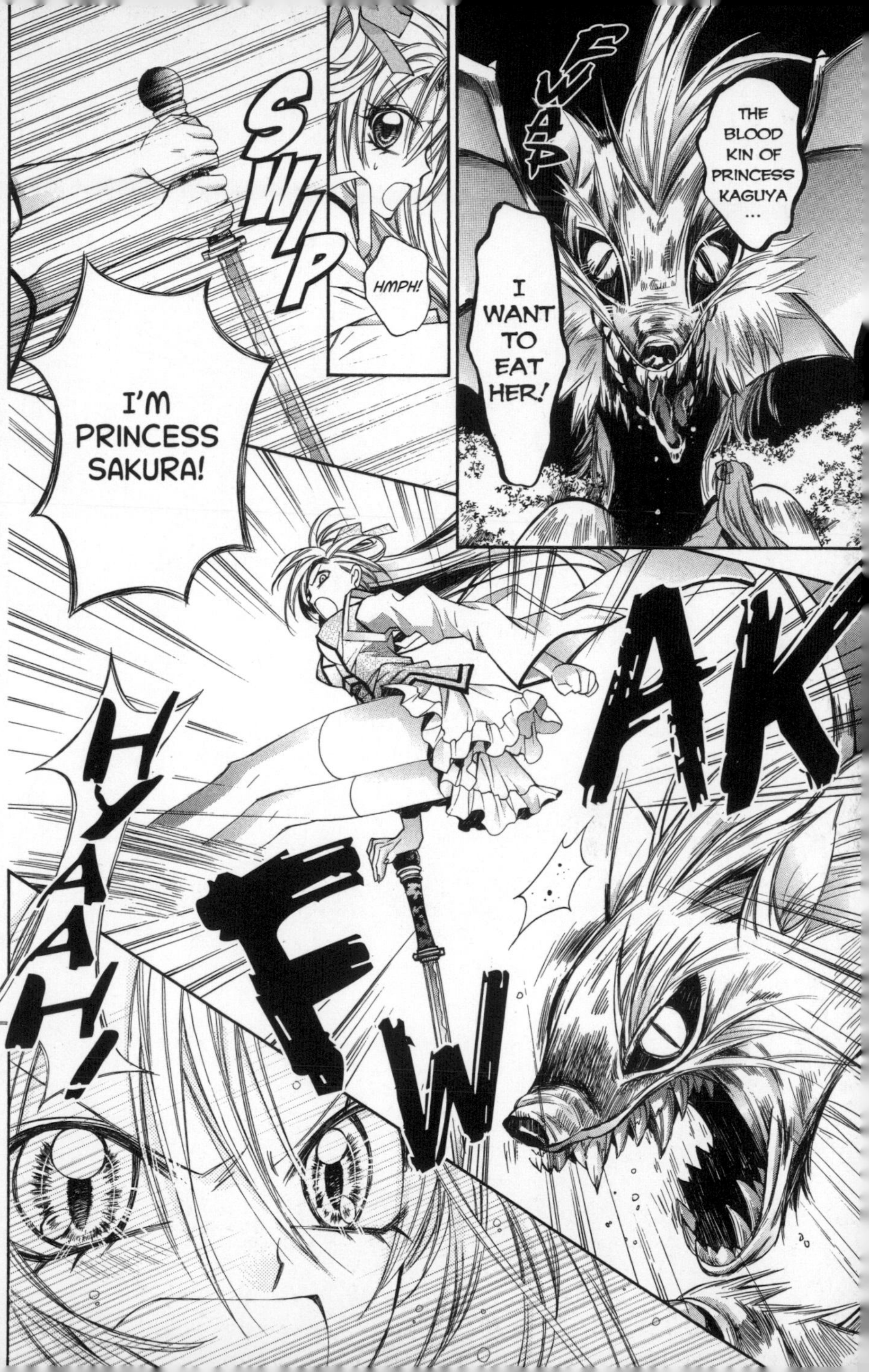

FWAP
THE BLOOD KIN OF PRINCESS KAGUYA...
I WANT TO EAT HER!
SWIP
HMPH!
I'M PRINCESS SAKURA!
AK
FW
HYAAH!

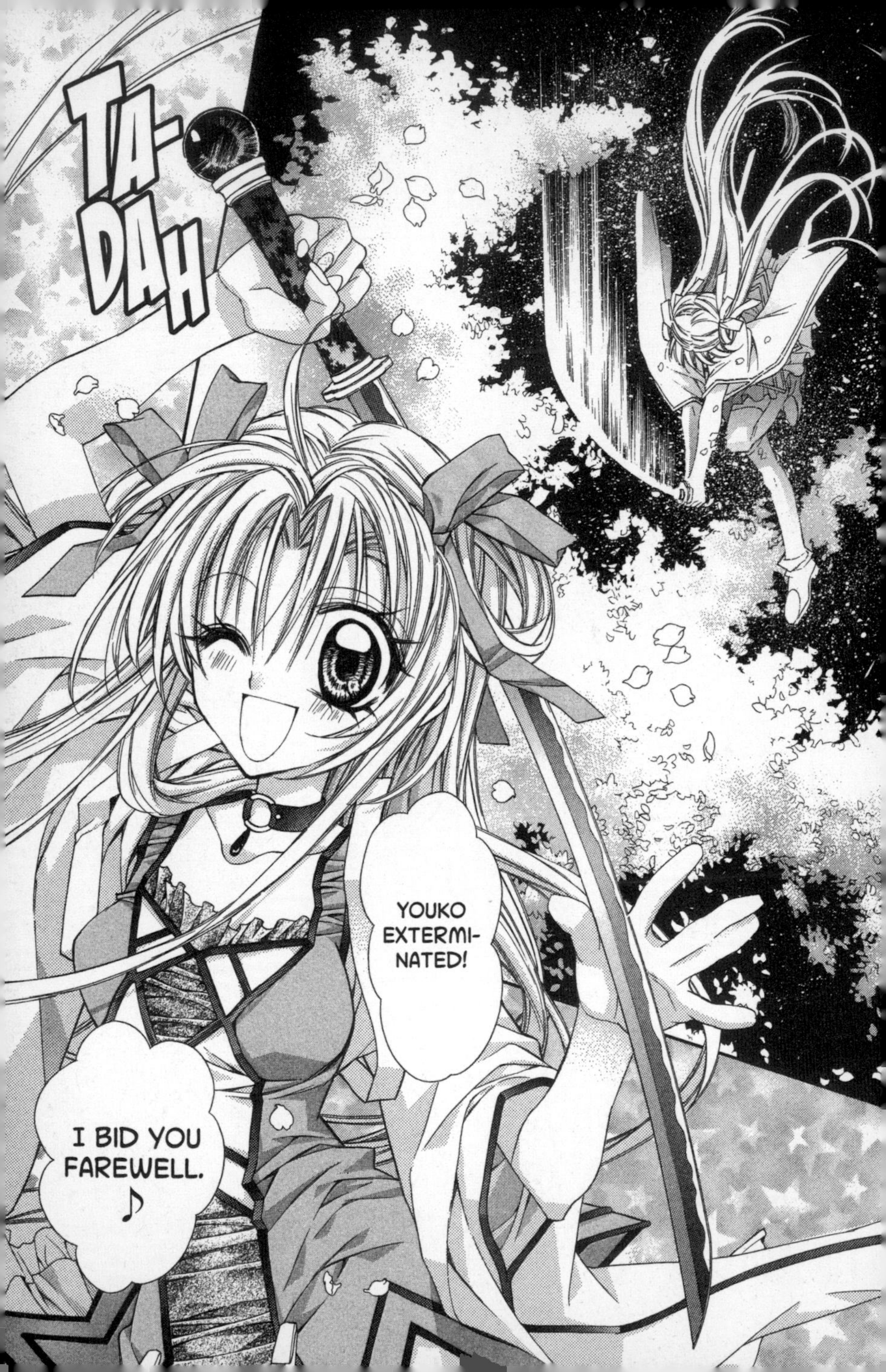
TA-DAH
YOUKO EXTERMI-NATED!
I BID YOU FAREWELL. ♪

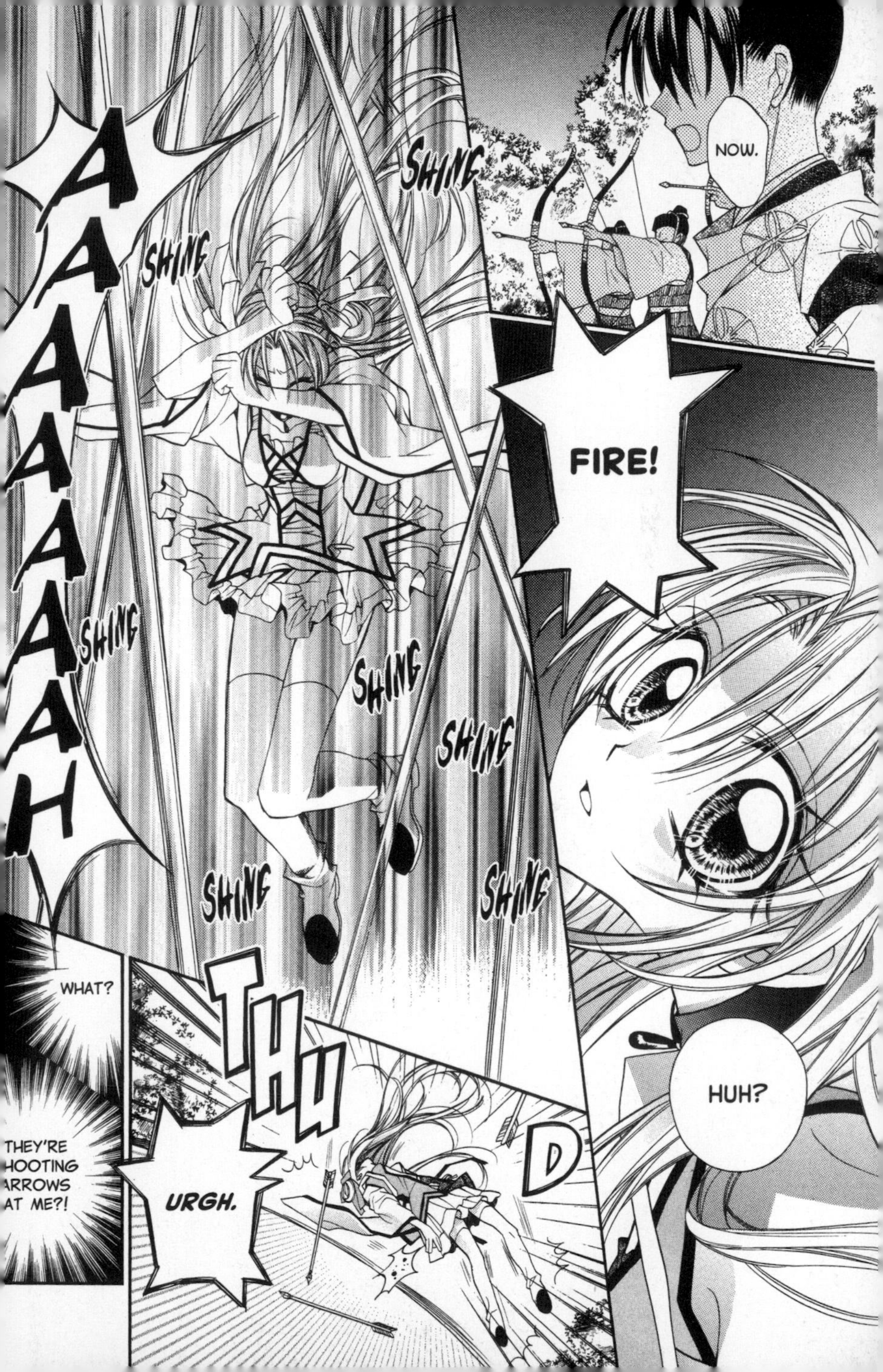
NOW.
FIRE!
HUH?
AAAAAAAH
SHING
SHING
SHING
SHING
SHING
SHING
SHING
SHING
THUD
URGH.
WHAT?
THEY'RE SHOOTING ARROWS AT ME?!

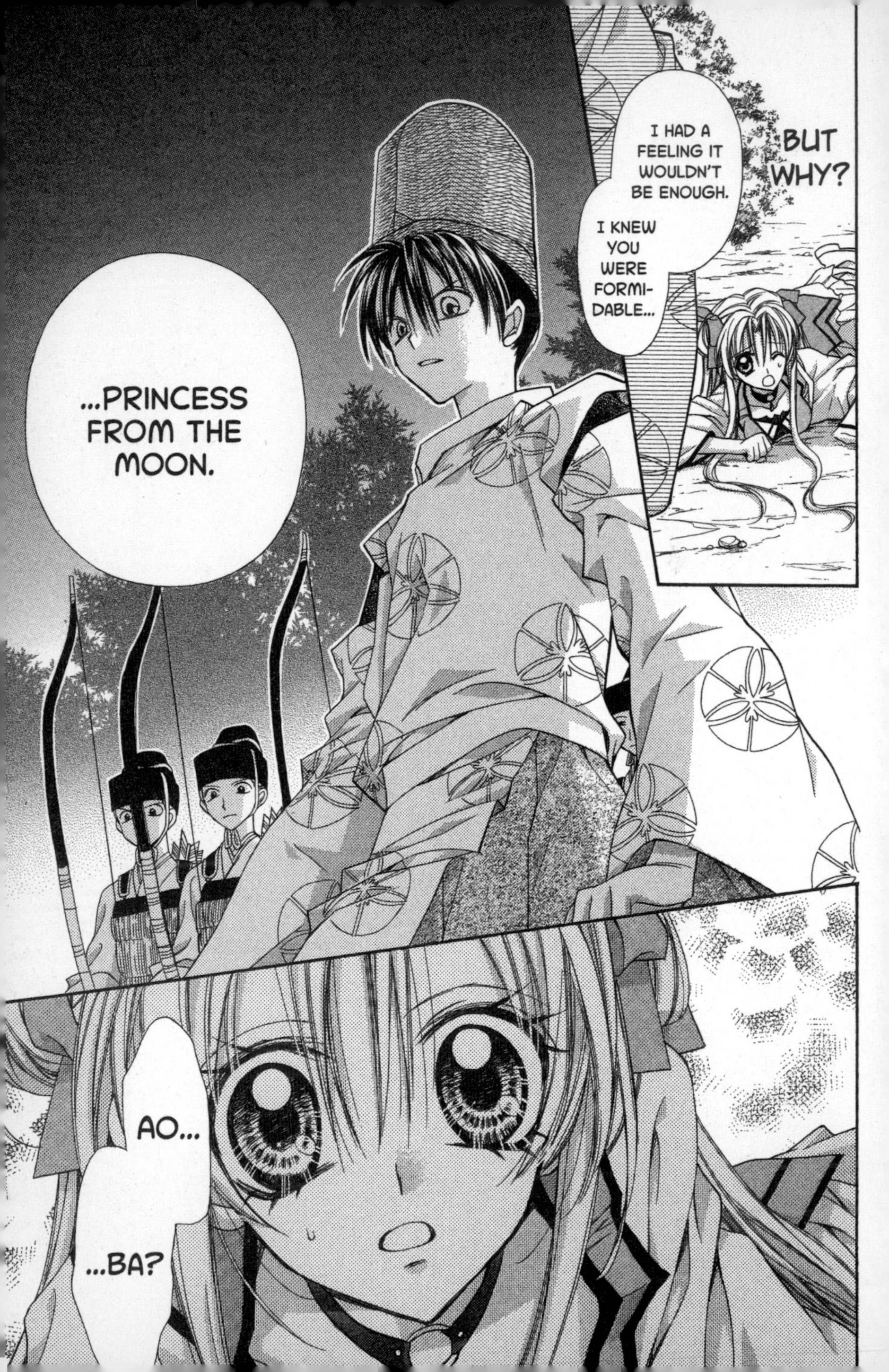
BUT WHY?
I HAD A FEELING IT WOULDN'T BE ENOUGH.
I KNEW YOU WERE FORMIDABLE...
...PRINCESS FROM THE MOON.
AO...
...BA?

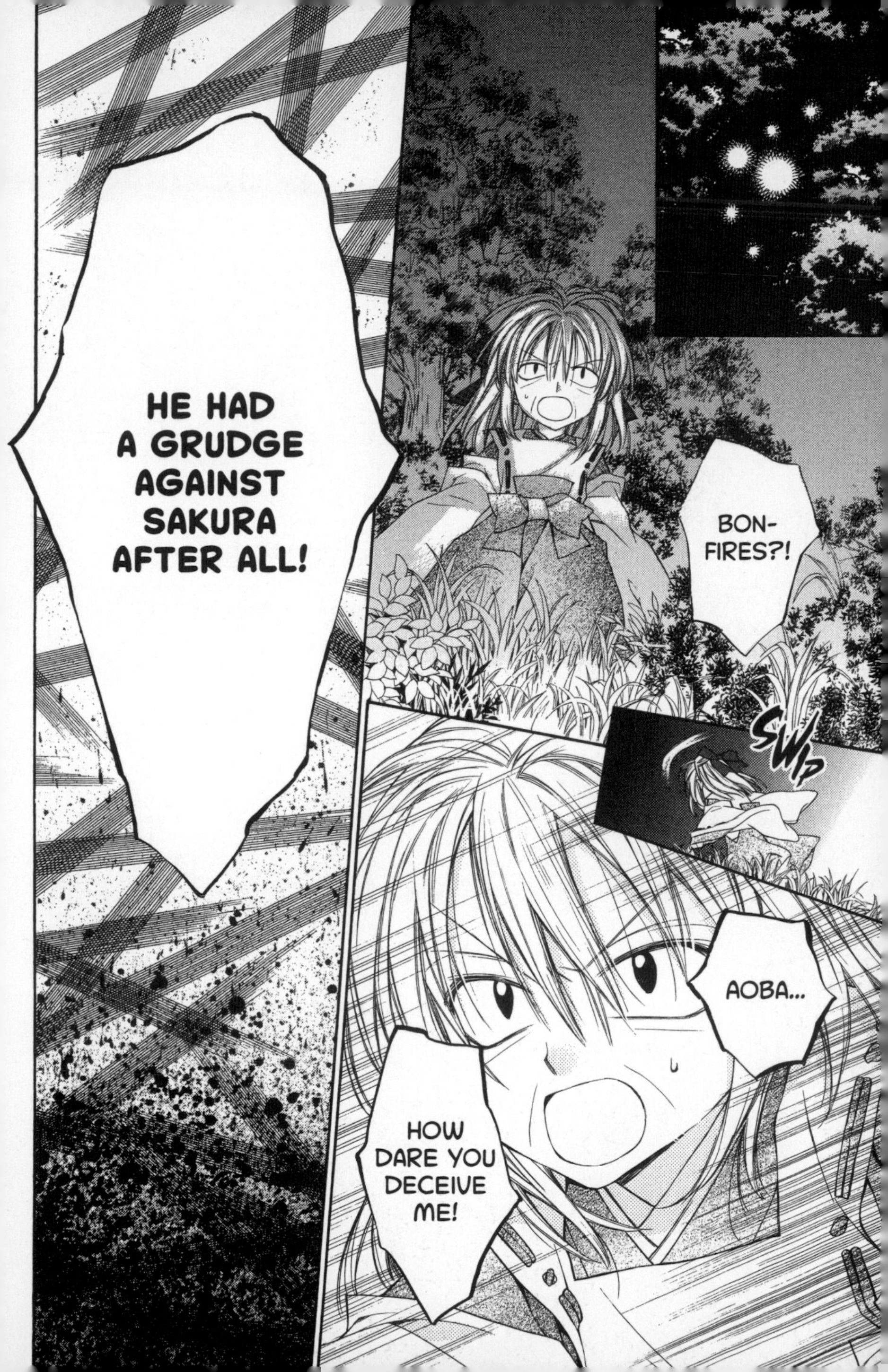
BON-FIRES?!
SWIP
AOBA...
HOW DARE YOU DECEIVE ME!
HE HAD A GRUDGE AGAINST SAKURA AFTER ALL!

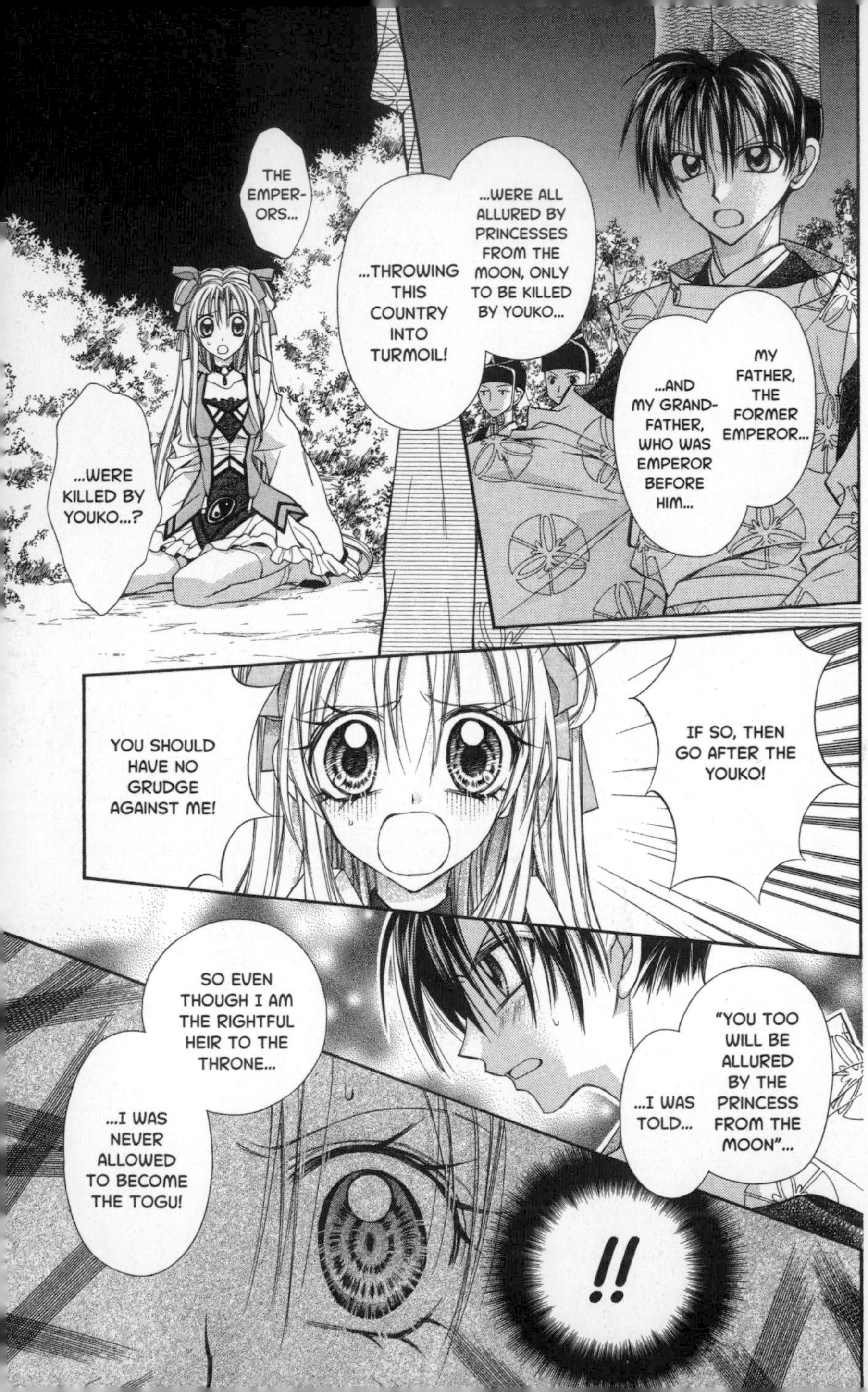
MY FATHER, THE FORMER EMPEROR...
...AND MY GRANDFATHER, WHO WAS EMPEROR BEFORE HIM...
...WERE ALL ALLURED BY PRINCESSES FROM THE MOON, ONLY TO BE KILLED BY YOUKO...
...THROWING THIS COUNTRY INTO TURMOIL!
THE EMPERORS...
...WERE KILLED BY YOUKO...?
IF SO, THEN GO AFTER THE YOUKO!
YOU SHOULD HAVE NO GRUDGE AGAINST ME!
"YOU TOO WILL BE ALLURED BY THE PRINCESS FROM THE MOON"...
...I WAS TOLD...
SO EVEN THOUGH I AM THE RIGHTFUL HEIR TO THE THRONE...
...I WAS NEVER ALLOWED TO BECOME THE TOGU!
!!

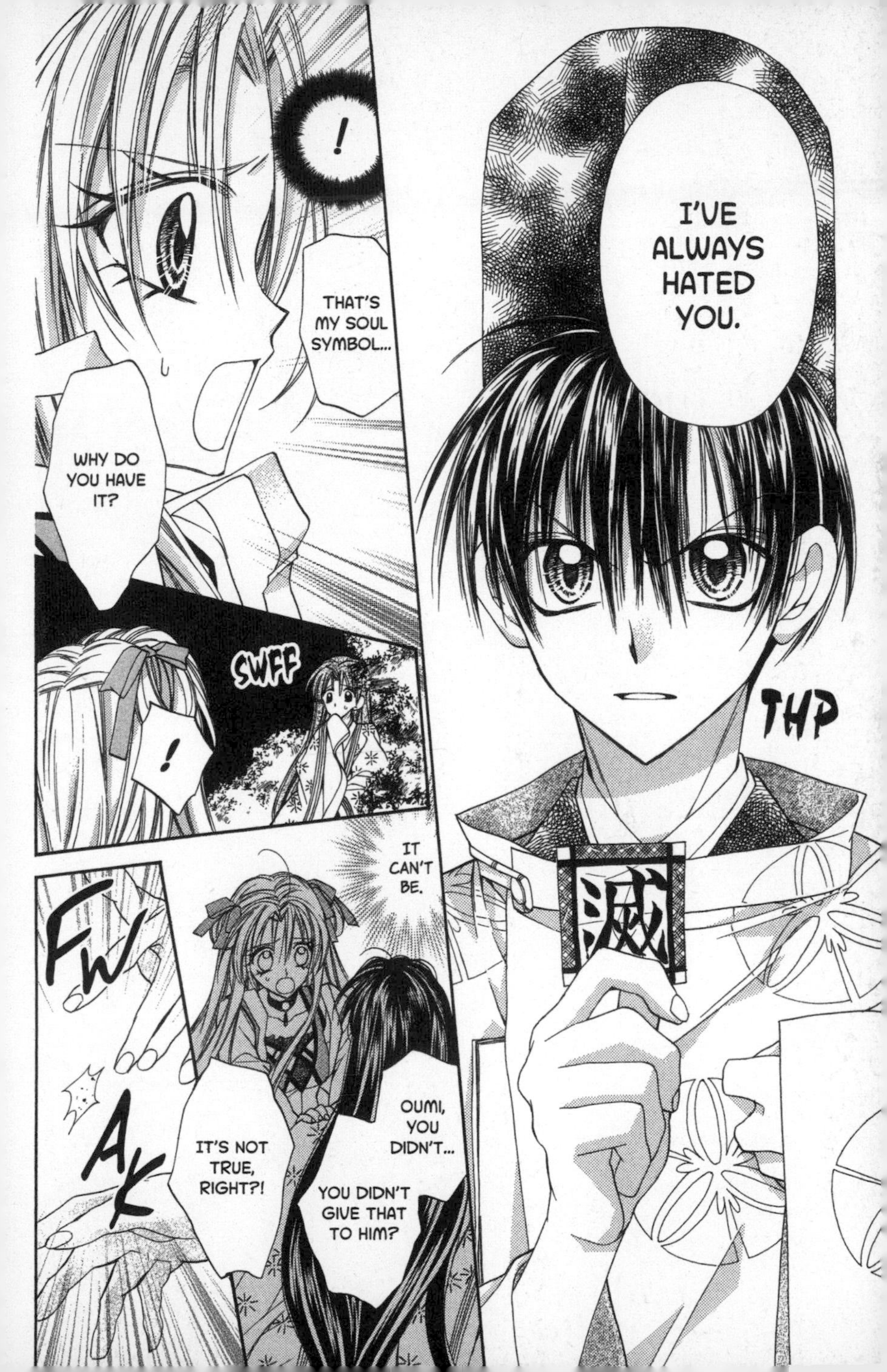
I'VE ALWAYS HATED YOU.
THP
滅
!
THAT'S MY SOUL SYMBOL...
WHY DO YOU HAVE IT?
SWFF
!
IT CAN'T BE.
FW
OUMI, YOU DIDN'T...
IT'S NOT TRUE, RIGHT?!
YOU DIDN'T GIVE THAT TO HIM?
AK

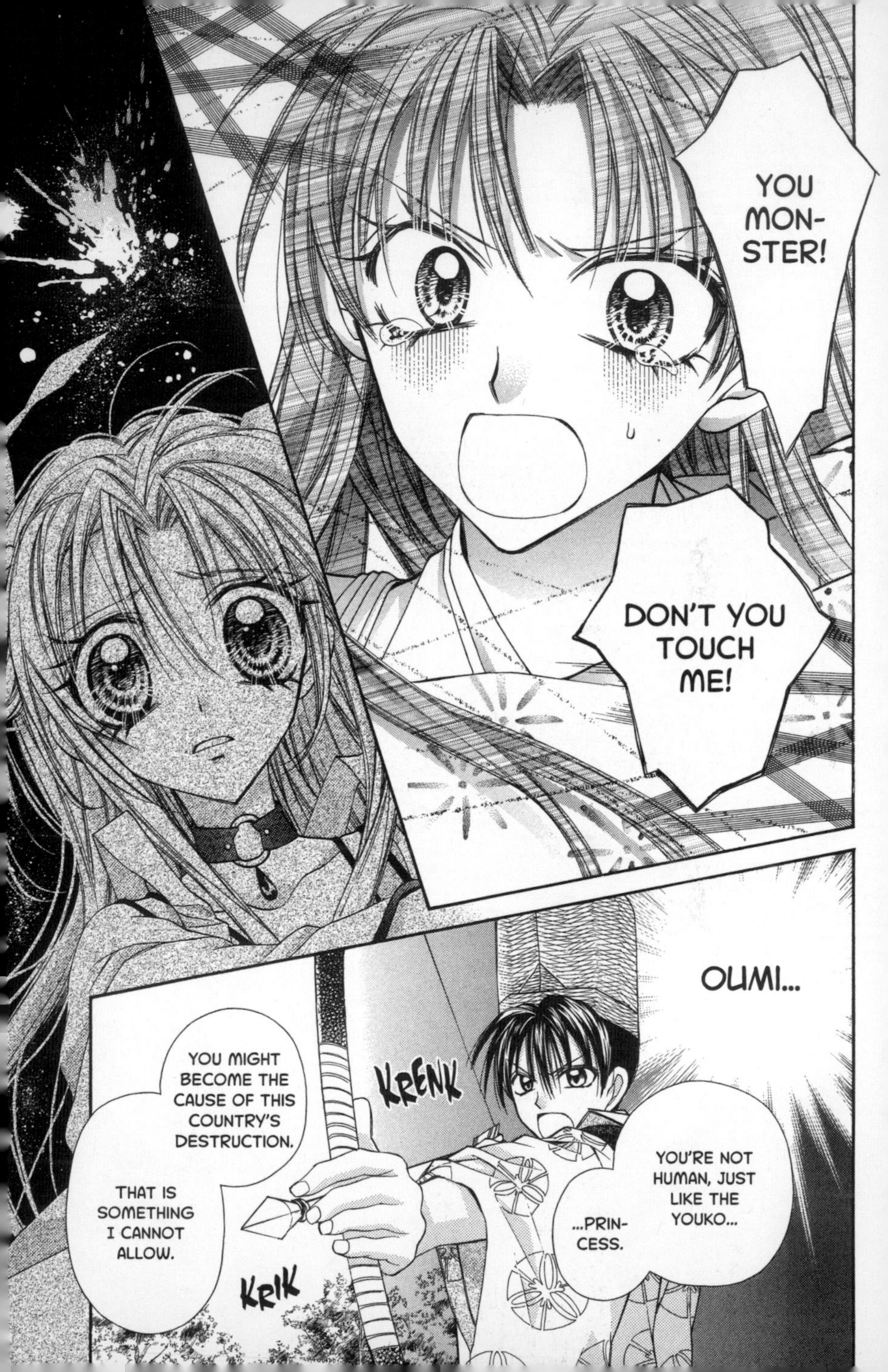
YOU MON-STER!
DON'T YOU TOUCH ME!
OUMI...
YOU'RE NOT HUMAN, JUST LIKE THE YOUKO...
...PRIN-CESS.
KRENK
YOU MIGHT BECOME THE CAUSE OF THIS COUNTRY'S DESTRUCTION.
THAT IS SOMETHING I CANNOT ALLOW.
KRIK

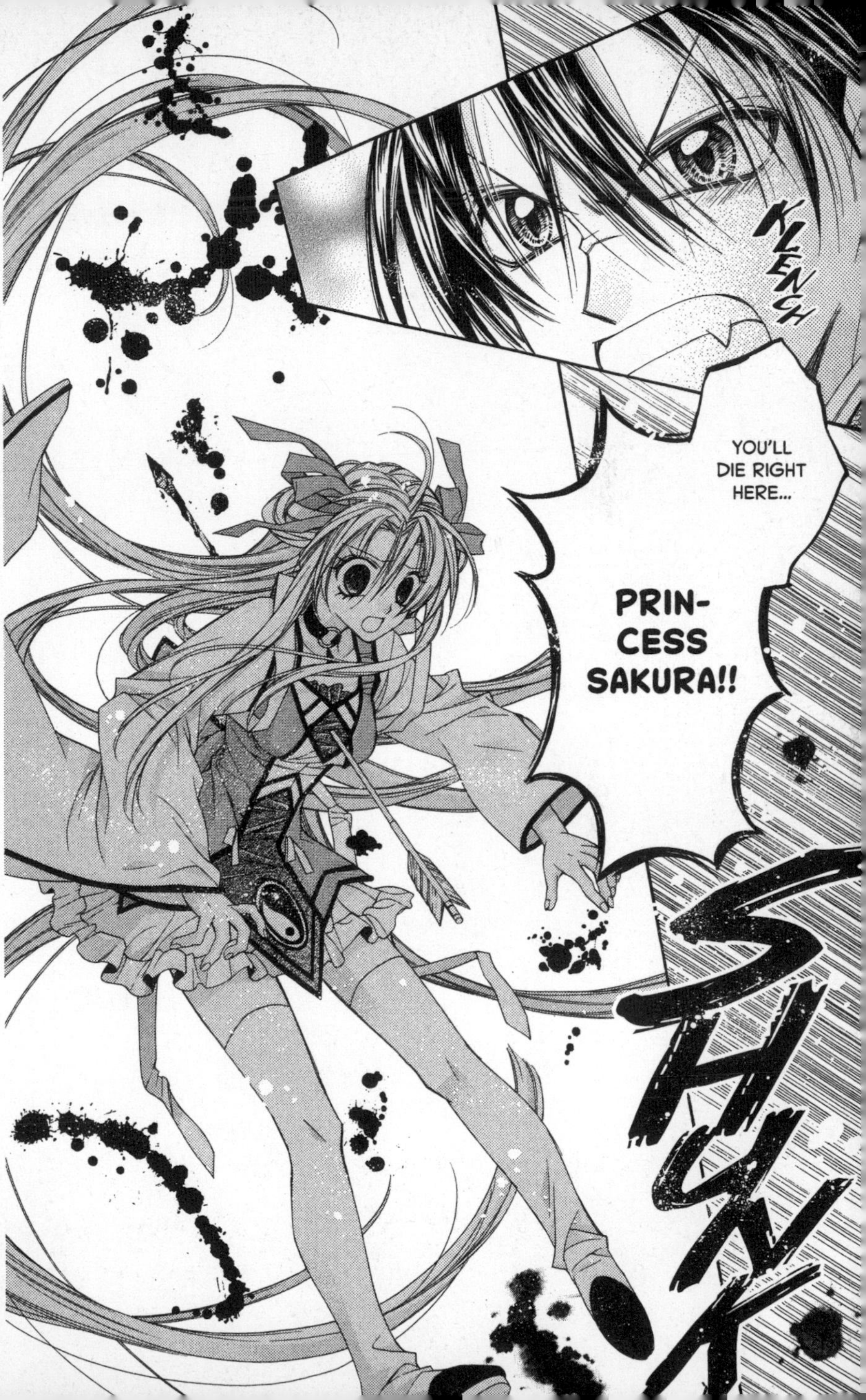
KLENCH
YOU'LL DIE RIGHT HERE...
PRIN-CESS SAKURA!!
SHUNK

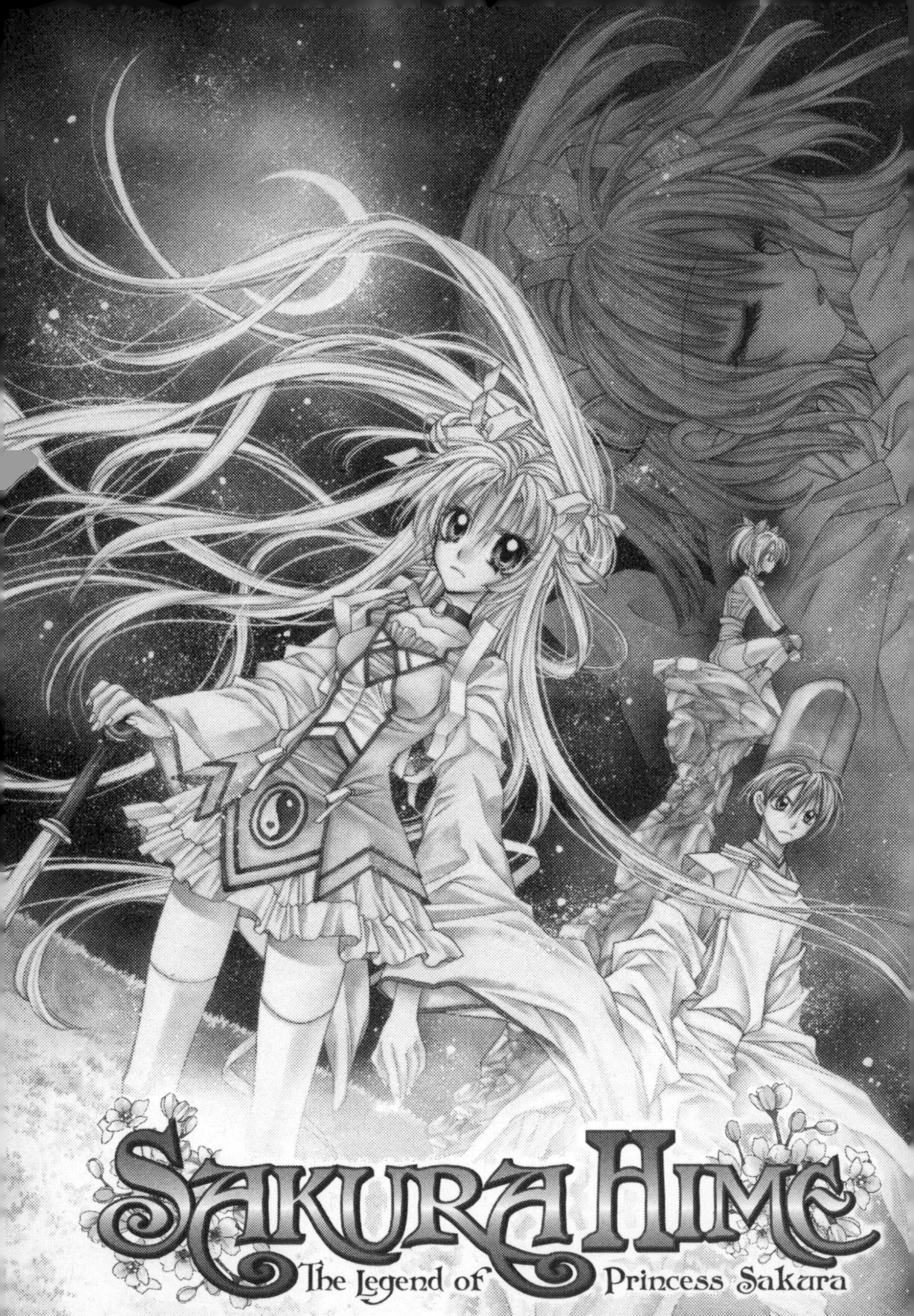
Sakura Hime
The Legend of Princess Sakura

## Chapter 3: Kohaku Appears! Humans and Those Who Aren't

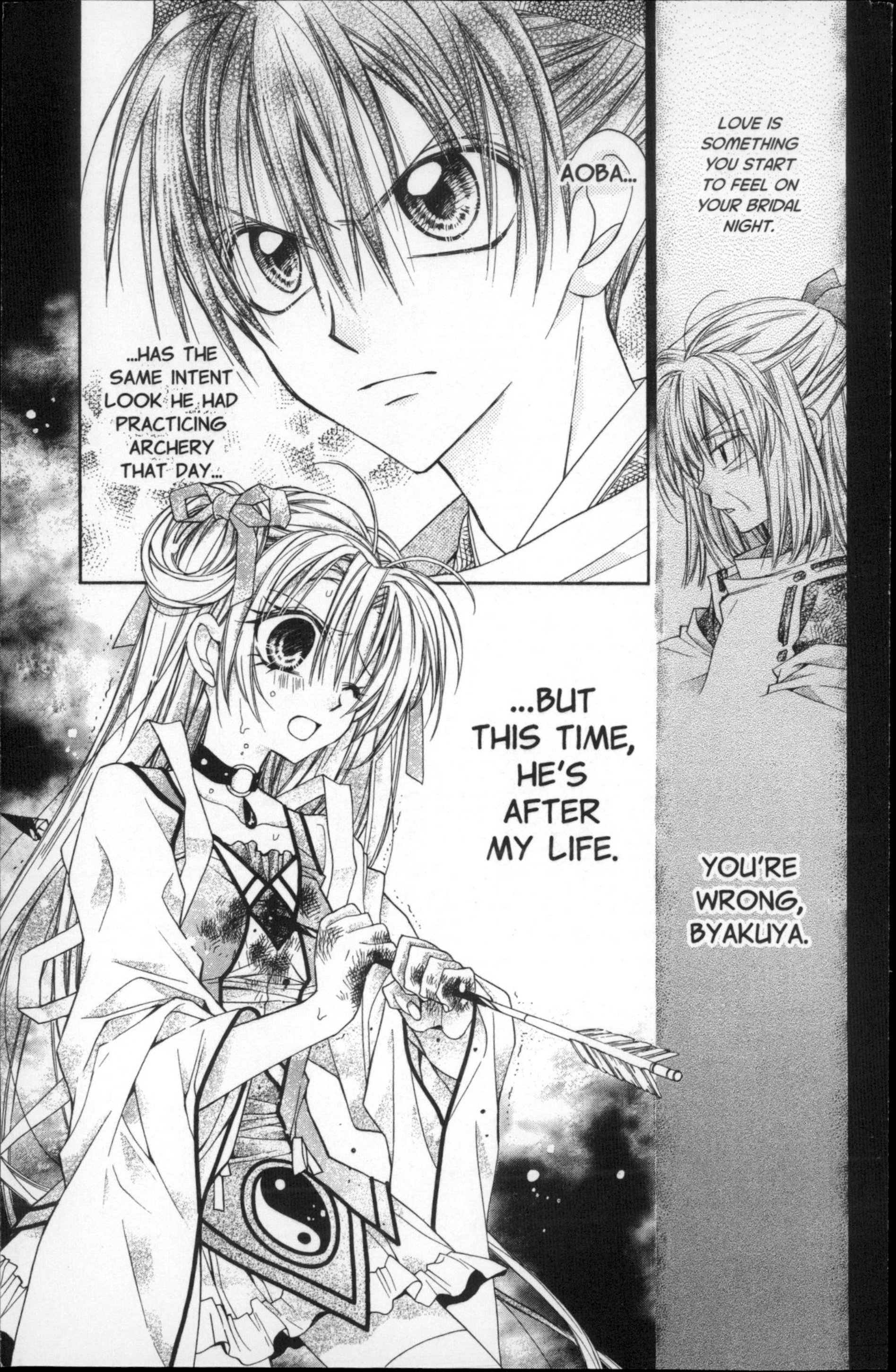
LOVE IS SOMETHING YOU START TO FEEL ON YOUR BRIDAL NIGHT.
YOU'RE WRONG, BYAKUYA.
AOBA...
...HAS THE SAME INTENT LOOK HE HAD PRACTICING ARCHERY THAT DAY...
...BUT THIS TIME, HE'S AFTER MY LIFE.

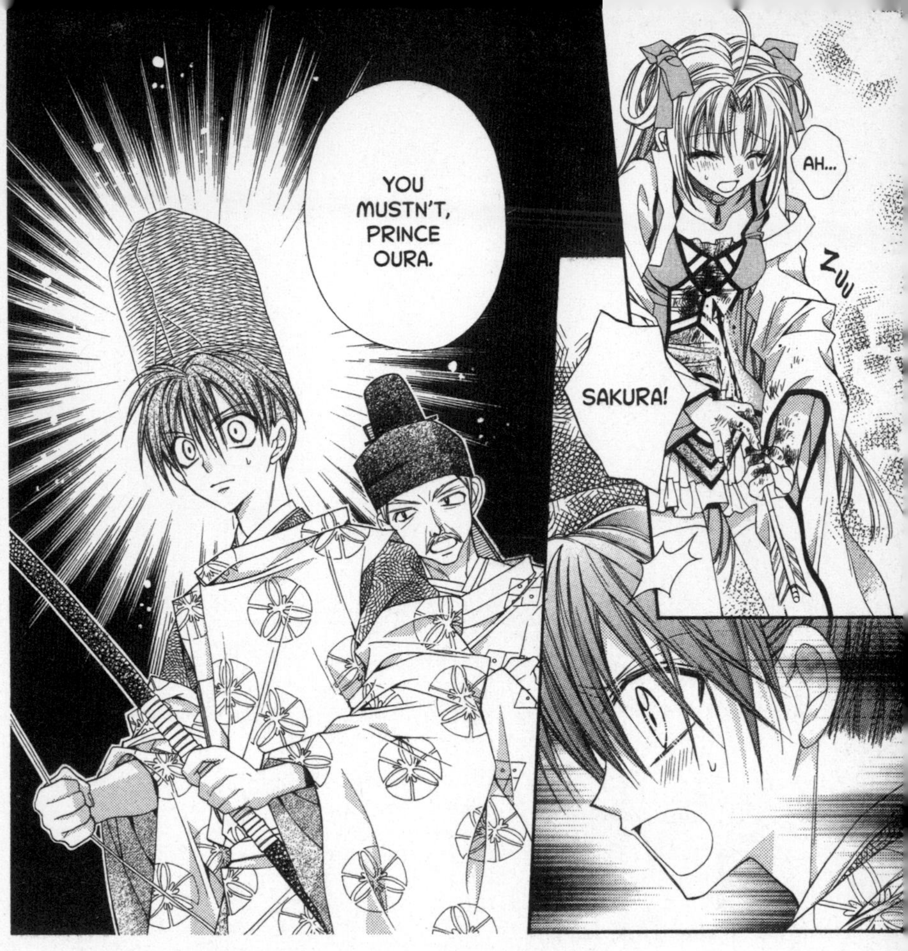
AH...
ZUU
SAKURA!
YOU MUSTN'T, PRINCE OURA.

**Chapter 2: Betrothed Since Birth** Lead-in Face your fate!

※ I'm giving away the story. Please read this after you read the chapter.
I always create the story in sections of "the so-and-so chapters," and usually they are three to five chapters long. The entire series is basically a composite of those. (The story doesn't read well unless it has various ups and downs.) The Aoba chapters start with this chapter. And this arc will be pretty long too. You may be surprised since the story has suddenly taken such an abrupt turn, but don't worry. Don't worry. Once you read the last chapter of his arc I'm sure you'll understand, "So that's why chapter 2 had to be like that"... But I still have a long way to go...

**Chapter 3: Kohaku Appears! Humans and Those Who Aren't** Lead-in Everybody has something they cannot yield to. But those feelings are always connected somewhere...

Dear Kohaku has finally made her appearance.
She takes the role of the cheerful klutz in this series. (*laugh*)
I like how her clothes aren't very cute.
When I was talking with Editor O, he said, "But they're both huge klutzes, right?" after taking a look at a scene with Sakura and Kohaku. I mistakenly said, "N-no, Princess Sakura is much more mature than Haine!" /// And then I realized afterward that I truly do think Sakura is more mature than Haine.
※ Haine → Haine Otomiya, the main character of *The Gentlemen's Alliance* †.

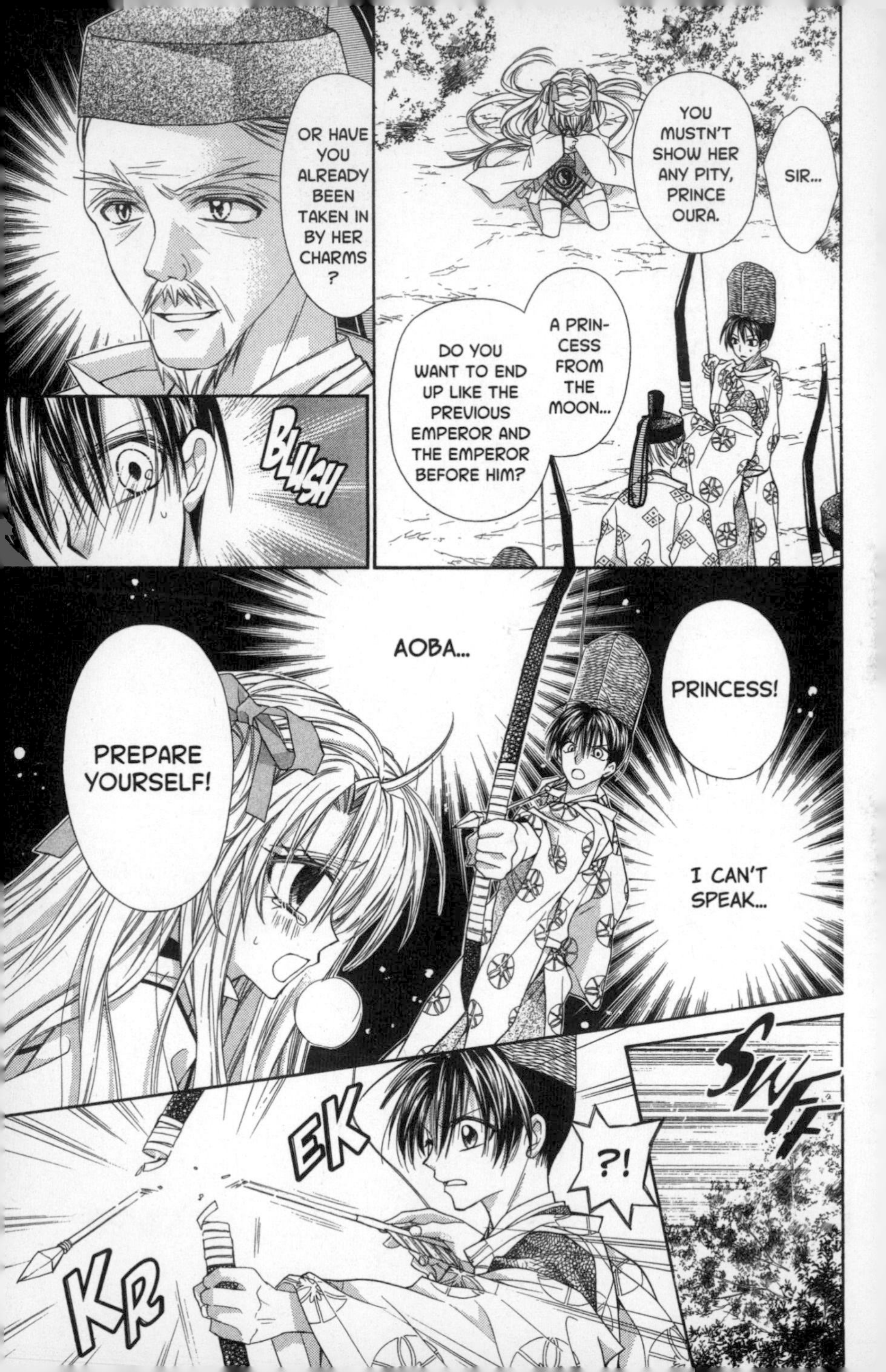
SIR...
YOU MUSTN'T SHOW HER ANY PITY, PRINCE OURA.
A PRINCESS FROM THE MOON...
DO YOU WANT TO END UP LIKE THE PREVIOUS EMPEROR AND THE EMPEROR BEFORE HIM?
OR HAVE YOU ALREADY BEEN TAKEN IN BY HER CHARMS?
BLUSH
PRINCESS!
AOBA...
PREPARE YOURSELF!
I CAN'T SPEAK...
SWFF
?!
EK
KR

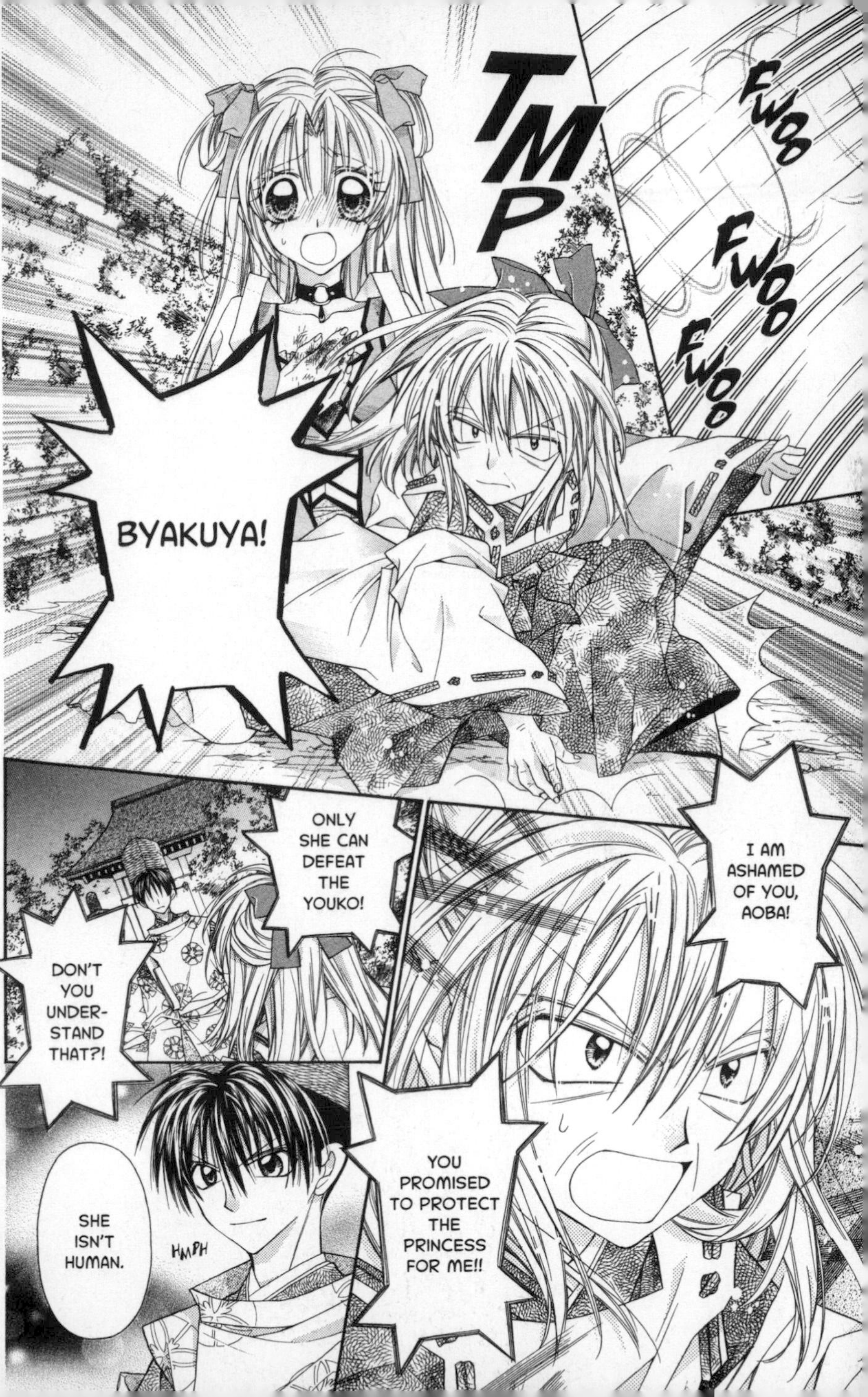
FWOO
FWOO
FWOO
TMP
BYAKUYA!
I AM ASHAMED OF YOU, AOBA!
YOU PROMISED TO PROTECT THE PRINCESS FOR ME!!
ONLY SHE CAN DEFEAT THE YOUKO!
DON'T YOU UNDER-STAND THAT?!
HMPH
SHE ISN'T HUMAN.

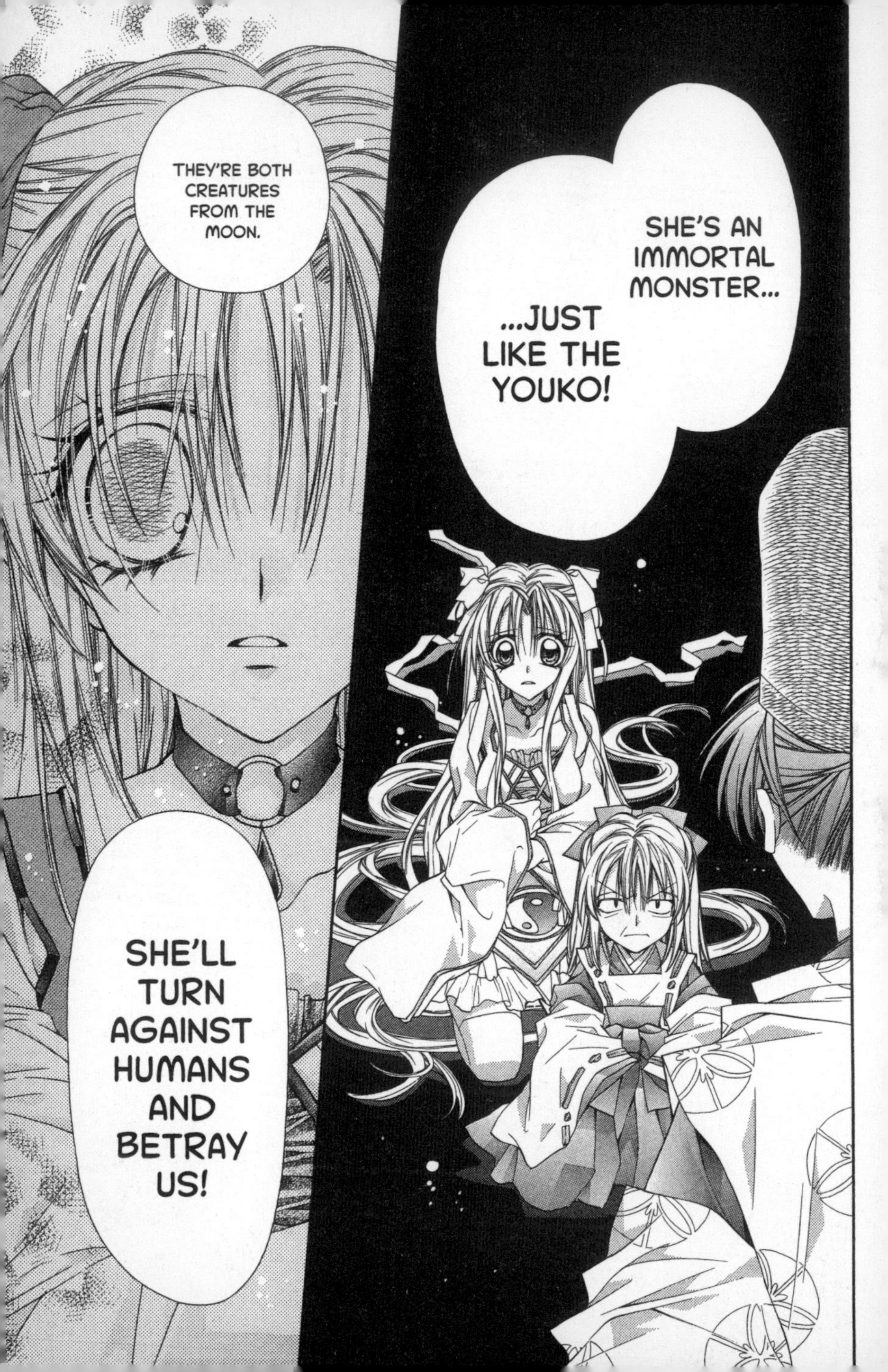
SHE'S AN IMMORTAL MONSTER...
...JUST LIKE THE YOUKO!
THEY'RE BOTH CREATURES FROM THE MOON.
SHE'LL TURN AGAINST HUMANS AND BETRAY US!

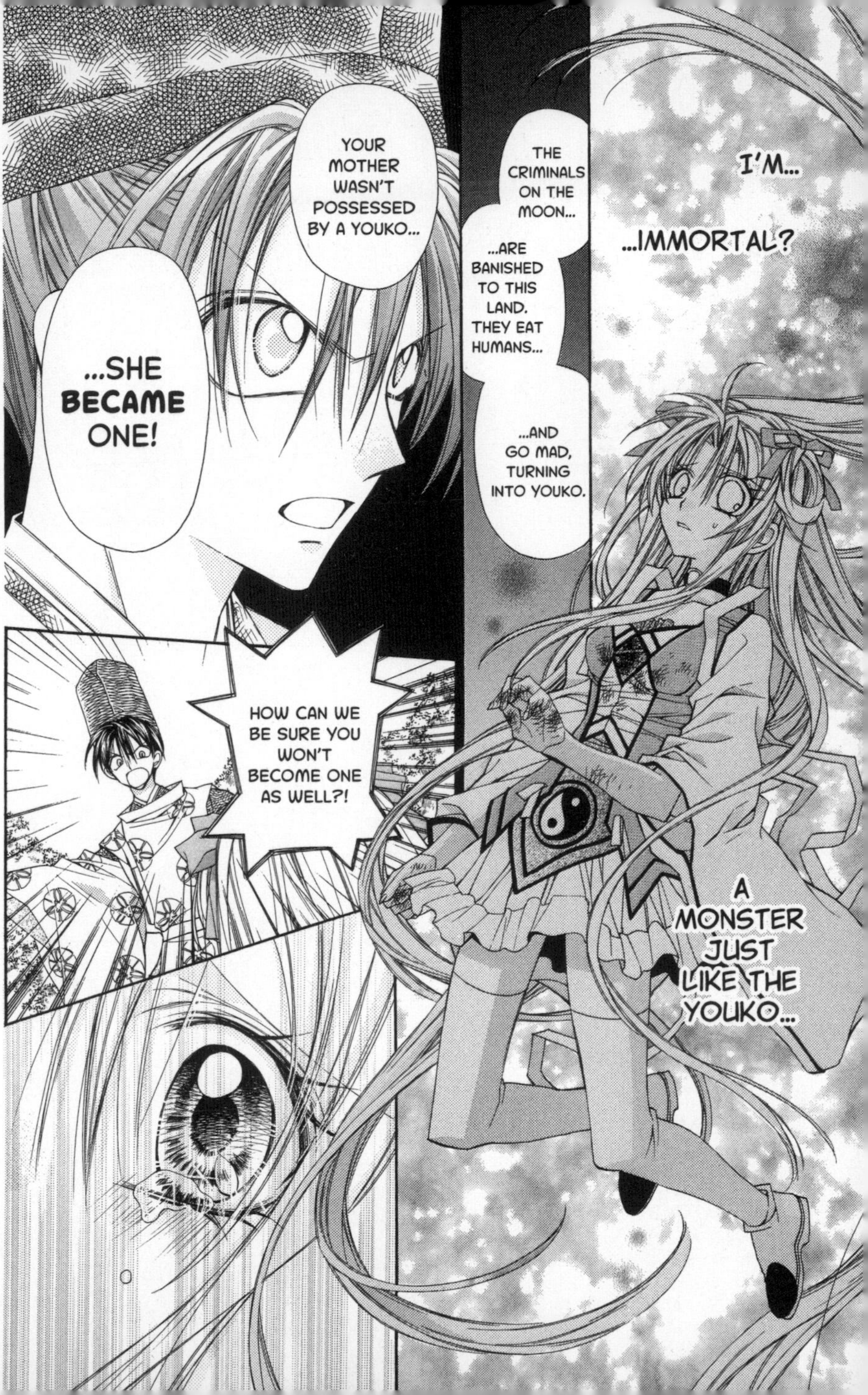
I'M...
...IMMORTAL?
A MONSTER JUST LIKE THE YOUKO...
THE CRIMINALS ON THE MOON...
...ARE BANISHED TO THIS LAND. THEY EAT HUMANS...
...AND GO MAD, TURNING INTO YOUKO.
YOUR MOTHER WASN'T POSSESSED BY A YOUKO...
...SHE **BECAME** ONE!
HOW CAN WE BE SURE YOU WON'T BECOME ONE AS WELL?!

Continuation of my reviews of Macross F songs.

"Do you remember love?"
I had the single for the Ijima version of this song. It seems Nakajima had a lot affection for this song, but maybe it was a little too much...? This song would sound better if you just sang it gently with a smile without thinking too much. The reason this version sounds so serious may be because of the scene in the anime when it's played. (I haven't seen that scene yet, so I apologize if I'm completely off the point.)
I just thought the grandness of this song would be expressed well if this song was sung happily and gently in a state of pure innocence. Sorry, I guess it's just a matter of taste.

"My Boyfriend Is a Pilot"
This song! I've been looking for the CD for this forever. I'm so happy I was able to get hold of the Ranka version as well. ♪
This is perfect for Ranka, isn't it?
She's so cute!

Minmay... It brings tears to my eyes...

"Lion"
I just loved the jacket of the CD single for this, so I bought it!
The image used for the karaoke screen is really nice, so I sing it over and over again. (I think it's the image for Joy Sound.)
I love the voices of Ranka and Sheryl, and I find myself feeling overcome by their power.

"Northern Cross"
I understand how good May'n is when I sing this myself... A song and lyric that deeply touches the heart. It's a song that ignites my mangaka soul. When I told Mizuse, "This is my favorite song," she told me, "That's so like you, Arina-chi"...

Do you think so?

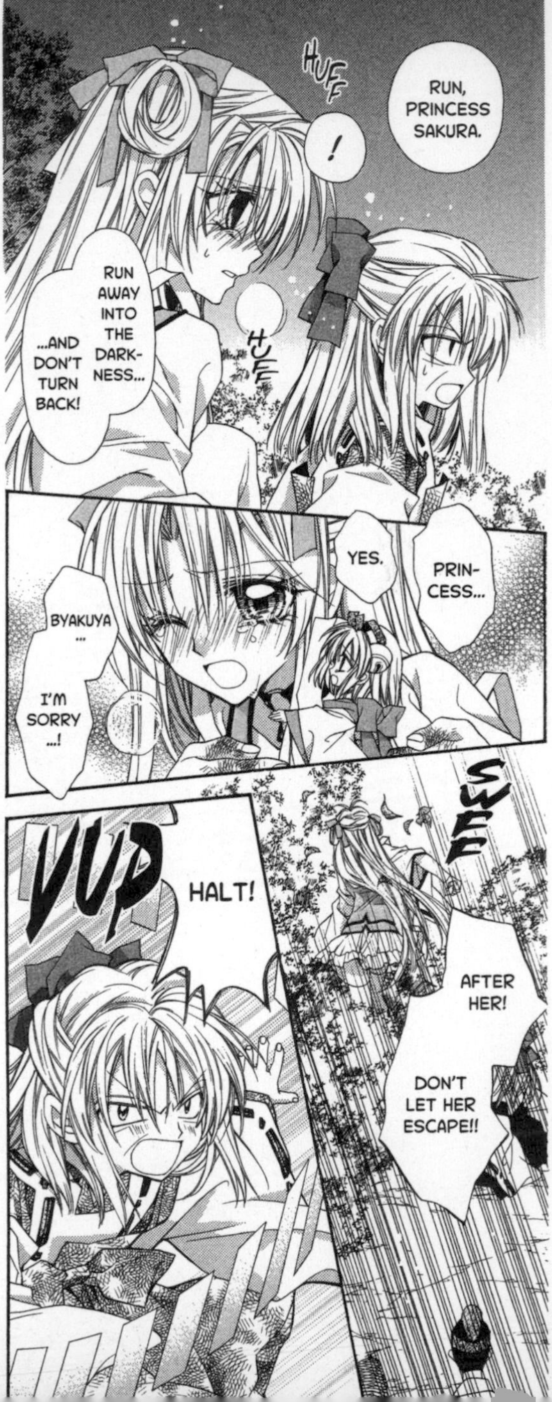
RUN, PRINCESS SAKURA.
HUFF
!
RUN AWAY INTO THE DARKNESS...
...AND DON'T TURN BACK!
HUFF
PRINCESS...
YES.
BYAKUYA...
I'M SORRY...!
SWEE
AFTER HER!
DON'T LET HER ESCAPE!!
HALT!
VUP

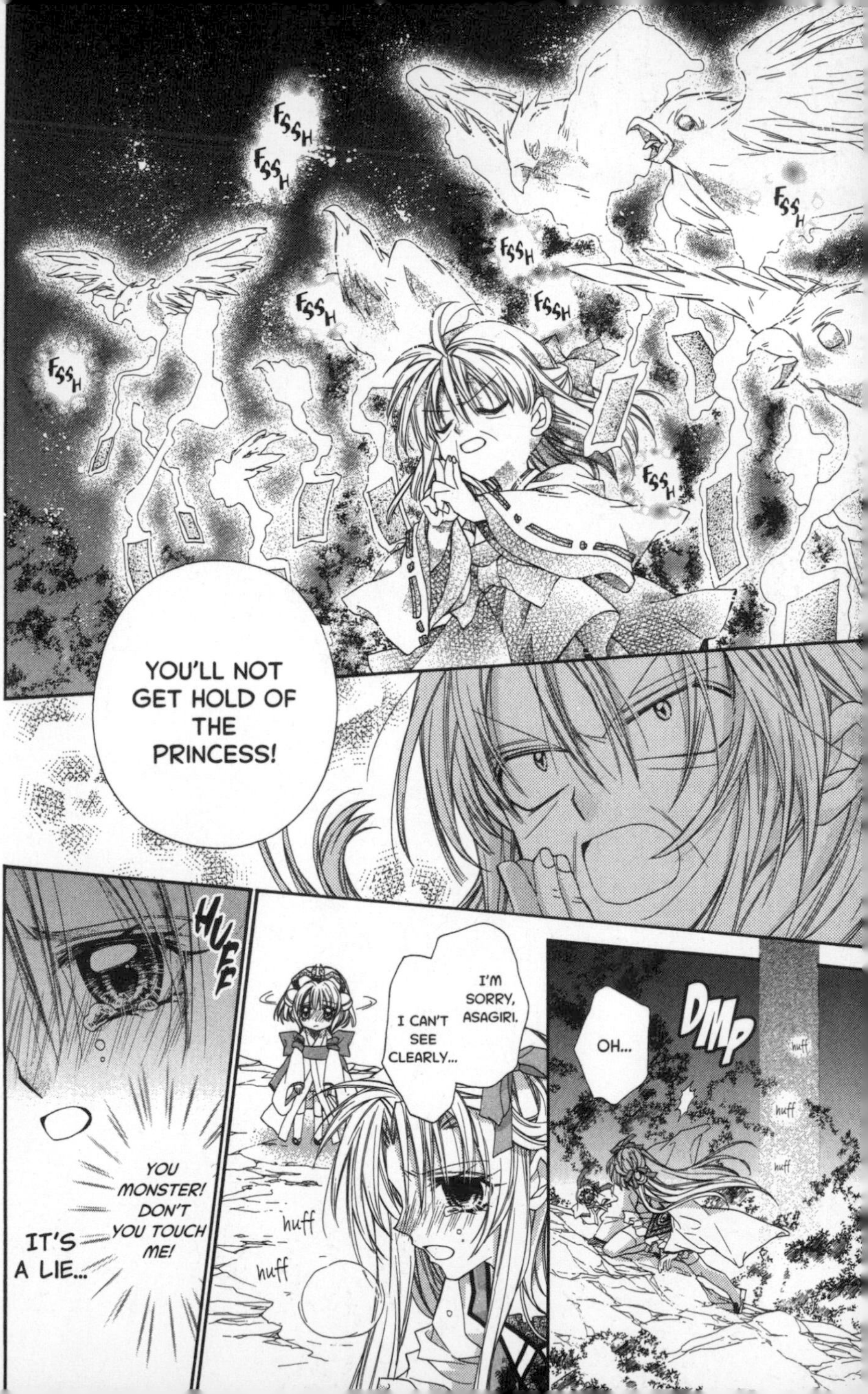
FSSH
FSSH
FSSH
FSSH
FSSH
FSSH
FSSH
FSSH
YOU'LL NOT GET HOLD OF THE PRINCESS!
DMP
OH...
huff
huff
huff
I'M SORRY, ASAGIRI.
I CAN'T SEE CLEARLY...
huff
huff
HUFF
YOU MONSTER! DON'T YOU TOUCH ME!
IT'S A LIE...

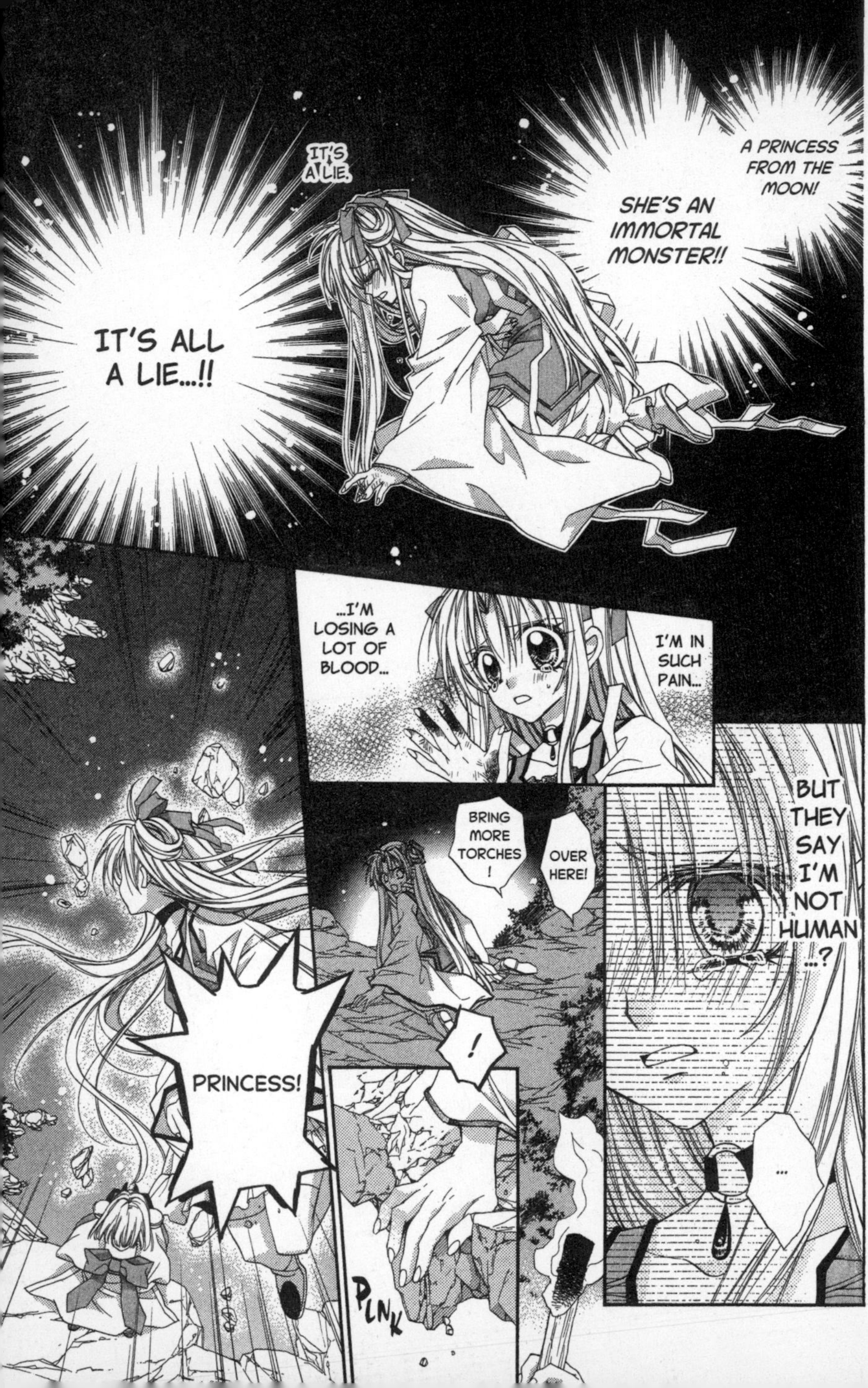
A PRINCESS FROM THE MOON!
SHE'S AN IMMORTAL MONSTER!!
IT'S A LIE.
IT'S ALL A LIE...!!
I'M IN SUCH PAIN...
...I'M LOSING A LOT OF BLOOD...
BUT THEY SAY I'M NOT HUMAN...?
...
OVER HERE!
BRING MORE TORCHES!
!
PLINK
PRINCESS!

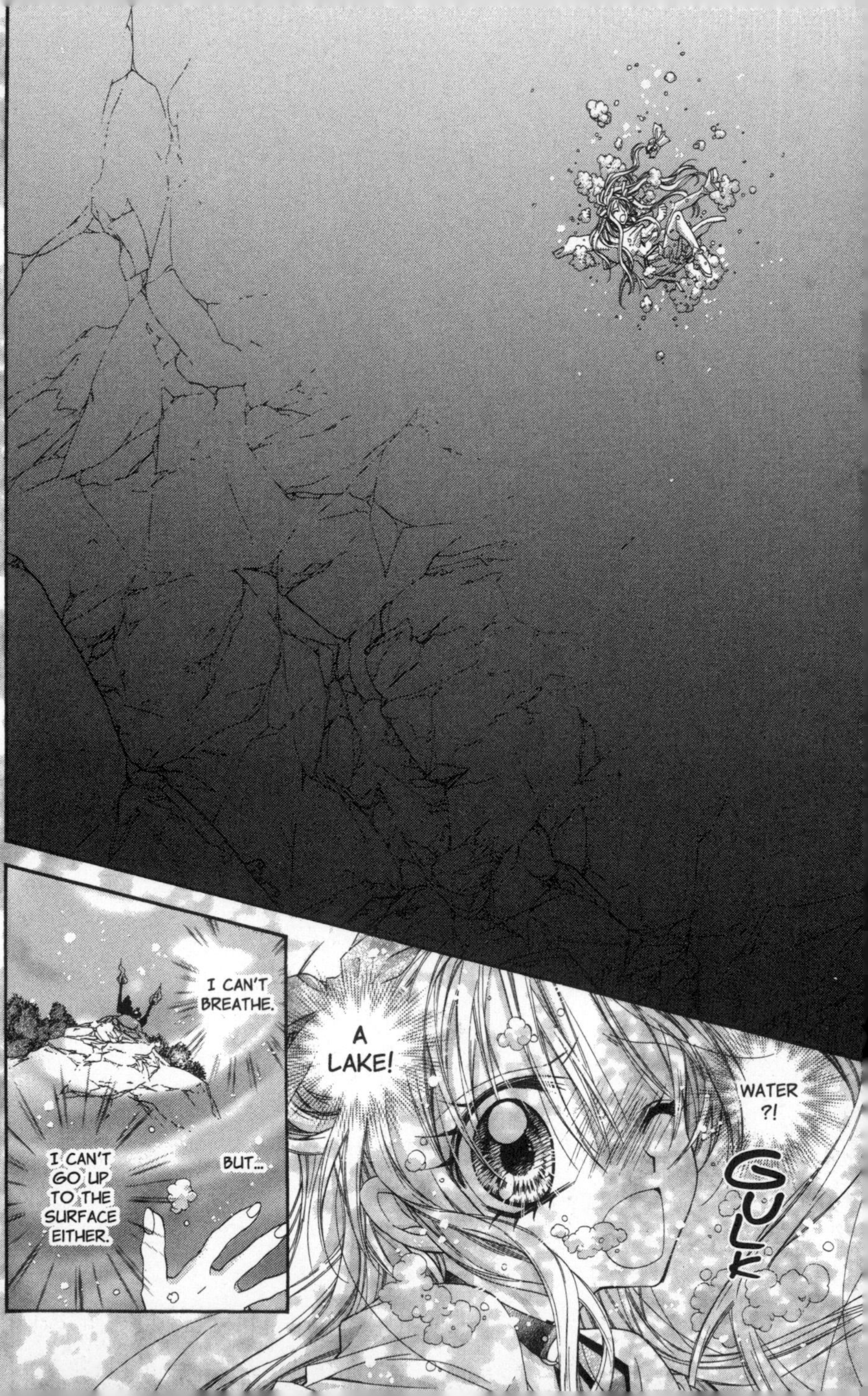
WATER ?!
GULK
A LAKE!
I CAN'T BREATHE.
BUT...
I CAN'T GO UP TO THE SURFACE EITHER.

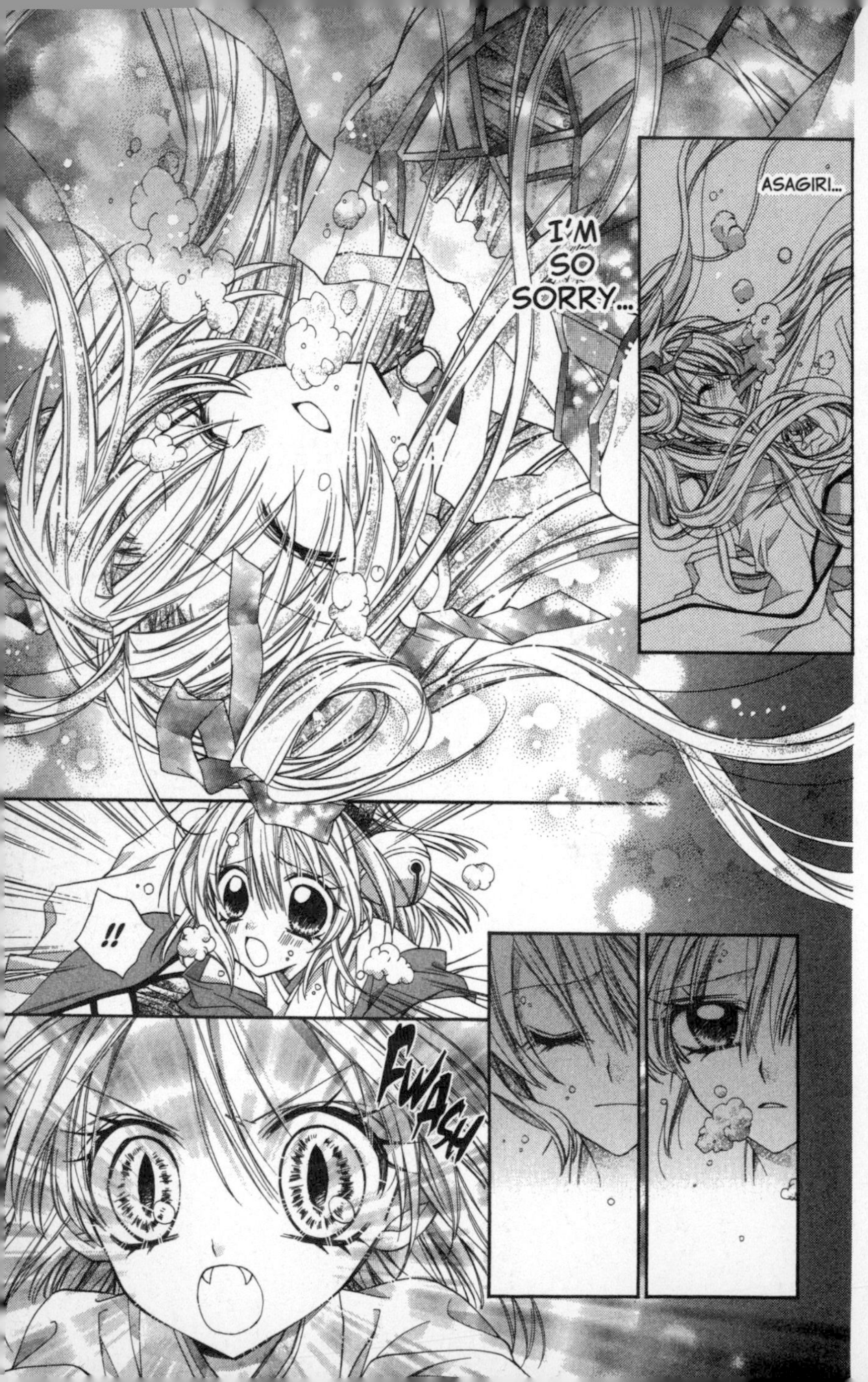
ASAGIRI...
I'M SO SORRY...
!!
FWASH

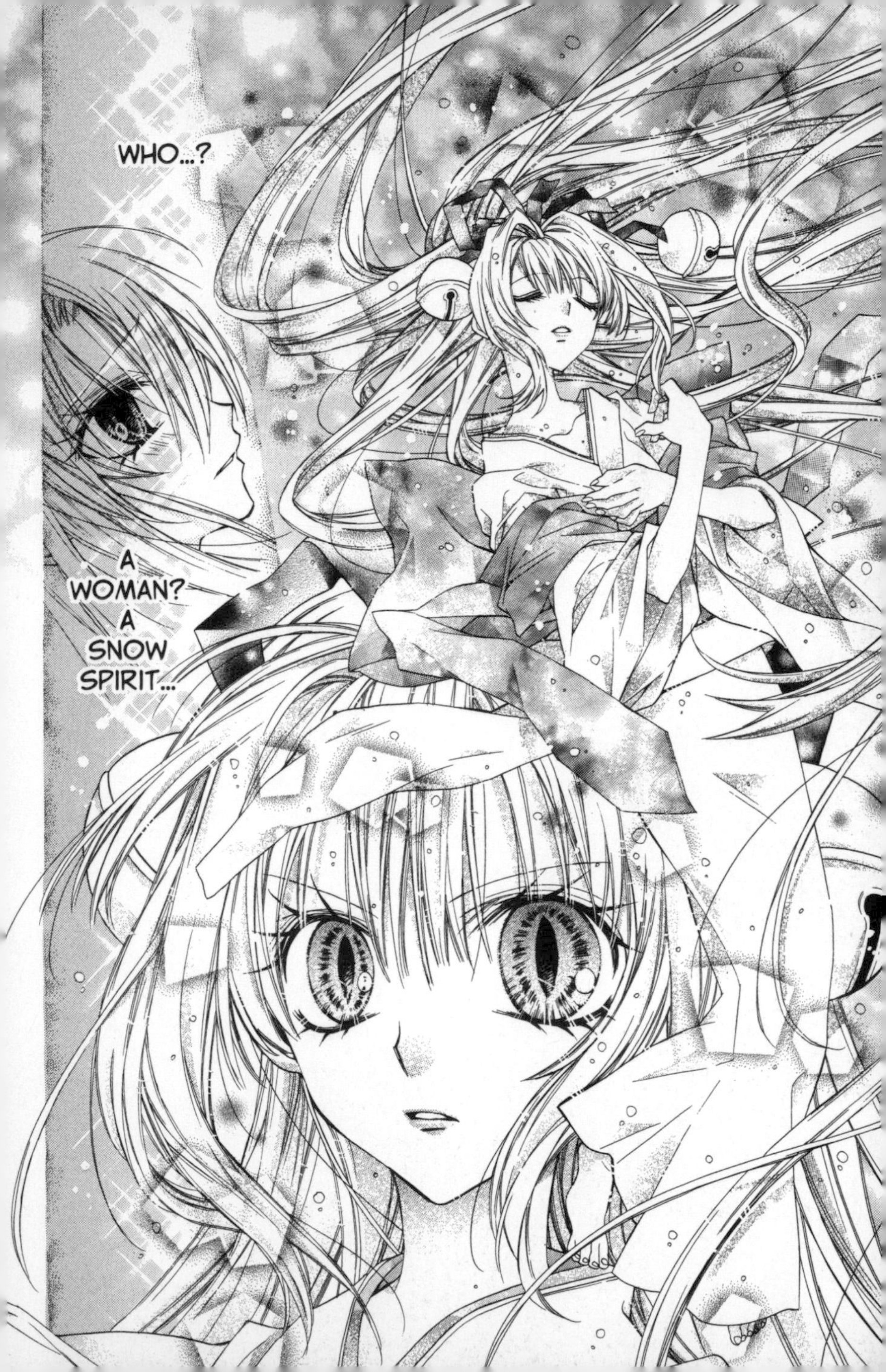
WHO...?
A WOMAN? A SNOW SPIRIT...

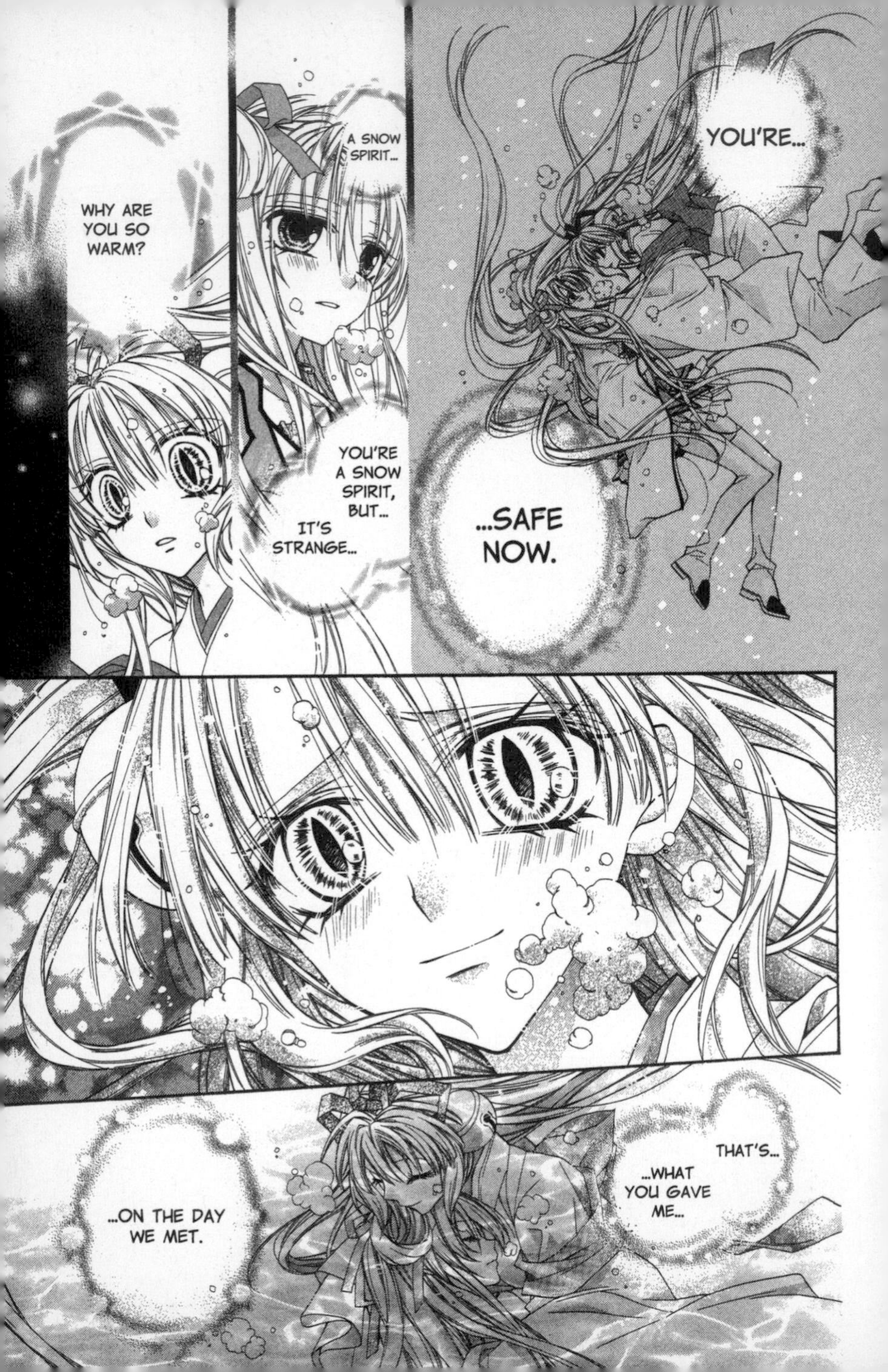
YOU'RE...
...SAFE NOW.
A SNOW SPIRIT...
YOU'RE A SNOW SPIRIT, BUT...
IT'S STRANGE...
WHY ARE YOU SO WARM?
THAT'S...
...WHAT YOU GAVE ME...
...ON THE DAY WE MET.

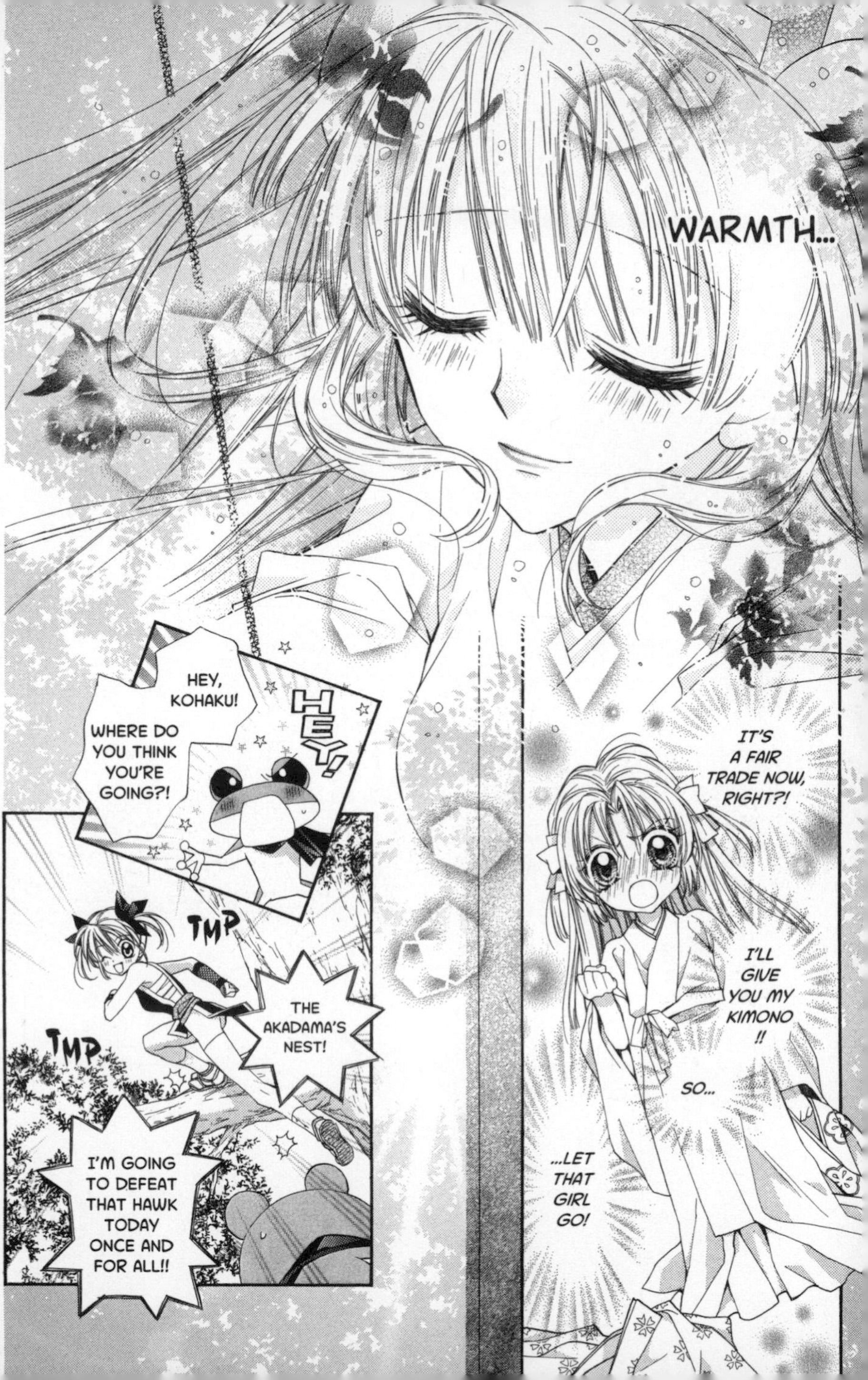
WARMTH...
IT'S A FAIR TRADE NOW, RIGHT?!
I'LL GIVE YOU MY KIMONO !!
SO...
...LET THAT GIRL GO!
HEY, KOHAKU!
WHERE DO YOU THINK YOU'RE GOING?!
HEY!
TMP
TMP
THE AKADAMA'S NEST!
I'M GOING TO DEFEAT THAT HAWK TODAY ONCE AND FOR ALL!!

Continuation of my reviews of the Macross F songs.

"Azure Ether"
The lyrics for this have a special place in my heart because Maaya Sakamoto wrote it, and it is one of the best songs Nakajima sings. (I don't know if she had assistance or just came up with it herself, but...) I can tell she sang it after giving it much thought. Her expressiveness is just wonderful. Her voice and the way she sings are a perfect match, and it enters your heart so smoothly. I like the title of the song a lot.

"Your Sound"
This is a song which only Ranka can sing, I think. (There are a lot of cover versions and self-covers in Macross F.)
Ranka sounds a little grown-up in this one, and that excites me too.

"Nyan Nyan Service Medley (Tokumori)"
The one in Nyan TRA was a nicely paced song too, but I love the live performance atmosphere of Tokumori! I'm looking for someone who'll sing it with me at karaoke. I want to do a chorus...

"What 'bout My Star?"
At first I got all tongue-tied and could not remember the lyrics so I was like ??... But you won't find many songs that are as fun to sing as this! So this is one of my favorites now.
I like how it sounds different depending on who sings it...♥ The slightly provocative lyrics differ from version to version, and that is fun too.

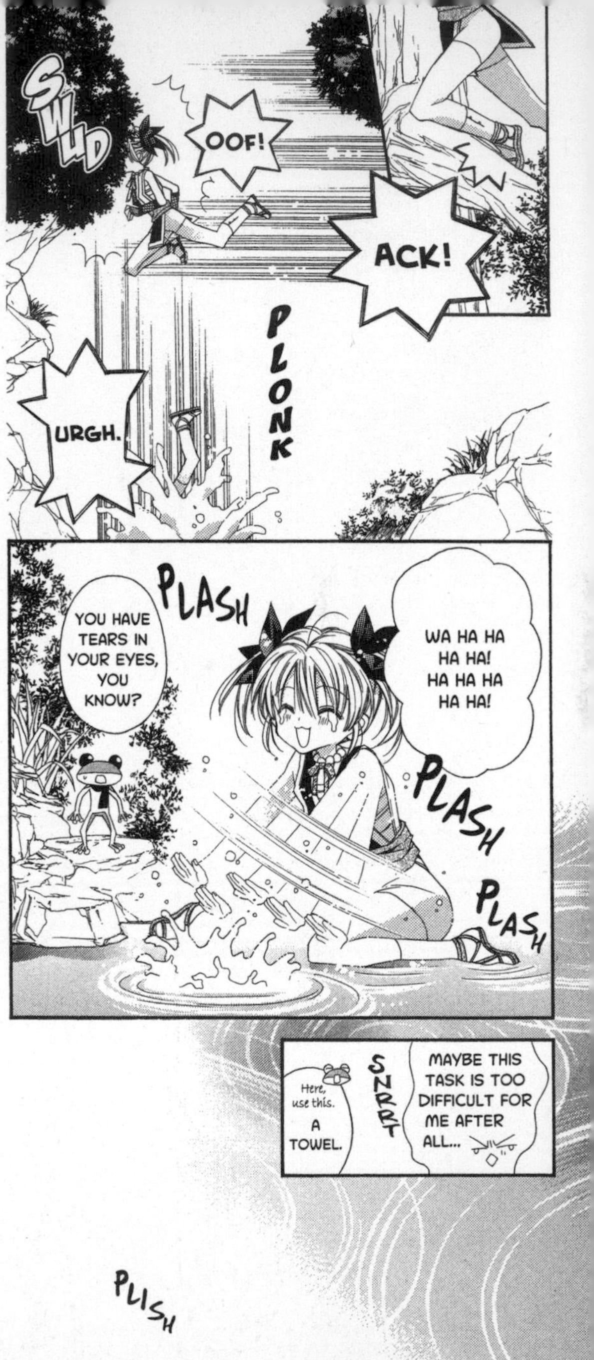
ACK!
OOF!
SWUD
PLONK
URGH.
WA HA HA HA HA! HA HA HA HA HA!
PLASH
YOU HAVE TEARS IN YOUR EYES, YOU KNOW?
PLASH
PLASH
MAYBE THIS TASK IS TOO DIFFICULT FOR ME AFTER ALL...
SNRRT
Here, use this.
A TOWEL.
PLISH

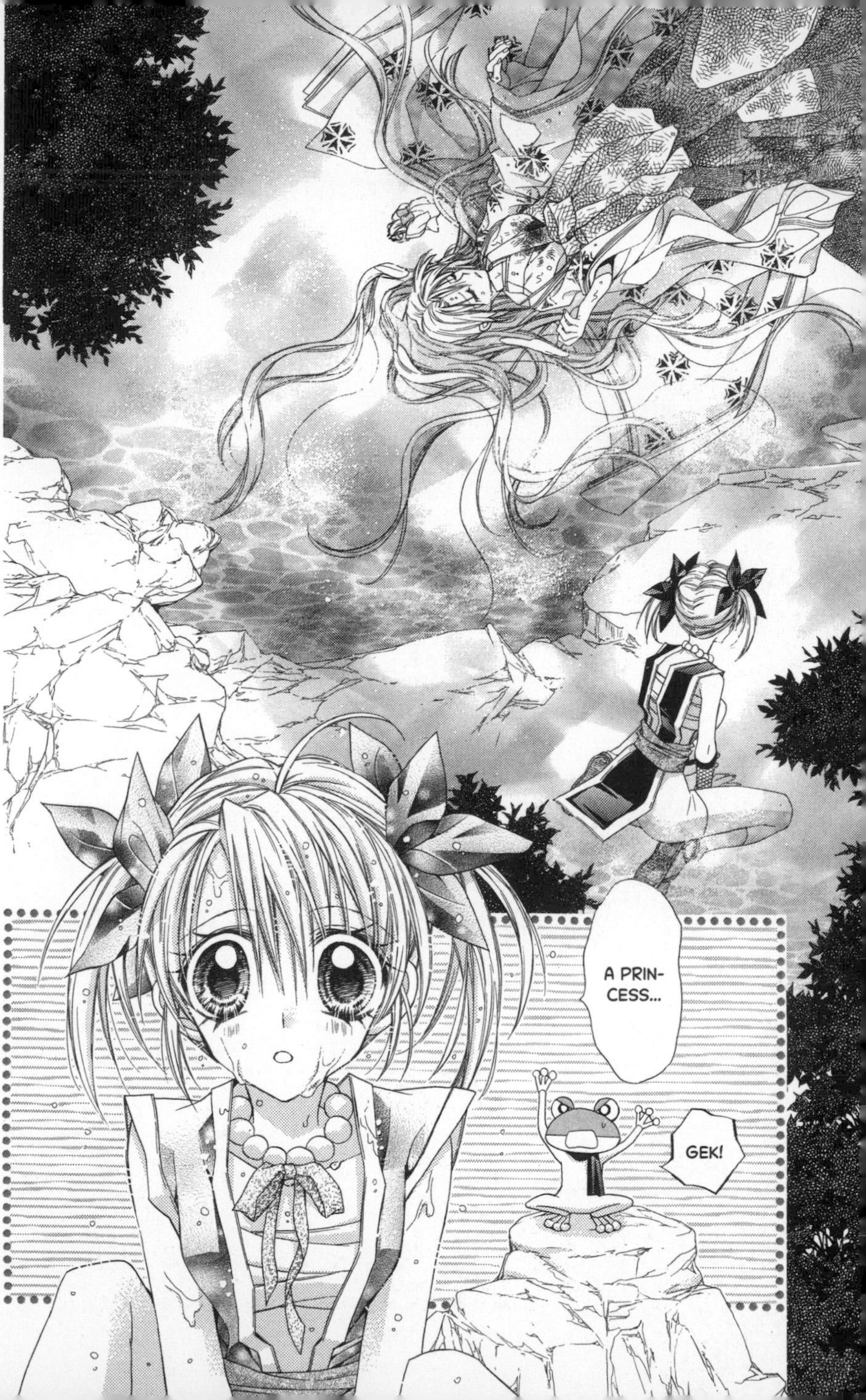
A PRIN-
CESS...
GEK!

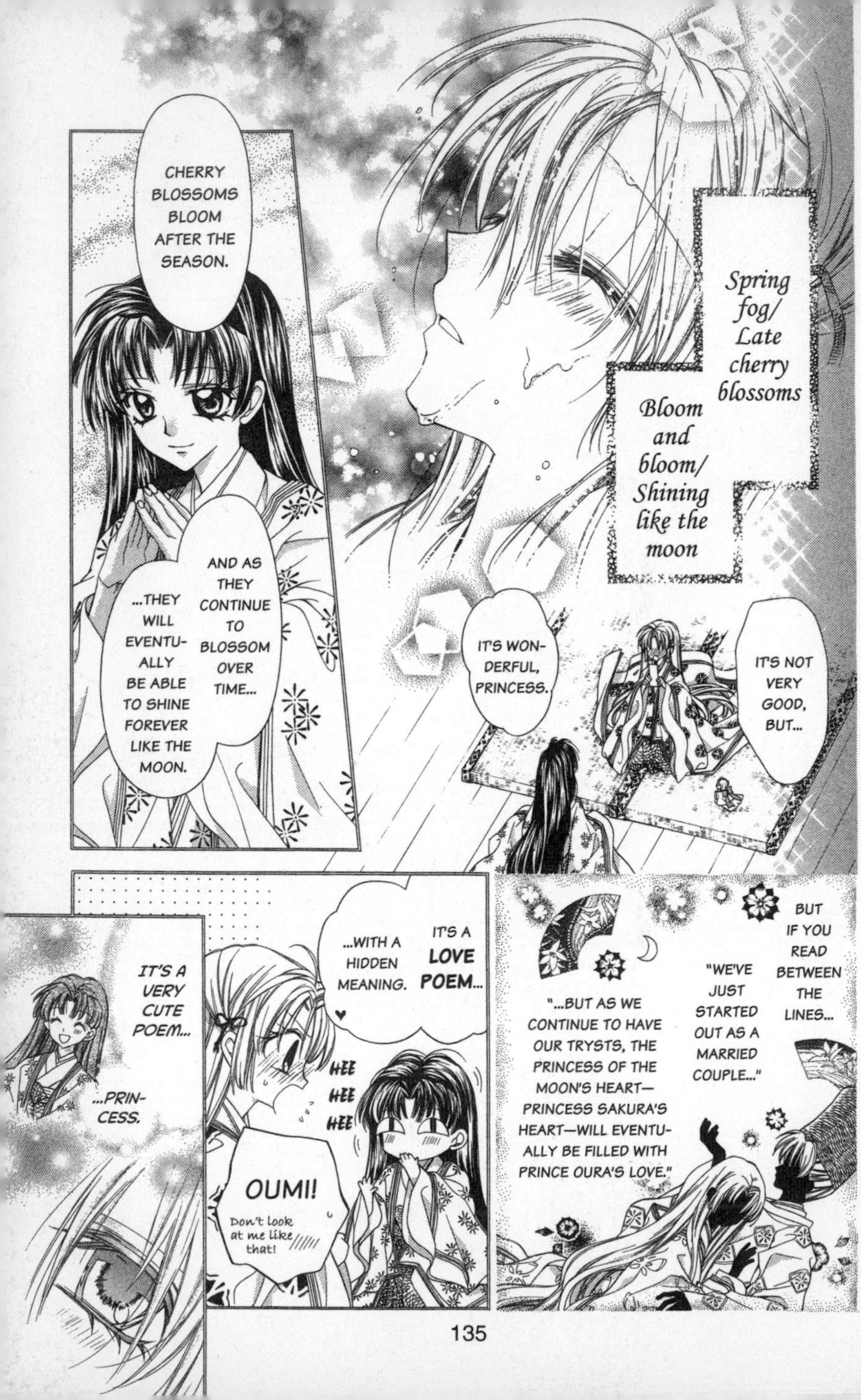
Spring fog/ Late cherry blossoms
Bloom and bloom/ Shining like the moon
IT'S NOT VERY GOOD, BUT...
IT'S WON-DERFUL, PRINCESS.
CHERRY BLOSSOMS BLOOM AFTER THE SEASON.
AND AS THEY CONTINUE TO BLOSSOM OVER TIME...
...THEY WILL EVENTU-ALLY BE ABLE TO SHINE FOREVER LIKE THE MOON.
BUT IF YOU READ BETWEEN THE LINES...
"WE'VE JUST STARTED OUT AS A MARRIED COUPLE..."
"...BUT AS WE CONTINUE TO HAVE OUR TRYSTS, THE PRINCESS OF THE MOON'S HEART—PRINCESS SAKURA'S HEART—WILL EVENTU-ALLY BE FILLED WITH PRINCE OURA'S LOVE."
IT'S A LOVE POEM...
...WITH A HIDDEN MEANING.
HEE HEE HEE
OUMI!
Don't look at me like that!
IT'S A VERY CUTE POEM...
...PRIN-CESS.

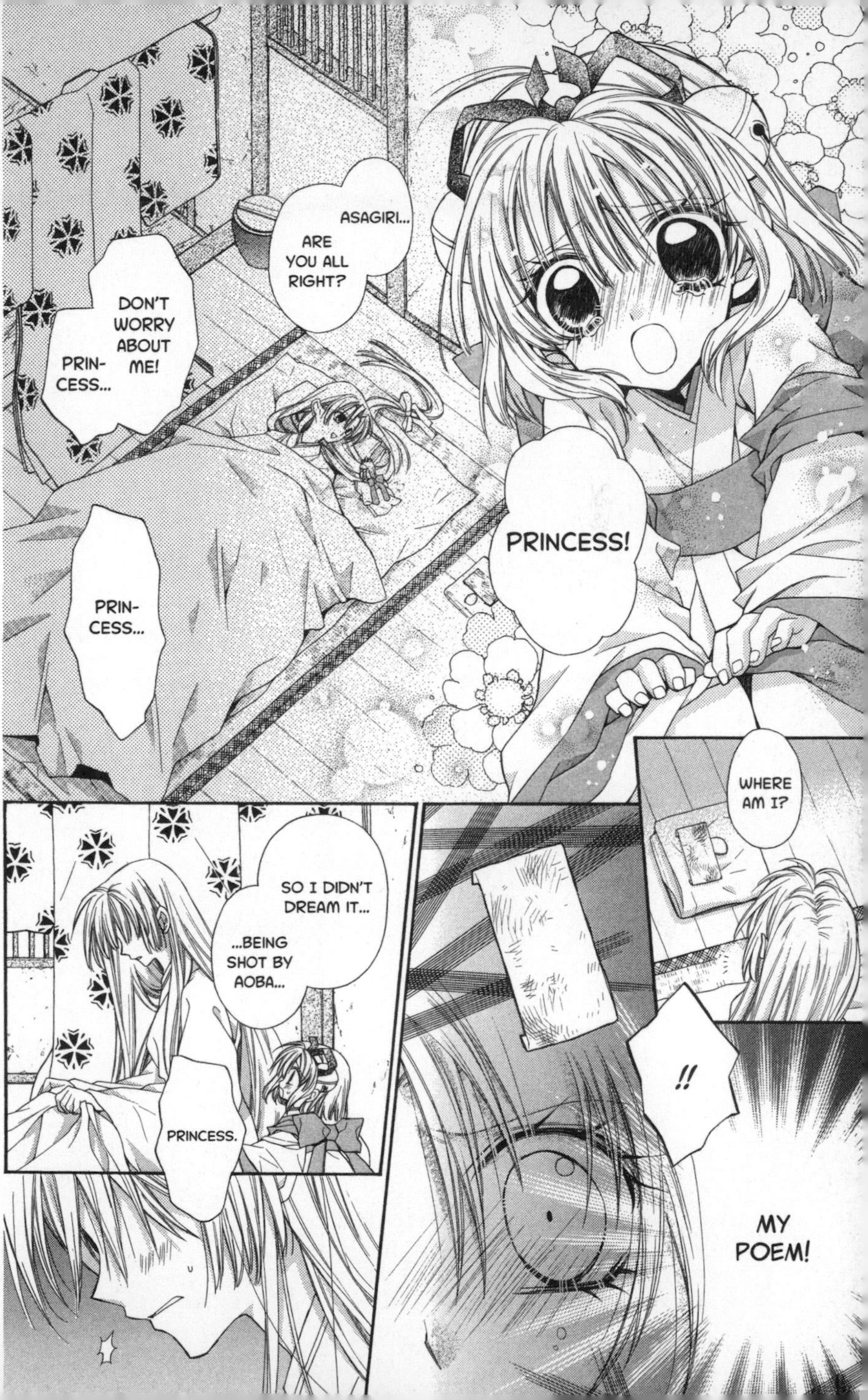
ASAGIRI... ARE YOU ALL RIGHT?
DON'T WORRY ABOUT ME!
PRIN-CESS...
PRINCESS!
PRIN-CESS...
WHERE AM I?
!!
MY POEM!
SO I DIDN'T DREAM IT...
...BEING SHOT BY AOBA...
PRINCESS.

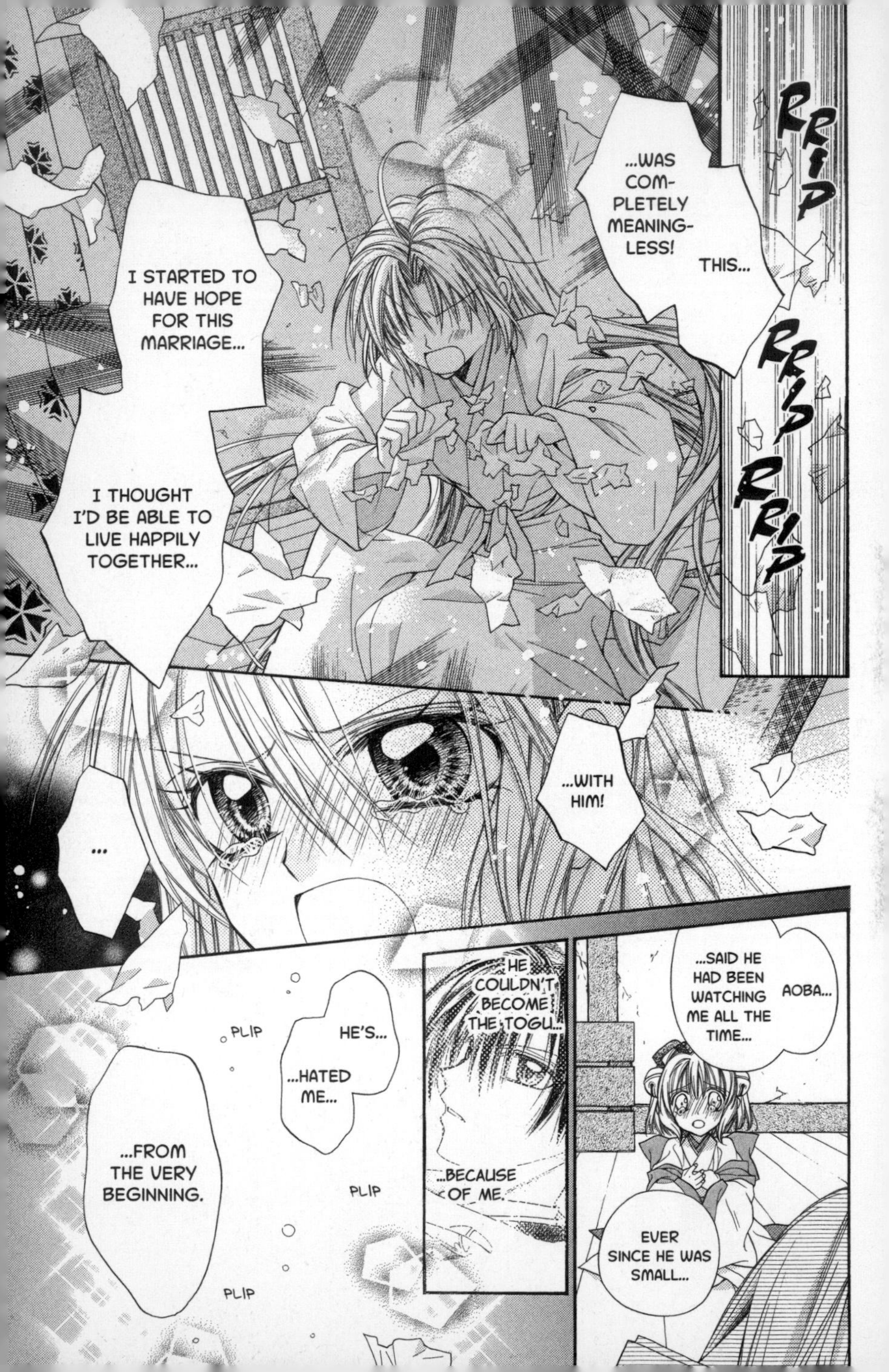

RRIP
RRIP
RRIP
THIS...
...WAS COM-PLETELY MEANING-LESS!
I STARTED TO HAVE HOPE FOR THIS MARRIAGE...
I THOUGHT I'D BE ABLE TO LIVE HAPPILY TOGETHER...
...WITH HIM!
...
AOBA...
...SAID HE HAD BEEN WATCHING ME ALL THE TIME...
EVER SINCE HE WAS SMALL...
HE COULDN'T BECOME THE TOGU...
...BECAUSE OF ME.
HE'S...
...HATED ME...
PLIP
...FROM THE VERY BEGINNING.
PLIP
PLIP

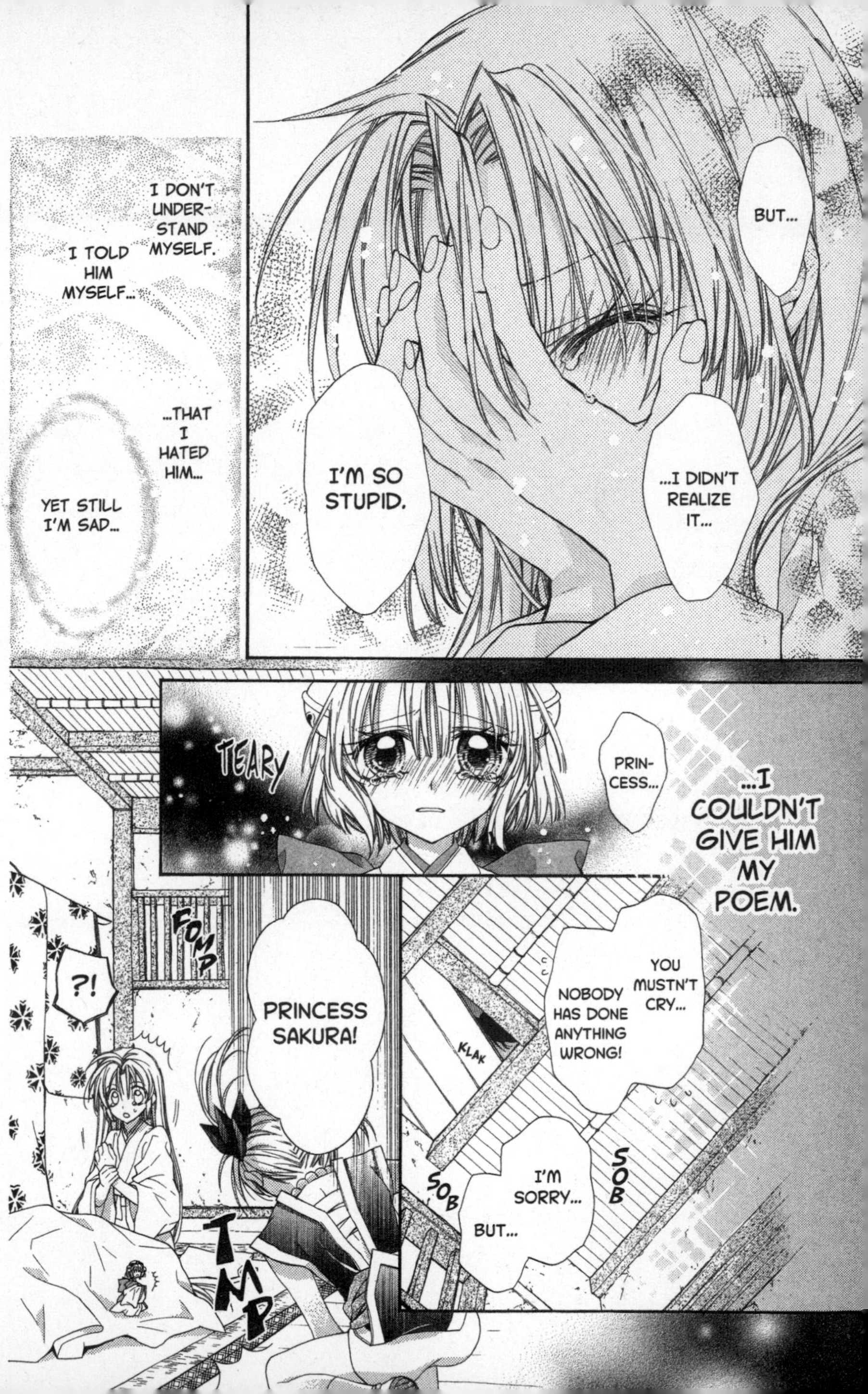
BUT...
...I DIDN'T REALIZE IT...
I'M SO STUPID.
I DON'T UNDER-STAND MYSELF.
I TOLD HIM MYSELF...
...THAT I HATED HIM...
YET STILL I'M SAD...
...I COULDN'T GIVE HIM MY POEM.
PRIN-CESS...
TEARY
YOU MUSTN'T CRY...
NOBODY HAS DONE ANYTHING WRONG!
KLAK
SOB
I'M SORRY...
BUT...
SOB
FOMP
PRINCESS SAKURA!
?!
TMP

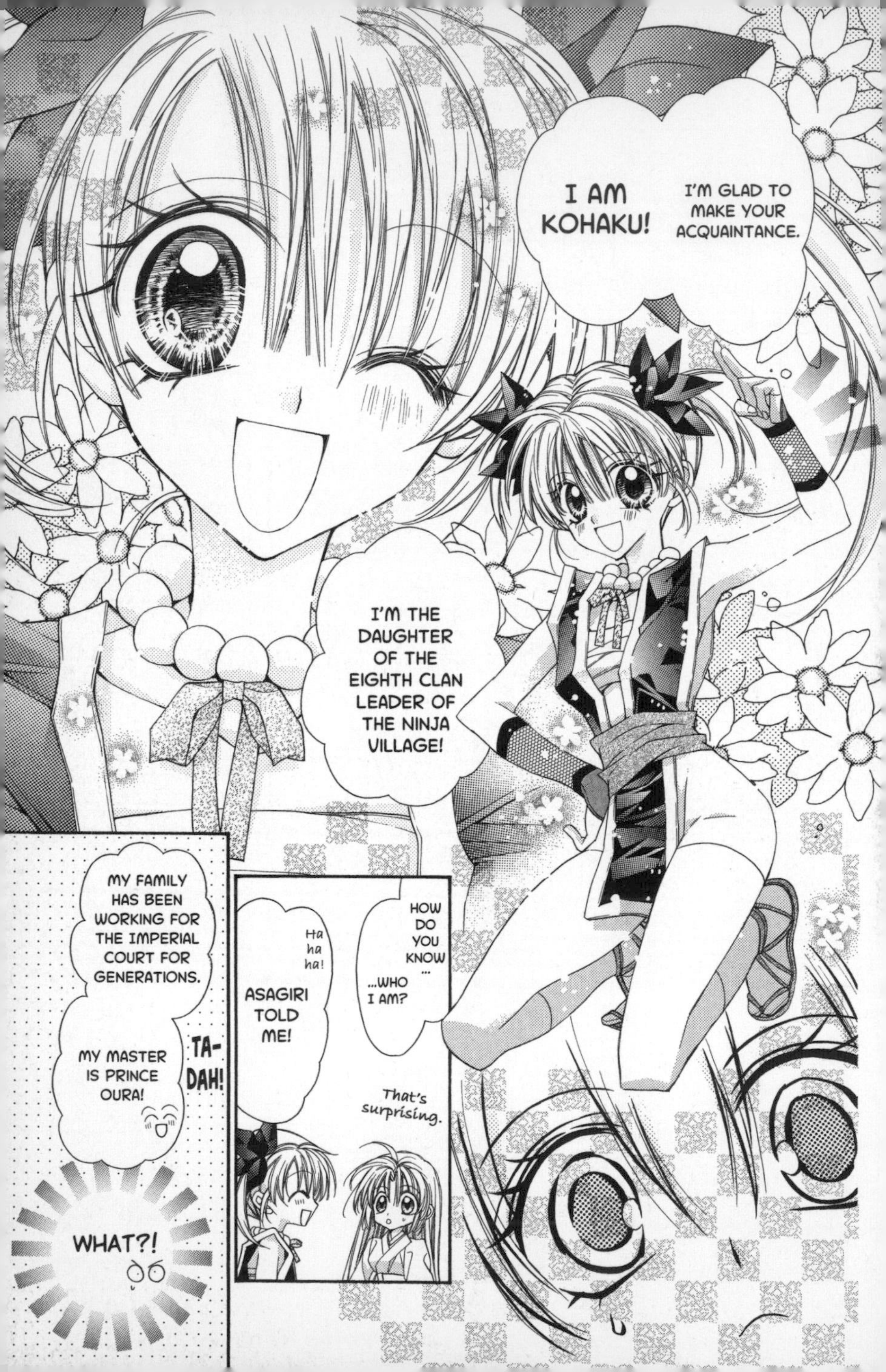
I AM KOHAKU!
I'M GLAD TO MAKE YOUR ACQUAINTANCE.
I'M THE DAUGHTER OF THE EIGHTH CLAN LEADER OF THE NINJA VILLAGE!
HOW DO YOU KNOW ... ...WHO I AM?
Ha ha ha!
ASAGIRI TOLD ME!
That's surprising.
MY FAMILY HAS BEEN WORKING FOR THE IMPERIAL COURT FOR GENERATIONS.
MY MASTER IS PRINCE OURA!
TA-DAH!
WHAT?!

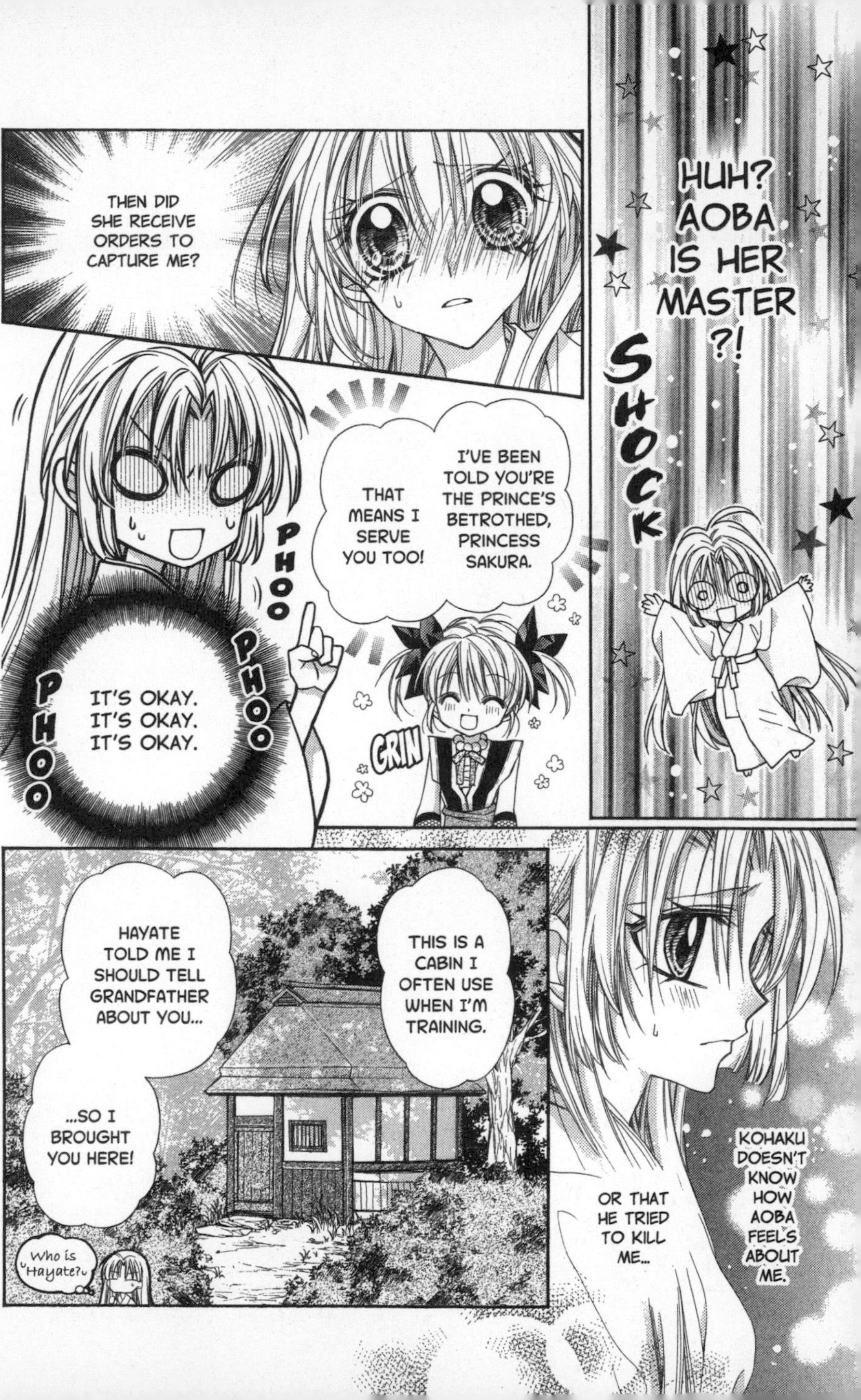
HUH? AOBA IS HER MASTER?!
SHOCK
THEN DID SHE RECEIVE ORDERS TO CAPTURE ME?
I'VE BEEN TOLD YOU'RE THE PRINCE'S BETROTHED, PRINCESS SAKURA.
THAT MEANS I SERVE YOU TOO!
GRIN
PHOO
PHOO
PHOO
IT'S OKAY. IT'S OKAY. IT'S OKAY.
KOHAKU DOESN'T KNOW HOW AOBA FEELS ABOUT ME.
OR THAT HE TRIED TO KILL ME...
THIS IS A CABIN I OFTEN USE WHEN I'M TRAINING.
HAYATE TOLD ME I SHOULD TELL GRANDFATHER ABOUT YOU...
...SO I BROUGHT YOU HERE!
Who is "Hayate?"

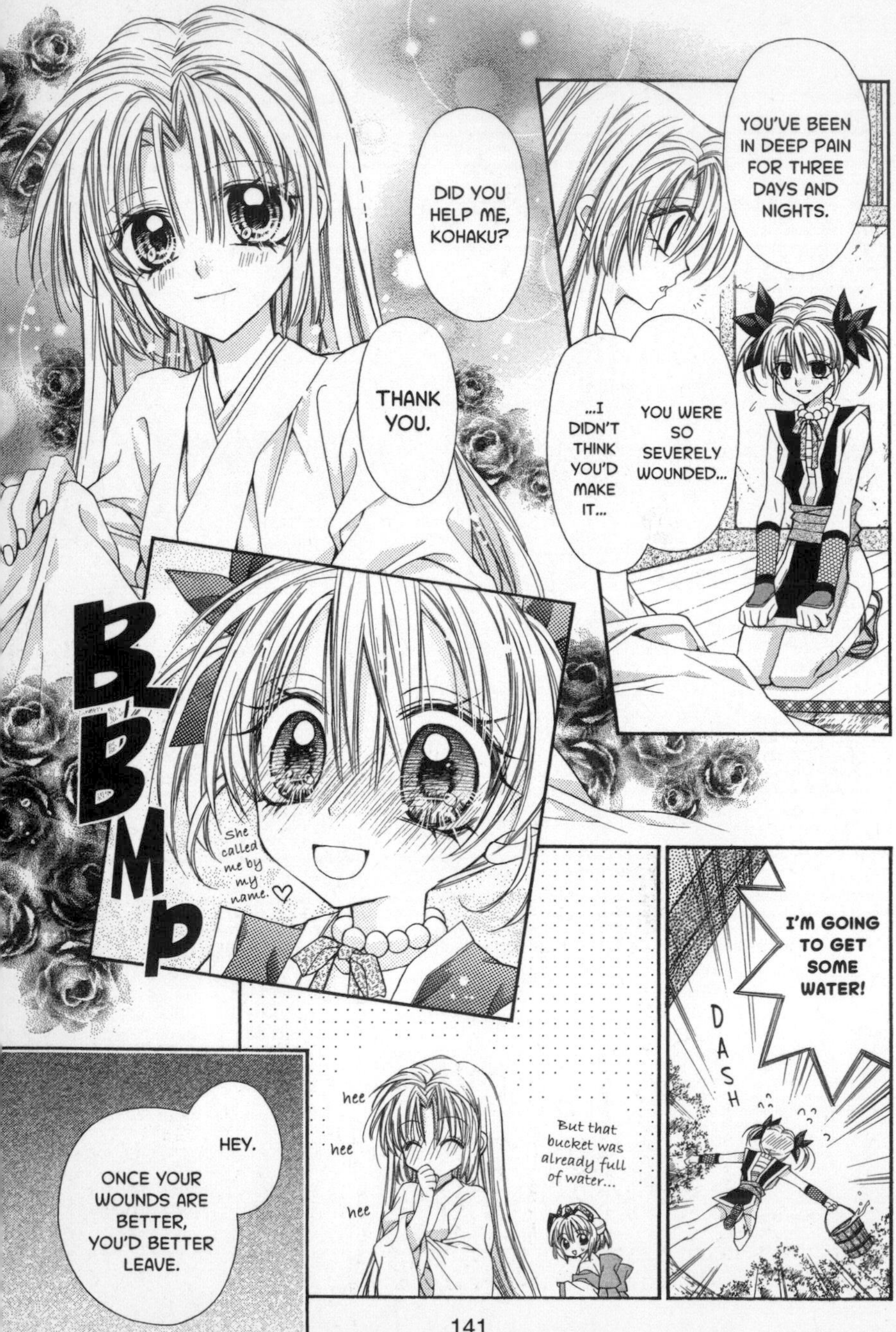
YOU'VE BEEN IN DEEP PAIN FOR THREE DAYS AND NIGHTS.
YOU WERE SO SEVERELY WOUNDED...
...I DIDN'T THINK YOU'D MAKE IT...
DID YOU HELP ME, KOHAKU?
THANK YOU.
BBMP
She called me by my name. ♡
I'M GOING TO GET SOME WATER!
DASH
hee
hee
hee
But that bucket was already full of water...
HEY.
ONCE YOUR WOUNDS ARE BETTER, YOU'D BETTER LEAVE.

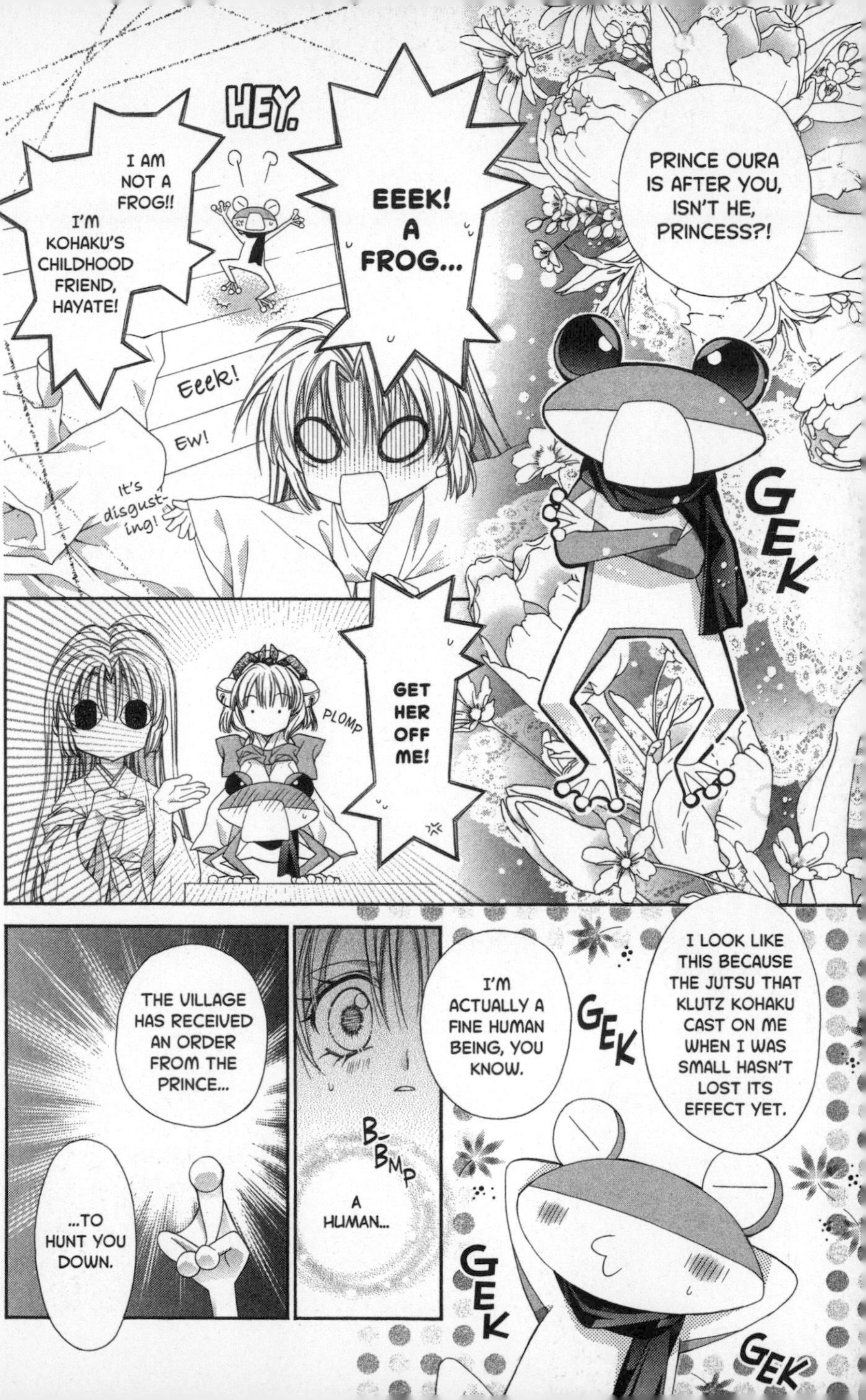
PRINCE OURA IS AFTER YOU, ISN'T HE, PRINCESS?!
GEK
HEY.
EEEK! A FROG...
I AM NOT A FROG!! I'M KOHAKU'S CHILDHOOD FRIEND, HAYATE!
Eeek!
Ew!
It's disgust-ing!
GET HER OFF ME!
PLOMP
I LOOK LIKE THIS BECAUSE THE JUTSU THAT KLUTZ KOHAKU CAST ON ME WHEN I WAS SMALL HASN'T LOST ITS EFFECT YET.
GEK
I'M ACTUALLY A FINE HUMAN BEING, YOU KNOW.
GEK
GEK
B-BMP
A HUMAN...
THE VILLAGE HAS RECEIVED AN ORDER FROM THE PRINCE...
...TO HUNT YOU DOWN.

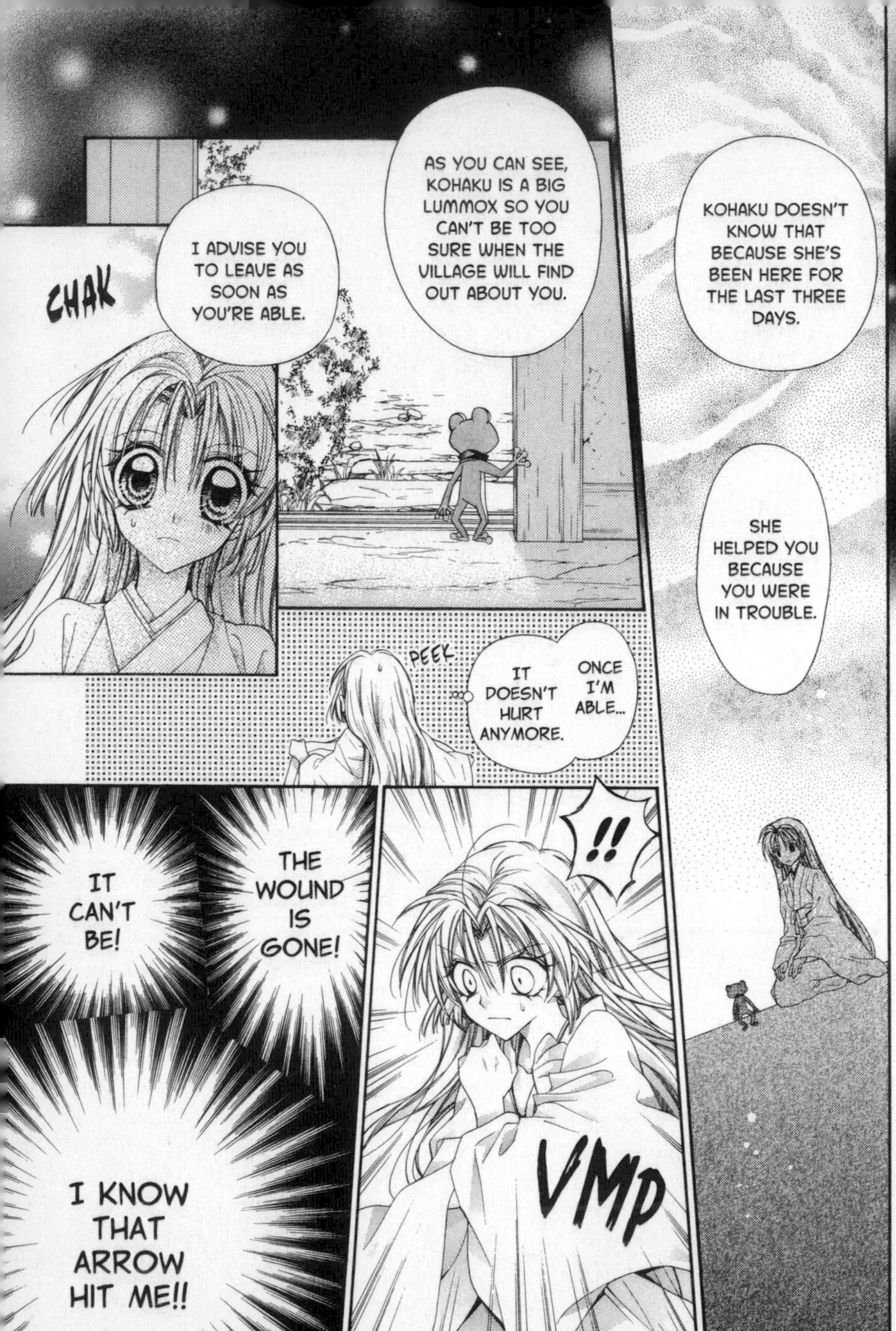
KOHAKU DOESN'T KNOW THAT BECAUSE SHE'S BEEN HERE FOR THE LAST THREE DAYS.
SHE HELPED YOU BECAUSE YOU WERE IN TROUBLE.
AS YOU CAN SEE, KOHAKU IS A BIG LUMMOX SO YOU CAN'T BE TOO SURE WHEN THE VILLAGE WILL FIND OUT ABOUT YOU.
I ADVISE YOU TO LEAVE AS SOON AS YOU'RE ABLE.
CHAK
PEEK
ONCE I'M ABLE...
IT DOESN'T HURT ANYMORE.
!!
VMP
THE WOUND IS GONE!
IT CAN'T BE!
I KNOW THAT ARROW HIT ME!!

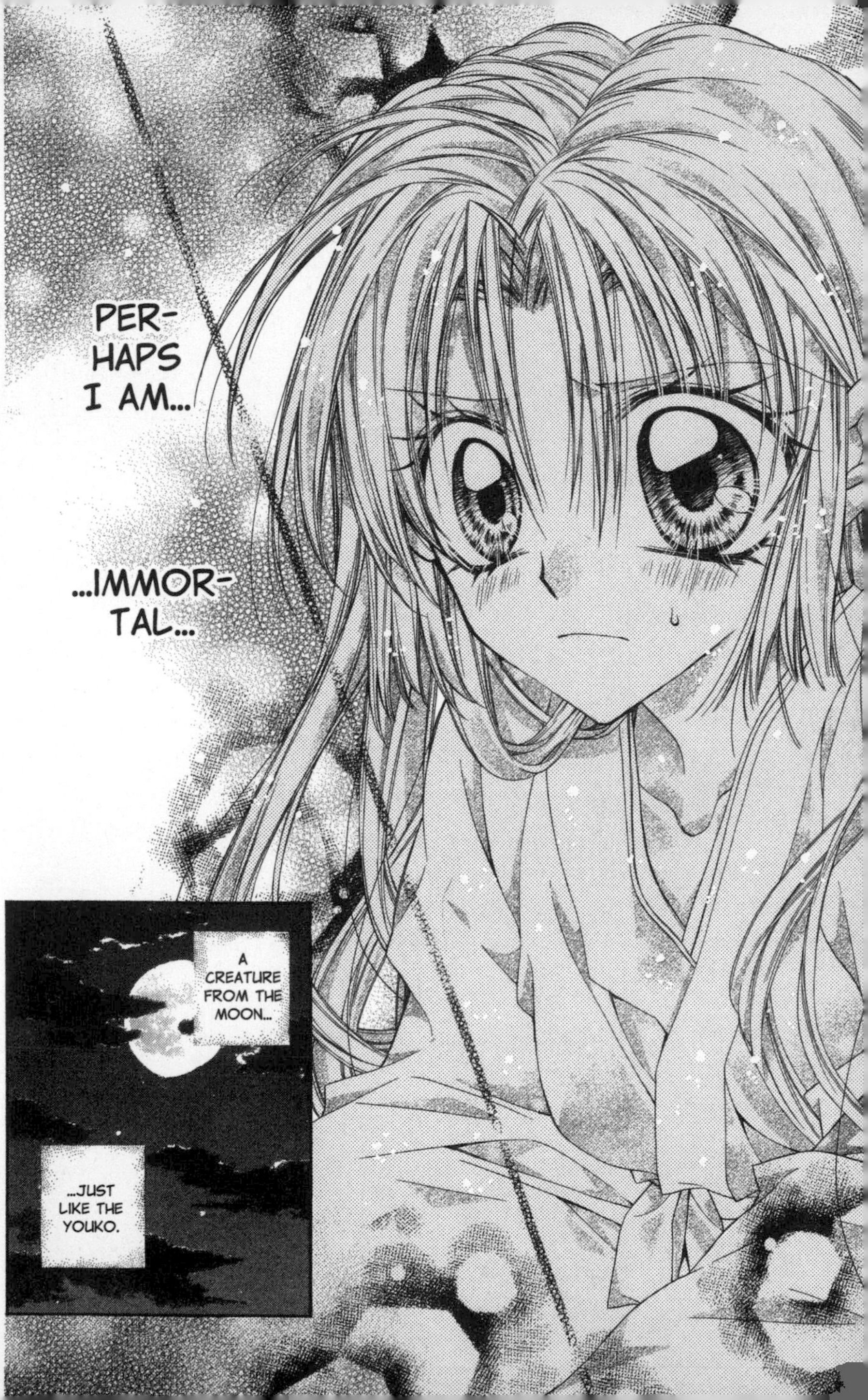
PER-HAPS I AM...
...IMMOR-TAL...
A CREATURE FROM THE MOON...
...JUST LIKE THE YOUKO.

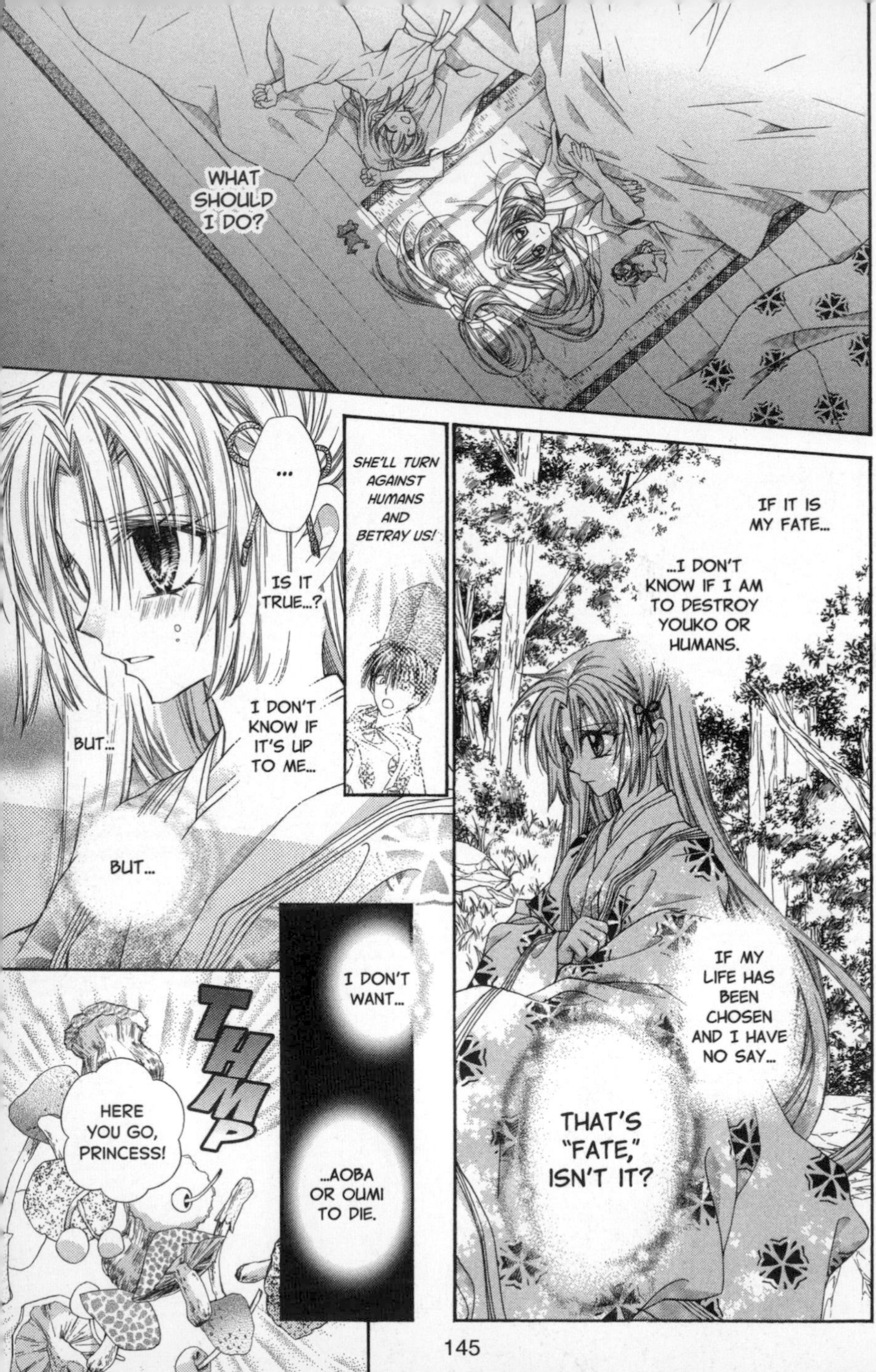
WHAT SHOULD I DO?
IF IT IS MY FATE...
...I DON'T KNOW IF I AM TO DESTROY YOUKO OR HUMANS.
IF MY LIFE HAS BEEN CHOSEN AND I HAVE NO SAY...
THAT'S "FATE," ISN'T IT?
SHE'LL TURN AGAINST HUMANS AND BETRAY US!
...
IS IT TRUE...?
I DON'T KNOW IF IT'S UP TO ME...
BUT...
BUT...
I DON'T WANT...
...AOBA OR OUMI TO DIE.
THMP
HERE YOU GO, PRINCESS!

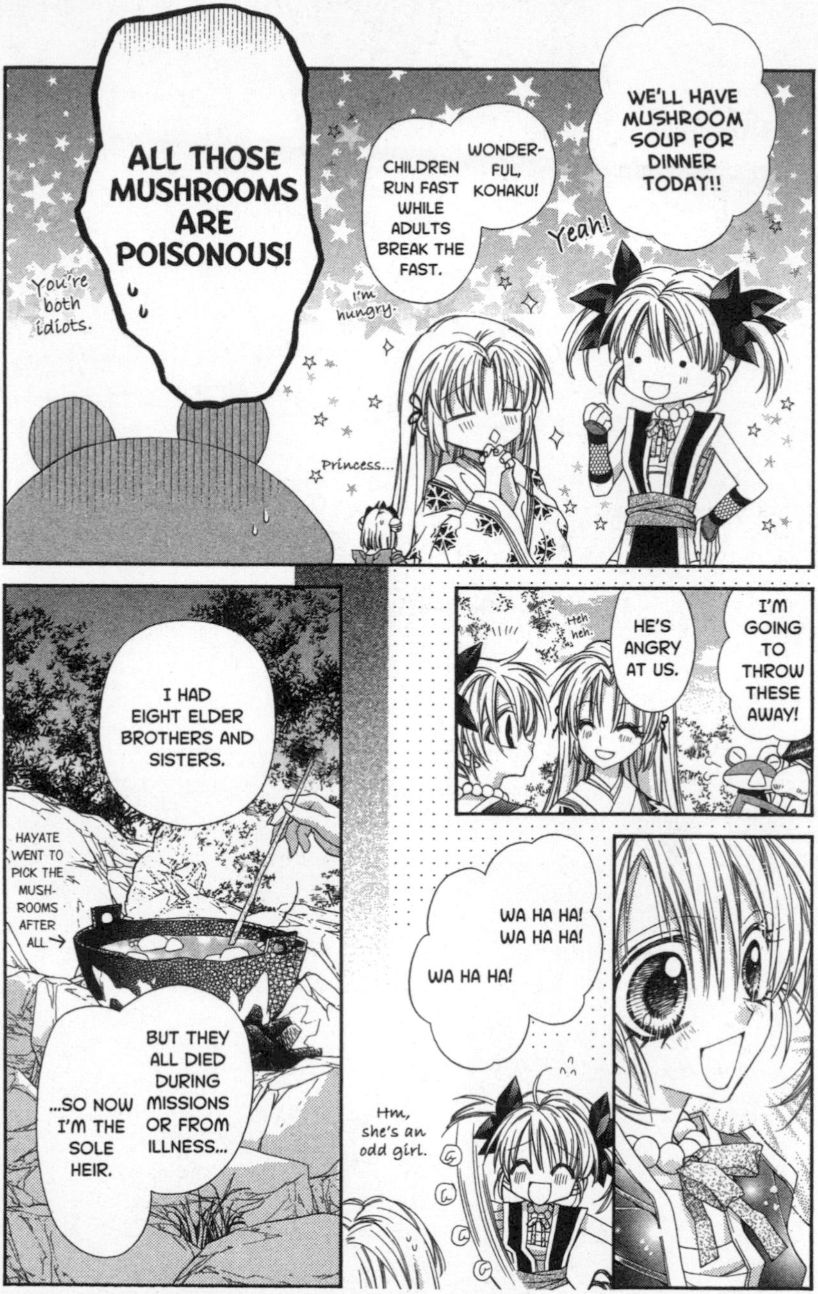
WE'LL HAVE MUSHROOM SOUP FOR DINNER TODAY!!
Yeah!
WONDERFUL, KOHAKU!
CHILDREN RUN FAST WHILE ADULTS BREAK THE FAST.
I'm hungry.
Princess...
ALL THOSE MUSHROOMS ARE POISONOUS!
You're both idiots.
I'M GOING TO THROW THESE AWAY!
HE'S ANGRY AT US.
Heh heh.
WA HA HA! WA HA HA!
WA HA HA!
Hm, she's an odd girl.
I HAD EIGHT ELDER BROTHERS AND SISTERS.
HAYATE WENT TO PICK THE MUSHROOMS AFTER ALL
BUT THEY ALL DIED DURING MISSIONS OR FROM ILLNESS...
...SO NOW I'M THE SOLE HEIR.

# AOBA

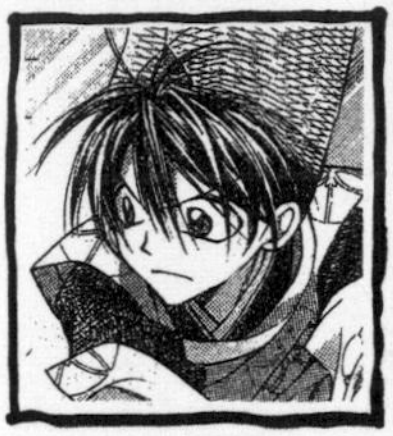

Prince Oura. Age 17.
Aoba is his childhood name.
(Sakura continues to call him Aoba because of the way they met.)

I haven't done anything unique with his character design.
He can easily be distinguished from the characters in my other series by his clothes, and also because I like black hair...
(Aoba actually has long hair.)

He is a person of great pride, and he has wanted to become the Togu because he cares deeply for his country.

He is awkward in that he doesn't know how to hold himself back.
He has mixed feelings for Sakura, but he is unable to be honest about them.

Of course (?) he doesn't like the Togu, Fujimurasaki.
He'll probably continue to dislike him.

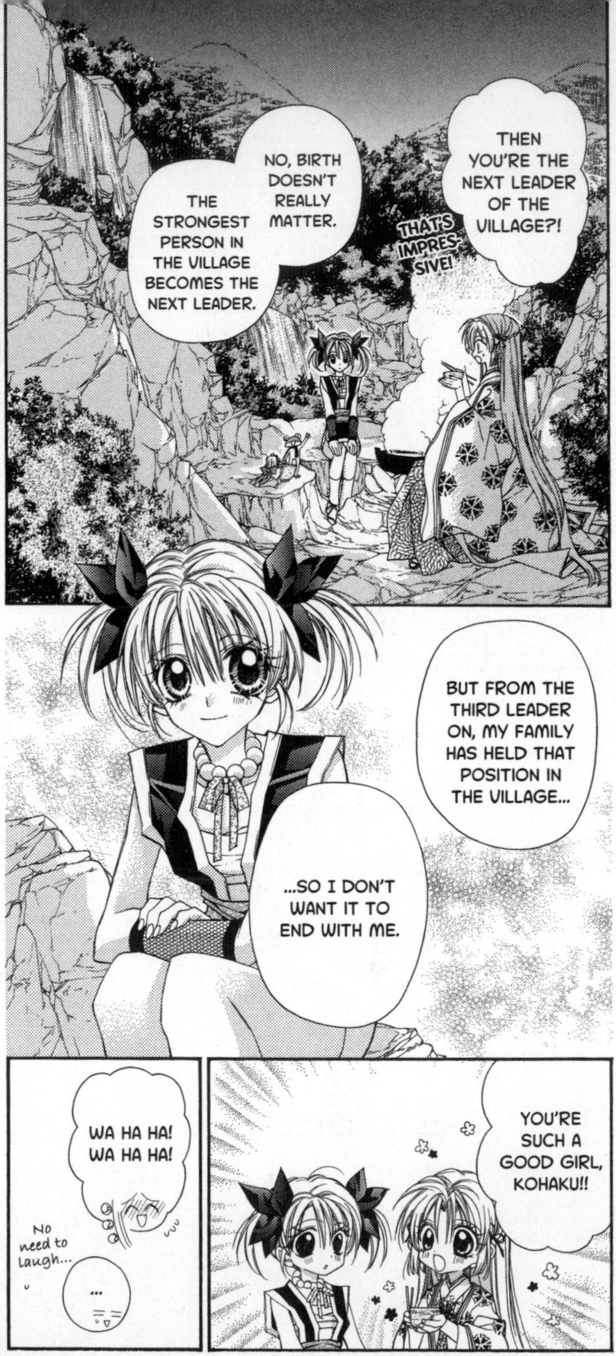
THEN YOU'RE THE NEXT LEADER OF THE VILLAGE?!
THAT'S IMPRES-SIVE!
NO, BIRTH DOESN'T REALLY MATTER.
THE STRONGEST PERSON IN THE VILLAGE BECOMES THE NEXT LEADER.
BUT FROM THE THIRD LEADER ON, MY FAMILY HAS HELD THAT POSITION IN THE VILLAGE...
...SO I DON'T WANT IT TO END WITH ME.
YOU'RE SUCH A GOOD GIRL, KOHAKU!!
WA HA HA! WA HA HA!
No need to laugh...
...

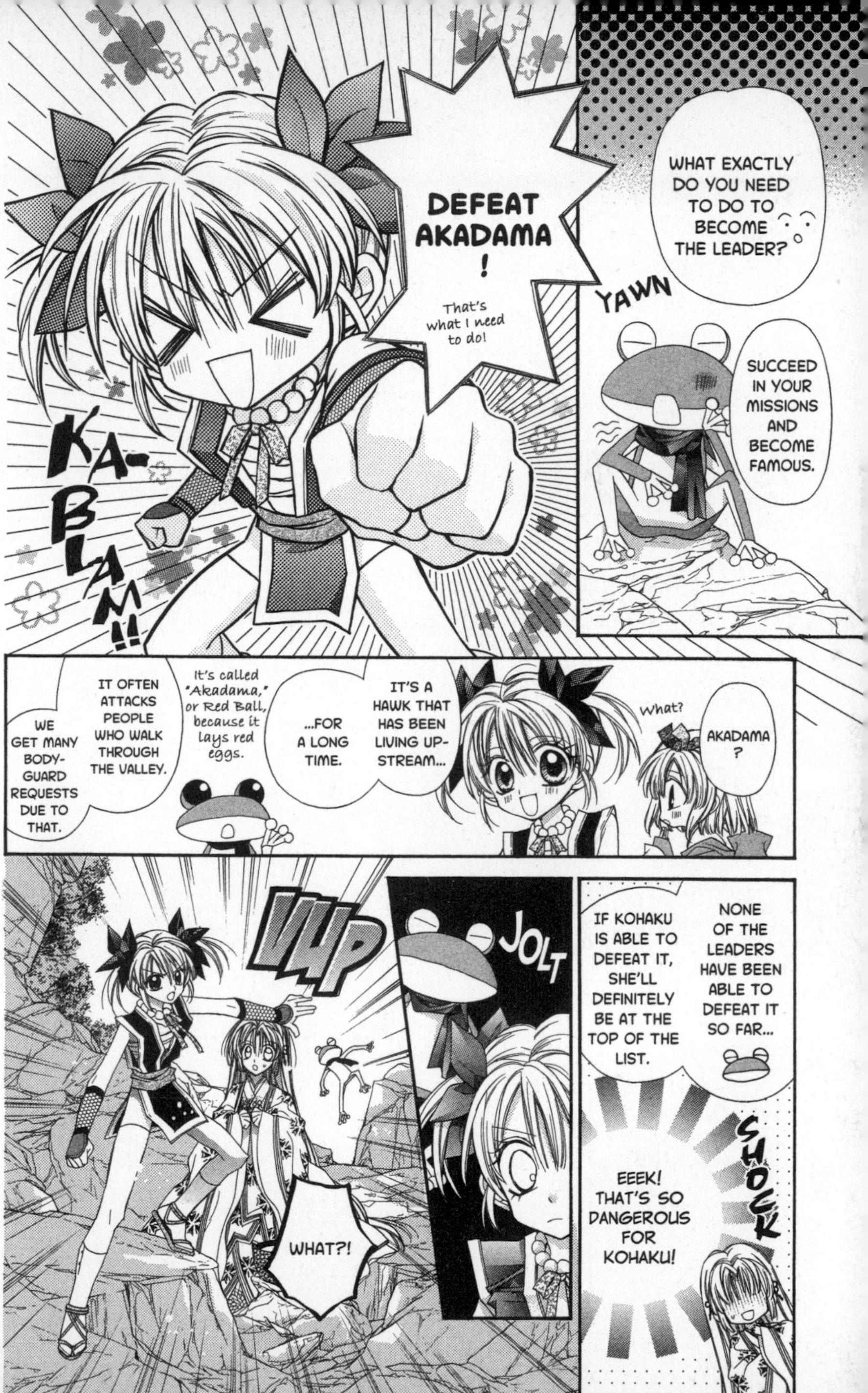
WHAT EXACTLY DO YOU NEED TO DO TO BECOME THE LEADER?
YAWN
SUCCEED IN YOUR MISSIONS AND BECOME FAMOUS.
DEFEAT AKADAMA!
That's what I need to do!
KA-BLAM!!
AKADAMA?
What?
IT'S A HAWK THAT HAS BEEN LIVING UP-STREAM...
...FOR A LONG TIME.
It's called "Akadama," or Red Ball, because it lays red eggs.
IT OFTEN ATTACKS PEOPLE WHO WALK THROUGH THE VALLEY.
WE GET MANY BODY-GUARD REQUESTS DUE TO THAT.
NONE OF THE LEADERS HAVE BEEN ABLE TO DEFEAT IT SO FAR...
IF KOHAKU IS ABLE TO DEFEAT IT, SHE'LL DEFINITELY BE AT THE TOP OF THE LIST.
SHOCK
EEEK! THAT'S SO DANGEROUS FOR KOHAKU!
JOLT
VUP
WHAT?!

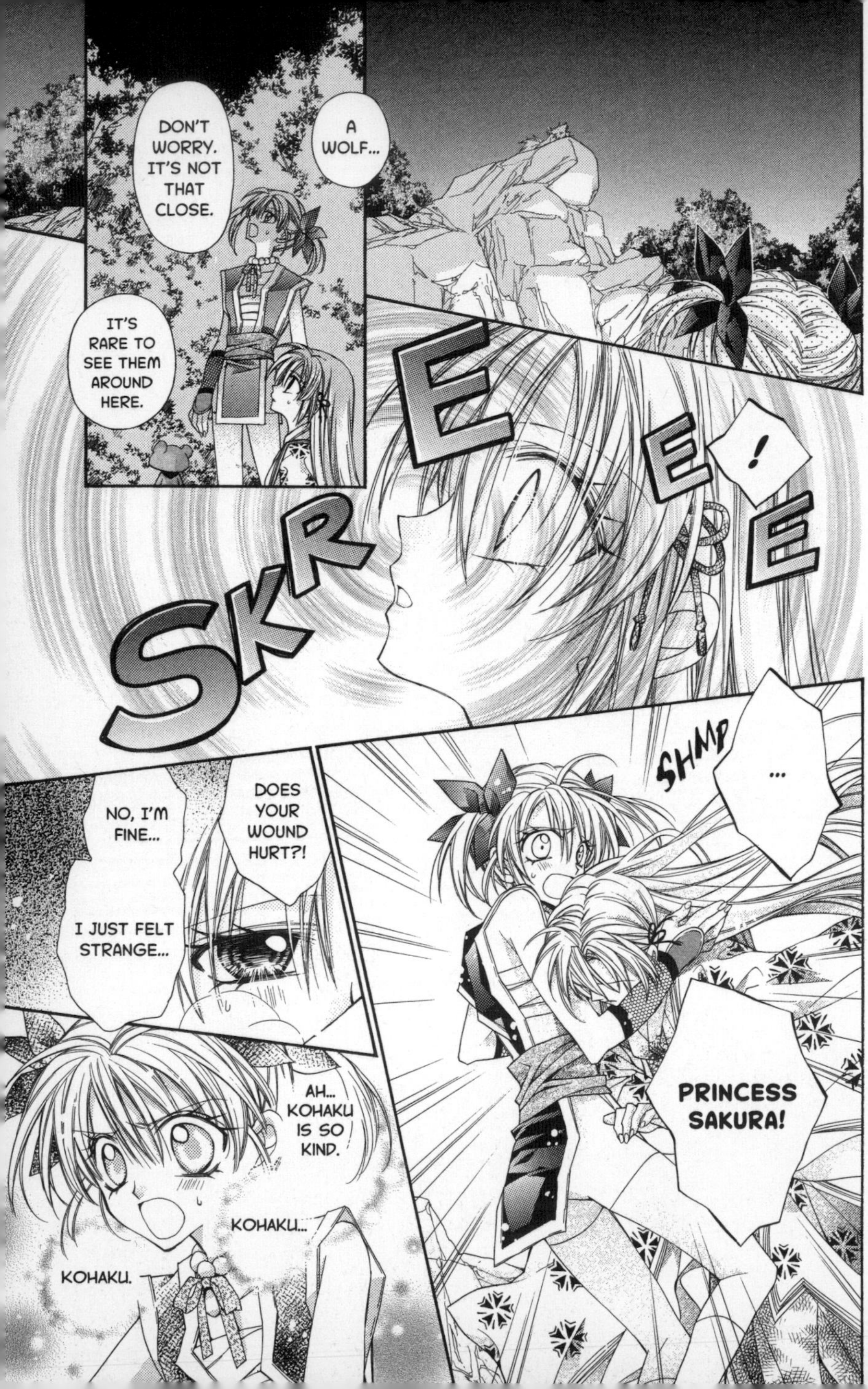
A WOLF...
DON'T WORRY. IT'S NOT THAT CLOSE.
IT'S RARE TO SEE THEM AROUND HERE.
SKREEEE
!
SHMP
...
PRINCESS SAKURA!
DOES YOUR WOUND HURT?!
NO, I'M FINE...
I JUST FELT STRANGE...
AH... KOHAKU IS SO KIND.
KOHAKU...
KOHAKU.

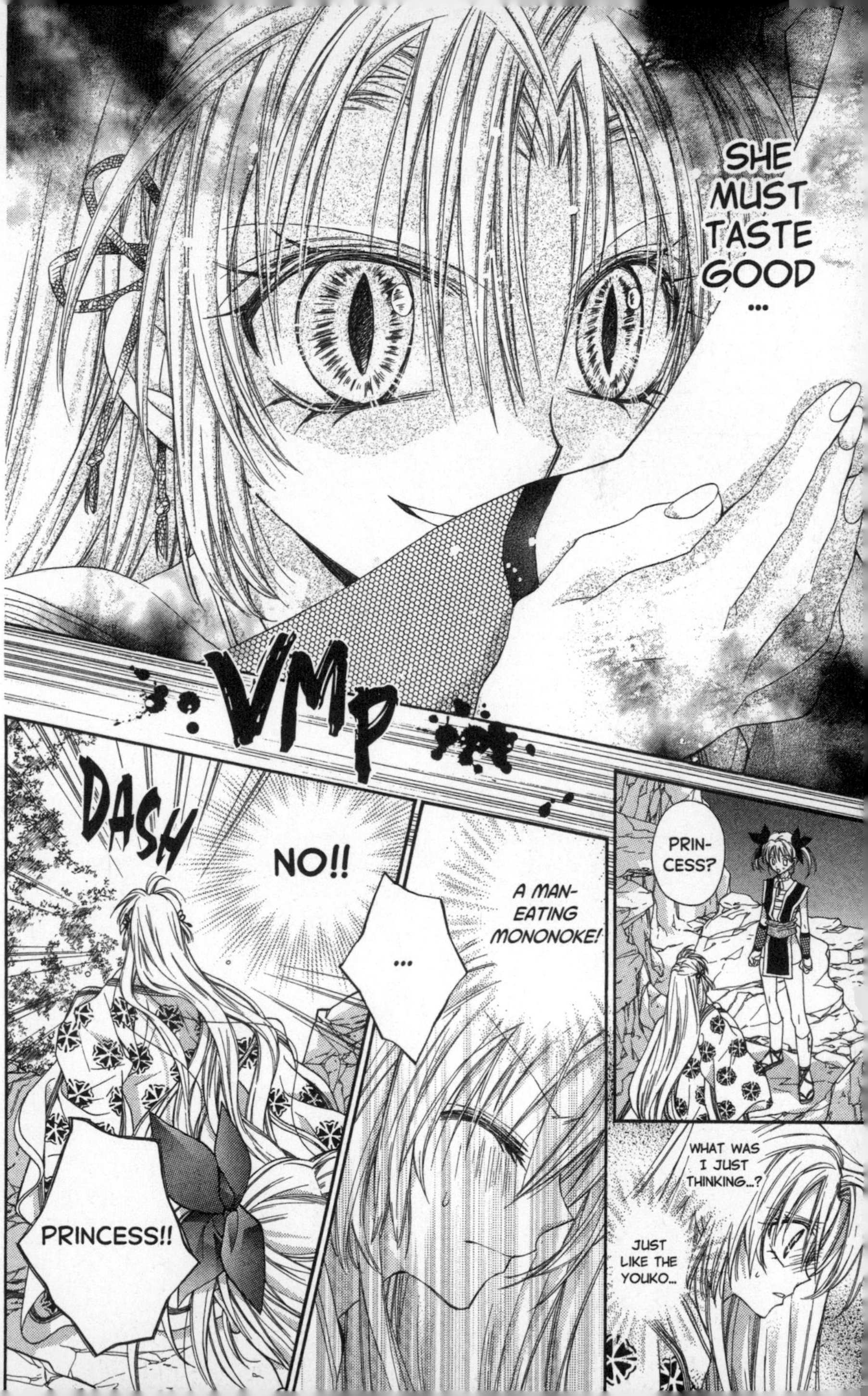
SHE MUST TASTE GOOD ...
VMP
PRIN-CESS?
WHAT WAS I JUST THINKING...?
JUST LIKE THE YOUKO...
A MAN-EATING MONONOKE!
...
DASH
NO!!
PRINCESS!!

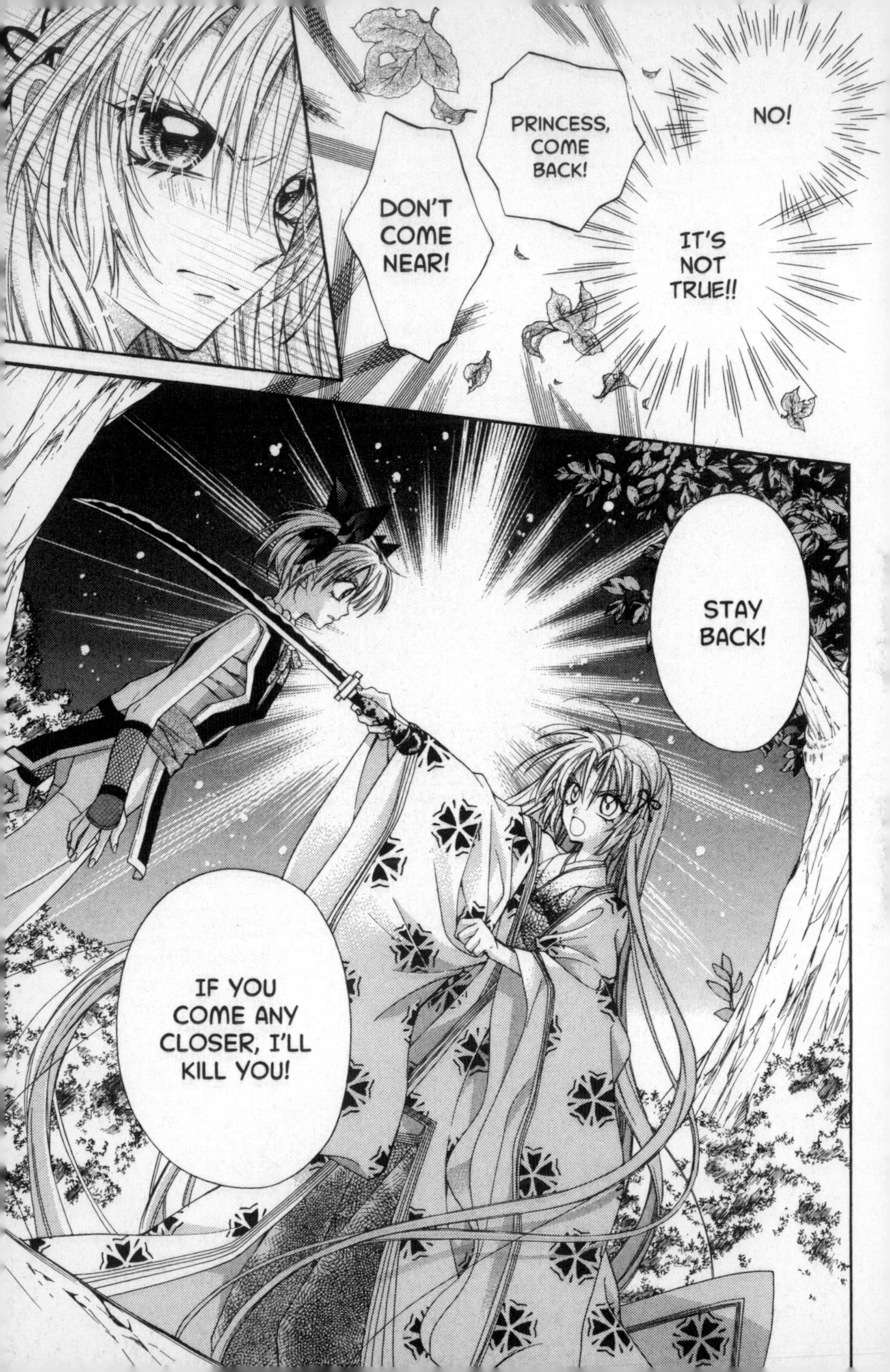
NO!
IT'S NOT TRUE!!
PRINCESS, COME BACK!
DON'T COME NEAR!
STAY BACK!
IF YOU COME ANY CLOSER, I'LL KILL YOU!

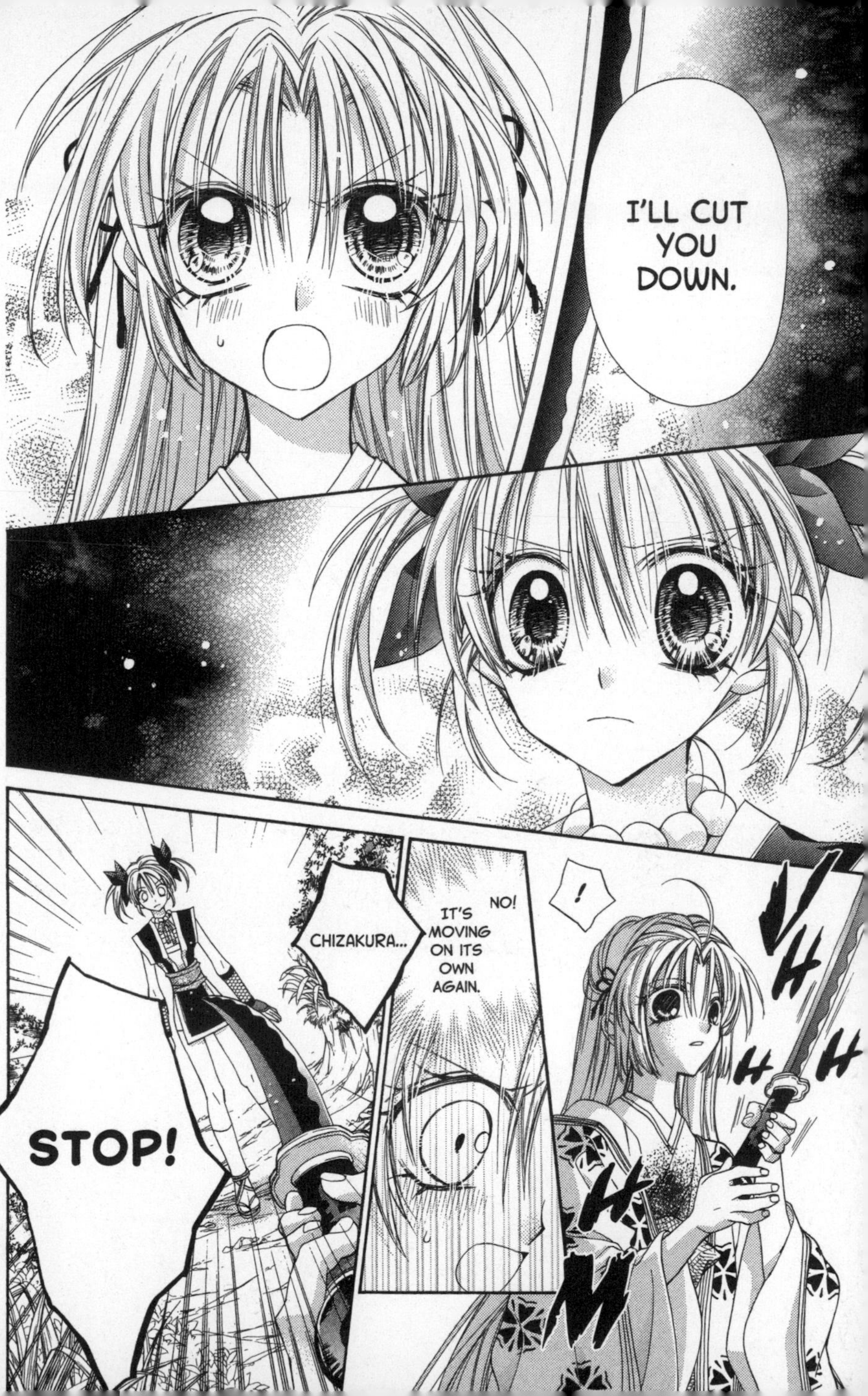
I'LL CUT YOU DOWN.
!
NO!
IT'S MOVING ON ITS OWN AGAIN.
CHIZAKURA...
STOP!

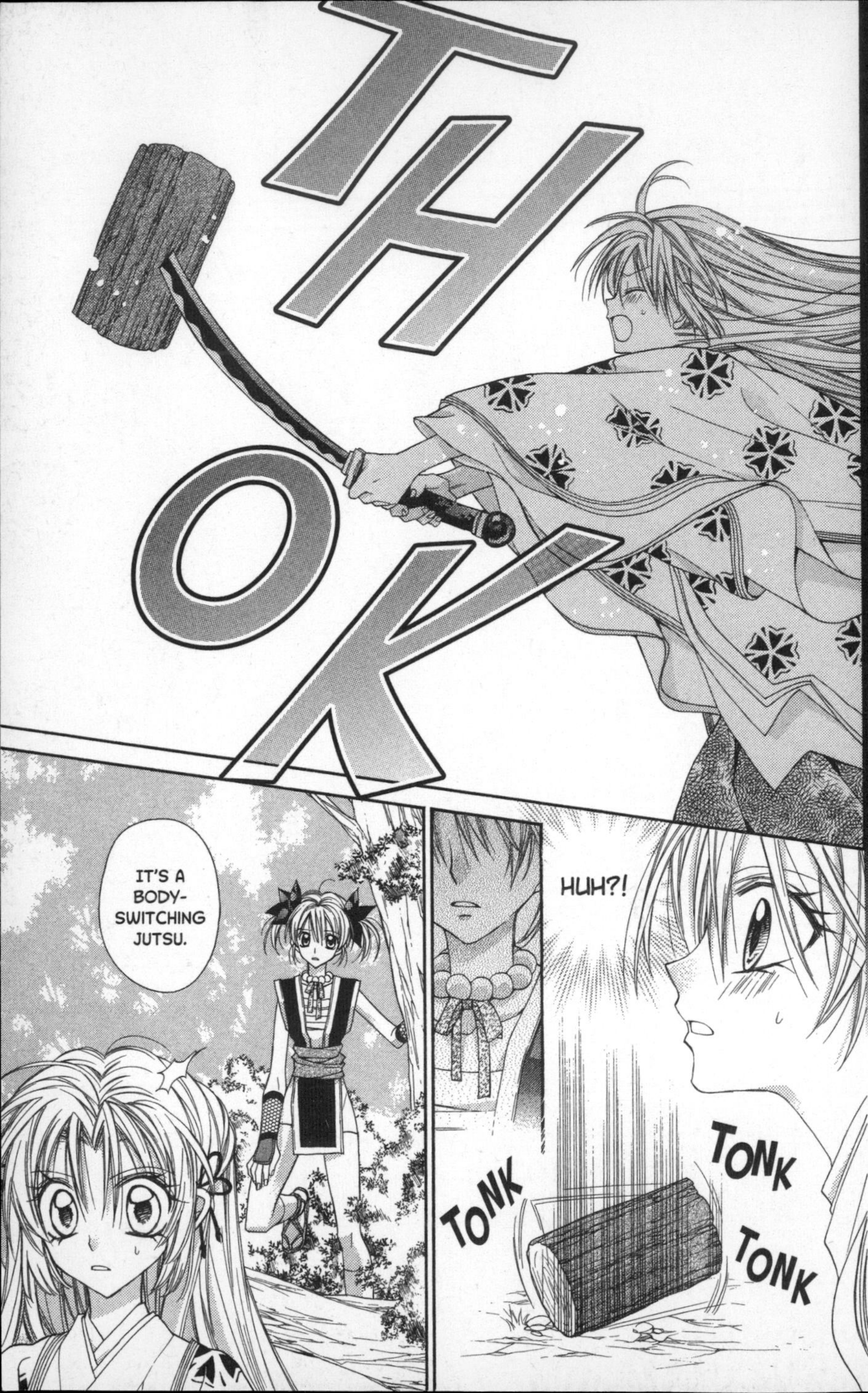
THOK
HUH?!
TONK
TONK
TONK
TONK
IT'S A BODY-SWITCHING JUTSU.

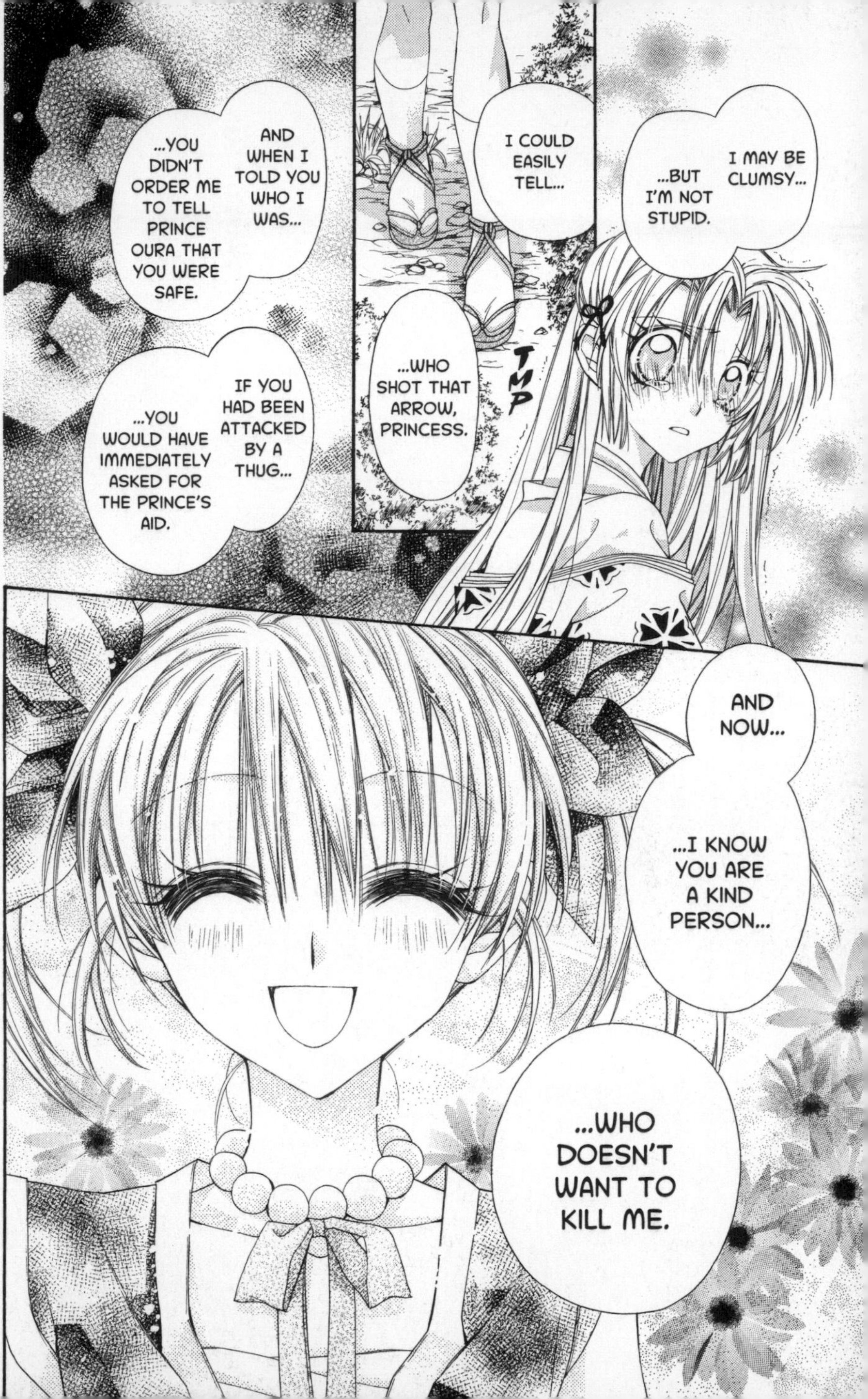
I MAY BE CLUMSY...
...BUT I'M NOT STUPID.
I COULD EASILY TELL...
...WHO SHOT THAT ARROW, PRINCESS.
TMP
AND WHEN I TOLD YOU WHO I WAS...
...YOU DIDN'T ORDER ME TO TELL PRINCE OURA THAT YOU WERE SAFE.
IF YOU HAD BEEN ATTACKED BY A THUG...
...YOU WOULD HAVE IMMEDIATELY ASKED FOR THE PRINCE'S AID.
AND NOW...
...I KNOW YOU ARE A KIND PERSON...
...WHO DOESN'T WANT TO KILL ME.

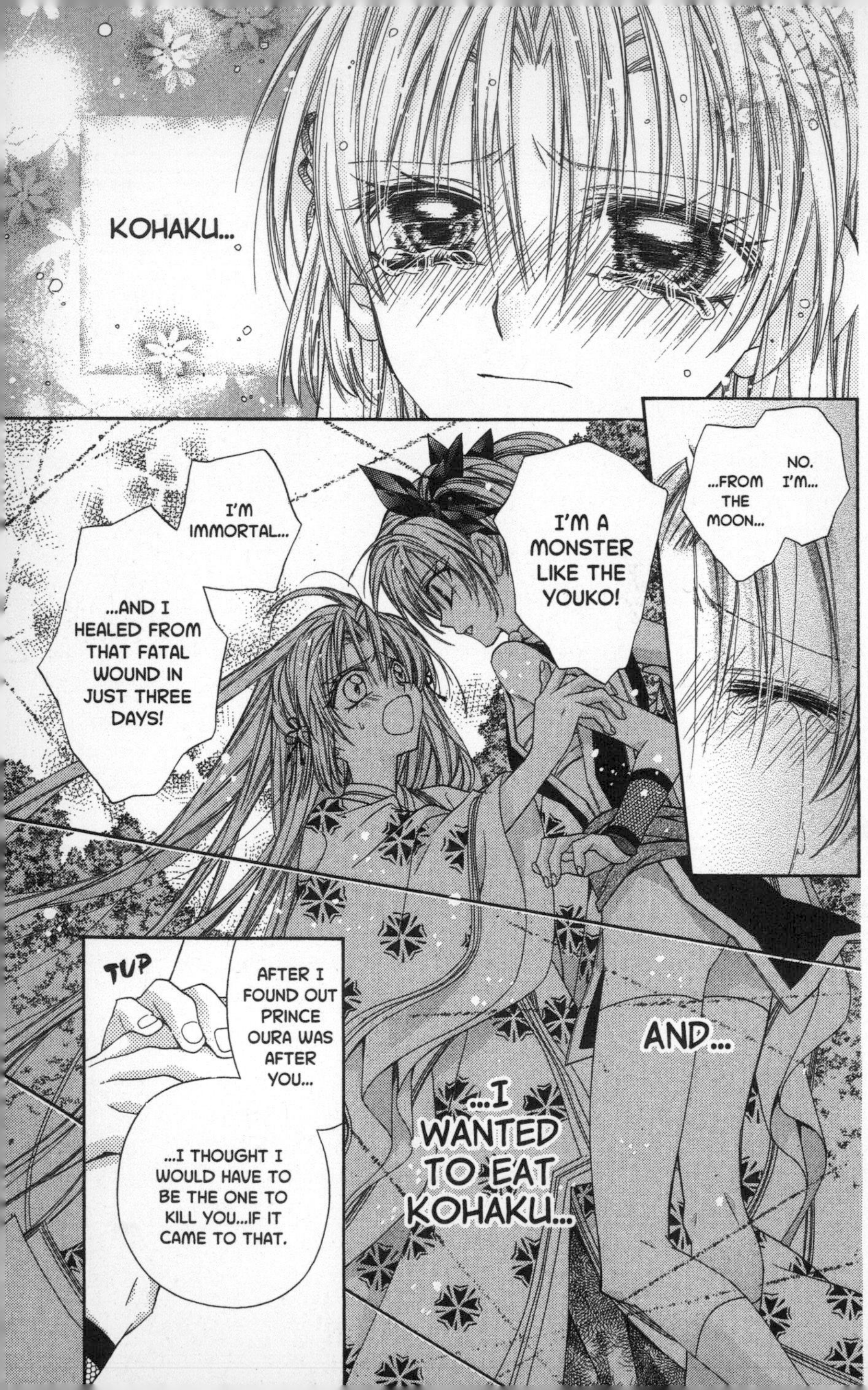
KOHAKU...
NO. I'M...
...FROM THE MOON...
I'M A MONSTER LIKE THE YOUKO!
I'M IMMORTAL...
...AND I HEALED FROM THAT FATAL WOUND IN JUST THREE DAYS!
AND...
...I WANTED TO EAT KOHAKU...
TUP
AFTER I FOUND OUT PRINCE OURA WAS AFTER YOU...
...I THOUGHT I WOULD HAVE TO BE THE ONE TO KILL YOU...IF IT CAME TO THAT.

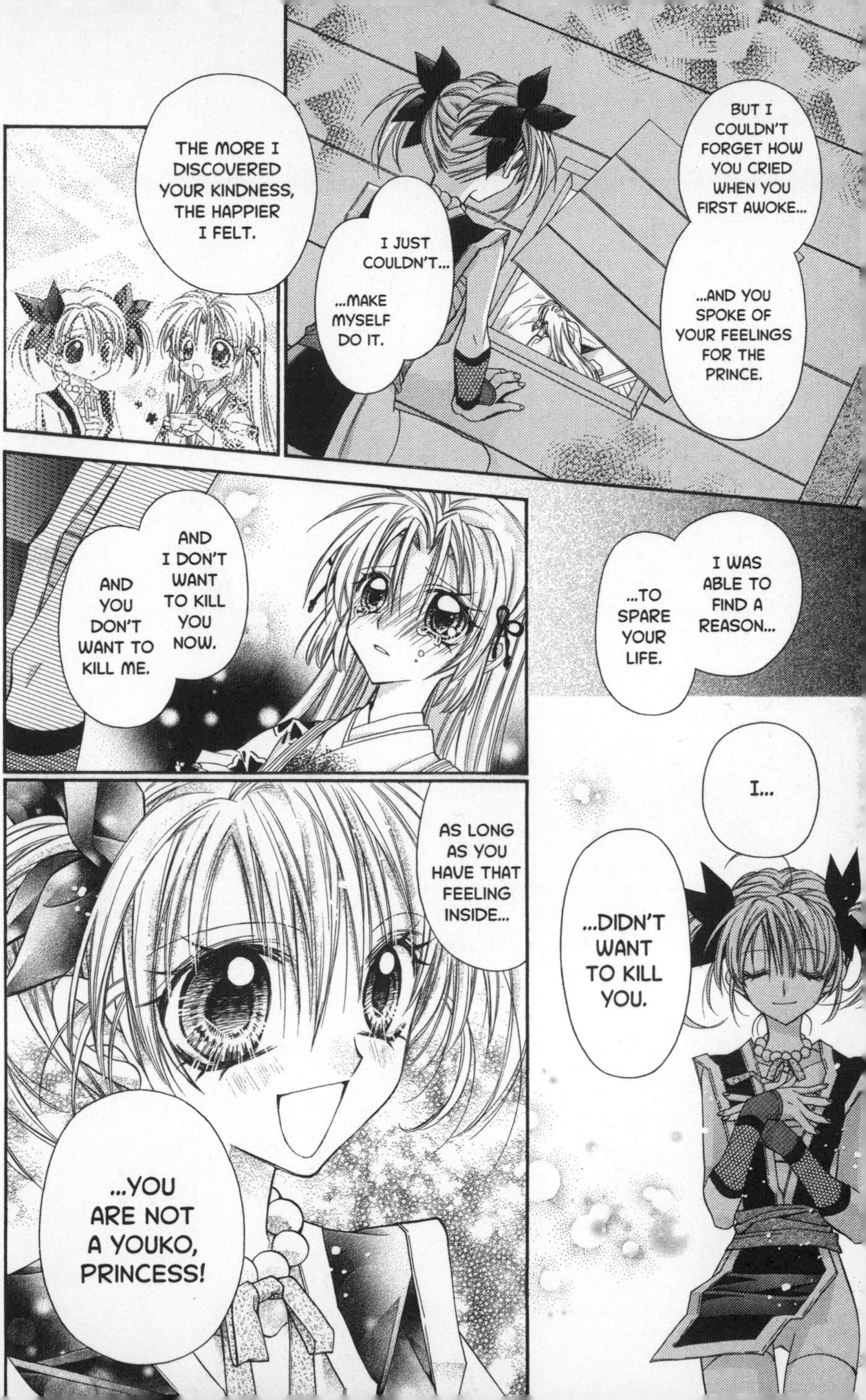
BUT I COULDN'T FORGET HOW YOU CRIED WHEN YOU FIRST AWOKE...
...AND YOU SPOKE OF YOUR FEELINGS FOR THE PRINCE.
I JUST COULDN'T...
...MAKE MYSELF DO IT.
THE MORE I DISCOVERED YOUR KINDNESS, THE HAPPIER I FELT.
I WAS ABLE TO FIND A REASON...
...TO SPARE YOUR LIFE.
AND I DON'T WANT TO KILL YOU NOW.
AND YOU DON'T WANT TO KILL ME.
I...
...DIDN'T WANT TO KILL YOU.
AS LONG AS YOU HAVE THAT FEELING INSIDE...
...YOU ARE NOT A YOUKO, PRINCESS!

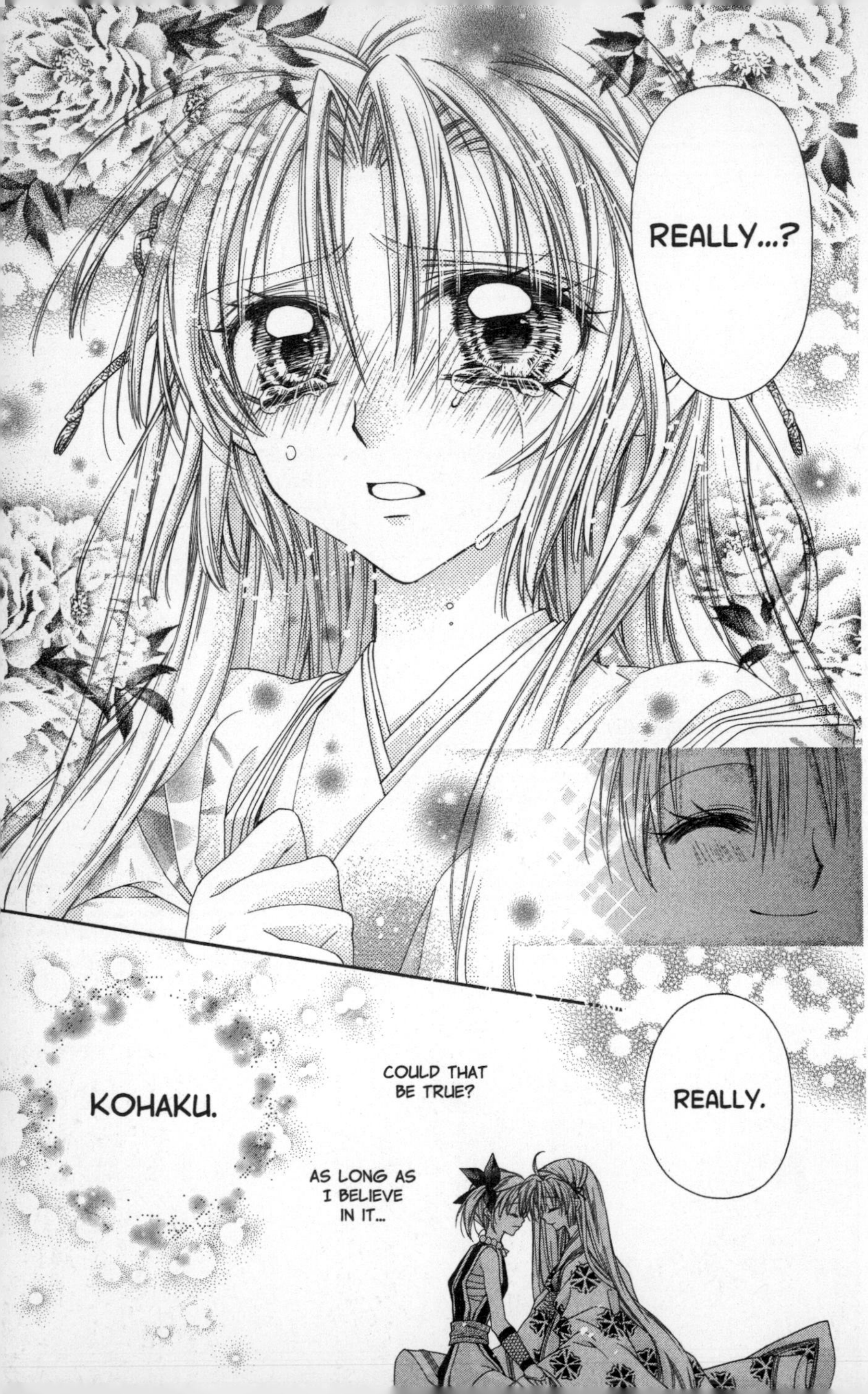
REALLY...?
REALLY.
COULD THAT BE TRUE?
KOHAKU.
AS LONG AS I BELIEVE IN IT...

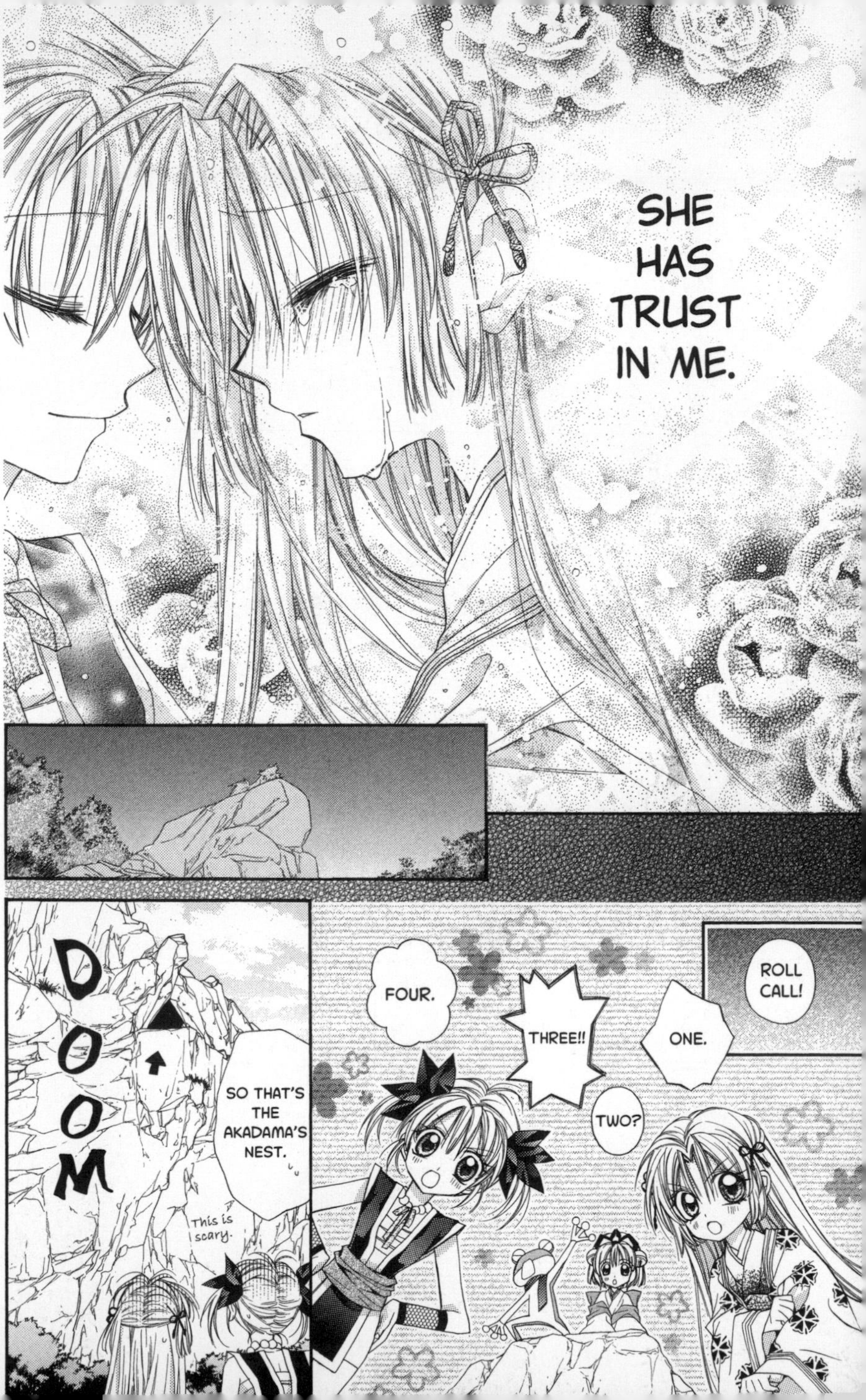
SHE HAS TRUST IN ME.
ROLL CALL!
ONE.
TWO?
THREE!!
FOUR.
DOOM
SO THAT'S THE AKADAMA'S NEST.
This is scary.

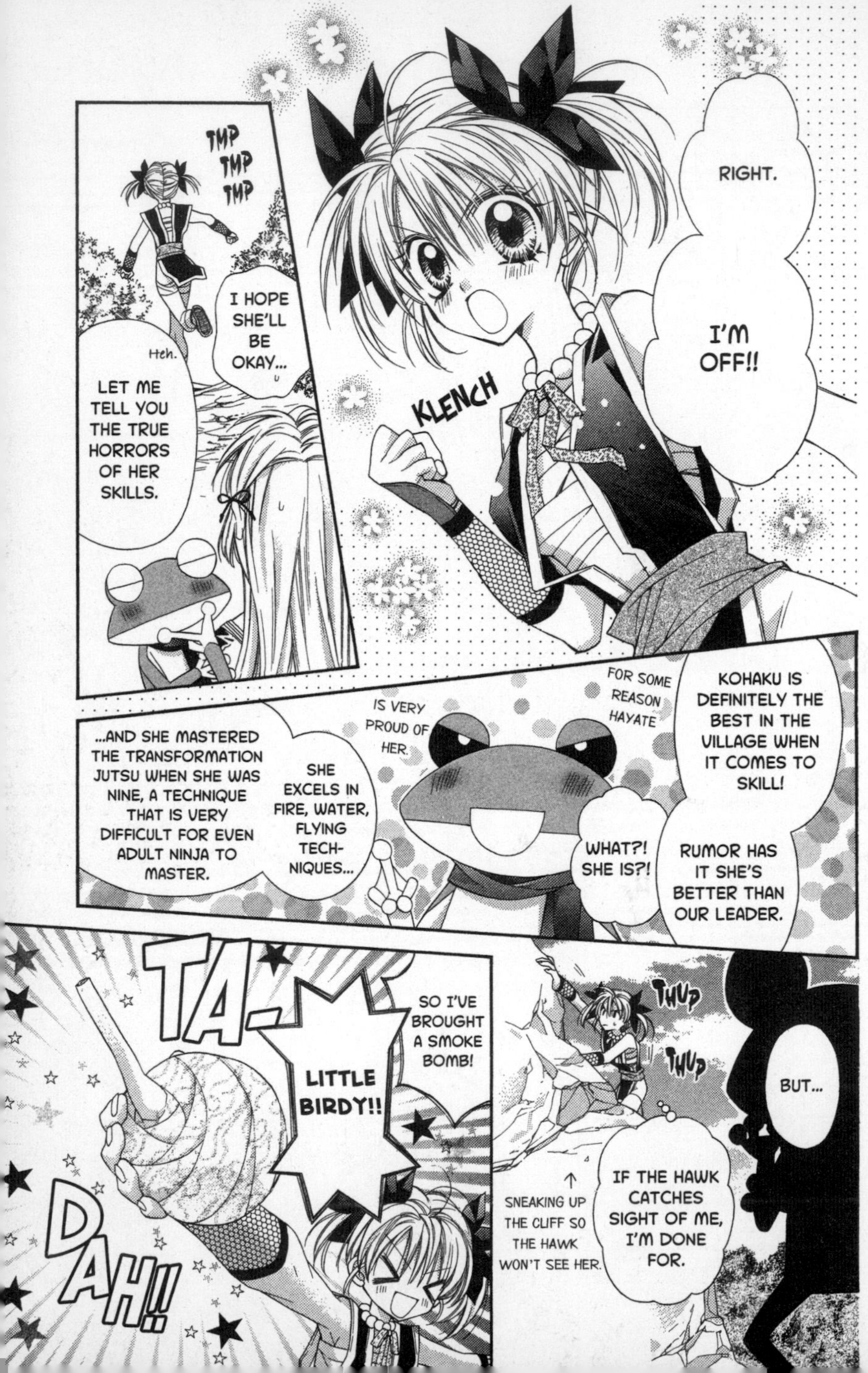
RIGHT.
I'M OFF!!
KLENCH
TMP TMP TMP
I HOPE SHE'LL BE OKAY...
Heh.
LET ME TELL YOU THE TRUE HORRORS OF HER SKILLS.
KOHAKU IS DEFINITELY THE BEST IN THE VILLAGE WHEN IT COMES TO SKILL!
FOR SOME REASON HAYATE IS VERY PROUD OF HER.
RUMOR HAS IT SHE'S BETTER THAN OUR LEADER.
WHAT?! SHE IS?!
SHE EXCELS IN FIRE, WATER, FLYING TECH-NIQUES...
...AND SHE MASTERED THE TRANSFORMATION JUTSU WHEN SHE WAS NINE, A TECHNIQUE THAT IS VERY DIFFICULT FOR EVEN ADULT NINJA TO MASTER.
BUT...
THUP
THUP
IF THE HAWK CATCHES SIGHT OF ME, I'M DONE FOR.
SNEAKING UP THE CLIFF SO THE HAWK WON'T SEE HER.
SO I'VE BROUGHT A SMOKE BOMB!
TA-
DAH!!
LITTLE BIRDY!!

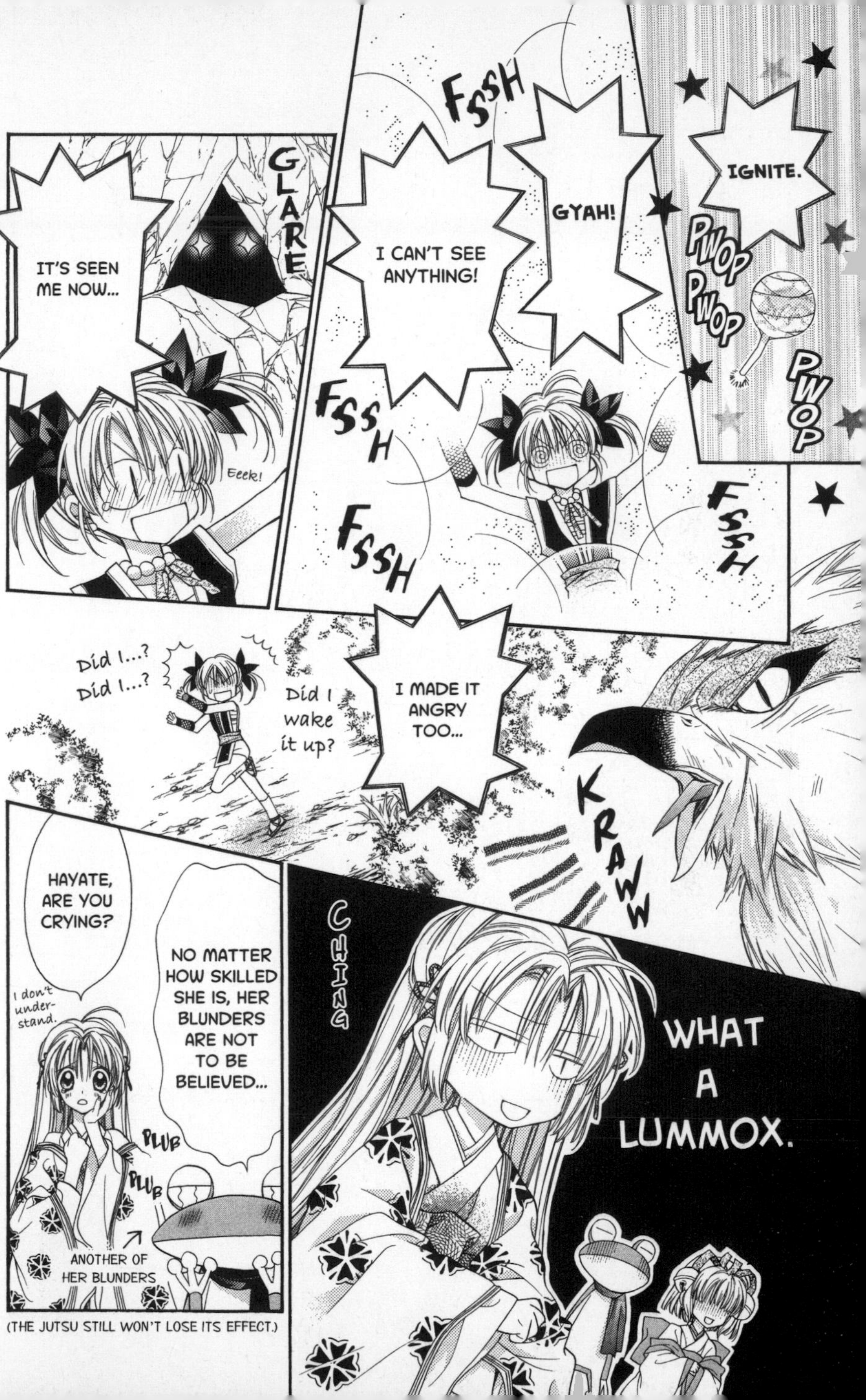
IGNITE.
PWOP PWOP
PWOP
FSSH
GYAH!
I CAN'T SEE ANYTHING!
FSSH
FSSH
FSSH
GLARE
IT'S SEEN ME NOW...
Eeek!
KRAWW
I MADE IT ANGRY TOO...
Did I wake it up?
Did I...? Did I...?
CHING
WHAT A LUMMOX.
HAYATE, ARE YOU CRYING?
NO MATTER HOW SKILLED SHE IS, HER BLUNDERS ARE NOT TO BE BELIEVED...
I don't understand.
PLUB
PLUB
ANOTHER OF HER BLUNDERS

(THE JUTSU STILL WON'T LOSE ITS EFFECT.)

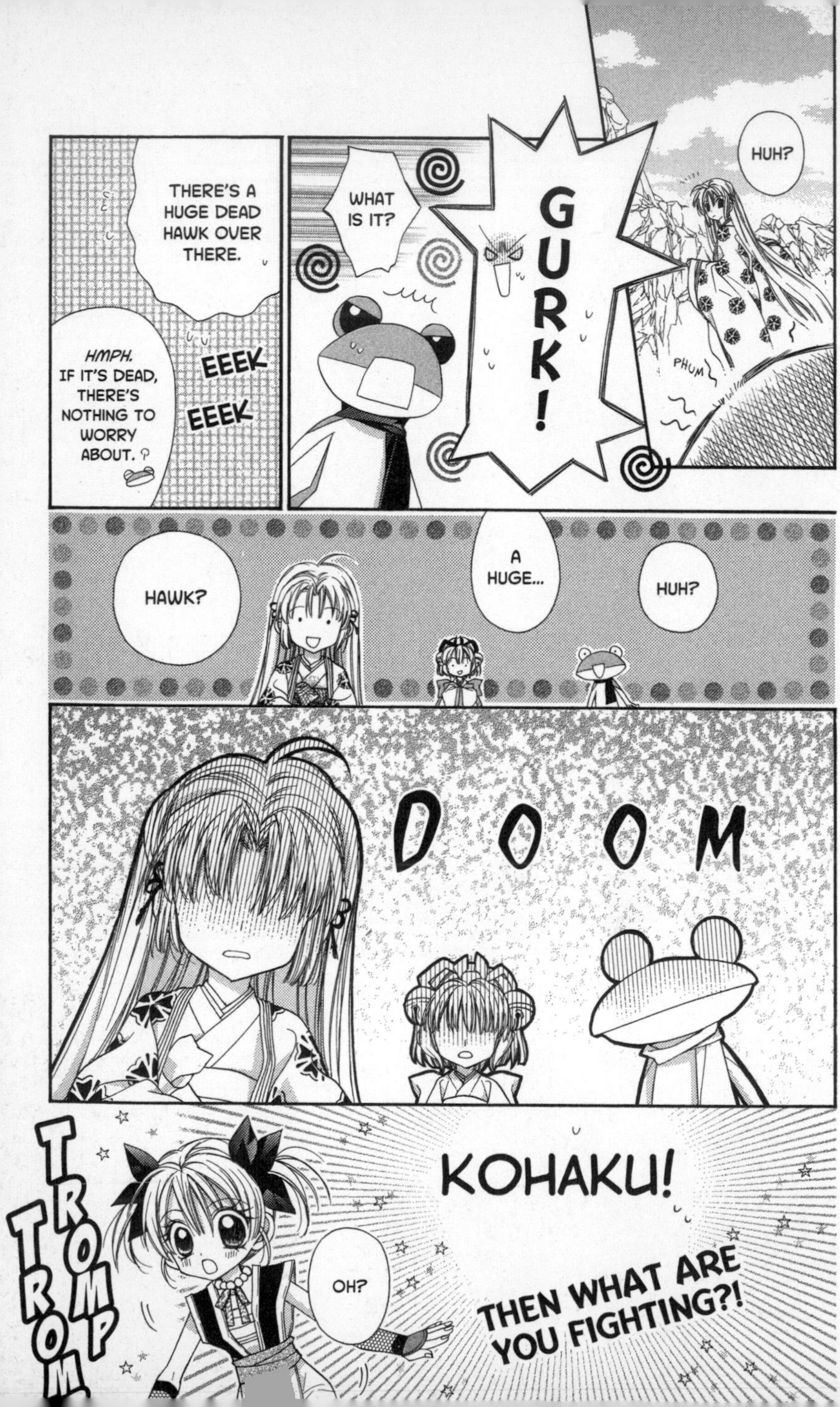
HUH?
PHUM
GURK!
WHAT IS IT?
THERE'S A HUGE DEAD HAWK OVER THERE.
EEEK
EEEK
HMPH. IF IT'S DEAD, THERE'S NOTHING TO WORRY ABOUT.
HUH?
A HUGE...
HAWK?
DOOM
KOHAKU!
THEN WHAT ARE YOU FIGHTING?!
OH?
TROMP
TROMP

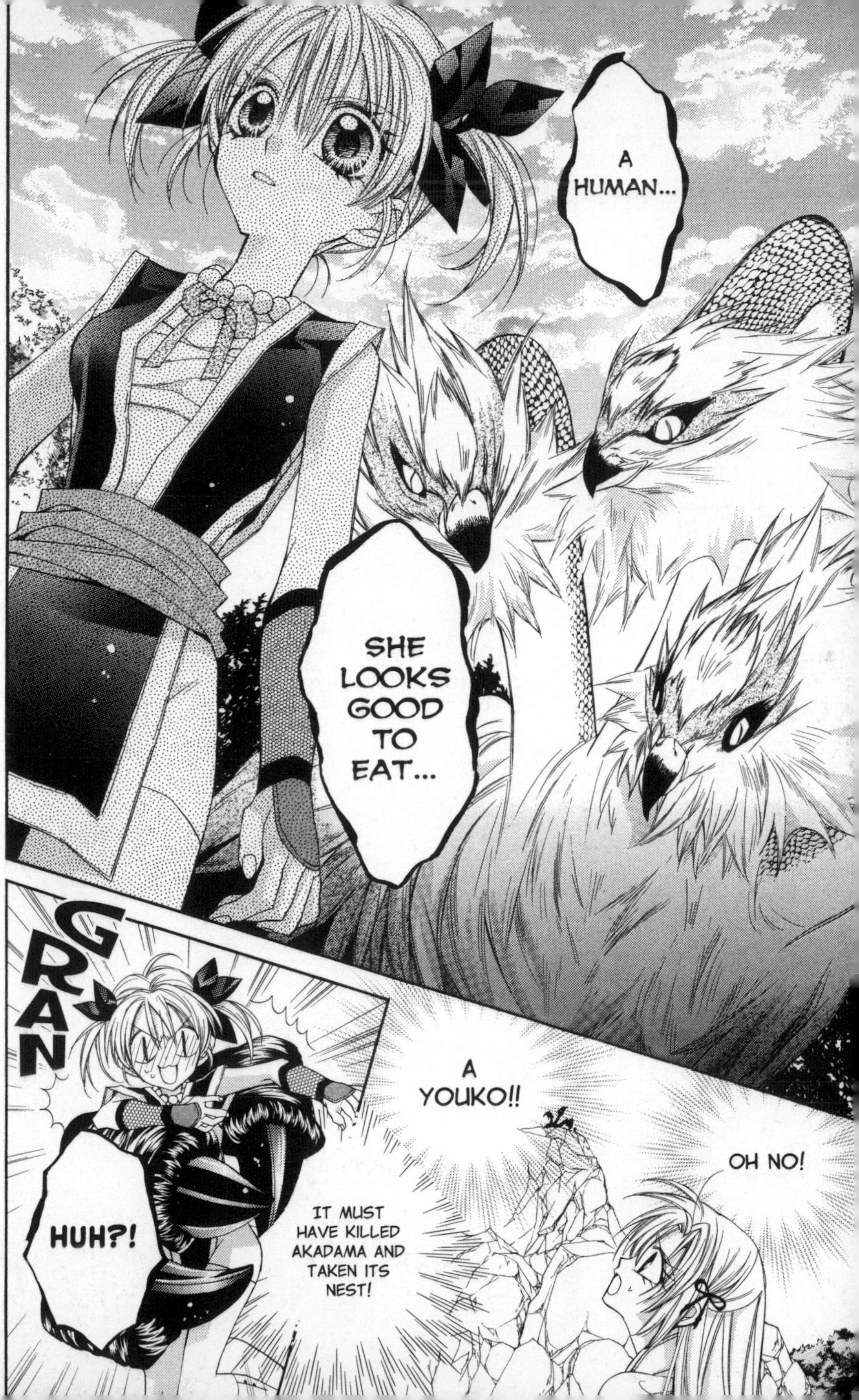
A HUMAN...
SHE LOOKS GOOD TO EAT...
OH NO!
A YOUKO!!
IT MUST HAVE KILLED AKADAMA AND TAKEN ITS NEST!
GRAN
HUH?!

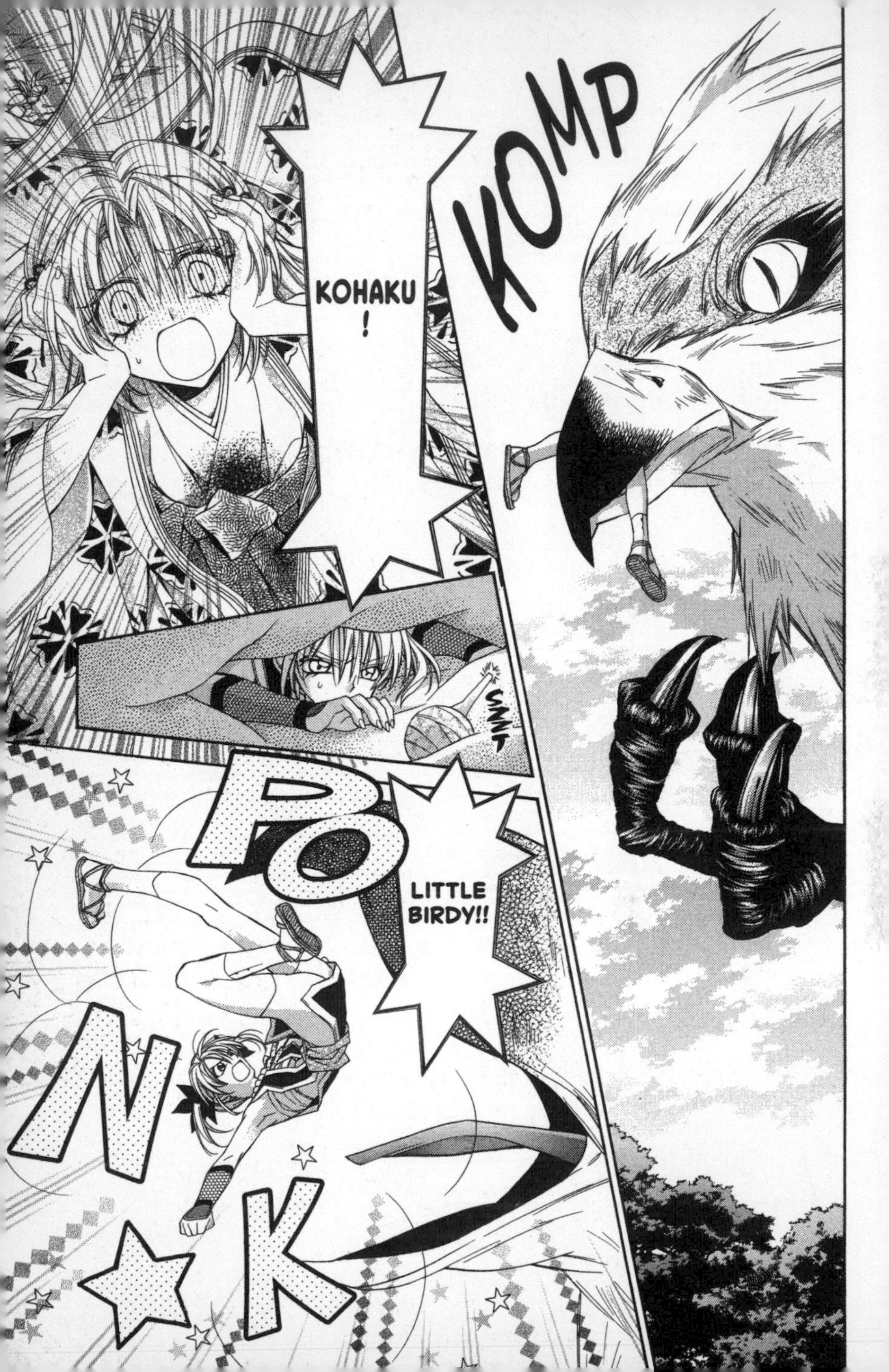
KOMP
KOHAKU!
PONK
LITTLE BIRDY!!

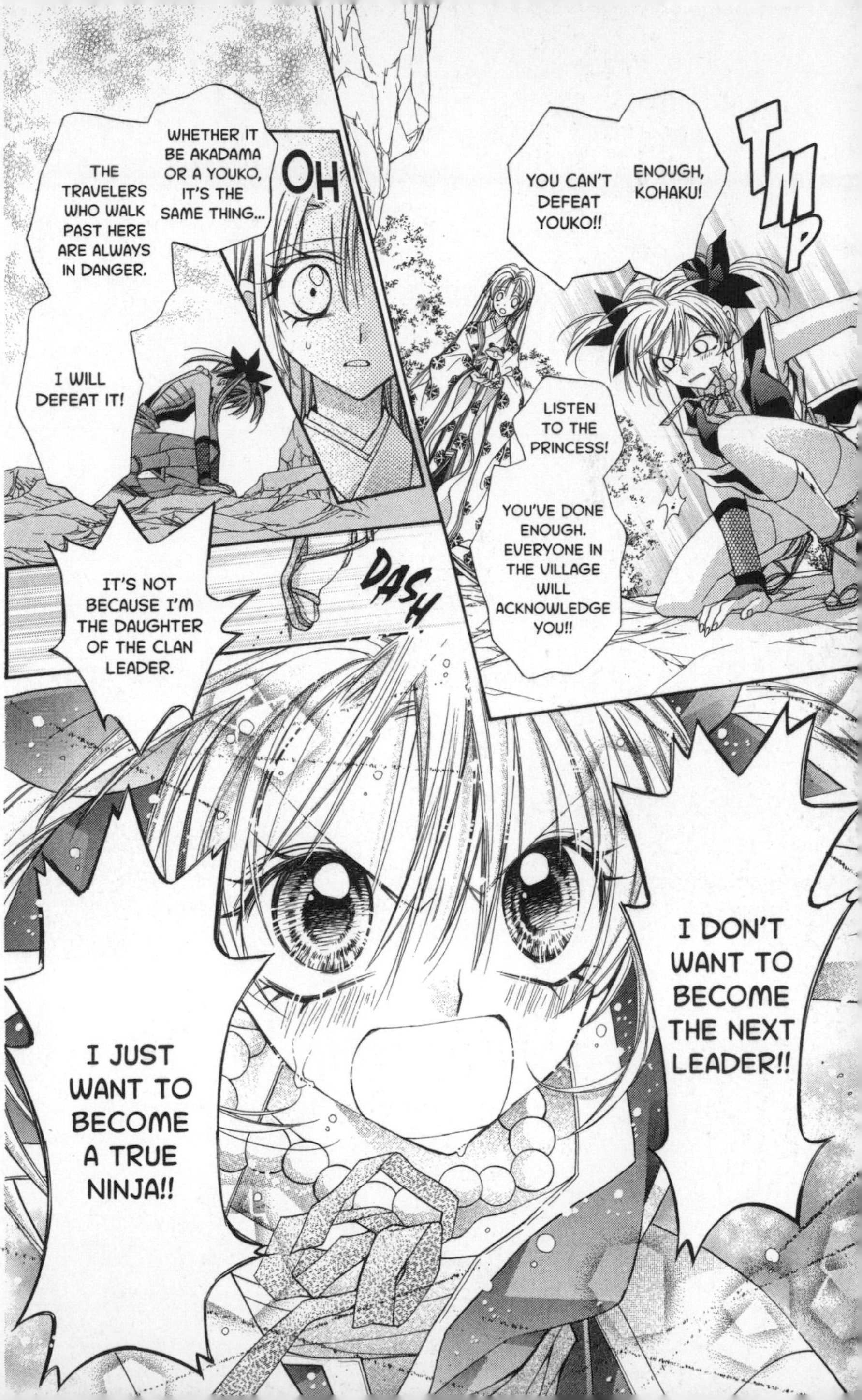
TMP
ENOUGH, KOHAKU!
YOU CAN'T DEFEAT YOUKO!!
LISTEN TO THE PRINCESS!
YOU'VE DONE ENOUGH. EVERYONE IN THE VILLAGE WILL ACKNOWLEDGE YOU!!
OH
WHETHER IT BE AKADAMA OR A YOUKO, IT'S THE SAME THING...
THE TRAVELERS WHO WALK PAST HERE ARE ALWAYS IN DANGER.
I WILL DEFEAT IT!
DASH
IT'S NOT BECAUSE I'M THE DAUGHTER OF THE CLAN LEADER.
I DON'T WANT TO BECOME THE NEXT LEADER!!
I JUST WANT TO BECOME A TRUE NINJA!!

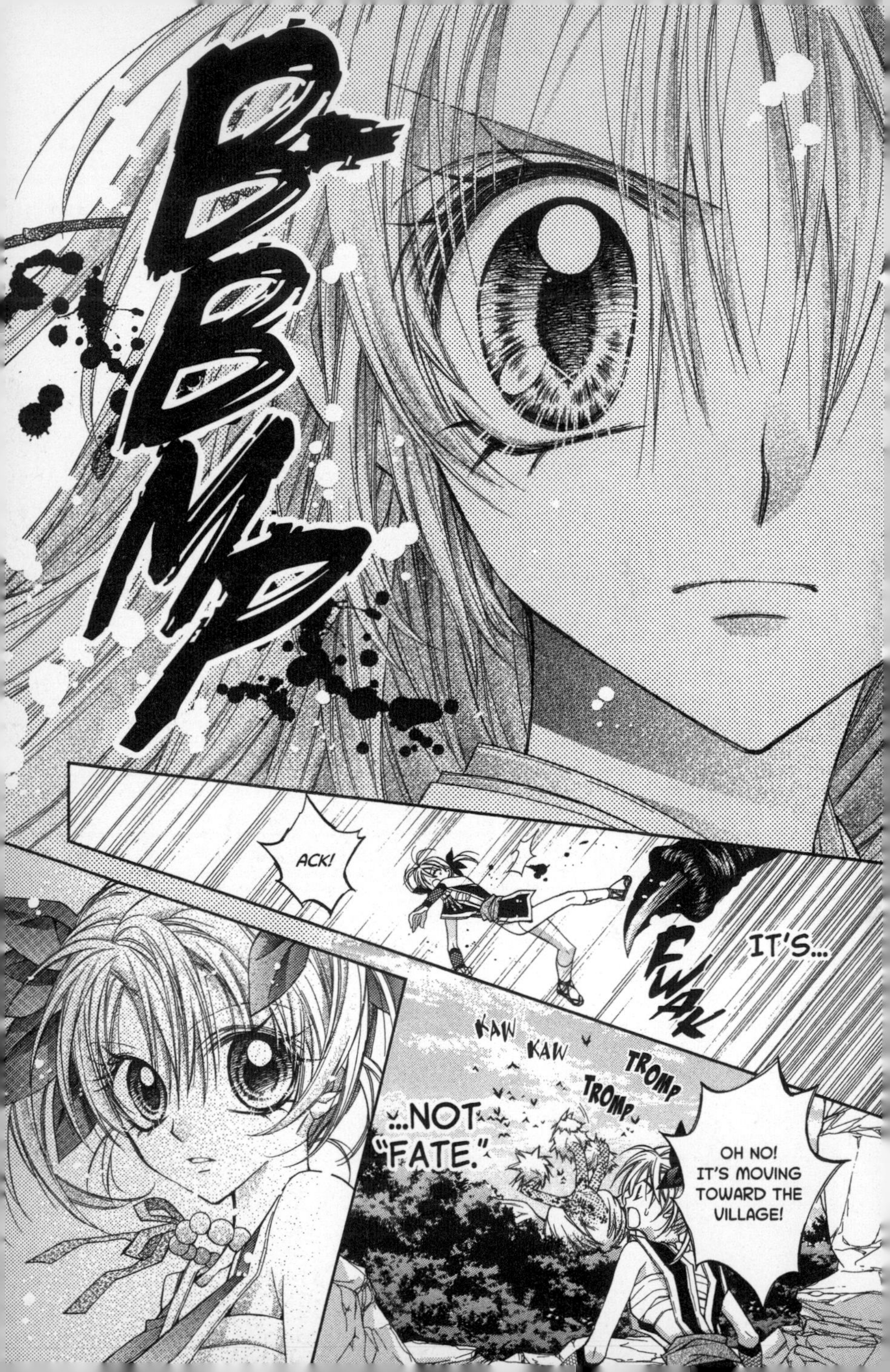
BOMP
IT'S...
FWAK
ACK!
OH NO! IT'S MOVING TOWARD THE VILLAGE!
TROMP
TROMP
KAW
KAW
...NOT "FATE."

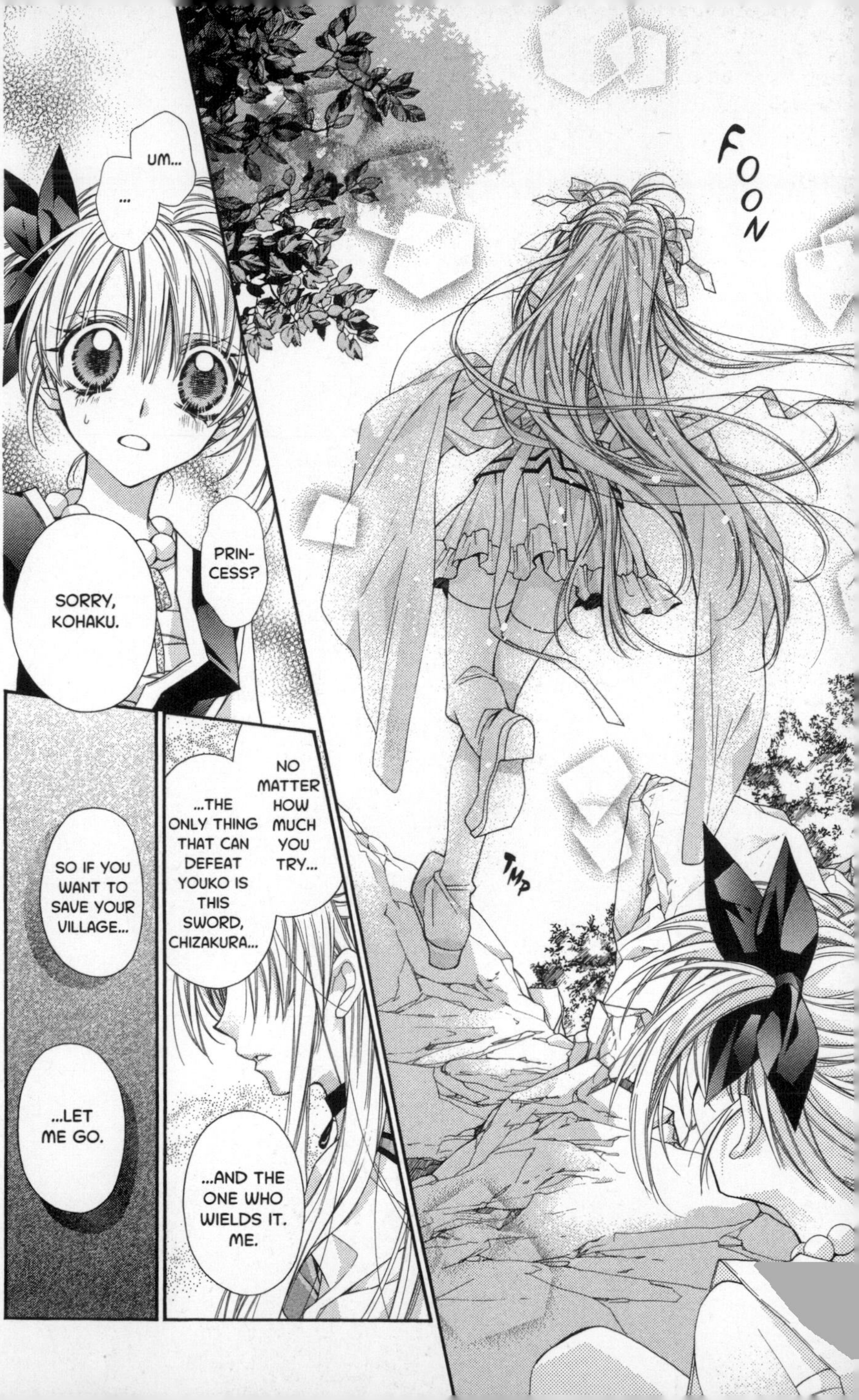
FOON
TMP
UM...
...
PRINCESS?
SORRY, KOHAKU.
NO MATTER HOW MUCH YOU TRY...
...THE ONLY THING THAT CAN DEFEAT YOUKO IS THIS SWORD, CHIZAKURA...
...AND THE ONE WHO WIELDS IT. ME.
SO IF YOU WANT TO SAVE YOUR VILLAGE...
...LET ME GO.

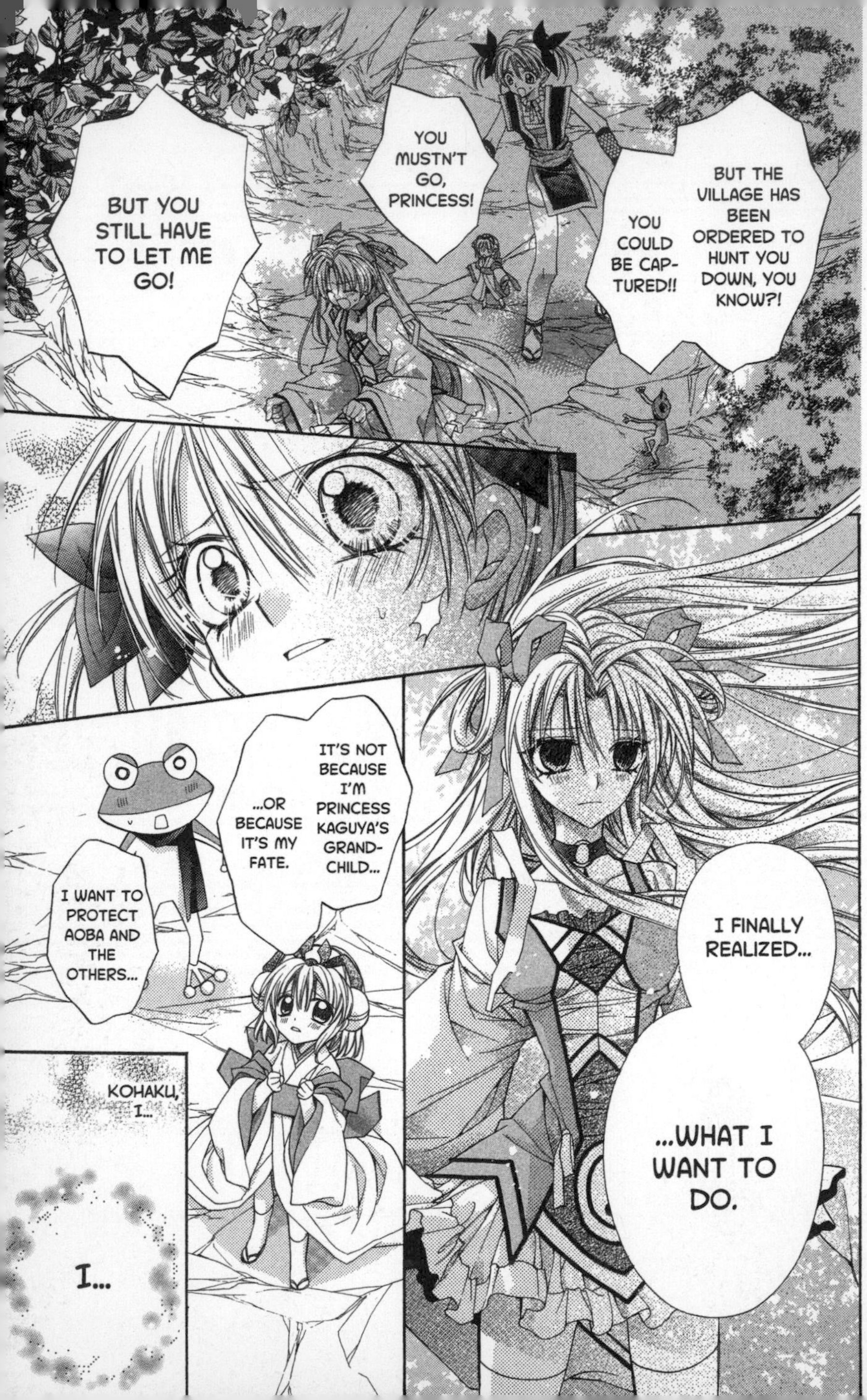
YOU MUSTN'T GO, PRINCESS!
BUT THE VILLAGE HAS BEEN ORDERED TO HUNT YOU DOWN, YOU KNOW?!
YOU COULD BE CAPTURED!!
BUT YOU STILL HAVE TO LET ME GO!
I FINALLY REALIZED...
...WHAT I WANT TO DO.
IT'S NOT BECAUSE I'M PRINCESS KAGUYA'S GRANDCHILD...
...OR BECAUSE IT'S MY FATE.
I WANT TO PROTECT AOBA AND THE OTHERS...
KOHAKU, I...
I...

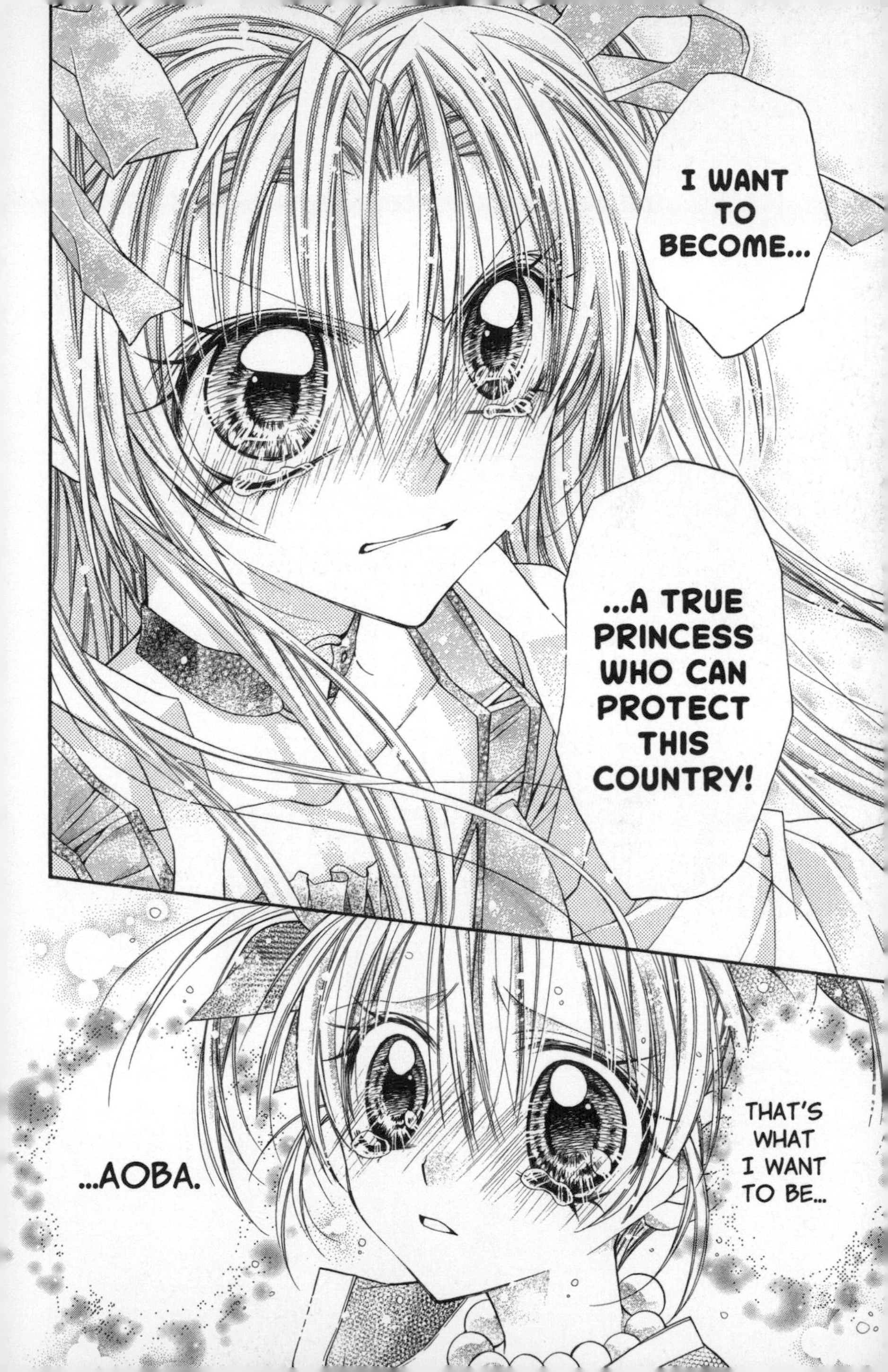
I WANT TO BECOME...
...A TRUE PRINCESS WHO CAN PROTECT THIS COUNTRY!
THAT'S WHAT I WANT TO BE...
...AOBA.

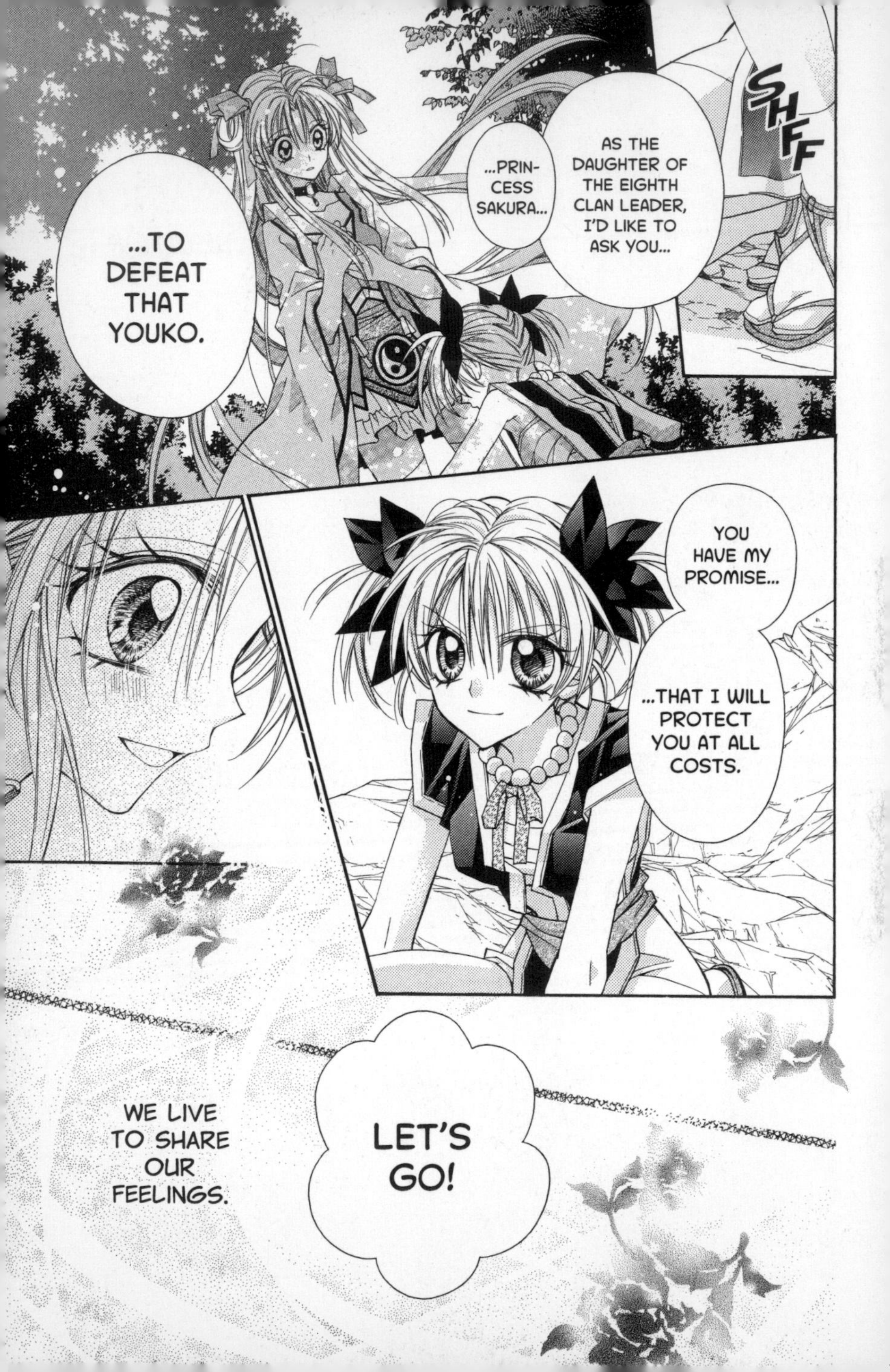
SHFF
AS THE DAUGHTER OF THE EIGHTH CLAN LEADER, I'D LIKE TO ASK YOU...
...PRIN-CESS SAKURA...
...TO DEFEAT THAT YOUKO.
YOU HAVE MY PROMISE...
...THAT I WILL PROTECT YOU AT ALL COSTS.
LET'S GO!
WE LIVE TO SHARE OUR FEELINGS.

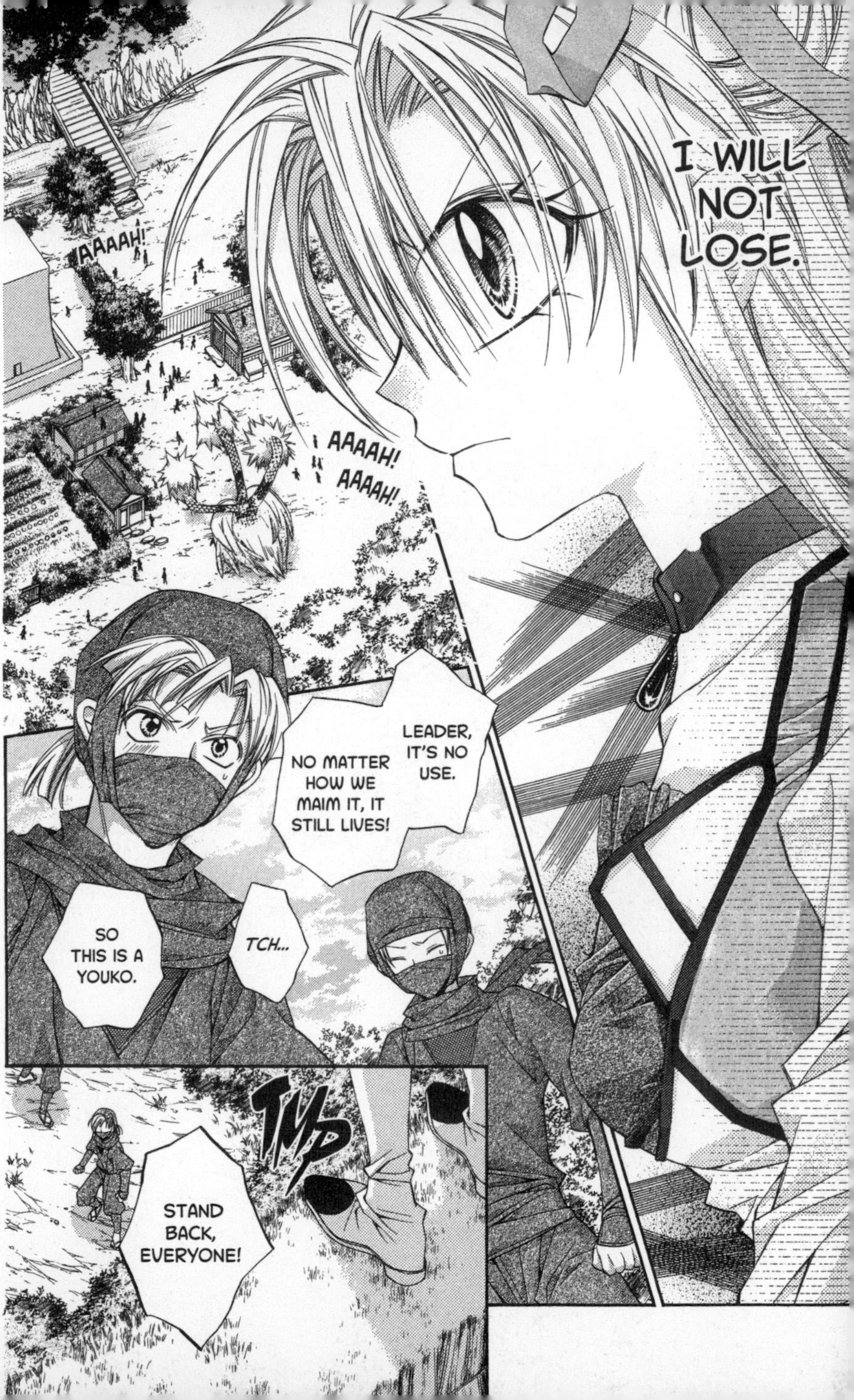
I WILL NOT LOSE.
AAAAH!
AAAAH! AAAAH!
LEADER, IT'S NO USE.
NO MATTER HOW WE MAIM IT, IT STILL LIVES!
TCH...
SO THIS IS A YOUKO.
TMP
STAND BACK, EVERYONE!

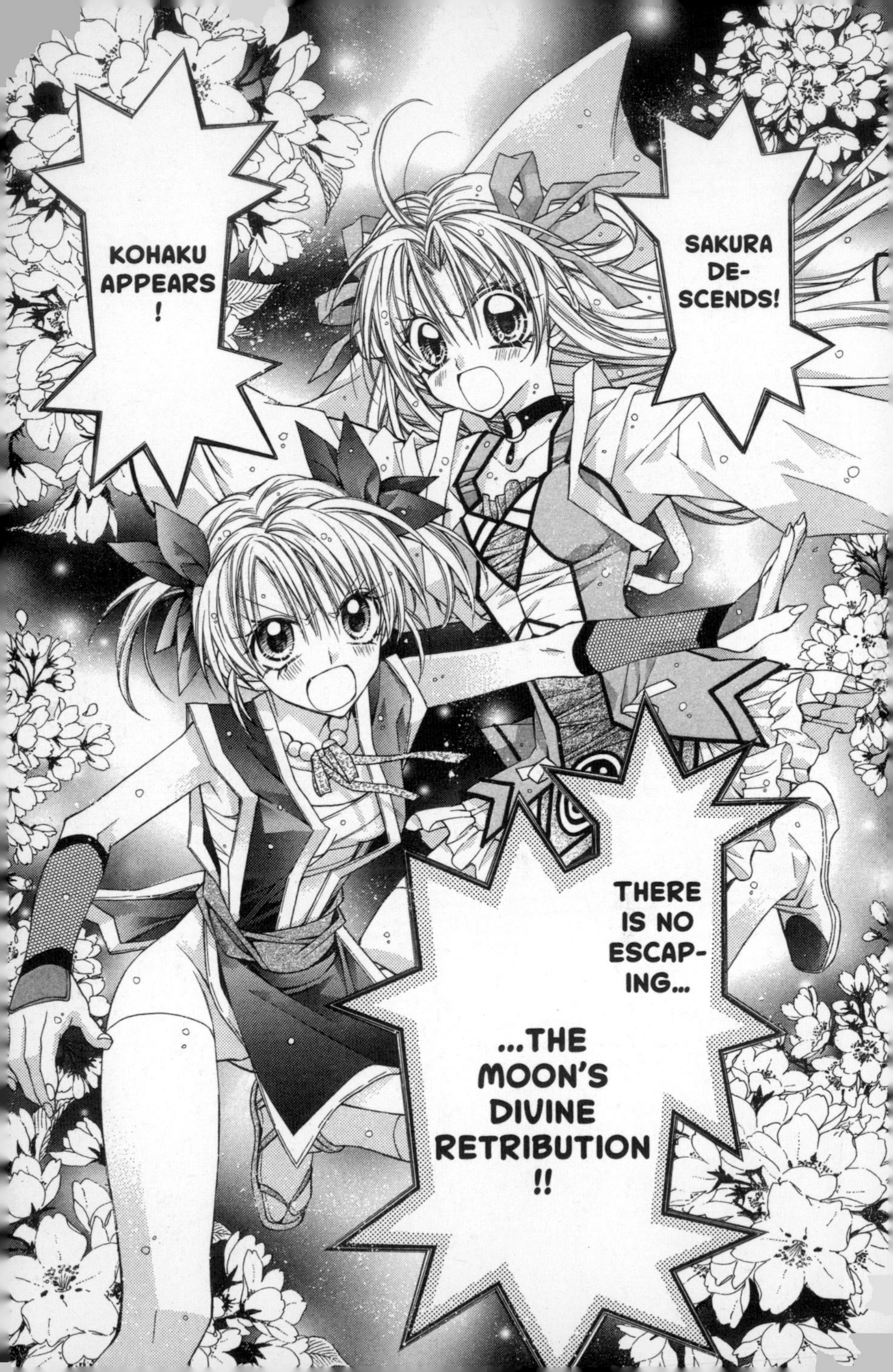
SAKURA DE- SCENDS!
KOHAKU APPEARS !
THERE IS NO ESCAP- ING...
...THE MOON'S DIVINE RETRIBUTION !!

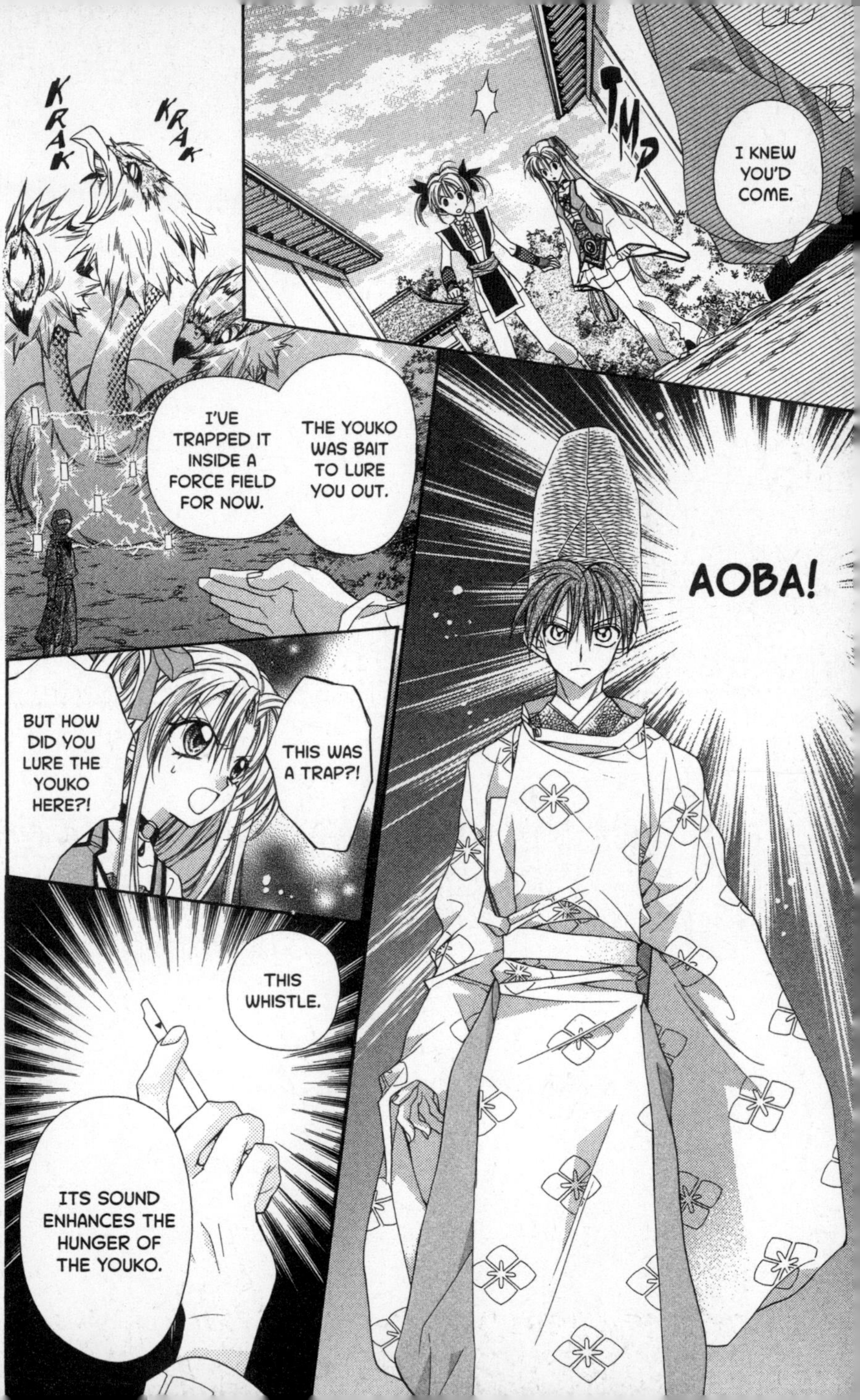
TMP
I KNEW YOU'D COME.
AOBA!
KRAK KRAK
THE YOUKO WAS BAIT TO LURE YOU OUT.
I'VE TRAPPED IT INSIDE A FORCE FIELD FOR NOW.
THIS WAS A TRAP?!
BUT HOW DID YOU LURE THE YOUKO HERE?!
THIS WHISTLE.
ITS SOUND ENHANCES THE HUNGER OF THE YOUKO.

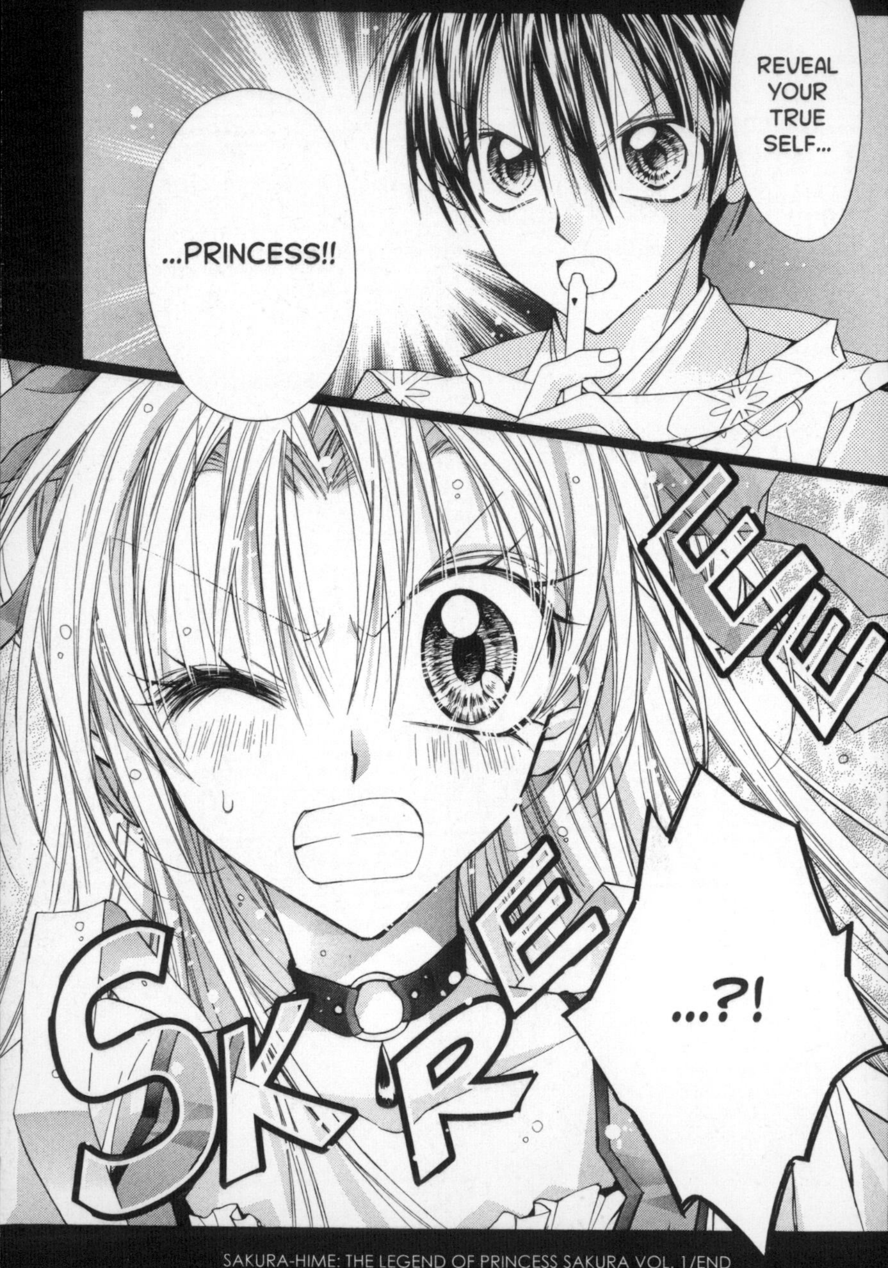
REVEAL YOUR TRUE SELF...
...PRINCESS!!
SKREEE
...?!

SAKURA-HIME: THE LEGEND OF PRINCESS SAKURA VOL. 1/END

✿ Current Things I Like ✿

Games → *Girls Mode*, *Chrono Trigger*, *Momotetsu USA* (after all this time...)

Manga → *Touch*, *Bokura wa Shitteshimatta*, *Koishitagari no Blue*, *Honey Hunt*, *Mei-chan no Shitsuji*, *Stepping on Roses*, *Mama wa Temparist*, etc...

DVD → *Game Center CX*, Down Town's *This Is No Task for Kids!!*, *Yappari Neko Ga Suki*, *The Story of Perrine*, *Moomin*, *Touch* (I bought the anime too), *Suberanai-hanashi*, Non Style, etc...

Music → *Macross F*, *Touch Best* (I'm hooked) (laugh), Berryz Koubou, Morning Musume

Drinks → Oi Ocha, Boss Café Latte

Food → Maruetsu's Garlic France, One Person Hotpot

Places I want to go → Maldives, Hot Spring, Okuhitachi Twinkle World

That's all. ♪

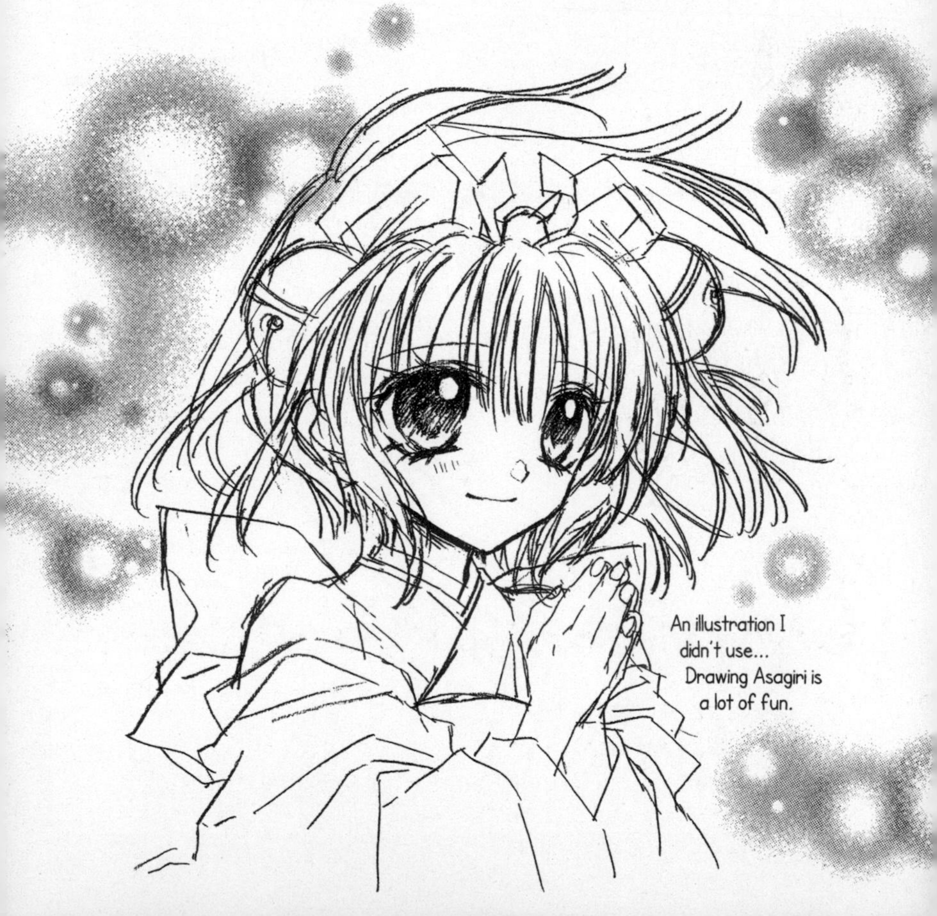

An illustration I didn't use... Drawing Asagiri is a lot of fun.

# Arina Tanemura Information

A colored illustration
for the DVD.
The you-know-what that
will be published soon...

[She's talking
about the *Paint Ribon*
art book in Japan. —Ed.]

Read more about
it on my blog or in
*Ribon* magazine.

❧ My blog, "Arina Diary"
  http://nikukai.arina.lolipop.jp/

❧ I'll be doing a series of essays on the magazine *Cobalt* starting April 1.
  "Arina's Seed": I hope you like it!!!!!

# The Legend of Princess Kaguya

*Princess Kaguya is a character in an ancient Japanese fable, "The Tale of the Bamboo Cutter." There are several variations to the fable, but here is how it relates to Sakura's story.*

There once lived an old couple who made their living from cutting bamboo and selling what they had crafted out of it. One day in the bamboo forest, the old man found a stick of bamboo glowing brightly. He cut the bamboo, and to his surprise he found a little girl about four inches tall. Having no children, he decided to take the girl back to the house to raise as his own daughter. After that, the old man found gold in the bamboo forest every time he went there, and the old couple gradually became very rich. In just three months, the little girl had already grown up to become a beautiful woman. She was named *Nayotake no Kaguya Hime*, or "Princess Kaguya Who Is Like Soft Bamboo."

Five noblemen sought the beautiful Princess Kaguya's hand in marriage, but she kept rejecting them, not wanting to get married. She said she would marry the suitor who could bring her what she asked, but she gave them impossible tasks.

When news about Kaguya reached the emperor, he asked for her hand in marriage too. Kaguya rejected him but later agreed to exchange poems. Three years after she started exchanging poems with the emperor, the old man and his wife noticed how Kaguya would keep looking up at the moon nostalgically, becoming more sorrowful each day. Kaguya told the old man that she was actually from the moon, and that she must return there. The emperor sent an army to protect Kaguya from the people of the moon who were coming to retrieve her. When the people of the moon did appear, the soldiers lost their will to fight and were unable to ward them off. The arrows shot by the soldiers all missed their targets.

The people of the moon convinced Kaguya to come with them by telling her that she should not live in an impure land for such a long time. As Kaguya departed, she left a letter for the emperor telling of her feelings for him along with a mystic robe and the elixir of life. The emperor saw no meaning in living for eternity in a world without Kaguya, so he had a group of his men climb the highest mountain in Japan to burn the elixir. And thus that mountain was named *Fujisan*, or "a mountain abundant with warriors." It's said the smoke of the elixir being burnt is still rising today, and the snow on its peak will never melt.